BLACKBOARD UNIONS

MARJORIE MURPHY

Blackboard Unions

The AFT and the NEA, 1900–1980

Cornell University Press

ITHACA AND LONDON

First published 1990 by Cornell University Press.
First printing, Cornell Paperbacks, 1992.

International Standard Book Number 0-8014-2365-1 (cloth)
International Standard Book Number 0-8014-8076-0 (paper)
Library of Congress Catalog Card Number 89-46175
Printed in the United States of America
Librarians: Library of Congress cataloging information appears on the last page of the book.

⊗ The paper in this book meets the minimum requirements
of the American National Standard for Information Sciences—
Permanence of Paper for Printed Library Materials, ANSI Z39.48-1984.

FOR PAT

first,
best,
and *always*

Contents

Acknowledgments

I began writing the history of teacher unionism in 1973 in a seminar conducted by Stephen Scheinberg at what was then Sir George Williams University (now Concordia) in Montreal. The seminar, my first, opened doors to a new life for me. For one year I studied history at McGill University and made lasting friends who have encouraged me over the years: Stephen Scheinberg, Michael Piva, John Thompson, and especially Frances Early. In that year I was also challenged by E. P. Thompson, whose *The Making of the English Working Class* I read while on my first visit to West Africa. The book and the location inspired me to appreciate the process of class formation beyond the familiar categories of labor history.

I brought my project with me to San Jose State University, where Dave Eakins and Robin Brooks helped me write a short history of Margaret Haley and the early Chicago Teachers' Union. The American Federation of Teachers gave me a small grant to complete my research that year, and with it I made the first of many pilgrimages to archives in Chicago and Detroit. Over the years Archie Motley at the Chicago Historical Society and all the staff in the manuscript, library, and photography sections have generously helped me. In Detroit, Warner Pflug and Philip Mason have warmly welcomed me back time and again to the wonderful collections they oversee.

In 1974 I began the Ph.D. program at the University of California, Davis. While there I studied with Ted Margadant, Roland Marchand, and Tony Judt. My fellow graduate students, Pat Hilden, Joe Fracchia, Mary Agnes Dougherty, and Maggie Creel-Washington, enlivened my seminars, taught me what they knew, and shared the triumphs and defeats of graduate life in what Mario Savio properly described as the "mechanism" of the University of California. Daniel Calhoun consistently urged me to read more widely, and then gave me hours of his time while I tried to sort out my thinking. David Brody skillfully guided my dissertation, providing me with the tough example of his excellent writing style and the challenge to meet his exacting standards.

I was fortunate to attend and later teach at the Newberry Library Summer Institute in Quantitative History in Chicago. These summer sessions and the Family and Community History Center at the Newberry Library were an incubator for the growing national interest in social history. I am grateful to Richard Jensen, who headed the center at that time, for his initial interest in my project and for his continuing support. I am also most grateful to Richard Brown and the Newberry Library for giving me a summer stipend and a research grant, which allowed me to complete a quantitative project on the social origins of Chicago public school teachers. The summer program also introduced me to several important friends—Nancy Fitch, Walter Licht, David Brundage, Susan Hirsch, Liz Cohen, and David Hogan—who continue to enrich my intellectual life. I also met there Dominic Pacyga, whose love of Chicago and understanding of ethnic political life continue to astound me. My most valuable friendship made in those Chicago summers, however, was with Jan Reiff, whose grasp of American urban history is unsurpassed. I completed my dissertation on Chicago teacher unionism, with the help of a Mabelle McLeod Lewis Fellowship, in 1981.

Another important influence on my thinking has come from studies in women's history. My teachers have been Billie Jensen at San Jose State University, Ruth Rosen at the University of California, Davis, and Mary Ryan, who taught a special seminar at the University of California, Davis. With Diane LeBow at Cañada College I participated in my first program in women's studies and shared with her the joys and frustrations of forging a new field. Ellen DuBois, Lillian Williams, Carroll Smith-Rosenberg, Ruth Milkman, Jane Caplan, Louise Tilly, Kitty Sklar, Alice Kessler-Harris, Sue Benson, and Barbara Melosh have helped, in their writings and in conversation, to shape my thoughts on the history of working women. Sue Carter, Dina Coppelman, and I share a special bond of interest in the history of public school teachers, and I have been enriched by sharing ideas with them.

The idea for this book formed in my mind in 1972 in the kitchen of Si and Rebbie Beagle. Si Beagle was a remarkable teacher unionist whose enthusiasm for progressive education outlived John Dewey. At the time I met him Si was promoting the More Effective Schools program, which had come out of collective bargaining agreements in New York City but which was under severe criticism by black teachers who rejected the old Progressive education formulas as racist. Undaunted, Si argued forcefully that a properly funded, child-centered classroom could overcome the debilitating effects of racism and class bias. As we argued, and we always argued, Si unfolded for me the history of the American Federation of Teachers. It was a story as confounding as our arguments over Ocean Hill–Brownsville, while it covered much of the turmoil of the twentieth century.

Other teacher unionists have helped me reconstruct this history. Marjorie Stern has always encouraged me and given generously of her time; she remains a real leader in the history of women schoolteachers. Mildred and David Flacks shared with me their experiences in Local 5, and Tima Tomasch also gave me insight into the trials of the radical and Communist teachers of the thirties. Informally, I have interviewed over a dozen union activists, while others have given me names, contacts, and ideas. Most important in helping me understand teacher unionism has been Raoul Teilhet, former president of the California Federation of Teachers. Few labor leaders of the sixties and seventies can claim Raoul's record of compassion and common sense. Miles Myers, current president of the California Federation of Teachers, has encouraged me in every step of this project. Bob Cherny of San Francisco State University gave me valuable leads on San Francisco history, and Evelyn Carstens filled me in on the history of both the Los Angeles and the Chicago locals. Hy Weintraub gave me insight into the socialist role in early AFT history. The late Mary Herrick gave me a long interview and continued to correspond with me, and Betty Balanoff gave me transcripts of her interview with Lillian Hernstein, also of Chicago. Jeffrey Mirel shared his knowledge of the Detroit locals; Paul Trimble sent me materials on the history of the teachers' union in St. Paul. I am also grateful to the members of Local 1493, the San Mateo Community College Federation of Teachers, who gave me my experience in teacher activism through which I was able to understand the issues that teachers' unions have faced. Judy Kirk and I shared a two-woman picket line, and she is still teaching me things about how classroom teachers read the educational power structure. Peggy Walker gave me exciting new insights into the issues of race and professionalism. I am also grateful to the teachers in the United Federation of Teachers (UFT) offices who helped me in the early years of my investigation. In the AFT's modern national offices I have benefited from the cheerful assistance of Paula O'Connor. Carl Megel, former president of the AFT, gave me an interview and shared with me his reminiscences. President Albert Shanker was most generous in providing me with an interview and his comments on recent history.

Lest the reader think all my influences derive from union experiences, I note here my first NEA experience was at a convention of the New Jersey Education Association in 1963, when the association began actively recruiting students. I have also been helped by Don Walker of the NEA archives, who has generously guided me with his knowledge of NEA history. I am also grateful to the staff at the Cornell University Labor Archives in Ithaca, the Robert Wagner Archives at New York University, and the Special Collections at the University of Oregon in Eugene.

I wrote most of the manuscript during a year's leave from Swarthmore College, supported by a generous grant from Eugene Lang. Several people have read portions of this manuscript and deserve to be thanked. Ruth Milkman and Paul Mattingly both offered critical and insightful comments. The book was much improved by their help. Andy Weiss also commented on an earlier version of the book. Peter Dimock and Richard Jensen commented on chapter 13. Ira Katznelson encouraged me to continue with the debate he laid out in *Schooling for All*. Patti Cooper and Lynn Weiner both read portions of the manuscript and gave me support and critical readings.

My colleagues and students at Swarthmore have patiently listened as I formulated arguments, and have responded gently as I canceled and put off engagements. Eva Travers, Ann Renninger, and Lisa Smulyan were especially helpful. Members of the *Radical History Review* collective have provided equivalent patience and encouragement.

Peter Agree, Laura Helper, Pamela Haag, and Kay Scheuer at Cornell University Press have provided cheerful support. Jim O'Brien's political judgment was nearly as crucial to the manuscript as his critical pen. Pat Manning, to whom this book is dedicated, I thank for always believing that someday I would write all of this down.

MARJORIE MURPHY

Swarthmore, Pennsylvania

Abbreviations

Newspapers
 CT   *Chicago Tribune*
 NYT   *New York Times*

Teacher Organizations
 AFT   American Federation of Teachers
 CTF   Chicago Teachers' Federation
 CTU   Chicago Teachers' Union
 NEA   National Education Association
 UFT   United Federation of Teachers

BLACKBOARD UNIONS

Introduction

In some ways this book is a standard account of unionization. That the workers are teachers and the industry is education, however, makes the study a bit unusual. Teachers are primarily women, and education is public employment. Teachers are also not well paid. These facts affect us and our children in profound ways. So this history is not so standard, because it is about a union movement in which gender difference had to be confronted; it is about an organization of public workers who first tested prohibitions against public employee strikes; and it is about a group of workers who were "scientifically" selected to fit a new norm of "professionalism." The union's problems in organization differed from those of blue-collar unions because the teachers' union was a new type of union for a new type of worker. Women white-collar workers are now underrepresented in the trade-union movement, but the failure to unionize is not entirely a failure of women workers. In this book I hope to set forth the historic obstacles to the unionization of public school teachers, to show how difficult organization was, and to illustrate the contradictions faced by public employees in unionization.

The growth of cities and the centralization of public school systems provided the basis for teacher unionization. Teachers faced a host of obstacles in achieving their union and collective bargaining strength. These obstacles dissipated as the century progressed, and there was an explosion of teacher unionism in the late sixties. The first and most enduring among the obstacles was the adjustment to centralization, which required a "professionalized" teaching force. The ideology of professionalism in education grew into a powerful antiunion slogan that effectively paralyzed and then slowed the unionization of teachers. Only in the last twenty years have teachers effectively challenged the confining definitions of professionalism to declare that their own personal well-being was in fact a professional concern. Of the two teacher organizations—the National Education Association (NEA) and the American Federation of Teachers (AFT)—the former claimed exclusive jurisdiction in professionalism while the later held stubbornly to its trade-union heritage. Finally in the late sixties, under pressure from union competition, the NEA entered the arena of collective bargaining and today rather prides itself on being called a union.[1]

Recurrent seasons of red-baiting were a second obstacle to teacher unionization. They created an atmosphere of fear that destroyed militant teacher activity and stifled teacher advocacy. Likewise, a chronic fiscal crisis in education, beginning at the close of the Progressive Era and continuing to the

1. Three dissertations discuss the issue of professionalization and public school teachers in Chicago. Robert Reid, "The Professionalization of Public School Teachers: The Chicago Experience, 1895–1920" (Ph.D. diss., Northwestern University, 1968), ignores the trade-union language of professionalization to interpret early teachers' unions as preliminary to professionalization. Cherry Wedgwood Collins, "Schoolmen, Schoolma'ams, and School Boards: The Struggle for Power in Urban School Systems in the Progressive Era" (Ed.D. diss., Harvard University, 1976), accepts Reid's interpretation except that she considers the inherent sexism in traditional professionalism and explains how feminist teachers came to professionalism through the use of Amitai Etzioni's notion of compliance in bureaucratic structures. My dissertation, "From Artisan to Semiprofessional: White-Collar Unionism among Chicago Public School Teachers, 1870–1930" (Ph.D. diss., University of California, Davis, 1981), pp. 1–9, refutes both Reid and Collins, arguing that they ignored teachers' efforts toward unionization and that professionalism was imposed from above by superintendents and educational managers in an antiunion campaign. Furthermore, I argued that by reading professionalization into the early history of teachers' unions, Reid's analysis badly misdirected Robert Wiebe's *The Search for Order, 1877–1920* (New York, 1967), which traces the rise of a new middle class through this new professionalization project. This misinterpretation was further confounded when Magali Sarfatti-Larson, in her *The Rise of Professionalism: A Sociological Analysis* (Berkeley, 1977), argued that American class formation was profoundly affected by the rise of professionalism and that this "strategy of professionalism holds sway on individuals and occupational categories which are inspired elsewhere by the political and economic strategies of the labor movement." Professionalism, Sarfatti-Larson correctly concludes, is ideological, but its history in the United States has been read outside the context of the history of the political and economic strategies of the labor movement. What we have is a history of professionalism that emphasizes outcomes and not struggles. Two new works in the sociology of professions give a new perspective on the history of professions: J. A. Jackson, ed., *Professions and Professionalization* (Cambridge, 1970); and Andrew Abbott, "Occupational Environments and Occupational Structure: Professions and Their Audiences in France and the United States" (Paper presented at the Social Science History Association annual meeting, November 1987). Abbott discusses not just the prerogatives claimed by professionals but the audience they appeal to in the process of negotiating more control. Appeals to local authorities, the public, and workplace colleagues constitute a dialogue of self-definition, Abbott maintains, which have different degrees of flexibility. Legal and public realms are more fixed and less conducive to change than those negotiated in the daily setting of the workplace. Taking this argument further, JoAnne Brown, in "Professional Language: Words That Succeed," *Radical History Review*, 34 (January 1986), pp. 33–51, examines the ways that professionals use language to legitimize their position in the division of labor. Professional work, she argues, needs some interpretation in order to gain the respect of its clientele. The need to popularize the professional service and at the same time monopolize it causes professionals to rely on metaphors to explain and simultaneously obscure the knowledge of their trade. This specialized vocabulary gives professionals a way of separating themselves from others. Brown criticizes sociologists and historians for not paying enough attention to the legitimizing function of professionalization's language, since "most of the action carried out by professionals is linguistic." Unionization for teachers, however, required direct action, the antithesis of professionalism's linguistic monopoly. In the history of teacher unionism, teachers give into the self-definition of professionalism only to discover that it is not merely a linguistic concession but a profound ideology that separates them from the community.

present time, has been an important obstacle. As the energies of teacher advocates were drawn into various schemes to develop national remedies, tax-conscious organizations blocked any attempt to move school funding away from narrow, local taxation. Within these confines, teachers managed to win more concessions but remained tied to a fiscally conservative tax system. These three obstacles—the ideology of professionalism, the recurrent red-baiting, and the also recurrent and not unrelated fiscal crisis—help explain the slow pace of unionism.

Though the central focus of this book is on unionization, it is not confined to the first teachers' union, the American Federation of Teachers (AFT). The origins of the union movement are found in a small, rebellious group of urban school teachers. They not only affiliated with the American Federation of Labor (AFL) but they also attached themselves to, and attended meetings of, the National Education Association. The history of teacher unionism, then, is a history of both the AFT and the NEA.[2] This book concentrates on the AFT only because the NEA has partially directed itself toward teacher interests; the book is not a comprehensive history of the NEA and the AFT as organizations but a study of the history of unionism itself: the idea of unionization and how it was carried forward by those most interested in it. The book is unique, then, in that it examines two rival organizations as they embrace and articulate the principles of teacher unionism.

There is another caveat in this history that may seem strange to the uninitiated reader. The NEA and AFT are organized in two distinct ways. The NEA has been a national organization with a visible presence in Washington, D.C., for over sixty years. Originally the NEA was organized along lines of separate departments, some of which grew quite powerful and dominated the organization's national affairs. Later, in the twenties, the NEA began to emphasize state associations. Only in the late sixties did the association pay attention to the strengthening of local chapters. The AFT, on the other hand, was organized on the basis of local unions. Its state organizations were weak, and it had little presence on the national scene. It moved its headquarters to Washington only in the early fifties, thirty years after the NEA. It was the beginning of collective bargaining in the early sixties that

2. The standard accounts of teacher associations and unions include Mildred Sandison Fenner, *The National Education Association, Its Development and Program* (Washington, D.C., 1950); Edgar G. Wesley, *NEA, The First One Hundred Years: The Building of the Teaching Profession* (New York, 1957); Carter Alexander, *Some Aspects of the Work of Teachers' Voluntary Associations in the United States* (New York, 1910); Celia Lewis Zitron, *The New York City Teachers Union, 1916–1964* (New York, 1968); William Edward Eaton, *The Social and Educational Position of the AFT, 1929–1941* (Washington, D.C., 1971); Eaton, *The American Federation of Teachers, 1916–1961: A History of the Movement* (Carbondale, Ill., 1975); Philip Taft, *United They Teach: The Story of the UFT* (Los Angeles, 1974); Timothy M. Stinnett, *Turmoil in Teaching: A History of the Organizational Struggle for America's Teachers* (New York, 1968). The first book to analyze the unionization of teachers in the context of educational change is Wayne J. Urban, *Why Teachers Organized* (Detroit, 1982). Mark H. Maier, *City Unions: Managing Discontent in New York City* (New Brunswick, N.J., 1987), directs attention to public employee unions in the context of urban politics.

gave it prominence. For the most part, the history of the AFT is a history of the locals, the strongest of which were in Chicago, New York, and (until 1957) Atlanta. Originally the Chicago locals were the most powerful; they kept the seat of the national union until after World War II; in the thirties the activities and size of the New York locals began to shift union power from the Midwest to the East. The organizational structures of the AFT and the NEA reflect the two traditions that teacher unionism drew on in its origins: centralized advocacy in support of the traditional professional mystique embodied in the NEA and the master-craft tradition of the American Federation of Labor, embodied in the AFT. In this book I hope to give the reader a sense of how very different these organizational traditions were and how, in the pursuit of unionism, teachers had to create a broader vision from both.

A final proviso concerns the very nature of the rivalry of the two organizations. The NEA, from its inception in 1857, was an organization of educational leaders, most of whom were school administrators. It was not until 1912 that classroom teachers were recognized with their own department and not until after the AFT was formed in 1916 that the NEA began actively to recruit rank-and-file teachers. In contrast, the AFT was an organization of rank-and-file teachers opposed to administrative hierarchy and close supervision. A few locals allowed school principals to join them, but the national consensus remained firmly against school administrators in leadership positions. Collective bargaining softened the lines between organizations. In the NEA members of the Department of School Superintendents left and formed their own independent organization of school administrators, and in the AFT, locals of school principals have been chartered. Although real differences have diminished with collective bargaining, the slogans of the past have become a shorthand signature for organizational difference. The NEA, while not denying that it is a union, often boasts that it is the "professional" organization, implying that the AFT is at a less-than-professional level; the AFT retorts that the NEA is the "administrator-dominated" organization. The intensity of this rivalry often obscures the real differences. The two organizations grew from two very different traditions but have grown in relationship with each other. The history of this relationship is the essence of the story of teacher unionization.

Teaching has been historically an avenue for social mobility. This book analyzes the meaning of that mobility in the context of unionization. I have argued, here and elsewhere, that teaching represented the aristocracy of labor for women workers; it was a high-status, low-paying job with the best available wages for women. For many entrants to teaching—women mostly in the Progressive period and ethnic men after the thirties—it was a step away from the blue-collar world of their fathers. Were teachers looking back to the system of social justice of their fathers and wending their way into white-collar work with trade-union values, or were they grasping at the values of their new social status, embracing middle-class ideals of respectability? It seems in this history that teachers responded to both calls—often in contradictory ways but in a consistent pattern that reveals the painful adjustments such class transformation can demand.[3]

The book is organized chronologically, beginning with the centralization of school life at the turn of the century. Centralization and professionalism were two very important features of the modern school movement. Early teacher unions emerged in opposition to this movement and began to give voice to teachers' grievances. In the first five chapters I outline the original rivalry between the AFT and the NEA through World War I. In chapter 6 I turn to the small AFT as it struggled with the AFL in the interwar years. A union of "brain workers," as AFL president Samuel Gompers called them, the teachers received a cold reception from the AFL, and returned the sentiment as women took over the helm of the AFT. This distance and the worsening fiscal crisis in education, outlined in chapter 7, left the AFT in an oddly isolated position. Radical factions grew in importance until finally, beginning in the depression years, the union devoted an entire decade to factionalism and the eventual ouster of several Communist locals; this factionalism is the subject of chapter 8. In chapter 9 I cover the era of McCarthyism and its effects on the union. In the following chapter I look at the history of civil rights and its impact on education in the late fifties and the early sixties. This story is continued in chapter 12, which covers the events of the Ocean Hill–Brownsville controversy and addresses the issues of conflict over race and class in the teachers' union. Chapter 13 traces the competition between the AFT and the NEA in the drive for collective bargaining. In the postwar years, it became increasingly clear that both organizations would pay more attention to civil rights, especially after the *Brown v. Board of Education* decision in 1954 pointed the way toward profound change. The AFT seemed to have an advantage because its formative years had been firmly based in radical movements that sought to better the position of American blacks. In contrast, the NEA struggled with a casual alliance with a predominantly black administrative organization and maintained many segregated state associations. Both organizations merged their interests with black teachers and sought to push the cause of civil rights along with their own collective bargaining interests.

But civil rights was not a stagnant movement, ready to be captured by competing teacher organizations. It was a dynamic, community-based movement, and here is where the last theme of the book emerges. When

---

3. The issue of social mobility is summarized in the work of Stephan Thernstrom, *The Other Bostonians* (Cambridge, 1973), and criticized by James Henretta. My understanding of class perspectives for public school teachers was largely shaped by the work of Daniel Calhoun, especially *Professional Lives in America: Structure and Aspirations, 1750–1850* (Cambridge, 1965). I have argued elsewhere that public school teaching was a privileged job for women that put them in the aristocracy of labor. See Marjorie Murphy, "The Aristocracy of Women's Labor in America," *History Workshop Journal*, 22 (Autumn 1986), pp. 56–69.

teachers first unionized against centralization, they had full community support because the language of centralization threatened neighborhood control. Teachers lost the battle against centralization and accommodated its terms, especially in regard to professionalism. In the late sixties centralization came under fire again as an obstacle to community control and the enfranchisement of an angry black community pressing for higher-quality education. Teachers' unions were by then organized and recognized by a centralized authority, so that teachers had a stake in the status quo of a system they once organized against. The unions were anxious to address the problems of quality in education but only through the centralized agency they negotiated their contracts with: the board of education. When parents of Ocean Hill–Brownsville asserted community control in the newly decentralized schools of New York, they were opposed by the United Federation of Teachers, AFT. The ensuing strike illustrated that the price of unionization—of overcoming obstacles created by professionalization, red-baiting, and consistently impoverished local tax bases—combined with the narrowing process of collective bargaining to alienate teachers from the communities they had originally intended to ally with.

Many books of considerable merit have been written offering various justifications on both sides of the issue of community control versus teacher unionism. None of them, however, has taken into consideration the sixty-year period of adjustment teachers went through to come to terms with administrative hierarchy in education. The union and the association seem to have switched political positions. Why does the union, which is the vehicle of progressive politics, seem now the agent of conservative thinking, while the association embraces the most progressive causes of the day? The explanation I offer here will disappoint a few who have partisan hearts in the matter, but I hope it will at least engage the issues of ethnicity, gender, and class in the politics of education. That teachers are both conservative and progressive in two different organizations seems appropriate from the perspective of the political economy of education.

What is striking in this history is the determination of teachers to gain a say in the educational process and the various avenues teachers tried before they were able to come up with the right combination for success. Many would argue that the success of unionism came at too dear a price, that teachers shed their radical politics and conformed to the worst of narrow self-interest. I think the readers of these pages will see that teachers took the only door that society held open to them. They explored other ways. Union leaders came on the scene and fought what they called "the good fight." They often gained a small foothold in the economic world, but in every encounter they lost ground on the political front until finally they had very little political ground to stand on at all. Teachers' unions, which are public employee unions, are narrow economic organizations because historically that is all our conservative society has allowed.

Chapter One

Turmoil in the Chicago Schools; 1902 and 1905

Two days after President Theodore Roosevelt orchestrated the dramatic settlement of the national anthracite coal strike in October 1902, the first school strike began at the Clarke School on Thirteenth Street and Ashland Avenue in the heart of Chicago's West Side district. It was a strike by students but it brought to the surface a smoldering conflict between neighborhood-based school teachers and a citywide school administration bent on imposing a centralized pattern on the city's schools.

Students and teachers had already lost patience with the school board and superintendent. The school water-supply system had been condemned by the Board of Health in August, and because a late summer typhoid epidemic had claimed hundreds of young lives, the Board of Education responded by urging the schoolchildren to carry water bottles to school. Many children had no containers and drank contaminated water from outdoor fire hydrants. Observing this death-defying practice, the increasingly harried teachers—already angry enough after having been once again denied a salary raise—began boiling water in school for the children to drink.

As if to complicate this potentially explosive situation, School Superintendent Edwin G. Cooley, in his second year of confident leadership, reorganized the administrative structure of the schools in September, eliminating five district superintendents from the West Side. Cooley argued that the district superintendents had too much local authority and that they blocked his attempts at uniformity and centralization. In place of the five demoted superintendents, Cooley assigned the elderly District Superintendent Edward C. Delano to head an enlarged West Side district, through which all superintendents would be periodically rotated to prevent the "objectionable features of the old system." Former District Superintendent Henry G. Clark became elementary school principal at the Clarke School, bumping, in turn, a popular female principal.[1]

The immediate cause of the strike was tied to Cooley's administrative reorganization and the attempt of a new principal to demand that children learn according to a centralized, citywide schedule. The new principal compelled teachers to follow rigidly a set course of excellence or fail any students who fell short of the standard. A teacher had insisted that children hand in perfect math papers or fail. The students argued that no one was perfect, but principal Clark insisted that the teacher continue with the procedure so that the students would conform to the expectations of the district superintendent. The students, threatening a general strike, walked out of the classroom. Parents in the neighborhood told reporters they supported the children's strike. The following day both principal and teacher relented, but the students decided that before they returned to the classroom they would have a parade. One student explained, "All strikers have parades, we will have one too."[2]

The strike might have ended there, but the central office felt the need to chastise the neighborhood. On the Monday morning following the parade, Compulsory Education Superintendent William G. Bodine and his squad of truant officers combed the streets in the immediate neighborhood of the Clarke School, north on Halsted and to the east, looking for truants. They rounded up two hundred children, but the community resisted the truant officers by slinging mud at them. Later, according to the *Chicago Tribune*, a "knife was drawn" and a "small riot" ensued on Maxwell Street. Bodine was the first compulsory education officer to abandon the former efforts at moral suasion and to rely instead on his "truant officers" to pull students into the schools. The officers became a regular feature in the school struggle, serving to inflame community tensions while representing the values and goals of the central office.[3]

A strike at Andrew Jackson School began with an incident three days after Bodine's sweep. Janie McKeon, a teacher, booted one of Bodine's foul-mouthed truants out of her fifty-five-member classroom for using abusive language against another student. The new male principal, another unpopular Cooley appointee replacing a woman, sent the recruit back to McKeon. She refused the student again, and this time her principal formally charged her with insubordination.[4] A week later, on November 7, Superintendent

1. The 1902 school strikes began 24 October 1902, involved eight public schools, and were reported in the *Chicago Tribune*. See the *Chicago Tribune* (hereafter cited as *CT*), 1, 4, 15, and 23 October 1902 for the coal strike in Chicago; see the Chicago Board of Education, *49th Annual Report*, 1903, and *CT*, 19 September 1902, for conditions leading to the strikes.

2. *CT*, 24, 25 October 1902. For the celebratory aspects of strikes, especially children's strikes, see David Nasaw, *Children of the City at Work and at Play* (New York, 1985), p. 168.

3. "Truant Officers Raid Ghetto," *CT*, 27 October 1902.

4. A co-worker characterized McKeon's suspension as "an outrage." "She is a splendid teacher and her suspension is a result of systematic persecution." *CT*, 30 October 1902.

Cooley officially suspended McKeon for thirty days without pay (she could not legally be dismissed until the end of the year unless a formal hearing were held).[5] On the day of her suspension, the Maxwell Street police station reported that two hundred striking students marched to the home of Alderman John Powers and demanded McKeon's reinstatement; two days later policemen labeled a crowd of four hundred students around the school "threatening."[6]

By appealing to their alderman, neighborhood residents chose the best way they knew to challenge the centralizing authority of the Board of Education. Powers had a reputation as one of the "Lords of the Levee," those tough Chicago politicians who ran the city's political wards like personal fiefdoms—"the levee" referred to Chicago's breakwater to Lake Michigan's watery intrusion. He was the official villain of the reformers around Hull House, Jane Addams's famous settlement house. She twice failed to defeat Powers. He was a clever politician who loved to choose his battles. But the student strikes represented a new type of community eruption. Backed by the most powerful business leaders in the city, the new school superintendent challenged the alderman, the neighborhood, and the teachers. The strike was a struggle at the confluence of change between the proponents of a centralized school system with a professional staff and the militant teachers supported by a resistant community.[7]

As the strike escalated in intensity, the class character of the struggle emerged: teachers assumed the language of trade unionism while the proponents of centralization responded in classic management terms. In response to the pressure parents put on the central office, District Superintendent Delano issued a statement that though McKeon was a good teacher, she had been insubordinate and would receive no hearing. The same day, students carrying union cards harassed the new principal, William Hedges, as he was marched under police protection to his car and made his escape from the neighborhood (Hedges lived in a "better" neighborhood in Hyde Park and was unfamiliar with the narrow streets surrounding the school he had come to direct). The teacher assigned to replace McKeon told reporters she was "imported labor" and had no students to teach in any case. Meanwhile, McKeon's lawyer claimed that his client had become the "victim of a conspiracy." McKeon's loyalty to District Superintendent Albert Speer, one of the demoted superintendents who had been popular in labor circles, coupled with her "fearless support of the Chicago Teachers' Federation,"

5. *CT,* 7 November 1902.
6. *CT,* 8 November 1902.
7. Jane Addams, *Twenty Years at Hull House* (New York, 1912), p. 223; Allen F. Davis, *American Heroine: The Life and Legend of Jane Addams* (New York, 1973); Residents of Hull House, *Hull House Papers, 1884* (Boston, 1895), housed at the Newberry Library in Chicago; the Hull House Association Papers, Manuscripts, University of Illinois, Chicago Circle; Lloyd Wendt, *Lords of the Levee: The Story of Bathhouse John and Hinky Dink McKenna* (Indianapolis, 1943); Carter H. Harrison, Jr., *Stormy Years: The Autobiography of Carter H. Harrison* (New York, 1935).

identified her with the teachers opposed to centralization and Superintendent Cooley. Teachers in Chicago had organized to oppose formal centralization bills introduced in the state legislature, and they were outspoken in their opposition to Cooley's de facto centralization program. McKeon took great pains to associate herself with parents in the neighborhood and the labor movement in the city in her refusal to operate under the new centralized school authority. She was not so much the victim of a conspiracy as she was an opponent of reforms that threatened to transform her job and change the schools irrevocably.[8]

To the school reformers, McKeon's identity with the community was precisely the problem with education in the city. The business community stood firmly behind Cooley, who referred to his seat at the city's best men's club as his "den." It was at the men's club that much of the new school reform was being mapped out. The tax-conscious businessmen and lawyers who spearheaded the movement for municipal reform in Chicago were Cooley's natural constituency. The *Chicago Tribune,* reflecting this atmosphere, called the student strike a "dismal burlesque."[9]

But parents, teachers, and students continued their resistance to the new policy. Their unity provoked the editors of the *Tribune* to remark that they were "shocked by the sympathy and support" parents had given their striking children. No degree of shock or outrage from the city elites could keep the spontaneous response contained. The most consistent grievance was against involuntary transfers of teachers, usually teachers who were close to the community. Another strike on the West Side erupted when a popular teacher was transferred because she had become too close to her students in a largely Bohemian district; the teacher herself was Czech.[10]

To contain the strikes that spread outside of the West Side, Superintendent Bodine sought desperately to avoid a repetition of the Andrew Jackson School confrontation. He brought school rebels from the South Side directly downtown to talk to Cooley. Under questioning, one of the student rebels "confessed" that he had heard about the strikes at other schools from the

8. For a portrait of Delano and Chicago school politics from the principal's perspective, see Chester C. Dodge, *Reminiscences of a School Master* (Chicago, 1941). See also *CT,* 9 November 1902.

9. *CT,* 11 November 1902. See the editorial in *CT,* 11 November 1902, p. 12. For more on Cooley, see Marjorie Murphy, "From Artisan to Semiprofessional: White-Collar Unionism among Chicago Public School Teachers, 1870–1930" (Ph.D. diss., University of California, Davis, 1981), pp. 54–70.

10. Two students were suspended because they would not sing; the newspaper reported that their refusal was a protest against the involuntary transfer of a music teacher. Students also complained that more than four hours of study resulted in "brain fag." *CT,* 11 November 1902. "The parents are even more incensed than the pupils and I am afraid this action on the part of the Board will cause trouble. Miss McKeon acted as she did to protect the innocence of the children in her room. The parents know this and they are more than indignant." *CT,* 13 November 1902. See also *CT,* 14 November 1902.

teachers. "Did the talk of strikes by the teachers suggest the idea to the pupils?" "Yes," replied the student leader, "yes, I guess it did."[11]

The explanation fit perfectly into Cooley's litany on the need for centralized school authority: teachers were unprofessional, they opposed centralization because of their ties to corrupt politicians, and they were using innocent young children to protect themselves against involuntary transfers. John Powers was one of the city's most powerful gray wolves, a big boodler who pocketed profits at the expense of clean government. In the case of the Andrew Jackson School, as the reformers saw it, Powers was abetting the teachers' attempt to return to a system of political pull that benefited badly trained teachers. The reformers saw a logical connection between all types of corruption—in city government, in municipal building contracts, and in million-dollar streetcar and subway scams—and the public school teacher with her ties to the community.[12]

In fact, teachers were required by law to graduate from normal school, be certified by the school district, and complete an apprenticeship program. They underwent yearly evaluations by their principals and were individually rehired by a vote of the school-management committee of the 21–member citywide Board of Education. If they were utterly incompetent, there was little that John Powers or any city alderman could do for them. Yet proponents of school centralization remained convinced (and sought to convince others through a compliant press) that teaching had become a sinecure gained through political favoritism rather than a position earned by merit. Board president Clayton Mark, a Chicago businessman, reported that "political pull" had been used in an attempt "to subvert an impartial and effective administration of the school system." But, he warned, the "strenuous efforts of friendship with teachers would cripple the school system by politicians and men of influence."[13]

The strike effort in Chicago fizzled after the students' forced "confession," but the issues of school centralization, professionalism, teacher militancy, and community resistance reappeared in varying forms throughout the

11. *CT,* 18 November 1902.
12. City reformers belonged to a number of city clubs. The Civic Federation and the Municipal Voters League were prominent, but the Union League Club and the City's Women's Club also had active educational committees. Between 1892 and 1919 Chicago hosted seventy reform groups in which 215 people participated in three or more. These activists came overwhelmingly from the upper class and included one-third businessmen, one-quarter lawyers or judges, and nearly 15 percent professors. See Stephen J. Diner, *A City and Its Universities Public Policy in Chicago, 1829–1919* (Chapel Hill, N.C., 1980), pp. 122–23; also David J. Hogan, *Class and Reform: School and Society in Chicago, 1880–1930* (Philadelphia, 1985), pp. 31–41; Samuel P. Hays, "The Politics of Reform in Municipal Government in the Progressive Era," *Pacific Northwest Quarterly,* 4 (October 1964), pp. 157–69, reprinted in Alexander B. Callow, Jr., ed., *American Urban History: An Interpretive Reader with Commentaries* (New York, 1969), pp. 417–39; in the same volume see Mosei Ostrogorski, "The Politicians and the Machine," pp. 301–29.
13. Chicago Board of Education, *47th Annual Report,* 1903, p. 18.

early Progressive Era as schools changed. The issue of disciplining school-teachers was more than an act of revenge: school reformers hoped to isolate teachers from the community, to separate their loyalties from immediate neighborhoods, and to wean them from community concerns. The student strikes illustrated a profound degree of solidarity between teachers and their communities. In order to change the schools, this association had to be broken and teachers had to be made to conform to a new image of profession-alism.

The Nineteenth-Century Schoolteacher

One major reason for the contention between the school superintendent and the teachers was the rapidly changing expectations of teacher qualifica-tions. Scholarly achievement was suddenly being used to determine the status and pay of the schoolteacher. Historically, however, female deport-ment and behavior had been valued above intellectual achievement in teach-ing. The history of the feminization of schoolteachers reveals a conscious effort to hire women because of their feminine characteristics, chief of which was their cheap availability.

Catharine Beecher, the originator of so much of what became proper female deportment in America, opened her training school for teachers in 1830, before women had become the dominant gender in the teaching profession. Beecher was prophetic in her opinion that women would become dominant in the field. She characteristically saw the job as a respectable alternative to marriage where the young woman "need not outstep the prescribed boundaries of feminine modesty." She was also insightful in arguing that moral influence, more than scholarship, would be the most important aspect of American education. "To enlighten the understanding and to gain the affections is a teacher's business," and "since the mind is to be guided chiefly by means of the affections, is not woman best fitted to accomplish these important objectives?"[14] Indeed, Beecher's early em-phasis on social behavior and its importance in a democracy became part of the job description for women teachers. In 1856, the Chicago school system opened its Normal Department in the high school, describing its students as "young ladies of our city, who distinguish themselves by correct deportment and superior scholarship."[15]

Deportment, moral character, social obedience, domestic virtue, and firm habits were virtues in teaching, whereas over exertion in academic subjects was sometimes actually frowned upon. When the psychologist G. Stanley

14. Kathryn Kish Sklar, *Catharine Beecher: A Study in American Domesticity* (New York, 1976), pp. 97, 223.
15. Chicago Board of Education, *25th Annual Report,* 1879.

Hall was invited to speak in Chicago, the Board of Education hesitated to let teachers attend the lecture lest his ideas prove too taxing.[16] Superintendent Benjamin Andrews warned that teachers were "not to expect too much from books," particularly psychology books, because the teacher's attitude was supposed to be "concrete and ethical," whereas the psychological observer was thought to be "abstract and analytical."[17] Another superintendent warned teachers not to study too hard but to wait for "gradual maturity."[18] These prescriptions were based on the notion that women had particular intellectual limits, which, once taxed, could lead to emotional and physical deterioration. What was valued in women was their "refining influence," their "finer moral sensibilities and nobler impulses."[19]

As long as education was to refine the moral and mental sensibilities, women were valued in the system. Most superintendents helped perpetuate the low regard for the intellectual achievements of teachers. One superintendent put it this way: "Most teachers are unqualified to present any original method of studying . . . and could do no better for their pupils than to follow a well-developed system with the necessary information regarding the subject presented in a textbook."[20] If a teacher ignored the feminine virtues of submission to this guideline and study, she could be reprimanded for over-ambitiousness. "Not a few of them have studied beyond their strength. With ambitious teachers the tendency to do this is a real danger against which I have repeatedly given warning."[21] So it was a delicate situation in which Catharine Beecher had placed the young women, not one of complete independence as she had hoped, but still better than the old submission under the strict Calvinist ideology Beecher was hoping to escape.

Teaching in the nineteenth century was steeped in paternalism; father-daughter relationships within the schoolhouse and the community flourished. After the Civil War most teachers were women, most principals men. Some principals played the role of benevolent master, guiding teachers in their intellectual growth while allowing them to experiment with their new knowledge. Margaret Haley, a sixth-grade teacher in Chicago, wrote that her school principal read poetry by John Boyle O'Reilly to liven up the teachers. He also brought them newspaper clippings on Board of Education decisions, and he urged them to become more involved. Haley was so taken by him that years later she often confused the date of his death with that of her father's death. Other principals were not nearly so benevolent, reminding teachers that they were often officially called assistants, that is, they had not yet achieved the status of a genuine teacher. In some towns the high school

---

16. Chicago Board of Education, *48th Annual Report*, 1902, pp. 103–4.
17. Ibid.
18. Chicago Board of Education, *27th Annual Report*, 1881, pp. 29–30.
19. Chicago Board of Education, *40th Annual Report*, 1894, p. 56.
20. Chicago Board of Education, *46th Annual Report*, 1900.
21. Ibid.

principal was also the school supervisor, and so normal department teachers would move from the classroom in the high school to the elementary classrooms as teachers and be supervised by their high school principal.[22]

In rural areas a young woman schoolteacher was isolated from family and supervisors. She nevertheless labored under the command of a school committee made up of local men, who would visit the school at any time. Often she would board in the home of a school-board member so that her personal life was under supervision. In Catharine Beecher's time the notion of boarding away from home offered women independence from the tyranny of family life, but by the late nineteenth century teachers recognized the tyranny of the community and preferred to live with their families. One teacher in the union later recalled that she turned down a rural job because there were so many Sunday school duties, Bible reading classes, and religious social obligations that she was afraid she would not be allowed to actually teach. The impersonality of urban life offered teachers some freedoms from these constraints.[23]

The major reason for the feminization of teaching was purely economic. School boards had very little money. Some schools operated strictly out of the old sixteenth-section provision of the Northwest Ordinance of 1787 which granted to the public domain every sixteenth section of land for the purpose of building schools. This portion of land was most frequently sold, although some districts simply rented the land or used it as collateral to borrow money for school construction. In small rural communities schools were built by community cooperation, whereas in larger towns and cities a portion of the county taxes were set aside for schools. Unfortunately for urban teachers and pupils, most taxes were based on land ownership or (less frequently) on real property. Rural-dominated state legislatures tended to hold down the tax rate for school purposes, making it difficult for urban schools to take advantage of the new wealth produced within their reach. In the late nineteenth century most cities were asking for separate taxes or were revising city charters to include special city taxes.

The problem became a crisis as the Progressive period began. Public utility firms, already under significant pressure as monopolies, and city streetcar franchises, also under attack for corrupt practices, tried to prevent tax increases for education. Most states moved away from a strict land tax,

22. Chicago Teachers' Federation Collection, Chicago Historical Society (hereafter cited as CTF Collection). The original version of the Haley biography is in the last section and is titled "1934 version" (hereafter cited as Margaret Haley's autobiography). Marjorie Murphy, "Progress of the Poverty of Philosophy: Two Generations of Labor Reform Politics: Michael and Margaret Haley" (Paper presented at the Knights of Labor Conference, Newberry Library, May 1979).

23. Evelyn J. Ounhey, "Factors That Govern a Teacher's Desire to Be Assigned to a Difficult School," Box 26/4, Chicago Teachers' Union Collection, Chicago Historical Society (hereafter cited as CTU Collection).

but a few remained dominated by rural legislators until well into the thirties. Teachers' salaries did not rise until unionization began.[24]

What teachers could not gain in salary in the nineteenth century they could gain in prestige. Teaching was a high-status occupation for women who had to work. Anzia Yezierska's autobiographical novel, *The Breadgivers,* provides a good example of the way teaching was perceived by working-class women. She portrays the making of a public school teacher as an incident in the troubled life of a poor immigrant family on the Lower East Side of New York. The heroine, Sara Smolinsky, "the hard hearted one," rejects the patriarchal tyranny of the family that had forced her sisters from the toil of the factory into miserable marriages arranged with cold economic calculation by her father. Sara follows instead the Horatio Alger formula of hard work and education to earn her place in the most lucrative and honorable position open to working women. The pinnacle of success for Sara Smolinsky was to become a public school teacher. A former New York public school teacher herself, Yezierska described vividly the moment Sara recognized her ambition. "A public school teacher—I. . . . It was like looking up to the top of the highest skyscraper while down in the gutter."[25]

Yet even Yezierska admitted that her teaching career was not all that satisfying. Known as a student who cut the education courses to take advantage of Columbia's broad liberal arts offering, Yezierska pursued a literary career. Her heroine expressed a similar disillusionment, admitting that teaching was not what she had wanted after all. Most who left teaching gave up in the first year. In Chicago the average teaching career for women was eight years; it was twelve years in Philadelphia. Those who stayed in teaching found that there was little room for advancement. In the pursuit of a uniform program, principals and superintendents were not anxious to give teachers new assignments. Supervisors' jobs often required a higher degree, which was nearly impossible for most working teachers to earn. Some laboriously attended night classes in college to become high school teachers in order to earn more pay, but the majority of career teachers stayed within their elementary classrooms for thirty and forty years.

These teachers expressed a growing concern over job security and pensions. Male public employees generally gained pensions and civil service protections in these years, and their victories presented female teachers with an attractive alternative to the adulation of the feminine, which would give them no financial solace in their old age. The idea of being free from political harassment as some civil service employees were, of gaining regular promo-

24. Marjorie Murphy, "Taxation and Social Conflict: Teacher Unionism and Public School Finance in Chicago, 1898–1934," *Journal of the Illinois State Historical Society,* 74 (Winter 1981), pp. 242–60.
25. Anzia Yezierska, *The Breadgivers: A Struggle between a Father of the Old World and a Daughter of the New* (New York, 1925), p. 75.

tions by examination, not by further education, and of getting a pension on retirement, appealed to the women schoolteachers. They underestimated the opposition to these reforms, but they were beginning to see themselves differently, beginning to look for more than words of reassurance. These changes were just the beginning of a teacher awakening that blossomed in the early days of school centralization.

Forces for Change

Much of the conflict over school centralization can be traced to the industrial revolution and its concomitant social dislocation. Rapid industrialization and the bitter contest between capital and labor transformed social relations in most American cities in the period from 1880 to 1920. In Chicago the accompanying protests swept through the city with the ferocity of a prairie storm. In the wake of this storm came the transformation of public education from largely unsystematic, decentralized congeries of informal networks into a bustling bureaucracy representing various ethnic neighborhoods and social enclaves. Fierce as the conflicts were in Chicago, the city was no exception to this basic pattern of change. Efficiency in business, that great call to eliminate crippling competition in the last depression of 1893, had been introduced into education and other social endeavors. The revolution in education, however, was not just a question of reorganization to imitate the methods of business (although centralization did follow business patterns). Instead it was an entire societal change in attitudes toward education prompted by the effects of industrialization on the job market.[26]

Changes in the job market—especially the decline in skilled labor and its replacement by unskilled or semiskilled blue-collar occupations and by clerical and lower-management jobs—brought workers and management together on the issue of the importance of education. Schooling was becoming more important to the working class. Immigrant workers and native-born laborers witnessed the transformation of work from an industrial setting run largely by artisans, craftsmen, journeymen, and apprentices to an altogether mechanized factory setting where only general education and a minimum of skill were needed. Blue-collar apprenticeship opportunities declined while

26. Hogan, *Class and Reform*, pp. 138–51; Harry Braverman, *Labor and Monopoly Capital: The Degradation of Work in the Twentieth Century* (New York, 1974), pp. 184–223, 424–26; Katherine Stone, "The Origins of Job Structures in the Steel Industry," in *Labor Market Segmentation*, ed. Richard Edwards, Michael Reich, and David M. Gordon (Lexington, Mass., 1975), pp. 27–84; David M. Gordon, Richard Edwards, and Michael Reich, *Segmented Work, Divided Workers: The Historical Transformation of Labor in the United States* (New York, 1982), pp. 76–99; David J. Hogan, "Education and the Making of the Chicago Working Class, 1880–1930," *History of Education Quarterly,* 18 (Fall 1978), pp. 227–70; Robert R. Albertson, "The Decay of Apprenticeship and Corporation Schools," *Charities and Commons,* 19 (October 1907), p. 815; Paul H. Douglas, *American Apprenticeship and Industrial Education* (New York, 1921).

opportunities in white-collar occupations multiplied. As fewer workers had the knowledge of how to do the work, the need for new managers increased. At the same time businessmen were concerned that the traditional democratic structure of education stood in the way of a less costly and more pragmatic education.[27]

Although substantially agreeing that education was important, labor representatives and members of the business community disagreed over the need for structural changes in education. The issue was not simply one of control: it was a definition of democratic methods on one hand and the desire for an operation that was unit-cost efficient on the other. The classroom then became a kind of contested terrain where the transition from a fairly simple, artisanal factory economy into a modern industrial complex attracted political and economic opposites to play the power struggles that the industrial revolution had introduced.[28]

Beyond these class-based battles, the problems in the schools reflected the chaos of dynamic urban growth that was unprecedented in the nation's history. After 1900 European immigrants flooded into American cities at the rate of half a million a year; farm workers, discouraged by the rising costs of transportation and farm equipment and the declining prices for agricultural products, migrated to the cities; and industrial workers who had once populated the agrarian factories in small villages and towns turned to the cities for more steady work. Chicago, New York, Philadelphia, Cincinnati, and Cleveland all reported record growth. As schools became difficult to administer, reorganization appeared inevitable. Growth, however, would not solely determine the direction of change. More working people placed their hopes in education. It was as if people had shifted their sights from industrialization to education to rediscover the perfectibility of humankind.[29]

The cities offered more than a free education. This was a diverse educational experience, one with graded classrooms and a classical high school. Public libraries, museums, and special vacation schools offered poor children, whether immigrant or native born, unheard-of opportunity. Consequently, urban schools were packed. Parents had difficulty getting their children into school, so they went to their city alderman, who in turn raised the issue at the local school committee. District superintendents worked to

27. Murphy, "From Artisan to Semiprofessional."

28. Richard Edwards, *Contested Terrain: The Transformation of the Workplace in the Twentieth Century* (New York, 1979), pp. 76–78, 136–39; Hogan, "Education and the Making of the Chicago Working Class"; G. M. A. Kerchensteiner, *Three Lectures on Vocational Education* (Chicago, 1911), pp. 8–12; Julia Wrigley, *Class, Politics, and Schools: Chicago, 1900–1950* (New Brunswick, N.J., 1982).

29. Selma Berol, "Public Schools and the Immigrant: The New York City Experience," pp. 31–43; Leonard Dinerstein, "Education and the Advancement of American Jews," both in *American Education and the European Immigrant, 1840–1940*, ed. Bernard Weiss (Urbana, Ill., 1982), pp. 44–60; Thomas Kessner, *The Golden Door: Italian and Jewish Immigrant Mobility in New York City* (New York, 1977), pp. 79–99.

upgrade their separate districts while aldermen and crooked school committeemen often appropriated profits on inflated costs for school sites in the overcrowded urban slums. The battle between the school-construction budget and the educational budget became an incessant struggle in what amounted to the greatest pre–New Deal public works project in all the major cities. In this context, corruption in education was perceived as the ordinary state of affairs. Teachers and school administrators viewed the burgeoning corruption in construction with alarm. It could potentially destroy the democratic promise and rob the common people.[30]

These aspects of education—inability to administer properly, corruption, and the battle over the budget—were largely settled in city hall or the central offices of the school districts, not in the neighborhoods. Only the district administrators, the school committeemen, the school principals, or the local aldermen had the power to broker for the interests of the neighborhood, and some of these men had their hands in the till.[31]

Even without corruption the old system of brokering in city hall could not solve the problems of ethnic rivalry and neighborhood change that had intensified before centralization was proposed. In some Chicago neighborhoods the schools were very badly placed. One school north of the Illinois and Michigan canal was particularly poorly located, standing on the border between a Bohemian and an Irish community. Stevedores on the docks, Bohemian and Irish men, literally fought in the streets for jobs while their sons brawled in the schoolyard. Folks in the community reported that every twenty years or so a fight in school ended in the death of a youngster; they would shake their heads and say that the school should never have been built there. In another neighborhood the school was uncharacteristically empty because the neighborhood had disintegrated in the face of new warehouses and factories, and classrooms were impossibly noisy because of the nearby railroad and foundry. Mothers complained that they could not hang out wash in the sooty air; open sewers from the factories produced an intolerable

30. David B. Tyack, *The One Best System: A History of American Urban Education* (Cambridge, 1974), pp. 177–78; Murphy, "From Artisan to Semiprofessional," pp. 17–19.

31. Mary J. Herrick, *The Chicago Schools: A Social and Political History* (Beverly Hills, Calif., 1971), pp. 75–112. Michael Patrick McCarthy, "Businessmen and Professionals in Municipal Reform: The Chicago Experience" (Ph.D. diss., Northwestern University, 1970), pp. 67–81. For more on business, reform, and education ties, see Donald David Marks, "Polishing the Gem on the Prairie: The Evolution of Civic Reform Consciousness in Chicago, 1874–1900" (Ph.D. diss., University of Wisconsin–Madison, 1974), pp. 89–141; Stephen London, "Business and the Chicago Public School System, 1890–1966" (Ph.D. diss., University of Chicago, 1968), pp. 61–65. For more on business ties, see George S. Counts, *School and Society in Chicago* (New York, 1928), pp. 133–53; and Counts, *The Social Composition of Boards of Education: A Study in the Social Control of Public Education* (Chicago, 1927). See also Charles E. Merriam, *Chicago: A More Intimate View of Urban Politics* (New York, 1929); Lloyd Wendt and Herman Kogan, *Big Bill Thompson* (Indianapolis, 1953); Fletcher Dobyns, *The Underworld of American Politics* (New York, 1932); Alexander Gottfried, *Boss Cermak of Chicago* (Seattle, 1962); Richard Bechr, "Edward Dunne: Reform Mayor of Chicago, 1905–1907" (Ph.D. diss., University of Chicago, 1958); and Harold Gosnell, *Machine Politics: The Chicago Model* (Chicago, 1937).

stench. Enrollments plummeted, while children blocks south were turned away because there simply was no space. The neighborhoods changed rapidly. Nor was the problem limited to Chicago. In Brooklyn whole new subdivisions opened without schools. A construction firm offered new school land at a premium price. Even if a school opened in a year, it would not be able to house the children in the new neighborhood. School location was a new administrative problem: it required accurate school censuses, the ability to predict population movement and new populations coming in. But who knew how many immigrants would come in the next year, the next five years, or thereafter?[32]

The new immigrants were not just from Ireland and Germany as in the past but from Italy, Slovakia, Croatia, Hungary, Russia, and Poland. They spoke new languages, sometimes as many as seven different languages in one classroom. Classes were too large to offer special attention to the children.[33]

Neither the old politicians, school committeemen, and district superintendents nor the new administrative centralizers had the resources and abilities to overcome the problems of education at the turn of the century. But the problems were so evident, so recurrent, with crowds nearly rioting outside the school-board doors every year, that few could overlook them. The question was: Who could be trusted to do the job? The school administrators meeting in the center city were often unaware of the neighborhood needs and the very informal agreements that tied communities together or (in the case of ethnic or social difference) badly divided them. The old politicians certainly knew that a neighborhood was more than a geographic location on a map, but they had neither the expertise nor the desire to change a system that had served them well.

The schoolhouse had been symbolically elevated to the level of the factory as a new arena for class struggle. Just as industrial idealists a century before had hoped that mechanization would redistribute wealth and elevate humanity, the educational idealists at the turn of the century looked to education as an open door that would fulfill the promises made by the industrial revolution. Big changes were happening; the issue was who would direct the changes and in whose interests. The question of leadership was central to the transformation in education.

Schoolteachers—common elementary school teachers, mostly women and usually the more experienced ones—began to assume leadership in the ensuing struggle over educational policy. Unlike society women, who were often invited and urged to participate with elite men's clubs in school reform, schoolteachers were scorned for stepping out of the feminine role at the same time they were harassed for not being professional enough. In a sense they

---

32. *CT,* 5 November 1904; *CT,* 6 December 1904; Edith Abbott and Sophonsiba Breckinridge, *Truancy and Non-Attendance in the Chicago Schools* (New York, 1970), pp. 298–307.
33. Annual school censuses sometimes reported ethnic breakdowns.

were elected by the communities they worked in, pushed by the conditions of their jobs, and pressured by the examples of other women coming into public life. In another sense they were ready to lead, ready to translate the new education into their own personal lives and grow with it. They welcomed the opportunity to abandon rote memorization for creative thinking, and the more they thought about education, the more political they became.

With formal election to employment, schoolteachers knew the educational system. They knew the neighborhood because if they did not live in it, they lived not far from it in the city. They were educated in the same neighborhoods, they came from familiar institutions, their fathers worked in the local economy. But contrary to what the centralizers would have the public believe, they were not necessarily tied to the political machine. They were voteless women. They were not interested in the lucrative political trade in education—the building contracts, schoolbook purchases, and equipment inventories. Everyone knew where the real corruption could be found. They did get their jobs on eligibility lists, and no doubt politicians did recommend people for jobs. But teachers themselves had to pass a test, and once elected, a teacher had to work closely with the school principal and the community, not the alderman, to assure her tenure.[34]

Teaching was not just a pleasant interlude for young prospective brides; it was a job for women that both illustrated the powerlessness of women in the city and promised them more independence than that which was available to their rural counterparts or to unemployed women. It was also a job at the center of social concern in the Progressive Era. Urban school teachers were the first to work with new immigrants. Before the settlement-house workers, social workers, or progressive reformers discovered the working immigrant and the poor factory hand, schoolteachers made the first contact with the human waves of newcomers. Teachers gave education its meaning, they helped shape the character of relationships within the community. So they were in a special position during a period of crisis. They could choose sides in the school wars or cut their own path. They chose to cut their own path, but they could not do it without the community.[35]

The strikes were unusual occurrences. They represented a time when young children expressed their involvement in an urban culture. Sensitive to the political winds and currents of school reform, schoolchildren could not miss the implications of centralization for their teachers. But more than a historical anomaly, these strikes illustrate the bonding between teachers,

34. For more on the image of teachers as boodlers, see *CT*, "Score Pull in Schools," 27 February 1900; "Want Anti-Pull Rule," 26 October 1900; 25 March 1903; "Pull Gone from Schools," 10 September 1903; "Clash Over Pull," 10 November 1903; "School Shakeup: No Pull," 29 September 1904; 4 December 1904; 28 December 1904. For an examination of the promotional system, see the report of Louis Post, Chicago Board of Education, *Proceedings*, 1906.

35. See my chapter "Teaching as a Job," pp. 89–146, in "From Artisan to Semiprofessional."

students, and communities. Curiously, this sense of solidarity was discouraged and misinterpreted to the point of condemning parents, teachers, and children. In an age when John Dewey's child-centered classroom was being introduced, teachers were being warned to stay out of the community. It is more curious when one considers how the further professionalization of teachers did create a distance between the student and the teacher—to the extent that when centralization was attacked in the 1960s parents and children attacked teachers whose interests then seemed to lie in the professionalization project and not in the neighborhoods. The relationship between teacher and student (and for that matter between therapist and patient or between social worker and client) is professionally defined as distant. Yet the best teachers, like the best therapists and the best social workers, establish close relationships with their clients. For schoolteachers the issue is further complicated by the politics of communities themselves and the fact that teachers often have little control over the political events that change the nature of the community. Still, the principle is the same: the professional teacher is warned to keep her distance while the most successful teacher has her ear close to the ground in her community and relies on her identification with parents and children in the community. The ambiguity in the definitions of professional behavior has added a painful irony in the history of teaching: early in the century teachers were damned for being too close to the community, and sixty years later they were damned for distancing themselves from it.

In the Andrew Jackson School neighborhood there was a definite spirit of solidarity of parents with their children and of children with the teachers. This relationship evolved out of the chaos of the new urban school, out of a sense of frustration with the entire educational project as it was being defined. The crisis over the typhoid-infected water was just a catalyst in a brew that had been simmering for some time. Fifty-five children sat in McKeon's classroom. We don't know what ethnic groups the strikers were from, but the census of the neighborhood tells us that their parents were born in Ireland, Russia, Germany, and Sweden. There were also a few Polish families, French Canadian families, a Chinese family, and several native-born families. The fathers were mostly laborers and teamsters, but there were pockets of peddlers, clerks, salesmen, and artisans from the building trades, and printers and printer feeders. The mothers were mostly housewives but not all of them. A few worked in the clothing industry located nearby, a few in the new white-collar occupations for women (clerks, stenographers, and telephone operators), and a handful in the old trades for women: a milliner, a seamstress, and a tailoress. The households were large. The women living in the Andrew Jackson School neighborhood had an average of four children. The average age for the male population was twenty-four; it was twenty-one for women. Over three-quarters rented their homes. In short, there was nothing extraordinary about the community, no common ethnic or occupational bond that would draw people together in this minor incident of resistance.[36]

There was also nothing clearly special about McKeon. She had taught in the system for nearly fifteen years, she was a member of the Chicago Teachers' Federation, but she was not an activist, and she never assumed any other leadership roles. Yet McKeon seemed absolutely certain that the parents resented Bodine's roundup of truant children and that they would resent the imposition of centralized authority in the operation of her classroom. She did not have to run to the neighborhood alderman to learn whether she could take her stand on this issue. Instead, she stood by the informal motto of her Chicago Teachers' Federation: "It was the right thing to do."[37]

36. Description of the neighborhood taken from the U.S. Manuscript Census, 1900 (Washington, D.C., 1900). I used estimates of the school neighborhood from school district maps.
37. Margaret Haley's autobiography.

CHAPTER TWO

Centralization and Professionalization

Centralization and professionalization were essentially two halves of the same walnut. Proponents of centralization wished to exert managerial control over the largest expense in the education budget, the teaching force. Educational historians have often referred to this process as an "organizational revolution," because of the hierarchical nature of the reform. But this phrase ignores the essential empowerment of the superintendent of schools to hire and fire personnel, which was the key focus of centralization. Unencumbered by any need for moral sensibility, political acceptance, or community favor, the new school superintendent would be able to function with the lightning power of Henry Clay Frick, the chairman of Carnegie Steel known for his tactic of locking out the hapless Homestead Steel strikers in 1892. What was needed was an ideology that separated teachers from the community, reinforcing their differences from the communities they came from and making them the hirelings of a new superintendent of schools who alone would determine their success in education. Professionalization became a tool for totally reshaping the lines of authority in school administration, for weeding out those of less desirable ethnic and social origins through requirements for higher education, and for instilling a sense of loyalty not to the community, but to the school principal, superintendent, and educational professoriate.[1]

1. For an overview of the centralization of schools, see David B. Tyack, *The One Best System: A History of American Urban Education* (Cambridge, 1974); Diane Ravitch, *The Great School Wars: New York City, 1805–1973* (New York, 1974); Marvin Lazerson, *Origins of the Urban School: Public Education in Massachusetts, 1870–1914* (Cambridge, 1971); David J. Hogan, *Class and Reform: School and Society in Chicago, 1880–1930* (Philadelphia, 1985); Martin Carnoy, *Schooling in a Corporate Society: The Political Economy of Education in America* (New York, 1972); Lawrence A. Cremin, *The Transformation of the School: Progressivism in American Education* (New York, 1964); Sol Cohen, *Progressive and Urban School Reform* (New York, 1963); David Nasaw, *Schooling to Order: A Social History of Public Schooling in the United States* (New York,

The teachers, though they benefited little from the confused and often contradictory existing lines of command, were wary of reformers who promoted such extreme centralization. These reformers were usually an assortment of schoolmen, business leaders, and prominent professionals, who sought to replace the informal networks of authority within neighborhoods by charging that the system was antiquated, rural, and corrupt. Significantly, they did not attack the obvious corruption in the construction end of the educational budget because these projects produced jobs for voting men in the community. Instead, they pointed to the efficiency of modern business establishments where lines of authority were centralized. They argued that the schools needed "one-man power" with the ability to hire and fire teachers, who were nonvoting constituents. Gender infuses the issues of centralization and professionalization in the language of "one-man power" and in the reality of the absence of political pull for voteless women.

The Push for Centralization

In 1893, Dr. Joseph Mayer Rice published a popular series in *Forum*, a national magazine, reporting that he had visited public schools in Chicago, St. Paul, Philadelphia, and New York City and found most teachers to be poorly prepared, barely literate, and wholly dependent on rote memorization as the basis of their teaching methods. Rice's examples pointed to the "absurd" methods of teachers whose educational background was often less than one year of high school preparation. Despite the sensational quality of Rice's critique, schoolmen, who lashed out against old conventional wisdoms, embraced this one with startling alacrity.[2]

Rice's book became the standard reference for the proponents of centralization, even though Rice's own observations failed to meet the standards of scientific and systematic procedure so popular with reformers. Careful quantitative analysis escaped Rice's attention and for that matter the notice of his admirers in the National Education Association. Focusing on one school in New York City, Rice argued that the school system encouraged rote learning of the extreme fashion he found during one classroom visit. "The school has been converted into the most dehumanizing institution that I have ever laid my eyes upon, each child being treated as if he possessed a memory and the faculty of speech, but no individualities, no sensibilities, no soul."[3] He objected strongly to the memorization of sets of questions and answers,

1979); Samuel Bowles and Herbert Gintis, *Schooling in Capitalist America* (New York, 1976); Raymond Callahan, *Education and the Cult of Efficiency: A Study of the Social Forces That Have Shaped the Administration of the Public Schools* (Chicago, 1962).

2. Joseph Mayer Rice, *The Public School System of the United States* (New York, 1893), p. 167; Cremin, *Transformation of the School*, pp. 3–8.

3. Ravitch, *Great School Wars*, pp. 128–29.

which constituted the main curriculum for the school he visited. Denying
that he meant to blame the teachers, he pointed out that they lacked incentives to improve their teaching since few were supervised and none could be
dismissed by the assistant superintendent. Rice had very little to say about a
new curriculum for teachers; instead he proposed a new structure for the city
schools in which a superintendent and twenty supervisors would work
directly with teachers and fire those who did not work up to new standards of
professionalism.[4]

Stung by Rice's criticism, teachers and principals pointed out that Rice
was a journalist whose experience in the schools was limited to his very
narrow view of one school. Of the four thousand teachers in the city, they
argued, Rice had observed the methods of one teacher and then condemned
them all. But the president of the Board of Education and the president of
Columbia University's Teachers College, Nicholas Murray Butler, publicly
endorsed Rice's recommendations, and the movement for the centralization
of New York's public schools gained new momentum.

The response to Rice's report on Chicago resembled the New York experience, except that board members were more vocal in condemning Rice in the
annual report: "Occasionally some notoriety-loving charlatan has assailed
our educational department and undertaken to criticize our teachers and has
given instances without names of gross ignorance." Still, in Chicago, the
board immediately reopened its normal school, and by 1898 former school-
board member William Rainey Harper, president of the University of Chicago, was heading a commission to study and propose a new organizational
structure for the schools.[5]

In the examples of New York and Chicago, we can see how the transformation into a centralized system was neither smooth nor without opposition.[6] The processes of centralization in the two cities were remarkably
similar even if the outcomes of legislation differed greatly. Both cities
achieved school reorganization through a political battle marked by the rise
of reform governments. In both cities, the economic depression of 1892–93
spurred on the formation of reform movements whose attention to municipal
corruption challenged the old parties either to clean up the city or to make
way for change. In New York the failure of school-reform legislation in 1893
set up a challenge to Tammany Hall officials in 1894. Forming a "Committee
of 70," the city's middle- and upper-class reformers built a citywide alliance
to overthrow the incumbents and vote in a reform municipal government
under William L. Strong. The beauty of Strong's election was that the new

4. Ibid., p. 130; Joseph Mayer Rice, "Our Public School System: A Summary," *Forum,* 15
(June 1893), p. 505.
5. Chicago Board of Education, *40th Annual Report,* 1894; Ravitch, *Great School Wars,*
pp. 126–31.
6. Margaret Haley's autobiography, pt. 1; *CT,* 10 February 1899, 23 February 1899, 26 March
1899.

government represented a coalition of Republicans and Democrats devoted to breaking the ties of patronage and bad government.[7]

In Chicago the reformers also appealed to the insecurity of the city's elites. Riots of unemployed workers in the fall of 1893 raised fears of renewed social disorder in a tumultuous city. When former governor John Peter Altgeld decided to run against Mayor Carter Harrison, Jr., the mayor was afraid he might lose his reforming, bipartisan, community support. The reorganization commission headed by Harper was the mayor's effort to achieve some major reform before the election. The Harper Report appeared four months before the election. Harrison sent the recommendations to the state legislature for approval, which he hoped would come a month before the election. In Chicago, as in New York, schoolteachers and principals, labor leaders and ward heelers traveled to the state capital to oppose the new school legislation.[8]

Reform governments in major cities were not strong enough to overcome opposition in the legislature. Chicago and New York had the same problem with upstate/downstate legislatures run by Republican-party machines whose interests in big-city politics had to be appeased in order to pass any law. In Albany the opposition of Republican boss William Platt, along with the considerable parade of school people from New York City opposed to the measure, defeated the second bill for school reorganization in the state. In Springfield the Harper Bill was adroitly defeated for much the same reasons. The final success of school reorganization in New York can be attributed to the persistent work of one man, just as the defeat of the educational bill in Chicago can be attributed to the dedication of one woman.

In 1895 and 1896 Nicholas Murray Butler led in the triumph of school centralization in New York City. A prodigy for the dons of Columbia University, Butler had earned a doctoral degree in his early twenties before going to study in Germany. Columbia welcomed him home and made him full professor before he was twenty-eight. He launched a new journal, *Educational Review,* and organized Teachers College before becoming president of Columbia University. Butler managed to integrate the old evangelical origins of the teacher-training movement with the newer demands for academic achievement. For Butler, centralization promised the kind of reform that would build his new teacher-training college while helping him launch a national reputation as an educational reformer.[9]

To achieve his purposes Butler cleverly enlisted the energies of middle-class women in the club movement to support his centralization campaign. The Public Education Association (PEA) began in New York as Butler's

7. Ravitch, *Great School Wars*, pp. 144–58.

8. Carter H. Harrison, Jr., *Stormy Years: The Autobiography of Carter H. Harrison* (New York, 1935), pp. 103–43; William Rainey Harper, chairman, *Report of the Educational Commission of the City of Chicago* (Chicago, 1898). See also newspaper reports on the Harper Report in *CT*, 22 January 1899, 23 and 28 February 1899.

9. Paul Mattingly, *The Classless Profession* (New York, 1975), pp. 148–49.

support group for school centralization but later became a national institution that recruited club women behind centralization movements.[10] PEA women launched an aggressive campaign for Butler's educational reform bill and served as his personal emissaries to the public schools. Their primary responsibility was to educate women schoolteachers in the importance of school reform. This was not an easy assignment. The women organized an informational meeting months before the bill was introduced to the legislature to explain the reform to the teachers. The teachers voted overwhelmingly to oppose the legislation. Later the PEA women tried small teas, organized in various schools, to persuade teachers not to oppose the bill; again their success was minimal. The teachers were angered by this intrusion, wondering why they had suddenly become the objects of such interest in the tea-and-biscuit circuit. Women schoolteachers in New York were often barred from city women's clubs because membership was by nomination. Furthermore, women's clubs met during the week, when schoolteachers were working. Working schoolteachers and nonworking middle-class women had little in common. Still it was an effective ploy to have women's club members testify for the educational reform bill in Albany when women schoolteachers testified against it. The bill passed the legislature in the spring of 1895.[11]

Butler was also a pioneer in using the press to his advantage to guide public opinion for his legislative reform. Reporters and editors were attracted by his colorful language and flamboyant combativeness against the opponents of reform. Schoolteachers who opposed him were all "incompetents" protected by local trustees whose jobs would be eliminated in his educational reform bill. He pictured the typical schoolteacher as a poorly educated girl whose interest in education was minimal at best. Protected by political hacks, teachers needed to be replaced by intelligent and well-trained women whose primary allegiance was to educational excellence, not to the job. Butler's dominance of the press through his connections and useful copy dampened the spirits of teachers, whose sporadic counterorganization proved useless in the campaign to defeat the bill. The bill became law in April 1896 despite the petition of 100,000 citizens against it.[12]

In Chicago, school centralization did not fare as well. William Rainey

10. Richard F. W. Whittemore, *Nicholas Murray Butler and Public Education, 1862–1911,* (New York, 1970), pp. 54–56.

11. *CT,* 22 January 1899. There is evidence from a later period that teachers resented very strongly "club" interference in school affairs. A perplexed school administrator, Clarence A. Weber, noted that "teachers cited the fact that school administrators usually belong to service clubs, take time off for lunch, and stay away till 1:30 or 2 o'clock . . . but teachers are usually, if not always, denied such opportunities." Weber, *Personnel Problems of School Administrators* (New York, 1954), pp. 16–17. See also Nancy Hoffman, *Woman's True Profession: Voices from the History of Teaching* (New York, 1971), p. 215; William McAndrew, "Public School Teaching," *World's Work,* 5 (March 1903), pp. 3188–89; Marjorie Murphy, "From Artisan to Semiprofessional: White-collar Unionism among Chicago Public Schoolteachers, 1870–1930" (Ph.D. diss., University of California, Davis, 1981), pp. 182–85.

12. Ravitch, *Great School Wars,* pp. 153–56.

Harper was clearly Nicholas Murray Butler's equal in scholarly achieve-ment, but could never match Butler's political skills. Harper earned his college degree when he was seventeen and like Butler worked for advanced degrees in Europe. The University of Chicago, however, was little more than the old Baptist College of the Midwest until oilman John D. Rockefeller took an interest and became a major contributor to the new prairie university. Harper wanted to build a university that combined the elegance and authority of Oxford University with practicality and vocational purposes. He too wanted a teachers' college to elevate the standards of public school teaching, and to this end he encouraged John Dewey to open an experimental school on campus and begin the work of teacher education. Harper's reforms, how-ever, differed markedly from Butler's.[13]

In New York, the original proposal, calling for a board of superintendents to oversee teaching, with another separate board to handle the business aspects of the schools, incorporated some of Joseph Mayer Rice's proposals. However, the dismantling of local boards of education, which had tradi-tionally controlled the firing and hiring of teachers, was something Rice could not endorse. Butler made local control the issue, arguing that without full professional control of the schools the board of superintendents would never be able to properly supervise the teachers.[14]

Harper's proposal called for more control centralized in one superinten-dent of schools with a smaller board of education: eleven members instead of the twenty-one members in New York. But Harper was even more specific in demanding a college education of all teachers and a special procedure for the hiring and firing of teachers. His report specifically criticized the feminiza-tion of teaching and called for efforts to hire more men, pay them higher wages, and promote them more rapidly in the school system. He was equally specific in outlining the authority of the superintendent. The eleven members of the board of education were not to have direct control over the schools. The former committee assignments of the old twenty-one-member board would be taken up by the superintendent and his assistants. Harper wanted to dismantle the policies of local control, but his plan was more centralized than Butler's policy and far more specific in what it would do for teachers. Butler knew that if he could get rid of local control, then the board of superinten-dents would take care of the teachers.[15]

In several areas Butler's strategies were not as workable in Chicago as they had been in New York. Butler had been able to keep his name out of his

13. Richard J. Storr, *Harper's University: The Beginnings* (Chicago, 1966); see also Steven J. Diner, *A City and Its Universities: Public Policy in Chicago, 1892–1919* (Chapel Hill, N.C., 1980), pp. 11–16; and Murphy, "From Artisan to Semiprofessional," pp. 40–41.

14. Whittemore, *Butler;* Ravitch, *Great School Wars,* p. 156.

15. Harper, *Report of the Educational Commission;* John Christian Pennoyer, "The Harper Report of 1899: Administrative Progressivism and Chicago Public Schools" (Ph.D. diss., University of Denver, 1978). See also Margaret Haley's autobiography, pt. 1; and Robert Reid, ed., *Bat-tleground: The Autobiography of Margaret A. Haley* (Urbana, Ill., 1982), p. 35.

reform bill, and he insisted that it be called the City Club bill or some other name. In Chicago, despite Harper's efforts, it was always the Harper Bill, even in its reincarnations in 1901, 1903, and 1909, after Harper had withdrawn from the fight. As for women's clubs, most supported the reform, but perhaps because of the decidedly antiwoman language of the report, they were not nearly as aggressive in their support as were the New York clubs. Finally, Harper had no campaign within the schools to divide the teachers. Indeed, there was a lot of material to unite teachers and defeat the centralization bill.[16]

Margaret Haley, a sixth-grade teacher in the Hendricks School, Back of the Yards, directed an effective campaign to mobilize schoolteachers against the Harper Bill and school reorganization. Schoolteachers in Chicago had organized briefly in 1895 to get a pension and again in 1897 to ask for a raise, but it was the campaign against the Harper Bill that first attracted Margaret Haley to the organization of teachers known as the Chicago Teachers' Federation. In Chicago the women's clubs had lost influence over teachers when they opposed the 1895 pension bill. Club women thought pensions would create a new dependence for schoolteachers, and frustrated teachers tried to explain the hardship of old age for working teachers. Haley accused the club women of caring for their maids better than schoolteachers. When the school-reorganization plan came before the public, the teachers had speakers to send to the women's clubs, and they organized their own afternoon teas in neighborhood schools.[17]

The University Women's Club took great offense at the idea that men should be paid more than women and pointed to equality in pay as one of the progressive aspects of Chicago schools. The Political Equality Club also condemned the Harper Report on the same basis. Club women had mobilized to nominate Ella Flagg Young to the office of superintendent and were sorely disappointed when the board nominated a man, an outsider whose political opinions on gold and silver issues counted for more than Mrs. Young's years of service. Finally, the language of the Harper Bill was extremely sexist. Filled with fears that feminization of school would destroy the minds of bright young men, the authors conveyed the sense that masculine authority would cure the schools of all ills.[18]

16. Murphy, "From Artisan to Semiprofessional," pp. 34–43; David B. Tyack, "Pilgrim's Progress: Toward a Social History of the School Superintendency, 1860–1960," *History of Education Quarterly,* 16 (Fall 1976), pp. 217–20.

17. Murphy, "From Artisan to Semiprofessional," pp. 45–48.

18. *CT,* 11 and 28 February 1899, 6 and 8 June 1899. The Harper Report recommended a higher salary for men than for women and lamented the decline of male teachers in the profession while extolling the positive effects men have on the male mind. See Harper, *Report of the Educational Commission,* pp. 22–27. One state legislator referred to it as "masculine economics" (*CT,* 23 February 1899). Harper began to oppose coeducation in 1902 and stirred resentments from women when he segregated classes and discouraged women at his university. Barbara Solomon, *In the Company of Educated Women: A History of Women and Higher Education* (New Haven, 1985), p. 58.

Another important issue raised by the teachers was the requirement for a college education. Very few Chicago teachers had college preparation, but a growing number had earned high school diplomas and some even managed to get a year of postsecondary education in normal schools. The call for a college education was the most elitist aspect of the report since very few of the teachers had had the opportunity to attend school beyond high school. Instead, most worked because their families needed their income. Teachers were not among the new generation of college graduates. Jane Addams and others like her had shunned school teaching because it was thought to be unfulfilling or perhaps beneath their status as middle- and upper-class educated women. A college education for women had become an elitist symbol that divided women, and schoolteachers who may have desired a college education were now being told that they were not fit for their jobs because they did not have enough education. The report had seemed to denigrate the value of experience in teaching in favor of book learning. One woman remarked that "learning how to teach from a college education was like learning how to cook from a cook book."[19]

Teacher opposition to a college education was not just another American exercise in anti-intellectualism. The teachers were not rejecting further training altogether but were protesting the forms of education the reformers wanted: the issue was control, not advanced education. In 1905 Chicago teachers were told that they had to take a certain number of courses to apply for a pay raise. The school superintendent expected them to take courses at the University of Chicago, Northwestern University, or the Cook County Normal School, though few public school teachers could afford to attend. The teachers decided instead to take education courses at the Art Institute of Chicago, where Anita McCormick Blaine (daughter of the famous Harvester king) had provided a refuge for the out-of-favor teachers of the old Normal College who were fired when the populist educator Francis Wayland Parker died. When they applied for the raise, the superintendent denied them the money, saying that the Art Institute was not a reputable institution. The point was that the superintendent could exert considerable control over the curriculum at the Cook County Normal School, where he expected teachers to attend classes. He also implicitly trusted the standards at the University of Chicago or Northwestern University. At the Art Institute, however, he had no influence on the curriculum; there teachers carried on the antiestablishment practices set by Francis Wayland Parker. In another instance a schoolteacher was denied a leave of absence because her plan of study did not include further education courses. Instead she wanted to study Greek and Latin, courses that pointed to the desire for a classical education. Clearly,

19. Murphy, "From Artisan to Semiprofessional," pp. 90–100; *CT,* 19 February 1899.

teacher education was for the purpose of furthering teaching, not the teachers themselves.[20]

Perhaps the main reason for the Harper Bill's failure, however, was that it called for a far more centralized reorganization than had been suggested in New York. Superintendent "Bulletin" Ben Andrews, in office at the time of the school-bill battle, gave teachers and their sympathizers plenty to complain about. Andrews, whose school experience was minimal, had been chosen over the more popular Ella Flagg Young because of his political connections. Throughout his entire administration he managed to offend the Chicago Federation of Labor, the mayor, and the school board. The teachers convincingly predicted disaster were he given more power.[21]

In February 1899, the National Council of the National Education Association held its semiannual meeting at a prominent Chicago hotel. Its leaders gave reporters accounts of the warm reception given Superintendent Andrews, the seriousness of the discussions over school problems, and the hope that Chicagoans would be enlightened enough to support the Harper Bill. Nicholas Murray Butler orchestrated the press in the same way he had done in New York and the effort proved timely: newspaper accounts were generous toward centralization and its benefits. Yet despite the administration's efforts to keep them from testifying against the bill, schoolteachers flocked to Springfield, and reports of their negative testimony filled the press. The final battles over the Harper Bill were fought in the legislature, while both the incumbent mayor and his opponent, the former governor, promised schoolteachers that their administration would give them better job conditions. The very atmosphere of the debate could hardly convince the people of Chicago that this reform would take politics out of the schools. The bill was defeated in 1899.[22]

As noted before, reformers attempted to pass the Harper Bill again in 1901, 1903, and 1909, but in each successive year teacher opposition grew stronger, and the proponents were unable to overcome the original objections to the bill. It was not until 1917, after the Board of Education had outlawed the teachers' unions and the state supreme court had upheld the untrammeled power of the Board of Education to fire and hire, that the centralization bill passed. Even after it was finally enacted, the politicos on the Board of Education did not step aside gracefully. For two years after the reform bill, one board of education fought for control with another, several board members were jailed, and a new superintendent was hired by one board of

20. Murphy, "From Artisan to Semiprofessional," p. 129; Chicago Board of Education, *55th Annual Report*, 1909; Otto Schneider, "President's Report," Chicago Board of Education, *54th Annual Report*, 1908; Chicago Board of Education, *Proceedings*, 1906.

21. *CT*, 11 and 19 February 1898; *Chicago Teachers' Federation Bulletin* (hereafter cited as *CTF Bulletin*), 6 March 1903.

22. *CT*, 10 February 1899; Murphy, "From Artisan to Semiprofessional," p. 53.

education only to be fired by another. This was hardly the era of a strong superintendency that the reformers had forecast.[23]

Few of the reform bills enacted in the country actually gave superintendents the powers of professional autonomy promised in the rhetoric of reform movements. Even in New York, the Board of Superintendents had to consult with a lay board, and it was not uncommon for its members to consider the superintendents their employees. District Superintendent William Maxwell complained bitterly when he was not allowed to attend the annual meeting of the National Education Association. Frustrated by the unwieldy forty-six-member Board of Education, Maxwell simply built his own framework for supervising the schools with very little consultation. When in 1917 the board was reduced to seven members, Maxwell had already gained considerable authority in school governance, which he had no reason to share with a streamlined board.[24]

The same kind of partly developed school-management system operated in other cities where the reorganization revolution had likewise begun sometime in the 1890s but would not be completed until the 1920s. In San Francisco a reform movement had brought about a new charter in 1898, which gave the mayor full responsibility for a professionally appointed staff. Four directors, paid three thousand dollars annually, and an elected superintendent ran the schools. But the system placed the elected superintendent in competition with the directors, and even though a strong superintendent dominated the schools from 1906 to 1923 there were complaints from the business community and professional educators that this dual system provided for divided loyalties among the staff and teachers. After a controversial report recommending a more corporate model of school governance appeared in 1916, schoolteachers and the superintendent united to oppose the new proposal. Despite these efforts, the once-defeated reform passed in a city referendum in 1920. The elected superintendent was replaced by a Columbia-trained professional who had just become NEA president, and thus the promises of the 1898 reform came to fruition in 1920.[25]

The San Francisco model was not unusual, for despite what professional schoolmen claimed, the revolution in school centralization was not an overnight success but rather a twenty-year struggle, and even in the decade of Harding and Coolidge, many school districts that had been reformed were not centralized. Massachusetts schools were a case in point. In 1901 a survey of 233 towns and cities in the state illustrated that superintendents were

23. Mary J. Herrick, *The Chicago Schools: A Social and Political History* (Beverly Hills, Calif., 1971), pp. 137–39, 166; George S. Counts, *School and Society in Chicago* (New York, 1928), pp. 94–100, 251–63; Henry Grant Dewey, "The Development of Public School Administration in Chicago" (Ph.D. diss., University of Chicago, 1937), pp. 148–59; John Howatt, *Notes on the First One Hundred Years of Chicago School History* (Chicago, 1940), pp. 33–42.

24. Samuel Abelow, *Dr. William H. Maxwell* (New York, 1930), pp. 105–6.

25. Tyack, *The One Best System,* pp. 147–66.

gaining duties formerly handled by school boards. Superintendents had the power to guide the curriculum, call teacher meetings, promote pupils, and supervise teachers. In ninety-two schools superintendents chose textbooks, and in ninety-five schools they could nominate schoolteachers. Hiring and firing were still board-of-education responsibilities, but the report optimistically pointed to the sixty superintendents who shared this responsibility with the Board of Education. In Boston a school-reform movement had pared down the old school committee to five members in 1905, and the committee hired a single superintendent to oversee the schools.[26]

These reforms seemed on the surface to point to greater autonomy for superintendents, but in school surveys made by George Strayer in the late twenties the reality of school reform was shown to be less than dazzling. In Lynn, Massachusetts, Strayer reported, the mayor was part of school deliberations, and the superintendent had to forward all decisions of appointment, transfers, and dismissals to the school committee. The superintendent and a secretary ran the schools, but the secretary was clearly the equal of the superintendent and had control over school finances, again subject to board approval. Strayer made various recommendations for the restructuring of the Lynn school system, but his picture of a typical Massachusetts school in 1927 clearly did not fit the image of the new, reorganized, modern school system. In a survey of the Boston public schools in 1944, Strayer again deplored the way in which members of the elected school committee handled administrative affairs, which he clearly felt belonged to the superintendent. "There are times," the report admonished, "when the Committee seems to consider itself a board of executives and the professional staff of superintendents its servants, who, leaving all initiative to the committee, are to operate in accord with its whims and desires. This is poor administration."[27]

Clearly the legal remedy failed to streamline the schools and strengthen the superintendent to the degree that the reformers had hoped it would. To bolster their position, superintendents had to find other means of gaining control over personnel decisions. One remedy was that of William Maxwell, who used the existing measure of school reform to circumvent the board and build his own bureaucracy. Edwin G. Cooley of Chicago found a different method, closer to blackmail, in which it was a school-board rule that members who were approached on school-personnel matters had to refer the matters to the superintendent or else face censure in the daily papers for succumbing to "pull" in the allocation of educational resources. A third method, and by far the most effective, was to shape policy so that the kind of schoolteacher entering school would be more amenable to the new administrative style demanded by the centralizers.[28]

26. Ibid., pp. 162–66; Polly Adams Welt Kaufman, "Boston Women and City School Politics, 1872–1905" (Ph.D. diss., Boston University, 1978), pp. 381–96.
27. Strayer Reports.
28. Murphy, "From Artisan to Semiprofessional," pp. 54–61.

By the twenties most school districts followed some plan of centralization, but the plans were pale reflections of the visions of the initiators—Butler and Harper. A few superintendents were able to enlarge the scope of their powers through informal arrangements with the Board of Education. Through these arrangements and experimentation in asserting control over teachers, superintendents began to see professionalization as the key to unlocking the puzzle over control. In other words, teachers whose dedication to teaching was measured by obeisance to the hierarchical forms of control—rather than devotion to the community or to educational ideals fostered in a non-hierarchical system—could be cultivated. That is to say, what could not be won in the halls of the legislature could be won in the halls of ivy.[29]

For their part, teachers offered little resistance to the call for further education. They would argue that a college education was not as useful as experience in the classroom, but perhaps because of the example of a new generation of college-educated, middle-class women they were not as adept at dodging this issue as they had been in confronting the issue of centralization. In part this was because the proponents of centralization pointed to advantages of professionalization through education, a commodity the teachers valued deeply. Formal education with a thorough pedagogical grounding, it was thought, would attract a higher caliber of student, eliminate the local daughters with neighborhood connections, and discourage certain unwanted ethnic groups and the children of unskilled laborers. By controlling entry requirements, superintendents began to reshape the teaching force.

A Profile of the New Teacher

Teaching as a job did not attract the first generation of women college graduates in great numbers. There were reasons for the bad reputation the job had gotten since Catharine Beecher's days, although Beecher herself taught less than the average stint of an urban school teacher. The schools were in bad physical condition, the pay was not increasing—indeed, in Chicago at the turn of the century teachers had gone twenty years without a raise—and as the new educational experts published their critique, teachers were getting a bad reputation as incompetent know-nothings. The early twentieth-century schools were not models of clean corridors and brightly lit classrooms. Teachers worked in typhoid-ridden neighborhoods and were exposed to all the diseases children brought to school. They worked in old buildings, or in storefronts and temporary buildings, often with no plumbing and dangerous ventilation systems. There were no fire escapes, very few schools had

---

29. Callahan, *Education and the Cult of Efficiency;* William H. Maxwell, *A Quarter Century of Public School Development* (New York, 1912), pp. 287–303. For more on the style of Edwin G. Cooley, see Murphy, "From Artisan to Semiprofessional," pp. 139–55.

playgrounds, and because coal contracts were political arrangements, con-
tractors would skimp on coal delivery unless the principal or schoolteachers
pressured the alderman for sufficient coal. There was little to attract the new
generation of college women, but in time this changed, as school centralization and professionalization developed hand in hand.[30]

The Progressive administrators, usually proponents and beneficiaries of
centralization, wanted a new teacher. They wanted someone who shared a
culture of middle-class values—the "culture of professionalism," as Burton
Bledstein described it—where character played a pivotal role. Control,
efficiency, and reasonableness were traits to be encouraged. Teachers were
not just to have jobs, they were to have careers commanding a much greater
and absorbing commitment. This new teacher would be self-sufficient and
somewhat removed from community life. "The new individual professional
life had gained both an inward coherence and self-regulating standards that
separated and defined it independently of the general community," Bledstein
writes. The new administrative Progressives were a product of the American
universities. They were the students of the great university leaders like
Butler, Charles W. Eliot, and Daniel Coit Gilman, who were determined to
reshape the American schoolteacher to become like themselves, committed
to the ideal of service, scientifically trained, and ambitious in their careers.
That the new concept was particularly apt for young, white, middle-class
males though the constituency they aimed at was female and ethnic did not
seem to dampen the ardor of the administrative reformers. New teachers had
to be recruited, molded, and educated to serve in the centralized school
systems.[31]

The reshaping of the schoolteacher to this new professional image took
time. A college education at the turn of the century was available only to
wealthier families. Moreover, the culture of professionalism was decidedly a
middle-class value system, something that not all schoolteachers shared.
The remaking of the teaching population required that certain attitudes and
values be replaced with ideals of success and ambition. Sometimes teachers
could borrow notions of excellence from their rural and industrial backgrounds that would serve them well in professionalization, but there seemed
always to be a catch. For example, artisans had long held the craft ideal,

30. *CT,* 26 April, 13 June, 29 October, and 8 November 1903; 6–7 February, 9 and 24 April, 5
and 13 May, and 10 December 1904; 14 May 1905. Chicago was not the only city with problems: see
Adele Marie Shaw, "The True Character of the New York City Public Schools," *World's Work,* 7
(December 1903), pp. 4204–21, as quoted in Hoffman, *Woman's True Profession,* pp. 226–27.

31. Burton J. Bledstein, *The Culture of Professionalism: The Middle Class and the Development
of Higher Education in America* (New York, 1976). In the words of Barbara Solomon, "On the
economic level it could not be denied that teaching offered a reliable means of earning a living, but,
as Sophonsiba Breckinridge noted bitterly in 1914, for all the so-called feminization of the teaching
profession, the schools were run by men—as superintendents and high school principals—with only
an occasional female post of authority." Solomon, *Educated Women,* p. 128; see also pp. 62–77, and
David Montgomery, *Worker's Control in America* (Cambridge, 1979), pp. 11–14.

which encouraged an individual craftsman to excel in his labor, produce the best product, and give creative expression to well-developed skills; it also contained an ideal of autonomy that gave the artisan a choice of time, a choice of apprenticeships, and a choice of method and style in completing a job. Young women who came from working families may have had this craft ideal, including its notions of autonomy. New Progressive administrators, however, were not using the concept of professionalism to promote further schoolteacher autonomy but, on the contrary, to exert further control over the teaching force. Professionalism then was a double-edged sword that cut in the directions of both autonomy and control.[32]

The tension between autonomy and control in the professionalization project promised teachers new freedoms from community control. Dress codes, strictures on behavior, and formulas of deference were common in most schools. Young women were monitored, especially in rural schools, to the point of making them daughters in the community rather than independent working women. Rural women teachers migrated with men into the cities not only to profit from the higher wages but also to enjoy greater private freedoms. Professionalism promised a distancing from that community while it restrained teachers from getting too closely involved in community mores. By taking their leave, the community teachers were losing political protections along with the hated behavioral restrictions. The paternalism of the community would be replaced by the hierarchical paternalism of the school. New teachers were to have allegiance to middle-class values, which of course was one of the reasons why unionism posed such a threat to the Progressive administrators.[33]

The formulas of the Progressive administrators quite clearly pointed to higher education for teachers, preferably a college education. The results of their campaign are hard to assess. Over the first twenty years of the century, teachers did have more postsecondary education than had been the case in the past. In 1921 most states did not have requirements for teacher certification, fourteen states required a high school diploma, and a handful required a normal school course of study, which could include secondary and postsecondary training. By 1937 thirty-two states required more than high school preparation, usually one to four years of college. The depression accelerated the qualifications for teachers: there were no jobs, so waiting schoolteachers acquired more education. Qualifications in cities varied immensely. Most cities began demanding some postsecondary education in the late 1890s. They often had their own normal schools (which were taken out of the high school departments and enlarged to offer at least one year of postsecondary

32. Ben Rust, *The Master Teacher and His Craft* (San Bernardino, Calif., 1954), p. 18; Murphy, "From Artisan to Semiprofessional," pp. 196–98; Mattingly, *Classless Profession*, pp. 7–16.

33. Willard S. Elsbree, *The American Teacher: Evolution of a Profession in a Democracy* (New York, 1939), pp. 535–48.

training) and training institutes for the entire teaching force. Chicago took over the Cook County Normal School and proceeded to require a single year of study until World War I, when for a short time two years and eventually three years of training were required for entry into elementary school teaching. High school teachers were not always required to have a college degree, but because cities built most of their high schools in the period starting in the Progressive Era, it was possible for administrators to demand and get qualified college-educated teachers in these schools. Since high school teaching was better paid, there were fewer posts and more applicants for the jobs. The main focus of reshaping the teaching force was on the elementary school level.[34]

Lotus Delta Coffman prepared a study of the social composition of schoolteachers in 1911 that would illustrate the depths of the Progressive administrators' problem in reshaping the teaching force. Coffman declared that "the kind of people we have in teaching necessarily affects the kind of teaching we get." He thought that differences in "race"—not just skin color but ethnic background—made a difference in the customs, traditions, moral and religious ideals, and language habits of the prospective teacher. It was important to have just the right teacher ethnically, religiously, and culturally. "Differences in social class," he went on to say, "to economic station, to intellectual maturity, to academic and professional training, and the like, must likewise be important factors affecting public opinion of the merits of the teacher and his work." Similar concerns were expressed by a number of school observers whose evaluation of schoolteachers included not only their educational attainments but their ethnic, racial, and class background.[35]

"Uncouth and uncultured," one schoolteacher complained in the Chicago Teachers' Federation *Bulletin*, "are terms which they freely apply to the unspecified element they desire to see eliminated from the schools." This teacher explained that the experts would probably consider a college degree a "certificate of culture." But Coffman was looking for more than simply educational requirements. Normal schools already existed and could be upgraded, as Ella Flagg Young suggested, to take urban teachers to a college degree. Progressive administrators, however, wanted more control over the type of entering teacher. A college education was not just a certificate of culture; it acted as a barrier to working-class women, one clearly perceived as a cultural divide for women in the school system. Postsecondary education could and did begin to change the very type of teacher who entered the field.[36]

34. Ibid., pp. 322–35; Lotus Delta Coffman, *The Social Composition of the Teaching Population* (New York, 1911); Willard Waller, *The Sociology of Teaching* (New York, 1932); Mary M'Ledge Moffet, *The Social Background and Activities of Teachers' College Students* (New York, 1929).
35. Coffman, *Social Composition*.
36. *CTF Bulletin*, 6 March 1903.

Coffman's 1911 study, although biased as a rural sample, showed that most teachers were sons and daughters of farmers (69.7 percent for the men and 44.8 percent for the women) and that women teachers' families were more blue-collar than white-collar (27.7 percent blue-collar and 24.6 percent white-collar for the women, 15 percent blue-collar and 14 percent white-collar for the men). Coffman's study confirmed the educational reformers' worst fears about the class origins of teachers. But reformers in fact had little to fear because the rise in educational standards had already begun to shrink the broad class and ethnic pool of prospective teachers.[37]

It is possible to study the effects of raising entrance requirements into teaching in cities using individual-level data for the census years 1880, 1900, and 1910, which span the period when requirements were raised. Because the data are difficult to collect, my study is limited to Chicago, a city in which teachers were just beginning to unionize at the turn of the century. In Chicago, 1880 predates the normal school requirement, 1900 was seven years after the one-year-training requirement, and 1910 was eight years after the three-year, postsecondary-education requirement.[38]

The results from these data indicate that the social composition of teachers had indeed begun to change before the administrative Progressives expressed their desire for a new type of teacher. Higher educational requirements restricted entry levels for women from blue-collar families and enhanced opportunities for women from high white-collar families. The statistics for Chicago indicate that in 1880 nearly half (47.7 percent) of Chicago teachers came from blue-collar backgrounds, another quarter of them (24.6 percent) came from low white-collar backgrounds, and only 15 percent came from high white-collar backgrounds.[39]

In 1880 more than half of Chicago's elementary school teachers had less than a four-year, high school education, even though they had some normal training. In Chicago and at the State Normal School in Bloomington, normal schools were either part of the high school program (and thus did not require

37. Coffman, *Social Composition*.
38. The United States Manuscript Census Schedules for Chicago, 1880 and 1900. The study is a 10 percent sample of schoolteachers and clerks for the years 1880, 1900, and 1910. Material was coded and analyzed using simple occupational codes.
39. U.S. Manuscript Census. Those who had completed a four-year classical high school course (25.2 percent) proudly listed their achievement with the name of their high school. These teachers had no formal teacher training except for the four-month apprenticeship period. Teachers who had a public school background with no normal school training were identified in the unspecified category. These teachers (11.9 percent of the total) may have received private tutoring, but the evidence suggests that the number of teachers with a grammar school education was close to 15 percent of the total. One university-trained instructor was a German language instructor. Less than a quarter of the grammar school teachers (23 percent) had experience teaching in country schools before coming to teach in Chicago. In 1880, 82 percent of the teachers in the Chicago schools received their training either within Chicago (80 percent) or elsewhere in Illinois (2.5 percent). Educational levels were taken from the Chicago Board of Education, *Annual Report*, 1879.

a high school diploma) or they were attached to grammar schools and functioned basically as training programs for practicing teachers no matter what their educational attainment.

The new requirements introduced by 1900 required at least one year of postsecondary training, a requirement that sent most local students to the city's normal school. A distinct shift in socioeconomic origins of teachers begins in this census year. Over half of the teachers came from white-collar backgrounds (50.8 percent), teachers from blue-collar backgrounds declined, and only half as many new teachers were from semiskilled families as had been the case twenty years earlier. By 1910 the decline in blue-collar origins became pronounced.[40]

Another concern of Lotus Delta Coffman and other new Progressive administrators was the immigrant teacher or the daughter of immigrant families. Most Progressives wished to impose some sort of Americanization in the schools, and by 1920 the Americanization of schoolchildren had become a national priority of the NEA. As recruitment patterns changed for teachers, the ethnic origins of teachers tended to become less representative of the population as a whole. In part this movement was a response to the changing population of the city. This was the era of the large waves of immigrants from southern and eastern European countries. A new population, these immigrants brought a strange culture to American cities that threatened the cohesiveness of the society. Americanization, it was thought, would at least introduce immigrant children to the culture and values of their new land. Americanization required American teachers, not daughters of immigrants.

The teachers who came from households where one or both parents were foreign born were likely to have fathers in blue-collar occupations. The change in educational requirements that cut the percentage of blue-collar families sending daughters into teaching also cut the pool of immigrant daughters. Semiskilled and unskilled heads of households of immigrant stock declined from 22.7 percent of family heads in 1880 to 7 percent in 1900. Old-stock parents of the same occupational categories increased from 5.9 percent in the semiskilled and skilled backgrounds to 8.3 percent in 1900. It seems safe to conclude that educational barriers discriminated most

40. Clerical workers provide an excellent control group with which to compare the teachers for the same period. After all, in the thirty-year period from 1880 to 1910, white-collar families increased as a portion of the general population, and the study could simply be reporting this increase. Clerical workers were in an expanding industry, and clerical work expanded much more rapidly than teaching in the same period. Entry requirements did not change drastically, even though the work was becoming more diversified and more and more women were entering the field. A comparison of teachers and clerical workers for the same period shows that while there were slight variations in the social origins of clerical workers' families these changes were not as dramatic as for teachers. In fact, while clerical workers tended to be more blue-collar in origins, in 1880 teachers' families and clerical worker families were not greatly dissimilar in occupational backgrounds.

against young women of blue-collar origins, especially those whose parents were immigrants and in the second wave of immigration. Chicago's teaching force became less representative of the city population.[41]

One aspect of the teaching population that Coffman most wished to change was that of the dutiful daughter living with her family and confined to the community she had grown up in. Public school teaching was often a job that the community could award to smart young women in widowed households. In fact, one-third of Chicago schoolteachers lived with widowed mothers. This was hardly the basis on which to build a career, but it also raises questions about the independence and autonomy of teachers. Although these women were not listed as heads of household and often worked with siblings to keep the family going, it is clear that their income was an important factor in the family well-being. The proposal that teachers be hired in an impartial system was aimed at avoiding commitments to such families. Exceptions to the married women's law, allowing women married to invalids, for example, to continue teaching, indicate that school systems followed the old paternalistic style of the village school, despite claims to the contrary. The proposal of the Progressive administrators, however, was to get rid of the socially dependent teacher and promote only the professionally trained, career-oriented teacher.[42]

41. As a city with more foreign-born than native-born residents at the height of the great migration, Chicago was at great risk to recruit immigrant daughters to school teaching. Unlike the teachers in Coffman's study, who were largely of native-born parents, Chicago's schoolteachers came from immigrant families (57.6 percent in 1880 and 61.1 percent in 1900). The large percentage of immigrant-family origins for the city as a whole (77 percent in 1900) meant that the teaching force fell far behind the city as a representative group. This distancing, the process of separating out a new population, seems also to have included children of immigrants. Chicago teachers who were of immigrant background were more likely to come from English-speaking stock; they were Irish (56.6 percent in 1880 and 48.9 percent in 1900), Canadian (12 percent in 1880 and 4.7 percent in 1900), English (15.8 percent in 1880 and 10.7 percent in 1900), and Scottish (3.3 percent in 1880 and 2.8 percent in 1900). Certain ethnic groups were underrepresented in the teaching force relative to their percentage of the total population. For example, first- and second-generation Germans were 34.5 percent of the city's population in 1900, yet they had only 9.1 percent of the teaching jobs. The Irish were overrepresented as an ethnic group: they were 27 percent of the teaching force in 1900 but only 17 percent of the population. The second wave of immigrants, the southern and eastern Europeans, who came later and were newest in the school system, were especially discriminated against. Italians were 2.5 percent of the city's population, and yet they had only .3 percent of the teaching jobs; Bohemians were 6.6 percent of the city's population but only 3.3 percent of the teachers. The fastest-growing segment of the immigrant population in 1900 was the Norwegians. They were 3.7 percent of the city's population but only 1.4 percent of the teaching force. The propensity for the raised levels of entry to prevent ethnic representation in the teaching force was, of course, tied to economic factors. Immigrants had a tougher time in the economy; they needed the income of children sooner than native-born parents.

42. U.S. Manuscript Census; see also Waller, *Sociology of Teaching*, pp. 273–409; Coffman, *Social Composition;* Strayer Reports. Teachers were very rarely the sole breadwinners in their families; in 1900, 10.8 percent of teachers in Chicago provided the sole family income as opposed to 9.2 percent of teachers nationally. As the second breadwinners in their families, Chicago teachers were once again head of the national average; 22 percent of teachers nationally and 30.2 percent of teachers in Chicago were second breadwinners. Nearly one-fourth of the teachers contributed a third income, and another 20 percent the fourth income. Daughters of widows were more frequently sole

Although the advanced educational requirements were just beginning in the cities at the turn of the century and became statewide requirements only in the thirties, it is clear that in this period a shift was happening in the way teachers lived. Most rural teachers, Coffman pointed out, boarded with families in the villages they taught in. This was a sign of dependence and paternalism in rural America. In the city, however, most women school-teachers lived with their families; if they were boarders, they lived in certain sections of the city where women were allowed to have their own apartments. Boarders in the rural areas were dependent, whereas boarders in the city were independent.

Even when women boarded together in the city, their independence was still relatively constrained. Women were not legally allowed to sign leases in Chicago until the depression era; often brothers or fathers would sign leases for them. Although women often boarded with widows who ran small boarding houses, a very few apartment buildings in the city would allow single women to rent rooms together, provided a male family member signed the lease. There were two sections of the city where this was allowed. The first was in the old Normal School neighborhood, where women had been coming from outside the area for some time; apartment buildings had women tenants and women heads of household. The second area was around the University of Chicago, where women entered the university and had to find housing around Hyde Park. Outside these two sections of the city, it was rare to find an apartment building where women were renting with other women. Occasionally in the southern part of the downtown Loop area or in fashionable Near North Side buildings, or in large complexes along Prairie Avenue, a building would open and advertise that women could rent apartments. This was, however, a rare occurrence. Nevertheless, boarding with friends was a sign of independence and autonomy, something that was rare before the administrative Progressives began their campaign for professionalism.[43]

National statistics reflect the fact that teaching was a boarding profession in rural America. In 1900, one in four teachers boarded. In only three other occupational categories were women more likely to be boarders—servants and waitresses, housekeepers and stewardesses, and nurses and midwives. Elementary school teachers in Chicago were relative homebodies; 67.2 percent of the teachers lived with their mothers and fathers in 1880, whereas only 18 percent boarded and the rest lived with other relatives. High school teachers, in contrast, were more independent: 36.5 percent of them boarded

breadwinners and second breadwinners along with male siblings. Only a few teacher households kept boarders, who were usually other schoolteachers. Of those living at home, 19.1 percent owned houses with mortgages, 52.8 percent rented, and the rest owned houses mortgage free. Teachers' incomes, then, were more likely to be paid toward rent than toward house ownership.

43. Frances Donovan, *School Teacher* (New York, 1939); *Statistics of Women at Work: Special Report of the Census Office* (Washington, D.C., 1907), p. 109.

and 59.5 percent lived with parents. Elementary teachers were younger—
their median age was twenty-four, and high school teachers' median age was
thirty-one.[44]

Perhaps a better sign of independence is the profile of households headed
by teachers themselves. High school teachers (17.6 percent of them in 1900)
far outnumbered elementary school teachers (2.7 percent) as independent
heads of household. Yet while teachers were not always living independently
alone, they were constantly being transferred in the city and often had to find
housing they could afford. They relied on family members to accommodate
them in areas where they might not be able to find single accommodations.
Of the total number of teachers transferred in 1880, for example, 52 percent
lived with members of their extended family (brothers, sisters, aunts and
uncles), 41.7 percent lived with their parents, and 5.9 percent boarded.
Those living with relatives may have achieved some independence in living
away from their homes of origin. Most transfers, however, were not voluntary but were made for the good of an expanding school system. So it is
reasonable to guess that the new accommodations gave teachers more autonomy from the old paternalistic village system, but transfers also illustrate
how teachers were at the mercy of the school administrators who put the
good of the system above the teachers' personal needs. Leaving the old
neighborhood of their youth, schoolteachers became a surprisingly mobile
population, changing addresses frequently and moving from one section of
the city to another.[45]

In 1900 the pace of transfers picked up, as it did again in 1910. More
teachers lived with their extended families, more teachers boarded. The
superintendent of schools handled transfers in Chicago after 1900; they were
no longer the function of a district committee. The same situation occurred in
Philadelphia, where teacher transfers continued to be an issue. In New York
City, schoolteachers made a special protest of involuntary transfers. Teachers in San Francisco made similar complaints. As an extremely important
teacher grievance, the transfer issue illustrates the degree of control the
superintendent was able to exert over schoolteachers. What the new Progressive administrators wanted and needed, as managers of the system, was the
ability to respond to the growing demands of the population in a school
system that was rapidly expanding and shifting from one district to another.
Whole sections of these cities were changing from residential to industrial or
commercial sites; middle-class, native, white neighborhoods were changing
to immigrant, working-class, overcrowded ghettos. Teachers and their families were moving in the city, but where they moved was determined by their
superiors. Although teachers were often forced to move out of their parents'
households, thereby gaining more autonomy, they were also being confined

44. Donovan, *School Teacher; Statistics of Women at Work*, p. 109; U.S. Manuscript Census.
45. Female-headed households.

to live with extended family members rather than in intellectual enclaves of the Cook County Normal School or the University of Chicago. Just how much autonomy they were gaining was questionable. Also, as the teaching population aged, older women teachers often moved in with a widowed female head of household. Transfers meant uprooting these special families. District committees were frequently sympathetic to such problems. A widow might have some connections in the neighborhood, through former associates of her husband, to protect her daughter and herself from an involuntary transfer. New career teachers had no such protections. Professional teachers had to find other avenues of redress, and in this way the union served as a positive buffer between teachers and the system. It was a weak guarantee to be sure, but it was all the teachers had.

The changes wrought by centralization paved the way to professionalization. Teachers were expected to be better educated. Feminine virtues were not only no longer praised but were seen as qualities emasculating education. Still, contradictions in the new role for women teachers persisted. The teachers themselves experienced ambiguity as they groped their way toward political independence. Although usually willing to concede that more education was a good thing, most teachers refused to accept that their inferior education should bar them from teaching. Experience, they insisted, should count for something. Margaret Haley often told the story of her father, an uneducated man, who built a few stone bridges over the Des Plaines River but was overlooked when the state began a bridge project in favor of a young, college-educated engineer. Haley's father watched the young man as he tried in vain to make the first connection from shore to shore and finally helped the man out. His daughter insisted that it was her father's experience that had made him knowledgeable, just as experience had given schoolteachers an edge over the better-educated, but more submissive, new-generation teachers. "They've got sheep's heads with those sheepskins," Haley remarked.[46]

Teacher Responses

Professionalism was not something that Progressive administrators could control, nor entirely define. Reshaping the teaching force was a long-term process, one that Progressive administrators could promote but not control. Ethnic and class origins of teachers changed slowly without drama. Certain groups, the daughters of unskilled workers and new immigrants, were effectively blocked from entering teaching. Professionalism, then, was Janus-faced. On one side it would inure teachers to a hierarchical system that automatically defined their subordinate position, first as perpetual student, and then in the classroom as subject of supervision. On the other side

46. Margaret Haley's autobiography, pt. 3.

professionalism promised autonomy and dignity, concepts that were very much in line with Bledstein's culture of professionalism. To promote professionalism was to tempt professional organization, to beg the question of salaries, and to instill notions of autonomy in the classroom. The professional élan, as we have seen, had already had an effect in making teachers more independent, allowing them to live away from home and, because of transfers, to move away from neighborhoods. The most important issue and the one that most clearly led from professionalism to unionism was the salary question.

The structure of teaching as a job was neither static nor filled with dramatic changes. A hierarchy was in place before centralization that was based more on class and gender credentials than on educational merit. As centralization gained support in urban schools, issues of gender and class arose, but they were answered by a new code of classification through educational merit, which appeared under the heading of professionalization. Although professionalization hindered promotions for women and kept certain ethnic and working-class daughters from entering the field, it had positive aspects that could not be contained. It was an ideological slogan, but it promised a prescribed autonomy and financial rewards. Women schoolteachers had been told that their demands for higher wages were unfeminine, that they had to perform their jobs selflessly, and that it was their feminine behavior more than their scholarly merit that was valued in the classroom. Professionalism negated that ideology; instead, professionalism promised that scholarly achievement would be rewarded financially, thus making the demands for higher wages no longer a question of stepping out of socially determined sex roles. Although there were fewer working-class daughters in the system, they were quick to pick up on the new freedom of making demands for their salaries and pensions. At the same time there was a growing number of college-educated women who discovered that, despite the meritocratic claims, professionalism still favored men with promotion, despite the higher educational achievements of the women. All that was needed to give life to a new movement was some political insight, some principle that legitimized women's entry into the arena of urban politics.[47]

It is no coincidence that the rise of teachers' organizations came with the rise of suffrage. Teachers recognized that education was a political football in mayoral contests. Their inability to vote had negative effects on their ability to negotiate (as policemen and firemen could). Centralization and profes-

47. Clyde M. Hill, *A Decade of Progress in Teacher Training* (New York, 1927); L. M. Chamberlain and L. E. Meece, *Women and Men in the Teaching Profession* (Lexington, Ky., 1937); Anon., "Married Women as Teachers," *Educational Review,* 25 (February 1903), p. 213; Thomas Woody, *A History of Women's Education in the United States* (New York, 1978), pp. 509–10; David W. Peters, *The Status of the Married Woman Teacher* (New York, 1934); Gerald Grace, *Teachers, Ideology, and Control: A Study in Urban Education* (London, 1978), pp. 97–102; Bowles and Gintis, *Schooling in Capitalist America.*

sionalism gave them, first, a grievance that rallied community support against certain administrative reforms and, second, a shift in the language of the debate away from the constraints of feminine behavior to the meritocracy that professionalism promised. For the teachers, professionalism was just as dangerous a tool as it was for the administrative Progressives, but it enabled them to raise their demands politically.

This historic intimacy between professionalism and centralization operates against the more traditional community-teacher alliance that operated in the Chicago strike of 1902. In the long run, as teachers embraced professionalism they lost political ground in the community. Much of the history that follows outlines the political isolation of schoolteachers as the professionalization project expanded. The teachers, however, did not immediately embrace professionalism as the panacea for their problems of autonomy. To the contrary, teachers were experimenting with new political forms, creating broad alliances, and seeking out labor as the vehicle for political change. Contrary to the ideology of professionalization and centralization, teachers argued that they needed to become political activists. Unionism implied both a political stance and a community agenda. Political activism implied a community alliance whereas professionalism implied hierarchy and isolation. It is significant that when teachers first organized they moved initially in the direction of unionism and politics.

When Catharine Goggin became president of the Chicago Teachers' Federation, she reminded her fellow teachers that they had contact with nearly a quarter of a million children, touching the majority of voting households in the city of Chicago. She told them quite specifically that they would be contacting those voters and bringing the issues of education to them, the working parents, to decide directly. It was a phenomenal statement, but it was not just a statement made in Chicago. In St. Paul teachers began a similar movement, and in New York teachers fashioned their own movement around the issue of equal pay for equal work. This was the call of unionization for public school teachers.[48]

48. In Goggin's words, "Its [the union's] endorsement should be a powerful aid, its disapproval equally mighty. It should so educate public sentiment that a newspaper which attempted to lower the teachers of the city should immediately feel the result of the attempt in its decreased circulation and depleted advertising columns. What a force that quarter of a million souls is and how much greater might be their power united for the common good. . . . The Federation should have a broader outlook. It should consider all which properly comes within the scope of intelligent citizenship." Herrick, *Chicago Schools*, p. 98.

CHAPTER THREE /

Unionism and Professionalism: The First Sparks

The success of early teacher unions depended primarily on their ability to improve wages and working conditions for teachers. In Chicago, despite impressive mass meetings, the voteless teachers remained largely unsuccessful until 1899, when Catharine Goggin and Margaret Haley launched what they called "the teachers' tax crusade." Examining the Cook County tax rolls, they uncovered two million dollars in unpaid taxes and forced local taxing agencies to collect the money. Though a series of court decisions reduced the award to the schools to six hundred thousand dollars, it was enough to give teaches a substantial pay raise. News of the teachers' success inspired other teachers to act. Goggin and Haley had especially targeted local monopolies in gas, electricity, and transportation, thereby connecting their cause with strong latent antimonopoly sentiment. They were women, so their story was one of the powerless empowering themselves, of women invading the county tax offices where no women had gone, of women standing up in courthouses citing the law to lawyers, of women defying the state legislature as it threatened to take away teacher's pensions. Neither verbal discouragement nor physical threats deterred the two women. They did what no male superintendent had done—they found money for their salary raise and they made corporations pay for it.

This success was possible only because the teachers had made allies with voting workingmen by affiliating with central labor councils. Only the unions could give women teachers the local political clout they lacked. But local organization was not enough. Teachers needed a national forum to face the changes in their jobs.

Nationally, women teachers brought their grievances to the National Education Association, even though the organization was hardly sympathetic to their salary problems. The NEA, tied to an older professional model that hampered the efforts of centralizers while it inhibited the full participa-

46 /

tion of women schoolteachers, resisted this backyard rebellion of rank-and-file teachers. Although the NEA underwent profound changes, leadership remained firmly in the hands of school administrators. Meanwhile, women teachers initiated new organizations that paved the way for genuine unionization. In all these developments, issues of gender were central. The old frock-coat professionalism explicitly omitted women while the newer, Progressive administrator sought women's consent in the wider centralization project. Women schoolteachers stood at the boundaries between professionalism and unionism as they assessed the two movements that dominated educational discourse.

Traditional Professionalization within the NEA

On the evening of 26 August 1857, a founder of the National Teachers' Association read a paper by William Russell entitled "The Professional Organization of Teachers of the United States," which argued that the association wanted teachers to "make their work a profession—not just an ordinary vocation." In the balcony two women teachers listened and later were asked to sign the constitution for the new organization that became the forerunner of the National Education Association.[1]

There is little to contradict Cherry Wedgwood Collins's apt remark that "professionalism was by tradition and current prejudice associated with men."[2] The gentlemen who organized the affair were members of a traditional professional elite, with one foot in the proprietary world they were born in and the other in the corporate, industrial world that was emerging.[3] In their vision, women were not really a vital part of the emerging economic order, so it was "with chivalrous inconsistency" that they allowed Mrs. D. H. Conrad and Miss A. W. Beecher to sign their founding document, which provided that women could be selected as "honorary members,"

1. Edgar G. Wesley, *NEA, The First One Hundred Years: The Building of the Teaching Profession* (New York, 1957), p. 23. See also National Teachers Association, *Proceedings, 1857,* pp. 15–24; and Paul Mattingly, *The Classless Profession* (New York, 1975), pp. 120–24.

2. Cherry Wedgwood Collins, "Schoolmen, Schoolma'ams, and School Boards: The Struggle for Power in Urban School Systems in the Progressive Era" (Ed.D. diss., Harvard University, 1976), p. 131. For more on women in the professions, see Patricia N. Feuler, *Women in the Professions: A Social-Psychological Study* (Palo Alto, Calif., 1979). See also W. J. Reader, *Professional Men: The Rise of Professional Classes in Nineteenth-Century England* (London, 1966), pp. 100–105; and Jacqueline Clement, *Sex Bias in Educational Leadership* (Evanston, Ill., 1975).

3. The engineer stood "between an earlier proprietary society and an emerging industrial corporate society." Daniel Calhoun, *The American Civil Engineer: Origins and Conflict* (Cambridge, 1960), p. 189. See also Magali Sarfatti-Larson, *The Rise of Professionalism: A Sociological Analysis* (Berkeley, 1977), pp. 30–31, 188–227. For a critique of Sarfatti-Larson, see Andrew Abbott, "Occupational Environments and Occupational Structure: Professions and Their Audiences in France and the United States" (Paper presented at the Social Science History Association annual meeting, November 1987).

though they were not recognized from the floor of the meetings. Instead, they could present, "in the form of written essays to be read by the secretary or any member whom they may select, their views upon the subject assigned for discussion."[4]

Women were quite aggrieved by the sexism of traditional professionalism well before the 1857 meeting of the National Teachers' Association. In 1853 Susan B. Anthony, a public school teacher in New York, was attending a meeting of the New York Teachers' Association and listening to a male colleague explain why no women appeared on the program or on any of the organization's committees. He declaimed, "Behold the beautiful pilaster of this superb hall; contemplate its pedestal, its shafts, its rich entablature, the crowning glory of the whole. Each and all the parts in their appropriate places contribute to its strength, symmetry, and beauty. Could I aid in taking down that entablature from its proud elevation and place it in the dust and dirt of the pedestal."[5] Unimpressed by this view of her appropriate place on the pedestal, Anthony waited until the men had discussed the question of why teachers did not receive the respect accorded to lawyers, doctors, and preachers and requested permission to attack the issue. Surprised by her audacity in breaking through the tradition of silence for women, the men on the dais discussed her request. Finally, a chagrined chairman granted her permission to address the audience. "It seems to me," she began, "that you fail to comprehend the cause of the disrespect of which you complain. . . . Do you not see that as long as society says that a woman has not brains enough to become a lawyer, doctor, or minister but has plenty to be a teacher, every one of you who condescends to teach tacitly admits before all Israel and the sun that he has no more brains than a woman?"[6]

Although the association was quick to grasp Anthony's point and voted full membership to women after the suffragist's speech, this approach did not infect the National Teachers' Association until 1866, when a similar fight changed the NTA rules to replace the term "gentlemen" with "persons." This, then, was the tenuous position of women in the earliest professional teacher organization, which was the forerunner of the modern National Education Association.[7]

A renaissance of professionalism developed within the now-named NEA during the 1880s and 1890s, based firmly on the old, male-dominated, traditional professionalism. The style of organization reflected the domi-

4. Wesley, *NEA*, p. 23. These restrictions, Wesley wrote, "caused reverberations at Indianapolis in 1866, at Trenton in 1869, and far away in time at Boston in 1910." The date in Boston would have been 1903, the occasion of Haley's challenge to Butler.

5. D. Emma Hodge and Lamont F. Hodge, *A Century of Service to Education* (Albany, N.Y., 1945), pp. 197–98, as quoted in Wesley, *NEA*, p. 23. This story was first recounted in Ida Justed Harper, *The Life and Works of Susan B. Anthony*, 3 vols. (Indianapolis, 1898–1908), and was reprinted by Margaret Haley in the *CTF Bulletin*, 29 May 1903.

6. Wesley, *NEA*, p. 323.

7. Ibid., p. 324; *NEA Proceedings*, 1872, p. 184.

nance of male superintendents and college professors, who made the July meetings of the association into "occasions for mild displays and elegance." Frock-coated Gentlemen delivered lectures to largely female audiences of classroom teachers: "The Prince Albert coats, flowing beards and vigorous mustaches of the speakers and officers naturally awed and impressed the audiences. While these badges of formalism and style were relatively harmless, they did induce a mild degree of self-consciousness that found its outlet in colorful words and emphatic pronouncements."[8]

"Formalism and style," though "relatively harmless" on the surface, created an atmosphere in which the hierarchical nature of school administration could be replicated in professional organization. This was especially the case as school centralization gained attention in the NEA. As for hierarchy, the old professional élan preserved traditional male and female roles. Male administrators addressed female teachers as they would young pupils. Within the NEA there were few constitutional mechanisms by which women could gain recognition. In 1870 women were granted the right to hold office in the NEA, but "as was quite natural," they tended to predominate in the kindergarten, elementary, child-study, and art departments. One woman, in 1888, became a member of the more influential Higher Education Department, but only two or three women entered into the Superintendence Department.[9] Women succeeded in penetrating this bastion of "formalism and style" only to a limited degree, and they protested their treatment in mild, humorous language, which accomplished little in terms of expanding their role in the organization. When, for example, in 1884 Mrs. Mary Wright Sewell protested the persistence of speakers' addressing the audience of women as "gentlemen," she did so as a lady: "Not withstanding the fluttering of fans and the fluttering of ribbons, and the gay waving of plumes and the glancing smiles, and the eloquent blushes from the audience, speakers have persisted in addressing their audiences as 'gentlemen.' "[10] More serious protests to formalism and style than Mrs. Sewell's comments were lodged as the feminization of the profession brought more and more women (frequently called "girls" by their superiors) to the NEA meetings. Still, union teachers referred to a "snobbishness" in the old NEA meetings: "A tradition of aloofness was formally established and rigidly respected."[11]

In the 1890s a new "spirit operating against these vanities" appeared in the NEA. Although the official history calls these "leveling rather than democratic" tendencies, they clearly marked the entrance of more militant women into the NEA. In order to appreciate fully these changes it is necessary to understand something of the old structure of the NEA.[12]

8. Wesley, *NEA*, p. 270.
9. Ibid., pp. 320–28.
10. *NEA Proceedings*, 1884, p. 153; Wesley, *NEA*, p. 325.
11. Wesley, *NEA*, pp. 270, 328.
12. Ibid., p. 320.

School administrators and college presidents dominated the old NEA in a unique system of separate organizations that set the agenda for the larger national meetings. School administrators were 50 percent of the active membership during the 1890s and classroom teachers only 11 percent. In 1896, 4 percent of the membership of the association was drawn from college and university presidents. Each group had its own department, but the Department of Superintendence and the Department of Higher Education dominated the central governing board.[13] In the 1890s these departments began to hold separate meetings apart from the national yearly meetings in July. The February meetings of the Department of Superintendence gave its membership special prestige in the course of the school year and allowed superintendents to meet in urban areas with full access to the press to distribute their ideas on education to a waiting, interested public. Summer NEA meetings grew less important but gathered a larger constituency of classroom teachers. The summer meetings had less formal business to transact and took on more of an educational role for classroom teachers. These were teachers' institutes in the guise of a professional organization.

The larger summer meetings kept the trappings of democratic decision making, though in reality a small group directed the organization. Superintendents and college presidents formalized an inner sanctum, as David Tyack calls it, in order to direct more definitively the course of the association.[14] This National Council drew its membership from each of one of the departments on an appointed basis, so that although it was not formally designed as an exclusive agency, it operated as one. The council represented primarily the Department of Higher Education, dominated by college presidents, and the Department of Superintendence, dominated by young, ambitious, male administrators. Up to 1907 a total of eighteen women had served on the ever-growing council, which had been limited officially to sixty members, although others attended the meetings. In the council, general policy issues were discussed and then forwarded to a Resolutions Committee, which, in turn, submitted the resolutions to the general body of the NEA for approval. This system was amended in 1896 at the suggestion of university professor B. A. Hinsdale, whose idea it was that the National Council send the convention "more general declarations" along with the resolutions. These soon became the NEA platform, emanating from the National Council for perfunctory ratification by the convention. To assure smooth functioning of this system, Nicholas Murray Butler took charge of the Resolutions Committee from 1897 to 1900 and again in 1903. For further assurance, a Nominating Committee was appointed, not elected, by the president. Members were chosen to represent geographic regions. This system changed in 1897 when

13. Ibid., p. 270.
14. David B. Tyack, *The One Best System: A History of American Urban Education* (Cambridge, 1974), p. 42; Wesley, *NEA*, p. 283. Haley called the National Council, which was formed in 1880, the "educational House of Lords." Margaret Haley's autobiography, pt. 1.

Nominating Committee members became subject to election, although the practice of electing presidents by acclamation continued.[15]

In short, the association was controlled by a small, male elite at a moment when more and more women teachers were coming to meetings. The teachers were concerned about centralization but found that the primary professional organization was committed to the new changes. Indeed the knot between centralization and professionalism was tied in the meeting halls of the NEA.

Nicholas Murray Butler, fresh from his campaign in New York City, graced the NEA with his leadership in 1895 and was a guiding light for the organization until 1910. Influenced by his grandfather and namesake, Reverend Nicholas Murray, President Butler brought to the NEA the sense of service that had dominated voluntary associations in the nineteenth century. Moralistic and even evangelical in their commitment to "service," these nineteenth-century ministers, teachers, and pedagogues thought a profession was close to a religious vocation. When he took the helm of the NEA, Nicholas Murray Butler married this vision of commitment with a more modern notion of professionalism, one which embraced educational training and scientific inquiry. In these years, "the NEA presented a public image of senior university, college and school superintendents cooperating as fellow professionals. Behind the scenes, holding it all together was Murray Butler."[16]

Butler's dedication to professionalism proved second only to his devotion to centralization. Viewing the profession as "a great trust administered by philosopher kings," Butler gained the respect and admiration of professors and school superintendents. Speaking from this viewpoint, Charles Eliot, president of Harvard and former NEA president, referred to this elite as a "thin" upper level in a democratic society, which consisted of the "managing, leading, guiding class—the intellectual discoverers, the inventors, the organizers, and the managers and their chief assistants."[17] Butler, Eliot, David Starr Jordan of Stanford, and others constituted what David Tyack has called the "architects of centralization."[18] Social rank could no longer command deference as educational achievement promised it would. Logically, it would seem, this system would eliminate the old sexism of traditional professionalism. Women found, however, that gender inequalities present at the founding of the NEA would not easily disappear under a

15. Wesley, *NEA*, p. 366; *NEA Proceedings*, 1896, pp. 27–30; 1897, pp. 28–29; 1898, pp. 34–36.

16. Collins, "Schoolmen, Schoolma'ams," p. 142; Richard F. W. Whittemore, *Nicholas Murray Butler and Public Education 1862–1911* (New York, 1970), pp. 54–56. Paul Mattingly pointed out to me the influences on Butler's life.

17. Whittemore, *Butler*, p. 54. Eliot is quoted in David B. Tyack, "Pilgrim's Progress: Toward a Social History of the School Superintendency, 1860–1960," *History of Education Quarterly*, 16 (Fall 1976), p. 284.

18. Charles W. Eliot, "Educational Reform and the Social Order," *School Review*, 17 (April 1909), pp. 217–20, as quoted in David B. Tyack, "City Schools: Centralization of Control at the Turn of the Century" (Stanford University, mimeographed), p. 4.

meritocracy. Indeed, much of the clarion call for centralization was couched in an attack on the performance of female schoolteachers. The transformation of professionalism and its complement of centralization within the NEA forced a realignment of new administrators away from college presidents toward newly organized teachers' groups. The realignment proceeded slowly from roughly 1903 to 1913, when Nicholas Murray Butler bowed out of NEA politics and new administrative Progressives replaced his leadership.

The NEA conventions, run in the middle of summer, had become an opportunity for frugal school marms to travel in large groups to exotic places in the United States. Protected by their large numbers, the women went to Buffalo, a favorite summer resort, or to Los Angeles on a three- or four-day train trip. Encouraged by boards of education and educational supervisors to go to teacher institutes where they could learn new teaching techniques, the teachers attended the NEA with much the same expectation. NEA meetings in the 1890s and 1900s were run like institutes, where women schoolteachers were expected to listen to papers delivered by male educational experts. But institutes also had a certain entertainment value, and the NEA also attracted teachers by choosing recreational areas, by including entertainment in the programs, and by helping to make travel arrangements for the teachers. Thousands of teachers responded favorably, and for this reason the Chicago teachers decided to launch their campaign for a national federation at the annual NEA meetings.[19]

The Teachers' Rebellion within the NEA

The questioning of male leadership by rank-and-file women teachers centered first around the issues of centralization, but soon the inequalities of

---

19. The old structure of the NEA, up to the 1890s, worked quite simply for the interests of school administrators and university professors, who dominated it. Of these two departments within the NEA (the organization had over a dozen departments at that time), the Department of Superintendence rose in importance in the 1890s. Supporting the issue of a strong superintendency, the department used its meeting as a propaganda machine to fuel the campaign of the proponents of the measure. Most important, the department was the mainstay of the National Council of Education, which proposed policy for the NEA and operated to control the organization.

The National Council drew its membership from each of the departments on an appointed basis so that although it was not formally designed as an exclusive agency it operated as one. The council was primarily representative of the Department of Higher Education and the Department of Superintendence. Until 1907 a total of eighteen women had served in the fifty-year history of the sixty-member council. General policy issues were discussed in the council, then submitted to a resolutions committee, which in turn submitted the resolutions to the general body of the NEA. Later this system was amended so that policy recommendations from the National Council were endorsed wholesale by the convention.

Leadership of the NEA was carefully preserved by an inner group through the nominating committee, which was appointed by the president in a geographically representative fashion. When in 1897 the convention decided that the nominating committee would be elected by delegates at the convention from the states they represented, the door opened a crack to the possibilities of rank-and-file control. Still, in 1897 the obstacles to change remained formidable. The curtain of formalism weighed heavily in the deliberations of the convention, and as always in the poisonous atmosphere of gender began to dominate the discussions. The women proposed their own vision of education that was based on experience in the classroom as opposed to university credit; they thought that knowing the community was more important than satisfying the top administrative personnel. In the beginning the women did not regard their battle as being particularly feminist; instead they modeled their cry for human dignity on the example set by the trade unions. Eventually, however, as the educational stage became more contested, they responded more self-consciously as working women and identified the inherent sexism in the educational establishment. The contest between classroom teachers and the university elite was again led by Chicago teachers, but as a movement of discontent it had a wide and varied appeal.

The first clash between the Chicago Teachers' Federation and Nicholas Murray Butler took place at the July 1899 meeting in Los Angeles. Members of the Department of Superintendence arrived earlier than the main body of teachers, a practice that accentuated their importance: most teachers had to wait until late June or the beginning of July to see if their boards of education intended to rehire them for the next year. Furthermore, by meeting earlier, the superintendents were able to consolidate their positions and maintain control.

In a holiday mood eight hundred Chicago schoolteachers boarded a train hired by the CTF. Catharine Goggin and Margaret Haley announced on their departure that they would organize the National Teachers' Federation in the NEA so that other classroom teachers could achieve the benefits they had gained from organization. But the teachers dallied on the way. They stopped in Salt Lake City to talk to Mormon women about polygamy, and again at Sulfur Springs, where they indulged in mud baths and play while the NEA convened. Rosy cheeked on their arrival in Los Angeles, they discovered that the NEA leadership had taken direct action to thwart their move to organize a new body. One reporter noted, "Every powerful influence has frowned upon the movement, and the existence of the Chicago body as an organization is being studiously ignored."[20]

Receiving the cold shoulder from the elements in control of the NEA, Chicago teachers were called "revolutionists" as high school and college teachers formally expressed a "critical" stance toward the CTF. Three years before the CTF formally united with the labor movement, it was accused of operating as a union, and to the credit of the teachers they would not deny it. But they were clearly daunted by their treatment and did not flaunt their union intentions either.[21]

---

consensus politics, the mildest dissent appeared revolutionary. Each year the NEA president was elected by acclamation. Each year the president was a man, and in the 1890s it was fashionable to elect a college president from the Ivy League. See *NEA Proceedings,* 1898; *CT,* 10 February 1899.

20. *CT,* 9 July 1899.

21. *CT,* 14 July 1899. Haley was extremely cautious yet consistent in recommending union affiliation. See David Swig Ricker, "The School-Teacher Unionized," *Educational Review,* 30 (November 1905), pp. 344–46.

Facing the censure of the group, the CTF decided the time was not propitious for the launching of the national organization. Resigned, they strolled into the last general session of the convention to hear Nicholas Murray Butler present a carefully prepared report from the Resolutions Committee, which condemned the CTF for "using political influence and protecting incompetents" in school affairs. Citing the teachers' opposition to centralization, Butler called the Chicago teachers insurrectionists and "union labor grade teachers," whose "pernicious" activities were offensive to the teaching profession. The CTF leaders, aghast at the charges, were denied recognition from the floor. The prepared resolution passed, and the new teachers' organization was officially censured before it had been organized.[22]

Before leaving the convention, Haley and Goggin noted that the NEA constitution provided delegate representation by membership, and since the CTF was growing by hundreds they would return and demand recognition. Butler's attack was "mean if not dishonest," the two teachers said, but they would fight it just as they fought in Chicago.[23]

There were two means by which the Chicago teachers could most effectively challenge the NEA old guard. The first was to use their numerical superiority within the deliberative general assemblies. This was easily accomplished, although in the next twenty years charges of packing the meetings were hurled back and forth. The second vulnerable spot for the old guard was its inability to cope with the problems of teachers' wages and the tax issue raised by the CTF. These issues plagued the new administrative superintendents, who listened attentively as the teachers took on the old guard.

Margaret Haley launched her attack at the 1901 Detroit NEA session devoted to public school finance. She chose as her target William T. Harris, the U.S. Commissioner of Education. Capturing the stultifying effects of these long, dull, and irrelevant sessions, Haley said that the discussants rose to "stumble over each other" and praise Dr. Harris at the conclusion of his address. "Each one began by stating that there was nothing to be said after Dr. Harris had spoken, for he always said the last word on his subject, and somehow they proceeded to say a later word."[24] One speaker suggested that "if some Rockefeller or Carnegie would extend their donations to public schools, then things would be fine." The next speaker, according to Haley, said the audience should return home with a feeling of complacency after Dr. Harris's address, because the educational sky was without a cloud. When the last speaker finished, Haley noted, "the audience was almost as stupefied as he was stupid." Desperate for the semblance of a discussion, the chair

22. *CT*, 15 July 1899; *NEA Proceedings*, 1899.

23. *CT*, 16 July 1899. See also J. E. McKean to Catherine Goggin, 25 December 1899, CTF Collection.

24. Margaret Haley's autobiography, pt. 1; *NEA Proceedings*, 1901, pp. 174–81.

opened the topic for discussion from the floor, the moment Haley had been waiting for. "I began by saying . . . that I hoped no Rockefeller or Carnegie would ever contribute from their ill-gotten millions to the public schools," Haley recalled. She thought such subsidies would quell the thoughts of teachers, "who of all people should have their eyes opened and should be free to state the facts."[25]

She went on to argue that "the educational skies were not without a cloud," as the second speaker had suggested, and feeling complacent was the very last thing teachers and educators should do when school revenues were low and school costs were rising rapidly as services expanded. She then explained the teachers' tax fight in Chicago, showing how they had received their well-deserved raise. When she finished there was a great burst of applause. Harris then rose and pointed his finger at Haley. He complained that she was hysterical and that if there were any further hysterical outbursts by exhausted grade school teachers, he would insist that the meetings not be held at the end of the school term. Such a policy would, of course, disenfranchise the growing number of women schoolteachers whose influence was obviously being felt in the upper echelons of the organization. Harris went on to say that the speaker was from Chicago, a city that was not a model for the country; indeed, it was "morbid, cyclonic and hysterical, and you can never tell what is going to happen in Chicago." He suggested that Haley read, among other things, Adam Smith's *Wealth of Nations,* perhaps an appropriate missal for the ideology of traditional professionalism.[26]

Sensing her political advantage, Haley rose again, and without being recognized, she pleaded guilty to Harris's charge of being a common grade school teacher. She challenged Harris to debate the question of taxes and school revenues, for she had just won the tax issue in Chicago and she thought the plan would benefit teachers everywhere. Finally, in a true rhetorical flourish, she said that if what she had done was hysterical, then she hoped it was contagious so schoolteachers all over the United States could gain the benefits. After a second round of applause, Harris quickly apologized, saying he had not recognized Haley, but he pointedly ignored the plea for a debate, and the session quickly ended.

Although Haley was not getting the audience she wanted, the pro-union teachers were making a point in the organization. They called into question the style of traditional professionalism, which may have offered status and prestige to aspiring male administrators but had little to offer the majority of women teachers. In the area of public school finance, the school superintendents were visibly lacking in leadership qualities. Even the newly centralized boards of education were incapable of fending off tax-relief programs that threatened the already shaky school-finance problem. Pressure from corpo-

25. Margaret Haley's autobiography, pt. 1.
26. Ibid.

rations to lower taxes was growing as the schools tried to accommodate the influx of hundreds of thousands of immigrants.[27]

Centralization, which was so heartily embraced by the National Council within the NEA, brought its own tax headaches. The amalgamation of often bankrupt boroughs and townships, as was the case in Chicago and New York, meant assuming a large debt for the sake of efficiency. Corporations were anxious to shift the burden of debt to home owners, while real-estate agents were just as determined to keep the tax base low. Often the laxity of public officials in collecting taxes, combined with the administrative diffi-culty of systematizing taxes in the newly created districts, meant that schools were not getting the money they needed to keep operations going as they had been, much less meet the increased load of immigrant children. Older forms of taxation suddenly seemed totally unenforceable. Private-property taxes, usually based on a variety of personal effects, proved especially impossible to police. Taxation of intangible property, particularly franchise rights for railroads, street cars, and utilities—which gave private concerns the exclu-sive right to conduct public business—remained an uncollectable item, at least until the teachers remedied the situation.[28]

The success of the teachers in Chicago effectively exposed the hypocrisy in the move to revive traditional professionalism. Haley analyzed it well when she pointed out that teachers were expected to introduce modern, scientific methods in badly overcrowded classrooms, with less than sanitary conditions in cities where politicians controlled budget allocations. She argued that "the distinguishing characteristic of the progress made in educa-tion in the last fifty years has been the demand for the freeing of the child." She insisted that the freeing of the child "can only be secured by the freeing of the teacher." She spelled out quite clearly what this freedom would be: "To the teacher it means freedom from care and worry for the material needs of the present and the future—in other words, adequate salary and old age pensions, freedom to teach the child as an individual and not to deal with children en masse. In other words, fewer children for each teacher. Last but not least, the teacher must have recognition in the educational system as an educator. The tendency is to relegate her to the position of a factory hand, or a taker of orders from above."[29]

The pioneering work of John Dewey and the child-centered classroom meant nothing if the expense of such education could not be met. Education of the quality demanded cost more money than taxing agencies were collect-ing. Some members of the NEA heard and understood Haley's message. Karly Mathie, president of the Wisconsin State Teachers' Federation, agreed

27. Marjorie Murphy, "Taxation and Social Conflict: Teacher Unionism and Public School Finance in Chicago, 1898–1914," *Journal of the Illinois State Historical Society,* 74 (Winter 1981), pp. 242–60.
28. Ibid.
29. Margaret Haley to Stella Reid, 18 September 1905, CTF Collection.

that the low wages of teachers easily led them to cast their lot with the labor movement. "There was a time when I thought that freedom in teaching was better than fine gold, but I see today that all forms of liberty are in a strange way based upon the conditions of employment."[30]

By 1903 Chicago teachers had begun to convert classroom teachers who attended NEA sessions. In Milwaukee, grade school teachers organized a delegate reception for teachers, which was a method of hosting the meetings and offering an alternative gathering place for women teachers. The Chicago Teachers' Federation had begun a publication, the *CTF Bulletin,* and it served as a national network for teachers in the country. Haley used it in 1903 to prepare teachers for a Boston meeting in which teachers promised to lay their case before the NEA. Three thousand schoolteachers met in Chickering Hall. Teachers from St. Paul and St. Louis, who had organized their own federations, attended the Boston meeting, as did teachers from Philadelphia, New York, and Washington. One speaker received "enthusiastic applause" for suggesting that the "high salaried officials who direct the destinies of the National Education Association . . . point out the way to educational perfection for the benefit of teachers who receive extremely low salaries." Yet this latter class, which she termed "the silent partners," had to "pay the bills for the support of the association in the main."[31]

Meanwhile at the official NEA proceedings, a floor fight ensued between Haley and Butler. Haley won and managed to get teachers on the Nominating Committee and to have her delegation recognized for its numerical strength. Butler tried to sandbag the coming reforms by appointing a committee to study teachers' wages, pensions, and tenure, the first important concession to the teachers' demands. This concession was not enough, however, as the teachers insisted that Haley be allowed to address the general assembly. Butler was forced to concede, and he ended the stormy NEA meeting with a gracious smile—and the full intention of stopping the classroom teachers' rebellion.[32]

At the 1904 NEA meeting Haley made a speech, which though it did not mark a substantial change in the organization, was a symbolic triumph. Indeed, the thousands of teachers who came to see the St. Louis World's Fair stopped first to hear Miss Haley give voice to the growing movement of teacher organization. She began emphatically by citing reasons why organization was needed: the corrupt state of urban politics, the inability of school boards or county boards to collect adequate school revenues, and the deplorable conditions shared by most urban school teachers. She explained that the significance of the tax suit was "not the disclosing of these humiliating facts nor the forcing of the corporations to return to the public treasury some of

30. *CTF Bulletin,* 23 January 1903.
31. *CTF Bulletin,* 11 September 1903.
32. *NEA Proceedings,* 1903.

their stolen millions" but rather "the agency" of the teachers who brought the suit. Though not openly advocating trade unionism, she insisted that industrial workers and teachers had a common cause "in their struggle to secure the rights of humanity through a more just and equitable distribution of the products of their labor." The important thing was for teachers to recognize that "back of the unfavorable conditions of brain and manual workers is a common cause." Ideology and the direction of the nation were at stake in this mission, Haley explained. "Two ideals are struggling for supremacy in American life today; one the industrial ideal dominating through the supremacy of commercialism, which subordinates the worker to the product and the machines; the other, the ideal of democracy, the ideal of the educators, which places humanity above all machines, and demands that all activity shall be the expression of life."[33]

Rhetorically a success, Haley's address demonstrated her notion that the role of educator was not restricted to public school teachers. Workers were also educators. This was heresy to the elitist expert educators gathered at the NEA, but it was not too distant from the views of the common school-teachers, who had little sense of professional exclusivity. Finally, the conflict of the two ideals that Haley saw struggling for supremacy in American life would destroy an aspect of teaching that Haley and other schoolteachers found worthy of preserving. The joys of teaching, the rewards of the service, were imperiled by the commercial ethos threatening the life of the demo-cratic society. "Those two ideals can no more continue to exist in American life than our nation could have continued half slave and half free. If the school can not bring joy to the work of the world, then the joy must go out of its own life, and work in the school, as in the industrial field, will become drudgery."[34]

Haley's poignant critique of the meaning of capitalism's changes and their impact on education impressed the schoolteachers and left the educational experts cold. Haley had originally asked to debate one of the educational experts, but she was turned down and told to prepare a speech instead and send it to the NEA months before the meeting. Aaron Gove, a superintendent from Denver, Colorado, rose after Haley's speech and, with the benefit of her prepared copy, delivered his debating points. Haley was never given the opportunity to rebut Gove's remarks. Granting that more attention ought to be paid to teachers' salaries, pensions, and tenure, Gove argued that teacher unionism would foster class division. He went on to defend centralization and warned teachers that they wanted nothing more than to usurp the new powers granted to superintendents. The very nature of the superintendency was admittedly autocratic, but Gove argued that it was a necessity: "Despo-

33. *CTF Bulletin,* 9 September 1904; also *NEA Proceedings,* 1904.
34. *NEA Proceedings,* 1904, pp. 145–52.

tism can be wielded with a gloved hand," he said.[35] As for the conflict between labor and capital, Gove said he would view teachers' involvement with alarm. He considered unionism fraught with danger in that it invited the "sordidness of our personal life" to undermine "idealism." He warned against descending "to a lower plane of social life" where "selfishness and acquisitiveness" replace "honor, integrity, patriotism and love," where teachers would strive "chiefly for a superiority of wealth over everybody, regardless of the truths of ideal manhood."[36]

Gove's rebuttal ended with the "truths of ideal manhood," and with the phrase ringing in the air, Haley was denied the platform. The tactics of the Prince Albert-coated educational establishment offended more than the classroom teachers. Reformers could not hope to attract college-educated women while they denied them a voice in the organization or belittled their claims for better living conditions. The Chicago Teachers' Federation did not have to point to the fact that men were being promoted to administrative posts and women were consistently overlooked. The new superintendents of schools needed to accommodate some of the teacher demands. The old guard was simply stifling a debate the superintendents wanted and was avoiding the changes needed to fit the new structure of education.

The NEA changed after this lively exchange, but not in the direction teachers or superintendents might have wished. First, through Butler's efforts the National Council consolidated its power and effectively blocked the growing power of local teacher delegations; it also controlled the treasury, and no more funds were available for the study of salaries, tenure, and pensions. Second, the NEA admitted a number of women's groups in 1907. Forming a new NEA department were the General Federation of Women's Clubs, the National Congress of Mothers, the Association of Collegiate Alumnae, the Women's Christian Temperance Union, and the Southern Association of College Women. In 1909 they were reorganized into the Department of School Patrons. Although these groups wanted to promote women in the educational field, their members were often upper-class women whose experience in education was limited to voluntary work. Third, the NEA incorporated the rhetoric of the teacher demands, thus addressing the gap between expectations and rewards. But it never conceded the basic problem of centralization: oversupervision and the loss of job control. In other words, the hierarchy would remain in place, but professionalism would

35. For Gove's speech, see *NEA Proceedings,* 1904, pp. 152–55. Wesley offers this description of Gove in 1884, as he attended the NEA meetings in Madison, Wisconsin: "A slender, dark gentleman in the early forties, with dark eyes and a heavy mustache that might have been dyed, was dressed in an elegant white wool suit, cut Prince Albert style, with a white stovepipe hat, tilted jauntily over one eye, and was smoking a long cigar. Surely some local sporting gentleman—but no it was Aaron Gove, Superintendent of Schools in Denver." Wesley, *NEA,* pp. 156–57, 260–61.

36. *NEA Proceedings,* 1904.

give lip service to the teacher-union demands. Finally, the organization would become more sensitive to women, giving them token positions, placing them on the program, and occasionally permitting them to speak from the floor.

The real change was the rise in influence of new administrative professionals in the NEA. They were largely the new superintendents who had benefited from centralization but who until the classroom teachers spoke out were more like obedient students under the tutelage of their educational superiors. The backyard rebellion of elementary and a few high school teachers gave the administrative professionals an opportunity to address unfinished problems that centralization had started. Not all school superintendents had gotten complete control over educational affairs, and many had very little to say over budgetary matters. These were not issues that concerned the old guard but were burning issues for the new superintendents and obviously for the teachers. The teachers then served as a vehicle for the administrative professionals who rescued the centralization and professionalization project from the more radical proponents of educational change. The new guard would use the teachers to overthrow the old while reshaping the terms on which modern professionalism would be based.

CHAPTER FOUR /

The Early Teacher Unions

Teachers formed the backbone of the suffrage movement. Several famous suffragists at some point in their careers earned a living teaching school. Susan B. Anthony was a teacher, Anna Howard Shaw taught school, Henrietta Rodman taught school. Rodman formed a Feminist Alliance in 1914 to protect married women from discrimination in the New York City school system. Susan B. Anthony wanted to help Margaret Haley in 1903 but was too sick to attend the teachers' convention, though she gave it her blessing. The new teachers' unions were not just woman-led; they were feminist. "Feminism," Nancy Cott tells us, seems to have come into common parlance around 1913. Suffrage was only a tool. "The real goal was a 'complete social revolution': freedom for all forms of women's active expression, elimination of all structural and psychological handicaps to women's economic independence, an end to the double standard of sexual morality, release from constraining sexual stereotypes, and opportunity to shine in every civic and professional capacity." The relationship between woman's new economic role and the need for the vote was especially obvious to schoolteachers. Affiliation with the union movement gave women new access to the halls of political power. Teachers in New York, Chicago, and Philadelphia, by their interest in unionism, encouraged the wave of unionization among women garment workers. By 1909 when thousands of clothing workers were challenging their employers, Margaret Haley and teachers in Chicago, New York, and Boston plotted to get a woman elected to the National Education Association. Unlike their unskilled colleagues, the schoolteachers scored a victory.[1]

Of all the new teachers' unions, the one organized by public school teachers in Chicago was the most powerful and influential. The leaders of the Chicago movement gave voice to the growing sense that self-supporting women were the exemplars of independent womanhood. Personal well-

1. Nancy F. Cott, *The Grounding of Modern Feminism* (New Haven, Conn., 1987), pp. 13–50.

being, in the form of higher wages and pensions, was a well-earned necessity. Self-sacrifice, the ultimate feminine quality on fiscally pressed school
boards relied to keep wages down, was viewed as just an employer tactic.
The gimmick of reminding teachers that the enterprise of education was
ultimately for the children would no longer hold these inspired women back.
"We wish to inquire," a teacher wrote in the Women's Trade Union League
journal, *Life and Labor*," about the child after he has left the school." What
about the welfare of children who could earn only meager wages in a
factory? How were the teachers to teach independence of mind if they had no
idea what it was? These new feminists embraced professionalism with the
same "profound ambiguities" found in the feminist movement. On the one
hand they expected to earn higher pay, pensions, and dignity on the job,
while on the other, they expected that as women they had a special contribution to make in the education and trade union movements.[2]

The old sexism of traditional professionalism had refused to recognize the
teachers' legitimate grievances, and when the Chicago Teachers' Federation
failed to organize a national teachers' union in 1901, it adopted a policy of
working within the National Education Association to wrest control from the
elite national leaders and allow teachers to find their own direction. This
policy was fairly successful until the NEA decided that a mass base of
practicing teachers would act as a foil to teacher unionization and competi-
tively out-organized the teachers' union. Other teachers, especially high
school teachers, adopted traditional AFL organizing strategies and sought to
build an independent union. The genesis of these two directions provides a
crucial insight into the union teachers' earliest decisions about the type of
organization they wanted.

The Chicago Teachers' Federation organized in 1897 with three constitutional goals: to gain a raise, to protect teacher pensions, and to "study
parliamentary law." The Chicago Board of Education promised a raise the
moment the fledging group announced that three thousand members had
signed up in an election year. But the salaries were not forthcoming, as
almost immediately after the election the board announced a permanent
deficit. Pension protection proved far too difficult to maintain because it was
underfinanced. Created in 1895, the pension favored women over men even
though men earned more money than women. The men were not about to
watch the women retire five years before they could and get the same amount
of money for a pension. A revised bill soon appeared before the Illinois
legislature, where legislators made it a voluntary program, thus threatening
its continuance. This bread-and-butter issue became the main focus of the
CTF for most of its existence and may very well account for the loyal
membership the CTF maintained despite its many detractors. In the first

2. Ibid.; Mary O'Reilly, "What Organization Means to Teachers," *Life and Labor*, 5 November
1915, pp. 166–68.

year, however, the pension seemed doomed to legislative alterations. Faced with these problems, the federation seemed to wander off the course of its original three goals. Instead of fighting for the wage increase and the pension, the first CTF president promoted the purchase of a retirement home in Wisconsin and promised stronger ties to the woman's club movement in the city.[3]

As we have seen earlier, both Catharine Goggin and Margaret Haley were well entrenched in the school system. Their rise to leadership was not unproblematic. The pretensions of the club crowd in the union alarmed a large faction that once again the original demands of the teachers would be subordinated to more clublike activities that called for less confrontation with the city.

Angered by what seemed to be a retreat for the new organization, charter member Goggin, who taught in the primary grades, challenged the CTF leadership in the first year. She was defeated in what many teachers viewed as a crooked election. Undaunted, she sharpened her political skills by taking seriously the "study of parliamentary law" and prepared for another challenge in the next year. Her opposition to school centralization became the focus of her campaign for federation leadership. In this campaign she was joined by Margaret Haley, a thirty-eight-year-old sixth-grade teacher interested in pensions and centralization. The two women based their campaign on the centralization issue, and Goggin won the presidency of the CTF. In her inaugural address she promised that she would devote herself to salary increases and pensions. Her impeccably organized election indicated that parliamentary law would reign in the union. Finally, she added a new scope for teachers, calling on them to be more political and more active. In making this last point she raised the curtain on a new type of teacher organization.[4]

As a team, Haley and Goggin built on each other's strengths in such a way as to inspire other women to act. Goggin was the niece of a popular city judge, one of five daughters, three of whom were public school teachers. She was known to be generous to a fault, helping destitute teachers make it through hard times. She promoted the pension and helped organize the federation. The soft-spoken Goggin was trained in the city's classical high school. Unlike many of her colleagues teaching in the primary grades, she had earned a high school diploma. Federationists thought of her as the general, the strategist of the union whose chief job was to unleash or rein in her more colorful colleague, Margaret Haley.[5]

Haley was the daughter of a stonecutter, whose shaky business deals forced Margaret's early entry into the work world at age sixteen. With little

3. CTF Minutes, Collection. See also Catharine Goggin, "The Chicago Pension Law," *School Journal,* 54 (May 1897), p. 542.

4. Catharine Goggin, "Early History of the Chicago Teachers' Federation," Box 35, CTF Collection.

5. See the poem by Anna Murphy, Box 35, CTF Collection.

more than an elementary education, Haley taught in rural schools and worked her way into Chicago, where salaries were higher and further education more available. Haley did not become interested in politics until after the Pullman strike in 1894.[6]

Goggin, a West Sider, taught in the downtown Jones School; Haley taught in the South Side Hendricks School in the Back of the Yards. They had an unusual grasp of the regional variation within the city. With over fifty years of combined classroom experience behind them, they were at an age when family burdens were less pressing and interest in political life seemed more compelling. They were both early feminists, taking their feminist proposals to their federation cautiously but still leading the teachers to endorse what were largely radical views of women's role in society. They faced a Catholic constituency that was initially opposed to suffrage primarily because it was seen as an elite movement requiring property qualifications for working women. The two women shared a belief that women were destined to assume a political role in American life, and together they generated a charismatic leadership that inspired literally thousands of public school teachers across the nation.[7]

It was in the field of school finance that Goggin and Haley made their lasting contribution to the teacher-union movement. They refused to believe that rich, bustling Chicago could not scrape together enough money in taxes to pay teachers a fair salary. In three short years, Goggin and Haley managed to win their tax decision in the Illinois courts. This dramatic accomplishment was achieved under the most arduous of political pressures. "It was nothing short of a miracle," Mary Herrick recalled.[8]

Aware of the drama of their achievement, Goggin sent Margaret Haley on the road for a national tour to speak to other teacher groups. This first foray outside Chicago provided the impetus for the formation of other female-led teacher organizations. In New York City the Interborough Association of Women Teachers (IBTA) formed in 1906, a year after the Chicago Teachers' Federation secured its raise. Arguing that teachers ought to receive the same salaries as men teachers, the teachers raised the issue of equal pay to the Board of Education. When the board turned the women down, they responded with mass demonstrations, a powerful membership drive netting fourteen thousand members, and lobbying efforts in the New York legislature aimed at changing the state salary schedules. Unlike the Chicago movement, the New York IBTA quickly succumbed to a bitter dispute over whether classroom teachers or administrators would head the organization. In 1907 Grace Strachan, a district administrator, emerged as head of the

---

6. Margaret Haley's autobiography, pt. 1. See also Robert Reid, ed. *Battleground: The Autobiography of Margaret A. Haley* (Urbana, Ill., 1982), pp. 3–33.

7. CTF Minutes, Box 2, CTF Collection.

8. Interview with Mary J. Herrick, Chicago Loop City College, January 1972.

teachers' organization. Strachan advised a moderate course and carefully steered through the 1911 state legislature a new law prohibiting discrimination in salary because of sex and giving women teachers a pay raise. The women's success in New York gave rise to a high school teachers' movement that was headed by Progressive men also interested in securing higher wages for teachers. The nucleus of this organization eventually grew into Local 5 of the American Federation of Teachers.[9]

The Goggin-Haley influence led directly to the formation in San Francisco of the City Federation of Teachers. Formed in 1906, the organization focused its energies on guarding the distribution of public lands by the Board of Education. In the West, the allocation of public lands for educational purposes had operated since the Northwest Ordinance as a means of funding public education. These special sixteenth sections of publicly owned property frequently sat at prominent intersections of growing cities. The property was often mishandled, and teachers knew that school revenues could be much higher if the properties were fairly rented. In Chicago, the Board of Education provided ninety-nine year leases for prime city sites at less-than-market value, while it claimed bankruptcy to the teachers. One year the Board of Education rented a floor of a building from one of its land tenants for the same price as the rental of the land. San Francisco teachers watched as the same mismanagement threatened their salaries. Protesting that selling the land was unpatriotic, the teachers tried to keep the Board of Education from making long-term leases. Like the New York City union, the teachers' union in San Francisco chose to use women administrators in its leadership. Dr. Margaret Maloney, a medical doctor and school principal, helped organize the federation and kept it going until the suffrage campaign of 1909 seemed to drain the organization's energies.[10]

Margaret Haley traveled to Baltimore, Philadelphia, and Boston during the Chicago tax crusade. In each city she found a basis for uniting the women teachers to obtain better wages. Between 1902 and 1910, over eleven of these organizations joined the American Federation of Labor. Others turned to suffrage or became discouraged, only to see a revival of the movement again in 1919. These cities and others, including St. Paul, Minneapolis, Atlanta, and Toledo, became the nucleus of the American Federation of Teachers.[11]

9. Patricia Anne Carter, "A Coalition between Women Teachers and the Feminist Movement in New York City" (Ed.D. diss., University of Cincinnati, 1985); Robert E. Doherty, "Tempest on the Hudson: The Struggle for 'Equal Pay for Equal Work' in the New York City Public Schools, 1907–1911," *History of Education Quarterly,* 19 (Winter 1979), pp. 413–34; Guild Papers, unprocessed files, New York University.

10. Harriet Talan, "San Francisco Federation of Teachers: 1919–1949" (M.A. thesis, San Francisco State University, 1982), pp. 2–9.

11. For reports on the tax crusade, see the *CTF Bulletin,* 29 March and 6 June 1902, 18 September 1903, 23 September 1904; see also corresponding dates in the *Chicago Tribune.* On other cities, see Joseph Whitworth Newman, "A History of the Atlanta Public School Teachers' Association: Local 89 of the American Federation of Teachers, 1919–1956" (Ph.D. diss., Georgia State

Taxes and Salaries

The tax issue was a popular success for teachers and liberal allies concerned with the rise of corporate greed. Journalists eagerly promoted Haley and Goggin and found other colorful women joining them, especially Margaret Maloney in San Francisco and Grace Strachan in New York. At a deeper level the tax campaign was part of the awakening of a municipal movement that characterized much of the Progressive Era. Municipal corruption, especially the blatant tax dodging that had become rampant in the nation's cities, angered a wide range of middle-class reformers. In Chicago the traction companies, led by the entrepreneur Charles Tyson Yerkes, had made a mockery of the political system by buying votes in the state legislature. What Margaret Haley discovered was that these same railway companies were dodging taxes under the noses of the same political hacks. By aiming her tax case at public services, she was attracting the attention of the politically astute in the city. As new public services were introduced into the city, such as public gas, lights, and telephones, the opportunities for further corruption multiplied. Schools represented another opportunity for special building contracts, for sweetheart contracts between realtors and political Board of Education members, and for jobs as janitors and school "engineers." It was Haley's genius to connect the municipal ownership organization with the teachers' federation movement. By serving as a watchdog for political corruption, the schoolteachers represented an ethical protest against urban corruption. In several municipal elelctions, every teacher in the city schools was armed with a petition, often calling for penny gas or penny phones, municipal ownership of traction companies, and elections for Board of Education members. Giving blank petitions to the students, the teachers were able to gather hundreds of thousands of signatures and deliver them under the cover of an appreciative press to the doors of the politicians. These alliances were invaluable for the voteless teachers, and the services of the teachers inspired Chicago's Progressive Era reform movement.[12]

Despite these successes, both in the press and in the courts, teachers in Chicago did not receive their pay raise immediately. Indeed, at the very moment the CTF won its court case, the state legislature emasculated the teachers' pension by making it voluntary. Haley said it was one of the keenest disappointments of her life and quoted one state legislator as warning her, "You can't hit the corporations as you have done and not expect them to hit back." Without the pay raise and damaged by the pension loss, Haley and Goggin had to return to their constituency and ask them to continue paying

University, 1978); Steve Trimble, *Education and Democracy: A History of the Minneapolis Federation of Teachers* (Minneapolis, 1979).

12. Ray Ginger, *Altgeld's America* (Chicago, 1958), chap. 2; Joel Arthur Tarr, *A Study in Boss Politics: William Lorimer of Chicago* (Urbana, Ill., 1971). See also the papers of the union at the time: Boxes 35, 37, and 39, CTF Collection.

the salary required to keep Haley in Springfield as a lobbyist. The teachers responded with great enthusiasm. But the solution to the teachers' problem was not through the legislature but rather through the local political system.[13]

The CTF, now five thousand members strong, affiliated with the Chicago Federation of Labor in 1902, and in doing so changed the direction of the Chicago Federation of Labor and the prospects for other women trade unionists. The affiliation issue was controversial within the CTF and other federations in other cities similarly inspired. In Chicago teachers called on Jane Addams to deliver a speech, which though it did not openly endorse teacher unionism, did little to dampen the spirits of a crowd clearly under the spell of Margaret Haley's rhetoric. The salary question outweighed objections to unionism. While the teachers were still struggling under the same salary scale, they were also serving in a school system that had no water, where students were on strike, and in an atmosphere where most working-class districts were enlivened by news of 1902's successful coal strike. Other organizations were not so fortunate. In San Francisco schoolteachers debated the union affiliation issue and decided against it. They were influenced by their own class prejudices and the cold reception given by the American Federation of Labor. In Chicago, teachers shared the same class prejudices, but they were swayed by new leadership in the local labor council.[14]

Cooperation between women teachers and local councils made an important difference in determining the success or failure of the earliest teacher organizations. Chicago represents a success but not a unique one. Teachers in St. Paul found allies early in the labor movement, as did teachers in Milwaukee. Chicago, however, was the model for others to follow, and nowhere else were the ties as firm as in the Windy City. John Fitzpatrick, who was serving as an organizer for the corrupt Chicago Federation of Labor, encouraged the women and steered their affiliation through AFL channels. In return for his help, the teachers were more than willing to help him overturn the CFL leadership in January 1903. This cooperation produced nothing short of a revolution for women workers in the Chicago area. Fitzpatrick, freed from the shackles of an uninspired union leadership, was able to focus on organizing women and industrial workers. The results for women were phenomenal. Within three years the CFL organized among the following women workers: milliners, packing-house workers, box makers, musicians, chorus girls, laundry workers, domestic servants, department-store workers, bookbinders, garment workers, and glove workers. In addition to its success with new women's unions, the CFL launched its first consistent lobbying effort through the work of Margaret Haley, who was

13. Reid, *Battleground*, pp. 42–85.
14. Marjorie Murphy, "From Artisan to Semiprofessional: White Collar Unionism among Chicago Public School Teachers, 1870–1930" (Ph.D. diss., University of California, Davis, 1981), pp. 174–80; *CTF Bulletin* 3, 24 October 1902; 14 November 1902.

elected union lobbyist. In 1903 the Women's Trade Union League formed and augmented the network of women's trade unions that the CTF had inspired. The teachers were the largest affiliate of the organization in Chicago and made up the backbone of the movement nationally.[15]

The most lasting effect of the affiliation was the final Board of Education 1904 approval of the salary increases teachers had earned from the tax suit. Judge Edward Dunne made the ruling that compelled the board to pay the teachers. In the next year he ran for mayor and won largely on the power of the CTF/CFL–Haley/Fitzpatrick combination. Dunne was so dependent on Haley in this election that he made it public knowledge that he consulted her on all his appointments to the Board of Education. The teachers' union in eight years had become a major power in city politics.[16]

The strongest argument for unionization and the best explanation for its early popularity was clearly economic. Teachers were interested in raising their salaries long before the debate over centralization or professionalization intruded into the educational world. Yet salaries became an issue, at first of contention between centralizers and teachers, but later of conciliation between professionalization and salary-poor teachers. It was difficult for administrators to argue that teachers should be better trained, more imbued with middle-class values, and less political while they kept teachers' salaries artificially low. "In most cases," Coffman reported in his 1911 survey, "the motive that starts teachers is economic pressure." Although parents of the average teacher earned approximately $800 a year, a good salary for the lower middle and working class, a large percentage of teachers in widowed

15. Women's Trade Union League of Chicago, *Biennial Report, 1911–1913*, p. 1. The turn-of-the-century growth of militancy among Chicago's women workers and the involvement of the CTF in supporting their unions is documented in newspaper accounts. For example, the milliners, whose wages were declining, formed a new union in 1902 (*CT,* 14 September 1902); three thousand women packers, nearly the entire female work force, struck a week later (*CT,* 21 September 1902); that same autumn, women box makers struck (*CT,* 12 October 1902), just weeks before the teachers affiliated with labor. In 1903, following the organization of musicians, chorus girls were dismissed for joining a union (*CT,* 3 March 1903); in May, women laundry workers struck for recognition in a bitter dispute (*CT,* 6 May 1903). The following year domestic servants in Chicago announced they were forming a union (*CT,* 9 January 1904); a month later, women department-store workers walked off the job when their leader blew a whistle signaling the beginning of a strike (*CT,* 18 February 1904); in October, women bookbinders were organizing a union (*CT,* 29 February 1904). The following spring marked the first move to gain union recognition for women garment workers, who walked out in March (*CT,* 19 March 1905); this led to a sympathetic strike by teamsters in May. Although the strike was lost, it did not halt women's organizing efforts, for five months later the Waitresses Union was seeking a club room to conduct organizing meetings (*CT,* 24 January 1905).

In the three years after teachers unionized, the movement toward women's unions took off. Mary McDowell exploited the teachers' obvious sympathies with this new movement when she told teachers that clothing workers and packers "are your proxies in industry" deserving support (*CT,* 15 May 1904). Teachers were generous in giving to organizing drives either through direct participation or through the organized activities of the Women's Trade Union League.

16. *CT,* 23 August 1904, 9 September 1904; Richard Becker, "Edward Dunne: Reform Mayor of Chicago, 1905–1907" (Ph.D. diss., University of Chicago, 1958).

families reported an average income of $250 a year, which was definitely poverty level.[17]

From family-budget studies printed in Chicago newspapers it is possible to reconstruct a teacher's relative contribution to the family economy. For a yearly income of $384 a year, a women's club, the Businesswomen's Exchange, calculated a budget of $182 for board, $78 for rent, $30 for car fare, and $26 for laundry, which left $32 for a winter coat, shoes, working shirts, thread, umbrella, time lost from work, medicine, and dentistry. The clubwomen concluded that a woman worker needed "twice that amount if she is to retain her health and self-respect." Beginning teachers rarely earned "twice that amount," or $786. The beginning salary was $550 a year, and the highest salary for teachers with more than eight years experience was $825 a year. That was the ceiling: no amount of further education could improve the teachers' earnings. Even though teachers earned more than other women workers, they did not move out of the family economy.[18]

Salaries for clerical workers, even at the lowest levels of employment, were higher than Chicago teachers' wages. In government service, where clerical wages were high, clerks began at $900 a year, $75 greater than grade teachers at the highest step. Clerks and public librarians earned between $650 and $1,000 a year, and pages earned between $450 and $600 a year, which was about the level of a beginning teacher. In private industry clerical wages were often lower than in public service but still higher than teachers' wages.[19]

Elyce Rotella has argued that as women entered clerical occupations, real wages declined. Women entered clerical work at the turn of the century in greater numbers not because of the wage levels but because of the high demand. Educational requirements for clerical jobs were not nearly as strict:

17. Lotus Delta Coffman, *The Social Composition of the Teaching Population* (New York, 1911), pp. 36–45. Coffman's general profile reads: "When she entered teaching both of her parents were living and had an annual income of approximately $800 which they were compelled to use to support themselves and their four or five children. The young woman early found pressure both real and anticipated to earn her own way very heavy" (p. 80).

18. If women contributed the low rent figure of $2.30 a week to the family, it seems that teachers could expect to contribute $260 a year, or a third of the salary of the highest paid teachers. Professional expenses, including the trip to NEA conventions, the purchase of special supplies, or the contribution of a piano to the school—a purchase that many teachers made despite the prohibitive cost of $800 for a piano—are not included in these budgets. As the third and fourth breadwinners in their families, teachers could afford to keep their union going and pay for the more expensive clothing they wore while working. *CT,* 6 May 1903.

19. Elyce Rotella, "Women's Labor Force Participation and the Growth of Clerical Employment in the United States" (Ph.D. diss., University of Pennsylvania, 1977), pp. 108–12; also Margery Davies, "Woman's Place," *Radical History Review,* 5 (June 1976) p. 218. Davies cites a study of average weekly earnings of 1,032 women workers in Boston in 1883, which showed teachers earning $5.00 per week, clerical workers including cashiers $7.43, telegraph operators $6.55, saleswomen $5.75, clerks $5.28, and errand girls $2.56; factory workers' wages ranged upward from $1.80, with a median of $4.23; domestic service workers earned $4.96 weekly, including board estimated at $3.00.

teachers could start in skilled occupations, such as stenography, at wages they earned in teaching after eight years, that is $800 a year. Clerical workers, like teachers, often lived with their families, but they were not subject to arbitrary job transfers. Indeed, the expanding labor market provided educated women a distinct advantage. The highest wages in clerical occupations were still paid to male clerical workers; women were never able to command the salary level the men achieved. As the requirements for entry into teaching rose, however, clerical occupations became more attractive. The expansion of the high school in the city made it easier for daughters of working-class and immigrant families to attain an income similar to that from teaching without foregoing years of income for further training.[20]

The pressure on salaries further emphasized the transformation of schooling. The price of professionalism, after all, was a higher salary. None of the educational reformers denied that professionalism meant higher wages. All the teachers had to do was to present their case. Yet not only were leaders in the NEA reluctant to allow women to speak on the issue of salaries, they were adamantly against making the same kind of tax-issue campaign that Chicago teachers had made. Centralization, after all, had gained the support of the business community on the proposition that it would make school government more efficient and less costly. Suits on back taxes would hardly make the new education palatable to a business community set on keeping taxes low. Nicholas Murray Butler worked hard to keep the salary and tax issue contained.

In 1903, when union teachers won a major concession by getting the NEA to institute a Committee on Salaries (with Catharine Goggin of the CTF as a member), Nicholas Murray Butler quickly had himself nominated to the Resolutions Committee. There he successfully blocked teachers' recommendations on salary policy. Butler's ploy was a major setback for union teachers, but not a permanent setback. The salary issue continued to draw teachers into unions at an alarming rate, while NEA meetings attracted more big-city women teachers who were aggressively verbal about their financial situation.

Relations with the AFL

Union leaders were scarcely more encouraging to the new teacher unions than the NEA old guard had been. AFL leaders, even some local Chicago leaders, suspected that the women had affiliated with the union movement only because it would give them ties to a voting constituency within the city. Haley and Goggin made no secret of their ambitions and never denied that the vote was an important attraction of schoolteachers to the union. But they

---

20. Rotella, "Women's Labor Force Participation," p. 108.

made eloquent class pleas as well, spoke idealistically of the potential of the labor movement, and pointed out that they would inspire other women workers to join the union. Unionists in other cities were more hostile and discouraged women from uniting with the AFL. In San Francisco, for example, women were actively discouraged. Although Grace Strachan of the New York teachers was notably cool toward labor, she alone could not have discouraged a groundswell movement; but labor itself responded equally cooly. One reason was that the issues early federationists adopted were specifically aimed at male privilege.[21]

Patricia Carter has shown that the earliest federations were faced with the issue of whether married women had a right to hold jobs. Most school districts insisted that when teachers married they resign their positions. It was quite common for teachers to marry secretly. In San Francisco, if a married woman asked for a leave of absence, it was assumed that she had resigned from her position. New York City had a law insisting that teachers resign on marriage; in midwestern cities no law existed, but it was generally assumed that a married woman's chief means of support came from a man. If a teacher was desirable, or had special talents or was simply well liked, her marital status could be overlooked. In hard times, however, it was assumed that married women would resign. New York City women argued that this was unfair, that the rule was indiscriminately applied, that teachers were being dismissed on account of sex and not for merit. When in 1903 the New York City Board of Education formalized its rule on forbidding married women from teaching, it set off a reaction from feminists, who followed closely the testing of the rule. In 1905 a married woman teacher maintained her position, despite the board's efforts against her, but the courts decided very narrowly on the question, and the board was still capable of refusing to hire married women. A survey of forty-eight cities in 1914 indicated that thirty-seven had regulations that prevented the employment or married women teachers.[22]

In some respects boards of education had a paternalistic attitude toward these city jobs, arguing that women did not need the income; often, however, married women with disabled husbands were allowed to return to the classroom. It was a shared community value that the family wage would support women and that teachers were no exception to the family wage. Martha May

21. Carter, "Coalition," pp. 107–39; Grace C. Strachan, *Equal Pay for Equal Work: The Story of the Struggle for Justice Being Made by Women Teachers of the City of New York* (New York, 1910); Talan, "San Francisco," p. 9.

22. The issue for teacher unionists flared up again in the thirties because the long-standing rules against marriage were conveniently applied by school boards anxious to unload their staff to save money during the depression. Also the idea that public works should provide family income, not pin money for bridge parties of single-career women, grew popular. Women were simply vulnerable to the politics of the depression that gave preference to male hiring. The American Federation of Teachers took a strong stance supporting married women teachers, but the union could never move the AFL on the issue. Carter, "Coalition," p. 139.

has shown that early labor support for the family wage changed in the Progressive period to become a general defense of male privilege, made especially by leaders of the AFL. Schoolteachers, by making their demands for equal pay and rights for married women, were defying of the AFL's support of the family wage. But child-labor laws were seen as a way of protecting jobs of adult men. Labor leaders interpreted these issues to be of special concern to women only, not crucial to the success of the new teachers' unions, nor even important to laboring men as parents. The AFL tended to lump these issues into a bag of women's issues, not labor questions. As women lobbyists joined forces in Congress to promote social change, their agenda was looked upon with suspicion by AFL leaders, who were firmly rooted in the family-wage mentality. In its earliest moments, the strong support of the teachers' union movement for working women's issues clearly ran against the grain of the labor movement.[23]

In the early twentieth century the AFL leadership had to exert little effort to discourage the fledgling unions. Haley and Goggin had their union accepted on the paternalistic attitude of protecting defenseless school marms; neither woman challenged the notion—they were happy just to get the go-ahead and affiliate with their local labor council. But Samuel Gompers, president of the AFL, neither sent out a national charter nor prepared for a national federation. In 1905 the San Francisco teachers were told they could not affiliate with the AFL because there was no national charter, and the convention had determined that locals had to belong to a national or international union. Seven years later, when men's locals were formed in Chicago and New York, they were issued local charters and Haley was called upon to pay dues to the national AFL. At that point Gompers opened the discussion about a national organization but obviously did not feel compelled to move until 1916.[24]

Haley and Goggin tried to organize their own national federation in 1901 and again in 1912 but without going through AFL channels. They turned to the NEA first, despite their estrangement from its leadership. There were simply more women within the NEA than within the labor movement, and women were welcomed at the national meetings.

Early teacher unions confined their AFL activities to a few local central labor bodies where they were not overwhelmingly outnumbered. Within these organizations, women schoolteachers were quickly recognized for their lobbying abilities at a time when lobbying was a relatively new tactic for labor organizations. Teachers were most interested in public legislation,

23. Martha May, "Family Wage," in *Women, Work, and Protest: A Century of United States Women's Labor History,* ed. Ruth Milkman (Boston, 1985), pp. 1–21.
24. For the affiliation of the CTF with the AFL in 1902, see *CT,* 1, 15, 20 November 1902. For San Francisco, see Talan, "San Francisco," p. 6. See also Blanche Rinehart, "Mr. Gompers and the Teachers," *Changing Education,* 1 (Summer 1966), pp. 12–17; and Charles E. Goss, "Before the AFT: The Texas Experience," *Changing Education,* 1 (Summer 1966), pp. 6–9.

and their unions were happy to turn over to them the occasional labor fight in the legislative halls. It was an arrangement that "worked" but did not integrate women into the full range of labor activities. With respect to national organization, few women's unions were encouraged, and as far as Gompers was concerned the new teachers' unions hardly existed at all.[25]

The Style of Feminism in the New Teachers' Movement

A new sense of confidence seemed to emerge from new women's organizations in these years, and schoolteachers seemed especially attracted to this new independence. Teachers considered themselves autonomous in the classroom and resented incursions on their autonomy. Catharine Goggin tried to explain that the high percentage of spinster teachers was due to the independence of schoolteachers. According to Goggin, a woman teacher "learns to govern, not to be governed. . . . Her ways become fixed and set; she cannot be molded to suit any man. Her individuality has become too strongly developed." Men, Goggin concluded, "would rather marry some young, submissive woman just out from under the mother's wing." Teachers were also role models for young women and reproduced a positive female image. Catharine Goggin once explained why she was "an old maid" and concluded that she could not bear to have a man call her "ducky."[26]

It was more than the promise of autonomy and the personality of the spinster that made the new teacher movement feminist. There was a tradition of feminism in the early days when women teachers first attended national meetings. Susan B. Anthony was a pioneer in challenging the authorities in her state teachers' association; in 1903, when Margaret Haley went to the Boston NEA meeting, she stopped to visit the ailing Anthony, who urged the women to press their demand for a spot on the program and encouraged them to assert their equality within the NEA.[27] Anthony also reiterated the program for working women that the old suffragists had pursued in Reconstruction. "Women must have equal pay for equal work and they must be considered equally eligible to the offices of principal and superintendent." The whole movement, then, had a decided air of attack on the male dominance of the profession. Haley made the attack specific when she considered the NEA programing: "The men are eight to one on the programs and the

25. Murphy, "From Artisan to Semiprofessional," pp. 174–80.
26. Catharine Goggin, "Early Days," Box 35, CTF Collection.
27. "I hope," Anthony wrote, "that you will maintain the right of women to be on the program committee next year, and that you will insist upon their recognition in all positions of honor and emolument equally with men. . . . Women must have equal pay for equal work and they must be considered equally eligible to the offices of principal and superintendent, professor and president. The saying that women have equal pay is absurd while they are not allowed to have the highest position which their qualifications entitle them to; so you must insist that qualifications, not sex, shall govern the appointments to highest office." *CTF Bulletin,* 11 September 1903.

women are twelve to one in the audiences and in about the same proportion in the schools."[28]

The feminism of the teachers was not strictly limited to their own job gains. Teachers also identified with other women workers and gave their time and energy to the success of women garment workers. In the 1910 Hart and Schaffner strike in Chicago, Emma Stagenhagen noted that the CTF "not only gave generous financial help but day after day sent for their members to speak in the forty-two halls widely scattered over the city where the strikers were meeting."[29] Although middle-class women with free time often took over the leadership of the Women's Trade Union League, teachers were the largest visible women's support group in the organization.

Finally, women teachers supported the rise of women's suffrage in the Progressive era. Margaret Haley was an officer of the Women's Suffrage Party of Illinois and was instrumental in gaining the vote for women in the state in 1913. She also worked in suffrage campaigns in California and New York. Grace Strachan was a leader in the New York City women's suffrage movement.

The feminism of the new movement was both its strength and its weakness. It strengthened the new movement to have such strong women leaders, and the enthusiasm for the movement was based on the larger push for suffrage. But once suffrage was won it was unclear what direction the movement would take.

The Administrative Professionals and Women in the NEA

The feminism of the movement also presented the danger that teachers' energies would be dispersed in local suffrage campaigns instead of focused on the struggle for higher wages. Teachers needed a national focus for their new activities. Although they had been stymied on the salary issue by the traditional professionals, they had gained considerable attention from new Progressive administrators, who were more sympathetic to the teachers' cause and certainly more cordial to female leadership.

The administrative professional group was diverse representing a range of personalities and ideas that differed from the old guard and the new teacher unions. They all benefited from the centralization movement; they were all career teachers with higher degrees; they were either superintendents of large urban school districts or were influential in the national organization through its publications; and, finally, they held liberal ideas about the role of women

28. *CTF Bulletin,* 1 May 1903.

29. Emma Stagenhagen, "Report on the Chicago Strike," *Life and Labor,* 13 July 1913. See also "The Chicago Teachers' Federation and *Life and Labor,*" *Life and Labor,* 3 (May 1913), pp. 146–47.

30. Box 38, CTF Collection; Strachan, *Equal Pay;* Carter, "Coalition," pp. 56–58.

in educational leadership positions. They did not welcome the Department of School Patrons. Indeed, when they were in firm control of the NEA in 1922, they disbanded the group, arguing that they were strictly a professional organization and did not welcome lay control. The superintendents were willing to ally with the women until the changes in the organization were accomplished. Determined to lead the educational world, they would focus the teachers' energies on their own agenda and ultimately work to defeat the concept of teacher unionism.[31]

Two examples of new administrative superintendents illustrate the shift of power within the NEA. William McAndrew and Ella Flagg Young, although exceptional in their own right, were also representative of a generation of school administrators who followed the first wave of centralization and who often invented their own techniques in the art of supervision. They were offended by the "style and tone" of the old frock-coat society and benefited from Haley's own pronouncements on class division and elitism within the organization. As modern professionals, they introduced flexibility on the issues of material needs, women's participation, and democratic process— within the framework of a newly redefined executive office of superintendent. Of the two, William McAndrew was a leader of the new, efficient, and modern superintendents.[32]

McAndrew liked to think of himself as a "salary expert," and because of this reputation he had been one of the few superintendents invited to the teachers' rally in Boston in 1903. He told the rebel teachers that the NEA leadership was "utterly impracticable" in its educational proposals, and he spoke of "woodenheaded board members" who paid teachers "next to nothing."[33] Subsequently he was named to head the committee on salaries, tenure, and pensions to which Catherine Goggin contributed her sage advice from her Chicago experience. McAndrew was well known by Chicago teachers because he had taught at the prestigious Hyde Park High School before becoming a district superintendent in New York City. He was a modernizer aptly described by Laurence Cremin as one of those new superintendents who managed "to be a progressive without incurring the stigma of radicalism, an opportunity that must have been appealing in an era when the average board of education was a group of businessmen, lawyers and farmers little interested in schemes to reform society."[34] In his younger days in Chicago, McAndrew flaunted his devotion to science and all things modern by riding a bicycle, "dressed in bicycle togs, which were just coming into

31. Murphy, "From Artisan to Semiprofessional," pp. 315–40.
32. Ibid., pp. 335–40.
33. *CTF Bulletin*, 11 September 1903.
34. "Here was no dabbling with the tricks of the trade that had been the earmarks of the Normal School," wrote Lawrence Cremin of this scientific pedagogue, "here was Wissenschaft with a vengeance." Cremin, *The Transformation of the School: Progressivism in American Education* (New York, 1964), p. 200.

vogue," as a principal described him. "His attitude made some of us feel that he considered himself a little better than the rest of us, but we may have been a bit prejudiced by his ultra modern attire."[35]

Later, in 1924, when business was in vogue, McAndrew became the superintendent of Chicago's public schools, and only then did the teachers learn the shallowness of McAndrew's former radicalism. He immediately called on all principals to check the teachers' punctuality, he viewed teachers' salaries as a unit-cost problem in a noncompetitive labor market, and he reinstituted an unpopular merit system that the CTF had defeated over ten years before. He refused to meet with any labor groups and contemptuously spoke of his distaste for meeting with "dowdy" elementary school teachers. He once complained bitterly that in public education, unlike any other industry, the physical plant was used only ten months of the year and in daylight hours; he stopped short of recommending that children attend classes in midnight shifts. His attitude toward the old guard in the NEA was genuine and never changed, but his early support of the demands of the Chicago teachers turned out to have been opportunism.[36] The merit of McAndrew was that he articulated the bread-and-butter issues that the teachers were raising, while he added the air of legitimacy through his position as a district superintendent. He was one type of new administrative superintendent to emerge who hitched his wagon to the rising star of the teachers' movement.

Other, less opportunistic, allies were the rare women who worked their way to the upper echelons of the educational system. Isolated and on the periphery of power, these women needed alliances in the educational world. Of them, Ella Flagg Young was an outstanding example of the new administrative superintendent. A former Chicago schoolteacher, she expressed an early and persistent interest in teacher education. She became head of the Chicago Normal School and from there in 1909 became the first woman superintendent of a large urban school system. Because she had worked her way up from the ranks she was representative of both men and women who had expanded their educational skills while working as principals and district

35. Chester C. Dodge, *Reminiscences of a School Master* (Chicago, 1941), pp. 100–101.

36. In 1911 he argued that "education is business and that a dollar-and-cents measurement is inevitable," and he pointed out that the professionals who regarded themselves above such considerations were old-fashioned. Opportunism was not uncharacteristic of McAndrew, but it was of the teachers who allied with him early in the century.

On McAndrew's love of rating teachers, see *School Review* 19 (November 1911) as quoted in Raymond Callahan, *Education and the Cult of Efficiency* (Chicago, 1962), p. 593. According to Callahan, "the real leaders" in "educational cost accounting were Franklin Bobbit and Frank E. Spaulding, but McAndrews followed their lead." p. 159. See McAndrews's comments in the Chicago Board of Education, *72nd Annual Report*, 1926, p. 26: "Chicago has a school plant valued at $120,000,000.00. This plant is in large part idle during the summer months. No industrial concern would voluntarily keep its plant idle for two months a year." For McAndrew's references to "mustard plaster" teachers and to teachers as "irritants" to school boards and legislators, see his "Appraising Radical Teachers' Unions," *School and Society*, 35 (February 1932), p. 191.

superintendents. Young was fortunate enough to have earned her doctoral degree under the tutelage of John Dewey while the two of them set up the University of Chicago's experimental school laboratory. Dewey claimed he learned a lot from Young, and certainly Young's alliance with Dewey gave her the credentials to overcome the qualms of educational elitists who balked at the new Horatio-Algers-of-the-classroom superintendents.[37]

Her most lasting achievement was to give recognition to the experience of older teachers and yet at the same time work hard for higher standards in teacher education. Like the administrative centralizers, she thought teachers should have a college education, but her proposal was to expand the existing normal schools to regular four year colleges and thereby keep them within the reach of young, working-class women. She had a lot of sympathy for the teachers' movement, and like McAndrew, benefited from the connection.[38]

In 1910 Margaret Haley successfully managed Ella Flagg Young's campaign for the presidency of the NEA, a turning point that was as much a victory for the new administrative superintendents as for women within the organization. Like her speech in 1904, Haley's campaign was controversial. She was able to capitalize on the efforts of other women leaders in the NEA who were pressing for women to gain power in the association. Katherine Blake had initially worked for Grace Strachan's nomination and wrote to Haley for CTF support shortly before Haley announced Young's candidacy. Haley was then able to capitalize on Blake's footwork and contact all of the women's organizations that planned to attend the convention. She arranged a special suite of rooms and receptions for Young's candidacy and had Blake manage Young's nomination in the Nominating Committee. Delegates wore badges for Young's election in a display unheard of in the old NEA. Young's victory was clearly a vote for the women professionals in the old organization—there was no question that the NEA would change. It was a dramatic transformation, one that would not be repeated until the election of a black woman as NEA president in 1967.[39]

For the first time, the NEA seemed ready to lend a sympathetic ear to the problems of classroom teachers. Young immediately prepared a resolution to create the Department of Classroom Teachers, to which the urban teachers' unions and associations readily signed up. Florence Rood, the

37. For Young's life history, see John T. McManis, *Ella Flagg Young and a Half Century of the Chicago Public Schools* (Chicago, 1916), especially on Dewey's debt to Young, pp. 119–20. Joan K. Smith has written a more broadly cast biography, *Ella Flagg Young: Portrait of a Leader* (Ames, Ia., 1979). See also Geraldine Clifford's review of Smith's book in the *American Historical Review*, 85 (June 1980), p. 727.

38. Young was the head of the Chicago Normal School from 1905 until she became Chicago superintendent in 1909. See the school reports, especially, Chicago Board of Education, *53rd Annual Report*, 1907.

39. Haley to Grace Strachan, 20 June 1910, CTF Collection; Smith, *Ella Flagg Young*. "Everyone regarded Mrs. Young's election as a feminist victory." Edgar G. Wesley, *NEA, The First One Hundred Years: The Building of the Teaching Profession* (New York, 1957), pp. 326–27; see also pp. 297–99; and the obituary for Mrs. Young, *NEA Proceedings*, 1918, p. 685.

union-affiliated leader from St. Paul, was elected leader of the new department and prepared an ambitious agenda, which included most of the salary and tax issues teachers had expressed interest in. But the National Council still controlled the purse strings, and the department became merely a forum for teacher grievances.[40]

Young was also successful in getting funding for studies of salaries and tenure for the first time since 1903, and this time the committee would include Margaret Haley and study major cities in the country. Young was not able to control the appointments to the committee, however, and soon Haley found it impossible to work with several male old-guard members. Swain, who was later to succeed Young as NEA president, soon took firm control. Instead of focusing on Chicago, New York, and San Francisco, as the rank-and-file teachers had hoped, the study focused on Denver, Atlanta, New Haven, and Hamilton, Ohio. Fewer women than men participated in the survey. Swain was able to hire economists and experts on political economy to present a sophisticated argument about the rise in the cost of living for schoolteachers. Even so, the report indicated that while the cost of living had risen 40 to 50 percent, teachers' salary increases were closer to 14 percent for elementary teachers and 25 to 35 percent for high school teachers. The report also indicated that more women schoolteachers had dependents than was usually thought.[41]

The Young revolution was a limited one. She had made a difference in some important areas. She steered through a resolution supporting women's suffrage. The Department of Classroom Teachers and the Salary Committee report were concrete measures of some change in the organization. A woman was elected president of the NEA every other year after Young's election, assuring women administrators that the sexism of traditional professionalism had at least been symbolically defeated. But although there were women eager and able to assume leadership roles in the new professionalism, the local political structure in which women had to operate remained largely male; consequently, so did the administrative posts. Ultimately Young's efforts brought few concrete benefits to the nation's female school administrators.

The changes that rank-and-file teachers were looking for, moreover, were far from achieved. President Swain in 1914 expressed his impatience with the "vigorous" resolutions of the Department of Classroom Teachers denouncing oversupervision and merit schemes. He reminded teachers to "keep the interests of the children in view."[42] The old guard was clearly retiring from NEA politics—Butler would resign during Young's term—and

40. Murphy, "From Artisan to Semiprofessional," p. 339; Wesley, *NEA*, pp. 280–331.
41. NEA, *Report of the Committee on Salaries, Pensions, and Tenure of Public School Teachers in the United States* (Winona, Minn., 1905); NEA, *Report of the Committee on Teachers' Salaries and Cost of Living* (Ann Arbor, Mich., 1913), pp. vii, 1–26.
42. Wesley, *NEA*, p. 280.

yet the organization was far from representing teachers' views. Firmly under the direct control of superiors, classroom teachers did not get the structural changes in their organization for which they hoped when they allied with the administrative superintendents. Indeed, the differences between teachers and the new administrative superintendents arose almost immediately.

The experience of early teachers' unions was nevertheless a positive one. Although Haley's organization in Chicago was by far the most heavily involved in union activities, it was also very active in NEA affairs. Early teachers' unions moved easily from their local union affiliations, which gained them political power on the urban level, to the national political world of NEA politics. Teachers needed local political power, something that the NEA could not offer, while at the same time they needed a national forum, something that the AFL was loathe to share with them. In the early years, then, teacher unionism was an amorphous movement. The tentativeness of the AFL meant that CTF leaders were reluctant to push union affiliation. Yet when teacher leaders like Grace Strachan threatened to discredit the union movement, the CTF was quick to isolate her and anti-union sentiment. All the participants recognized that some national organization of teachers would emerge, and until 1913 most teachers believed that it would be within the framework of the NEA. As disappointment grew over the role to which the NEA's new Department of Classroom Teachers was limited, teachers became more serious about national union affiliation. Changes within the AFL, especially through the efforts of the Women's Trade Union League, made this possibility increasingly viable. Meanwhile, school superintendents, harrassed by local teacher organizations for higher salaries and pressured by local business leaders for cuts in taxes, began to exert control to rid themselves of the teachers' rebellion.

CHAPTER FIVE

Professionalism, War,
and the Company Union

In the last years of the Progressive Era the idea of unionism spread rapidly among teachers. A new union formed in the steel town of Gary, Indiana, a local struggled into existence in Atlanta, and in Washington, D.C., a group of teachers considered joining the teachers' union movement. The CTF continued to influence many elementary school teachers, and high school teachers were drawn to unionism because of a rising interest in the labor movement generally and the growth of vocational high schools in urban centers, where teacher unionism was popular. Chicago added two new locals: the Men's High School Union in 1912 and the Federation of Women High School Teachers in 1914. In New York teachers organized and began publishing their own paper, *American Teacher,* which was welcomed since the CTF had been unable to continue its publication. Teachers in Gary, St. Paul, and San Francisco organized, and other teacher groups in Boston, Philadelphia, and Cleveland wrote enthusiastically of their short-lived but nonetheless union-oriented teacher groups.

Talk of a national organization had been in the air, but the CTF, the largest union of all, seemed to drag its feet regarding a national union. In large part this was because feminist union leaders had developed an antipathy toward Samuel Gompers which prevented the CTF from formally affiliating with the AFL in 1902, even though formal requests for a national charter had been raised by CFL representatives that year and were approved by the convention. Gompers never followed up on this initiative, and the elementary school teachers never pursued the possibility of paying for the honor of being ignored. High school teachers affiliated automatically and jealously pointed out in 1914 that the elementary school teachers were getting the benefits of labor affiliation with the CFL yet they had not paid a cent to the national. It was not until the crisis over the Loeb Rule, described below, that the CTF affiliated and the national, AFT was founded in 1916.

In 1915 the Chicago Board of Education passed a simple, yellow-dog contract, declaring that teachers who belonged to unions would not be rehired. Aimed at the heart of the movement, the Chicago Teachers' Federation, the move was not just an idle threat. An intense campaign against the union, against the leadership, against the entire idea emerged in the Chicago newspapers and was broadcast across the nation. Women schoolteachers who joined unions were branded as either mindless dupes or city toughs who had no business in the classroom.[1]

The Loeb Rule, as the Board of Education regulation was called, challenged the whole idea of unionism not from the professional perspective but from a perspective outside the profession, from the boards of education that were packed with businessmen. In this sense it was a classic anti-union drive. For the budding teachers' movement it was a disaster. One Chicago teacher remarked, "Chicago has been free of floods, earthquakes, volcanic eruptions and tidal waves. Still it had its Fire of 1871 and its Loeb Rule of 1915."[2]

In defiance of the attack by boards of education, a small group of teachers organized the first national teachers' union in the country in April 1916. From its inception, the American Federation of Teachers was self-consciously asserting a new role for classroom teachers in the house of labor, while preserving its legitimacy in the schoolhouse.

It was not long before the opponents of teacher unionism within the profession, sensing an additional advantage in the war hysteria of World War I, hatched plans for the movement's demise. The new administrative progressives who led the NEA took aggressive steps to bring teachers into their organization, claiming a legitimacy that unions could never offer. In the period between 1913 and 1922, professionalism and unionism became two opposing forces, not because they were inherently in opposition but because unionism was so adamantly opposed by the new administrative Progressives within the NEA.

Yellow-Dog Contracts and the Birth of the AFT

Opponents of the CTF on the Chicago Board of Education had talked of passing an anti-union bill in 1905, but the teachers were simply too powerful

1. For an account of the Loeb Rule fight, see Marjorie Murphy, "From Artisan to Semiprofessional: White-Collar Unionism among Chicago Public School Teachers, 1870–1930" (Ph.D. diss., University of California, Davis, 1981), pp. 70–74. For more on the attack on the teachers, see Jacob Loeb, "Stenographic Report of Address," 2 February 1917, CTF Collection.

2. Freeland G. Stecker, "The First Ten Years of the American Federation of Teachers" (1946), Arthur Elder Collection, Walter Reuther Archives, Detroit. For more on the business composition of school boards, see George S. Counts, *The Social Composition of Boards of Education: A Study in the Social Control of Public Education* (Chicago, 1927).

in the city. The first yellow-dog contract offered to teachers was in Peoria, Illinois, in 1913, where a new teachers' union died instantly after the Peoria Board of Education decided to force teachers to sign contracts declaring that they had no association with any trade union. The effectiveness of this approach, and no doubt the influence of similar anti-union campaigns in private industry, emboldened the CTF's enemies on the Chicago Board of Education. All that was needed was an occasion, and when one did not immediately arise it was manufactured.[3]

In the summer of 1915, before the Board of Education had passed the Loeb Rule, Ella Flagg Young and Margaret Haley became the subjects of a state investigation by a group called the Baldwin Commission into the finances of the public schools. Haley was at first fooled into thinking that this was a legitimate inquiry that could become a platform for her progressive ideas on taxation and public salaries. She was quickly disabused of this idea when Young was called to testify and was publicly attacked by the state's attorney. "Frenzied Feminine Finance," newspapers quoted from the investigation, as Haley desperately tried to stop the investigation and the adverse publicity aimed at Young. Critics pictured Young as virtually giving away the store to public school teachers out of her feminist sentimentality, her Catholic sympathies, and her alleged near-senility. Haley quickly perceived that the attack was based on opposition to the new salary scale that Young had introduced, and in response she arranged for Chicago labor leaders to attend the sessions to intimidate the state senators on the investigatory commission who depended on labor's vote. The move worked, and the commission temporarily adjourned. Haley later discovered that the resolution to create the investigation in the first place was never passed by the state legislature but instead inserted into the minutes by some mysterious persons.[4]

Before its bogus existence was uncovered by Haley, the Baldwin Commission had achieved one important end: it had seriously called into question the leadership of both Young and Haley. If nothing else it was a testing ground for the attacks on Haley's union that followed. Even more than Young, Haley, who was pictured as a "lady labor slugger," could be slandered at will. The fight over the yellow-dog contract in Chicago, then, was not simply a chapter in the story of anti-unionism in the Progressive period; it had the additional ingredient of smearing female trade-union leadership.

Jacob Loeb, the Board of Education president who went about the city of Chicago explaining why Haley and the CTF had to be isolated, always explained that he had no particular interest in the schools but was a businessman and, he added, a good one at that. He charged that Haley "counsels that class distinction be brought to the attention of immature minds." He added that she "preaches anarchy." Her greatest sin appeared to be her political

3. *American Teacher*, 5 (May 1917).
4. *Margaret Haley's Bulletin*, September 1915; *CT*, 6 July to 8 August 1915; see especially 9 and 24 July 1915.

abilities: she was "an astute and designing politician." He told stories of innocent schoolteachers who were captured by the union and forced to conform to the "dominance" of the women leaders in the CTF. These teachers, "contemptuous and rebellious towards those in authority," Loeb argued, would "send forward children who in turn are likely to be dissatisfied, contemptuous and rebellious towards authority, and who have no regard and no respect for law and order."[5]

In 1916 thirty-five teachers, most of them in the CTF and one in the men's local, were fired from their teaching jobs. Rumors of the board's intentions to fire all teacher unionists, including high-school teachers, circulated widely throughout the movement in the United States. The high-school men teachers handed over their charter to the Illinois State Federation of Labor, "for safe keeping, with the intention of keeping alive somehow" the idea of teacher unionism. Haley continued to test the legality of the Loeb Rule in the courts as she labored for a revision of the law to provide for permanent tenure. In April 1917 the Illinois Supreme Court upheld the Loeb Rule, allowing the Board of Education to enforce its ban against the CTF. Haley quickly reorganized her union, disaffiliated with all union contacts, and turned her attention to paying legal bills on dues from a substantially reduced membership. The reorganized CTF no longer had the powerful ties of a voting, male Chicago Federation of Labor. Reduced to the status of a woman's club and no longer officially a union with a paid lobbyist in Springfield, connections to every ward in the city, and a place in the network of pro-union politicians who depended upon labor support at election time, The CTF had become permanently crippled by the yellow-dog contract. The success of the rule, as we shall see, also made it difficult for the new national union that was organized in 1916 during the height of the Loeb Rule crisis.[6]

The Formation of the AFT

Over spring vacation in April 1916, representatives of four unions met in South Chicago to organize a national American Federation of Teachers. Three of the locals were from Chicago: the Chicago Teachers' Federation, the Federation of Women High School Teachers, and the Chicago Federation of Men Teachers. The fourth local was from the steel town of Gary, Indiana, just across the Illinois border from Chicago. From a distance, the New York Teachers' Federation sent its warm regards and regrets for not being there.

5. Loeb, "Stenographic Report"; Martin Lazerson, "Teachers Organize: What Margaret Haley Lost," *History of Education Quarterly,* 21 (Summer 1981), pp. 261–70.
6. *Bulletin of the Chicago Federation of Men Teachers and the Federation of Women High School Teachers,* 4 (September 1917) and 3 (February 1917); Chicago Board of Education, *Proceedings,* July 1916, pp. 1227–39; Stecker, "First Ten Years"; Chester C. Dodge, *Reminiscences of a School Master* (Chicago, 1941); *American Teacher,* 5 (May 1917).

Word was that locals in Atlanta, St. Paul, and Washington would join in the effort to create a new national organization of teachers' unions. Gompers promised that if the teachers organized he would grant a national charter. There had been plans for Haley to launch the union a year earlier, but her activities had been curtailed by the financial investigation. When the teachers' locals did meet in 1916 and Gompers granted their charter, Haley was busy on the Loeb Rule and could not attend. The Board of Education was planning to fire the thirty-five union teachers, including Haley's sister, an elementary school teacher in the South Side. Rumors of firings were rampant.

There was an overpowering sense of doom at this inaugural meeting. "With a price on their heads, as it were, they organized a union," Freeland Stecker recalled. High school teachers predominated at the meeting and argued that in such a crisis they needed strong leadership. They argued that Margaret Haley of the CTF did not fit the bill, and they chose instead to make Charles Stillman of the Chicago Federation of Men Teachers president of the new organization. The choice proved decisive for the AFT.[7]

There were three immediate results from the AFT's choice of Stillman. First, it endangered the alliance with the CTF, opened the door for Haley's withdrawal from the union a year later in 1917, and brought about the first grievance within the union. Ida Fursman of the CTF protested the election of Stillman. She later explained that she "took it for granted that Miss Margaret Haley, nationally known leader of the CTF, would be the natural choice for head of the new national union."[8] High school teachers found it "difficult and embarrassing" to convince Mrs. Fursman that the choice had been made not because of lack of appreciation for Haley's work "but rather because of differences over the scope of a national organization." The subsequent break by the CTF would prove very important to the fledgling national union, because the CTF had by far the largest membership of the locals and its loss to the union meant a substantial loss in income. It was in partial recognition of this fact that Haley was appointed national organizer of the union.

The second impact of the leadership decision was on the relative direction of the union. By choosing a man from the men's local—and by remarking that they had to do so because they needed strong leadership in times of crisis—the teachers were privileging male leadership in the union at its inception. Although women presidents were to follow, the tone of the leadership was set early: it was an affirmation of male abilities and in effect a rejection of the style and methods of the feminist leadership of the CTF. Third, the union became a high school teachers' union. Elementary teachers, notably the St. Paul Federation, stayed in the union, but there was little

7. Stecker, "First Ten Years." Freeland G. Stecker to Blanche Rinehart, 29 December 1959, Arthur Elder Collection, Access 75/2.

8. See Ida Fursman to Lucie Allen, CTF Collection; also Jennie Wilcox to Henry Linville, Linville Collection, Box 2, Walter Reuther Archives, Detroit.

growth in AFT locals among elementary teachers throughout most of the first thirty years of the union's history.

In part this can be attributed to the rejection of Haley's strategy of boring from within the NEA. Indeed, Atlanta had one of the largest unions, including a large elementary school constituency that was also affiliated with the NEA. Haley's strategy of organization was to advertise the benefits of unionism at the NEA meetings where most activist teachers gathered. Although the AFT had several meetings in conjunction with the NEA, the scheduling was not part of an organizational strategy. Furthermore, the NEA was anxious to rid itself of Haley and teacher unionism. No sooner had the AFT organized its first meetings than the NEA launched its first organizing campaign, a campaign aimed at finally ridding the educational world of teacher unionism.

In the union, left-of-center teachers, including the feminists, lost their patience with Samuel Gompers and by extension Charles Stillman over the question of whether the union would support Woodrow Wilson and his war effort. Samuel Gompers convened a conference of executive union leaders in Washington, D.C., in March 1917 in anticipation of Wilson's declaration of war a month later. Stillman eagerly responded to Gompers's call. After the sinking of the *Lusitania,* the Zimmerman note, and the resumption of German submarine warfare, labor anticipated an effort to support Wilson should war be declared. Demonstrating his loyalty to President Wilson, Gompers asked the executive leaders of the union to pledge their support for war with Germany. Without consulting his executive board—which included Margaret Haley, a vocal opponent of war preparedness and later of the war effort itself—Stillman enthusiastically committed the union to Gompers's policy. Neither the organizational meeting of April 1916 nor the convention of December 1916 considered the issue of war, although the union had from its inception issued resolutions condemning "militarism" in the schools, especially the ultrapatriotic formation of a training corps of young men for "preparedness." The teachers' revulsion to the growing war hysteria should have given some pause to Stillman's unqualified support of the war, but it appears that he acted, as did many union presidents, without consulting the union leadership or its members.[9]

Events moved quickly after Stillman's pledge to Gompers of support from his union. Ten days after the United States declared war, the Chicago Teachers' Federation, at Margaret Haley's direction and under pressure from

9. American Federation of Teachers Collection (hereafter cited as AFT Collection), Series 13, Accession 348, Walter Reuther Archives, Detroit. See notes and proceedings from the 1916 convention; also Arthur Elder Collection, Accession 75:1/10; Linville to Clara Stutz, 23 February 1919, Linville Collection, Box 1, Accession 373. "Some of the Chicago women think Stillman is reactionary": Wilcox to Linville, Linville Collection, Box 2, Walter Reuther Archives, Detroit. Mary O'Reilly protested the fact that Stillman had no convention in 1917. The first AFT convention was in April 1916, the second in December 1916, and the third in July 1918.

a court decision upholding the ban on teacher unionism, withdrew from the city labor federation and in 1917 withdrew its nearly three thousand members from the AFT. Haley left Stillman in charge of a shell organization of less than one thousand members. Gompers responded generously to his friend Stillman. Recognizing the unpopularity of Stillman's pro-war stand in his own union, Gompers helped Stillman and the AFT by paying Stillman's full salary and eventually giving the union five organizers. Gompers's largesse bolstered Stillman's prestige at an important juncture, but it was never enough to quell entirely those teachers who opposed the war and anticipated that the union would at least take a stand of silent opposition to the war effort. Others simply resented Stillman's high-handedness and expressed growing concern over Stillman's efforts to please the AFL hierarchy.[10]

Among the discontented were the socialists, women, and elementary school teachers. Margaret Haley was furious: she openly condemned the war and questioned the value of the new union. Haley and the Chicago Teachers' Federation were out of the union, however, and Chicago high school teachers were split on the war issue, with the men supporting it and the women opposed. Indeed, Stillman's stand may account for the stagnation in the women's local while the men's local nearly doubled its membership. The women high school teachers' union was led by a group of socialist women who were actively supporting peace candidates in local elections. Stillman quietly sought affirmation of his policy at the 1918 convention, which passed a resolution affirming the union's loyalty in the war but also condemning militarism in the schools.[11]

As long as the AFT grew in membership, Stillman's alliance with Gompers went unquestioned. Only Haley had been strong enough to launch a vocal protest, and she was out of the union. New locals appeared regularly, but they were short-lived. The high school locals brought in fewer than five hundred members. The defeat of the yellow-dog contract, Stillman's position on the war, and the impact of the war itself eroded early AFT strength. Fundamental divisions among the teachers raised the possibility that the union would not hold.

The union waited until 1918 before drawing up a statement of general principles from which a constitution could be drafted. At the initial meetings

10. Linville Collection, Box 1: Wilcox to Linville, 1 May 1918, "Gompers is Anti-Labor"; Wilcox to Linville, 19 January 1919. Selma Borchardt Collection: Linville to Borchardt, 14 December 1914, "of course we all know the AFL is about as slippery as the proverbial eel, but that should not discourage us."

11. Ida Fursman, president of the Chicago Teachers' Federation, was running for office on the Socialist ticket in the twenty-seventh ward of Chicago; Mary O'Reilly was a staunch opponent of the war. In the high school unions, Ethel Beers was the socialist leader followed by Jennie Wilcox; both of them opposed the war. For the platform of the 1918 convention, see *Proceedings*, 1918, AFT Collection, Series 13, Box 2. Further, it is important to realize that Stillman moved the convention to Pittsburgh, away from the center of antiwar sentiment in his hometown Chicago. Material on the Chicago locals can be found in the *Bulletin of the Chicago Federation of Men Teachers and the Federation of Women High School Teachers*.

the divisions within the teachers' union movement appeared more pronounced. There was, for example, deep antagonism between New York and Chicago men teachers, between men teachers and women teachers (especially over the war issue), and, finally, between elementary and high school teachers.

High School versus Elementary School Teachers

The rejection of Haley's strategy by the AFT had been more than a disagreement over tactics. It represented a deep chasm between high school teachers and elementary school teachers. When the first AFT meeting elevated male high school teachers and ignored Haley, the move was not entirely sexist; some of the women who were part of the decision considered themselves quite feminist and radical. The bypassing of Haley was primarily due to distinction in class between the college-educated high school teachers and the normal school graduates in elementary schools.

Class distinctions grew as school districts expanded the number of high schools in a city. This expansion led to the preservation of collegelike conditions in high schools and offered new opportunities to recently college-educated women. There was only one high school in Chicago in 1870; by 1910 there were seventeen, and by 1920 there were twenty-five. High school teaching required subject-oriented teaching in which a woman could specialize in a field of study as a college student and apply her specified knowledge in the classroom. High school teachers therefore seemed to be closer to the ideal of specialized knowledge—closer to a professional élan—than elementary school teachers, whose knowledge was general. High school teachers also taught set periods in a day, with breaks between classes as students rotated from subject to subject. Elementary school teachers worked with the same students from the beginning of the day to the end; their responsibility to the student was continuous. High school teachers were organized in departments in which their immediate supervisor was a department head who could negotiate a better deal for teachers with the school principal. Elementary teachers reported directly to their principal. Some high schools allowed teachers to elect their department heads or rotated the authority among the several members.[12]

This distribution of supervisory personnel gave high school teachers a greater opportunity for autonomy. Elementary school teachers were subject to severe overcrowding when a sudden influx of immigrants unpredictably overwhelmed a neighborhood. Some elementary teachers in Chicago had

12. Chicago Board of Education, *Annual Reports*, 1879–1920; See also the reports on high school teaching in the records of the New York City Board of Education, Manuscript Collections, Teachers College, New York. See also NEA, *Teachers Salaries and Living Conditions* (Washington, D.C., 1905), pp. 138–78.

classes of seventy children who spoke several different languages. High school teachers were spared this unpredictability. High schools served regions, not just neighborhoods. Removed from the immediate scrutiny of the surrounding community, high school teachers did not need to maintain ties with the community. At the same time, because of class differences and because there were fewer high school teachers than elementary teachers, a high school teacher was more likely to know the district superintendent and the superintendent of schools.

High school teachers were also better paid than elementary school teachers. The reason for the better pay was in part historical and in part a recognition for higher educational achievement. The classical high school drew a largely middle-class constituency preparing for higher education or terminal diplomas that gave recognition to the scholarly achievement of a select few. The teachers were respected by influential members of the community, their status was somewhat higher than that of other teachers, and they were largely men, although women held a significant proportion of the positions. Their total compensation represented a smaller percentage of the school budget—in contrast to elementary school teachers' salaries, which were the bulk of the budgetary expenditures in competition with school-building programs—and it was money well spent in attracting the best teachers.[13]

Scholarly achievement also figured in the higher compensation of high school teachers. High school teachers in Chicago, of whom there were only forty in 1880, were far better educated than elementary school teachers. Two-thirds of them had a high school diploma or better, and only six claimed a normal school education (less than high school). The majority of high school teachers received their training in Illinois, as did the elementary school teachers, but 45 percent were trained outside the state.

The most irksome aspect of higher wages for high school teachers was that high school teaching, because it was at a higher level, was perceived by the public as more difficult—a point that well-trained kindergarten and primary grade teachers persistently and successfully challenged. Certainly G. Stanley Hall's notions about the importance of childhood development, Freud's emphasis on personality formation in early years, and Piaget's notions of childhood imagination and learning, contributed to counterarguing this point. But change was difficult to achieve. Even Ella Flagg Young, who accepted the argument that teachers ought to be compensated equally regardless of grade level, when faced with strong opposition from high school

13. Margaret Haley was most articulate in pointing to the differences between elementary school and high school teachers' salaries, an issue that divided teachers when Ella Flagg Young in 1913 proposed a salary increase. Haley called the high school teachers "the elect of the Lord." Margaret Haley's autobiography, pt. 2, section on the Loeb Rule; NEA, *Teachers Salaries*, pp. 177–78; Willard S. Elsbree, *The American Teacher: Evolution of a Profession in a Democracy* (New York, 1939), pp. 449.

teachers, fell back on the argument that merit, or educational attainment, was the reason why elementary school teachers were paid less.[14]

The pay differential was not negligible. Teachers in high schools often earned a third more than elementary school teachers. In Chicago, teachers in high schools earned from twelve hundred to sixteen hundred dollars a year whereas the highest elementary school scale was eight hundred dollars. Moreover, even after 1900, when high school teachers had a college degree, elementary school teachers with the same or higher qualifications were not given more compensation. There was an incentive for high school teachers to complete a masters degree or doctorate, but for elementary school teachers an advanced degree did not change their compensation. The elementary school teacher, if she had higher education, often transferred to a high school assignment, but she was not given compensation for her elementary school teaching experience. Short of becoming school principal, which required more responsibility and often less compensation than high school teaching, promotion to high school teaching was the only means for elementary school teachers to move up.

The distinctions in the structure of the job of teaching between elementary and high school teachers as well as the pay scale and degree of autonomy exaggerated potential conflicts between teachers. These differences simply never arose in the NEA, and they surely never came up in an atmosphere where teachers' wages themselves went unnoticed. Once teachers were outside the organizations in which school administrators predominated, these distinctions became immediately paramount.

Mary Herrick, a Chicago high school teacher and later a leader in the American Federation of Teachers, explained how the slight educational advantage of the high school teacher served as an important distinction over the grade school teacher. "When Maggie Haley became CTF leader, the average elementary school teacher had no more than a high school education, and that didn't amount to very much." Haley had even less than a full year of high school. "And she was the one," Herrick explained, "who could do all these magical things with the suits and the taxes. There was nobody like her." Everyone in the teacher-union movement agreed that Haley's first tax suit was a stroke of genius. Her leadership style, however, got mixed ratings. "All she had to do was to say, 'This is what we're going to do,' and they believed her!" "And the high school people didn't, you see," Herrick concluded. "They never accepted her on that basis."[15]

Of course Haley was a difficult leader to get along with; she antagonized many high school teachers. She was angry in 1913 when Ella Flagg Young gave a 10 percent raise to high school teachers while elementary school

14. Chicago Board of Education, *25th Annual Report,* 1879; NEA, *Teachers Salaries,* pp. 157–69.

15. Interview with Mary J. Herrick, Chicago Loop City College, January 1972.

teachers received only a 5 percent raise. She called them "high and mighty." Members of the Federation of Women High School Teachers complained that their association with Haley prevented membership growth, although Haley's eventual withdrawal from the union did not lead to a surge in its growth. In Philadelphia years later, Mary Grossman discussed similar difficulties encountered in bridging the gap between two constituencies; in New York, Henry Linville had great contempt for Grace Strachan's organization because Strachan was an administrator. But the New York union had honored many of its own school principals with membership—the antagonism looks suspiciously like a male/female, elementary/high school difference. Women predominated in the elementary grades, but they held less than half the high school jobs.[16]

When the AFT decided to ignore Margaret Haley and elect high school teacher Charles Stillman instead, it took a decided direction in the history of teacher unionism. Reminders of Haley's old movement remained in the union, especially through the leadership of Mary Barker of Atlanta and Florence Rood of St. Paul, both of whom headed classroom-teacher groups with a history of working within the NEA. Yet the feminist quality of the original movement was somewhat lost; the connection with the NEA was also less important, and the community ties, which were so important to elementary teachers attacking monopoly privilege, were no longer as strong. High school teachers were more likely to drive automobiles; they were more likely to be from outside the community, and many were originally from out of state. The character of the early AFT, then, was slightly different from the original movement.

The War and the NEA 100-Percent Campaign

Warfare between the NEA and the AFT began in the war years, when the new superintendents were carefully retaking control of the NEA. A proposal for a representative assembly threatened to disenfranchise urban teachers who had been the vanguard of the teacher rebellion and unionism. State organizations, where administrators were often in control, would elect representatives to the national organization. The proposal sharply divided teachers nationally. Some were new to the organization and could only see changes in recent years that had come about largely through the efforts of the CTF. They favored the state representation plan. Others were alienated when the NEA took a strong pro-war stance and devoted the organization to "preparedness" in 1916 and 1917. In 1918 a plan based on wartime disci-

16. Robert Reid, ed., *Battleground: The Autobiography of Margaret A. Haley* (Urbana, Ill., 1982), pp. 216–17; Margaret Haley's autobiography, pt. 2; Mary Grossman Papers, Urban History Archives, Temple University, Philadelphia, Box 1; Linville Collection, Box 2.

pline emerged to wrest control of the NEA from the teacher activists who attended the yearly conventions.

At the 1918 convention the National Council proposed a Commission on the Emergency in Education. The emergency was a "calamity" that had led to "the collapse of the teaching profession" and was "aggravated" by war rather than caused by it. The commission was intended to "nationalize education," for "of our collective enterprises, education alone remains hampered and constrained by the narrow confines of an obsolete conception." The commission would pursue "compulsory Americanization" in education and emphasize the "exclusive use of the English language in instruction." Intelligence testing in the army had revealed that "the young girls" who taught school had not done their job. It was not their fault, the commission argued, but they had to be better trained. Most of all, the commission urged, this was a national emergency, and to underscore this point they sent James W. Crabtree to Washington to begin the operation needed to meet the "emergency."[17]

Crabtree was instructed to help in the recruitment drive to get these "girls" to sign up with the NEA so they could become more professional. There were only 8,466 members when he took office in 1917, but by 1920 he had raised membership to 87,414. A research division was established to produce volumes of statistics on teachers' salaries, the tax base, and school budgets. The *NEA Journal* appeared at the doorstep of every new recruit. The entire campaign fit very neatly into the professionalization project; at last the NEA presented a distinct alternative to the unionization project begun by the teachers.[18]

Suddenly the war effort gave a language to the NEA by which it could incorporate the teachers' grievances within a new professional drive. *Research Bulletin* One cartoon appearing in the *NEA Research Bulletin* entitled "Uncle Sam Insures America's Future," seemed to assure teachers that rising costs of education would be met and that the federal government would somehow solve the problems for corporate America. Indeed, the NEA was moving in the direction of demanding federal involvement in education. First, however, it wanted to assure teachers that it was now committed to salary increases. The NEA would become a lobbying effort for teachers nationally. It was a novel concept, one that came directly from the new leaders in the NEA.[19]

The chair of the emergency commission was George B. Strayer of Columbia University, and the secretary was Lotus Delta Coffman of the University

---

17. Edgar G. Wesley, *NEA; The First One Hundred Years: The Building of the Teaching Profession* (New York, 1957), pp. 300, 371. "Thousands of unprepared girls were teaching." *NEA Proceedings,* 1918, p. 62; see also pp. 68, 129–31, 187–89, and 205–7.

18. Wesley, *NEA,* p. 301; *NEA Proceedings,* 1918, pp. 40–41.

19. "Uncle Sam Insures America's Future," *NEA Research Bulletin,* 10 (November 1923), p. 170. See also "A Worthy Campaign," *NEA Research Bulletin,* 6 (December 1917).

of Minnesota. Strayer had a strong sense of mission as he took over the NEA. Committed to further centralization and professionalization of the schools, Strayer organized a team of investigators to visit school systems and analyze progress in both areas. Firmly committed to professional salaries, Strayer was equally committed to sound school finance. He was not interested in advocating teachers' salaries outside the context of the overall administration of the school district. Above all, he wanted to ensure that teachers met the new standards of educational achievement.[20]

Lotus Delta Coffman was especially interested in the classroom teachers' professional behavior. He once scolded teachers at the Department of Classroom Teachers meeting in 1919 because he had heard that some of them wanted to eliminate supervision; he expressed the fear that "class dictation might evolve from class consciousness" in their meetings.[21] Both Strayer and Coffman wanted a united profession, and to accomplish this, their "most important work," in the "perspective of the time," was to bring "thousands of teachers into the NEA." Strayer called this "professional solidarity."[22]

Membership in "professional organizations" became a sign of professionalism, and school administrators were encouraged to insist on membership in the NEA as a professional duty. Loyalty to the school, loyalty to the country, and loyalty to the profession were manifested through the instrument of an NEA membership card. Membership in "militant" organizations was, by the same token, "unprofessional."[23]

Robert Reid, in his study of the professionalization of schoolteachers, has shown that local administrators linked unions to strikes in order to intimidate teachers during the NEA membership drive. After the war, when pent-up worker demands led to more strikes—which were met with violent repression—unions were pictured as associations of thugs and criminals. The calamity that Strayer and Coffman confronted was the rising popularity of teacher unionism inside and outside the AFT. Teachers would no longer submit unquestioningly to the ascendancy of the superintendents. Arguing in pure class terms, teachers rejected the traditions of professionalism because the traditions had never been to their benefit. As one teacher characterized the NEA leadership, "They never offered us support, and had not treated us

20. See the extensive reports on school systems published by George B. Strayer: *The Report of a Survey of the Public Schools of Pittsburgh, Pennsylvania* (New York, 1940); *Report of the Survey of Certain Aspects of the School System of Chattanooga and Hamilton County* (New York, 1932); *Report of the Survey of the Schools of Lynn, Massachusetts* (New York, 1927). See also Strayer's remarks in the *NEA Proceedings*, 1918.

21. Wesley, *NEA*, p. 282; *NEA Proceedings*, 1916, pp. 637–52; 1917, pp. 615–22; 1918, pp. 381–87. Coffman was also part of the lament for professional activity: see Lotus Delta Coffman, *The Social Composition of the Teaching Population* (New York, 1911); and "Teachers Associations," *NEA Research Bulletin*, 8 (April 1920).

22. *NEA Proceedings*, 1918, p. 68; George B. Strayer, "Plan to Meet the Emergency in Education," *NEA Research Bulletin*, 6 (September 1918), pp. 10–15.

23. Wesley, *NEA*, p. 300; Robert Reid, "The Professionalization of Public School Teachers" (Ph.D. diss., Northwestern University, 1968), p. 295.

as being of their number."[24] Samuel Gompers argued similarly, in an attempt to woo teachers to the AFT: "Teachers have tried to keep the atmosphere and traditions of a profession lest they lose caste with 'influential' citizens. What has it profited them? Their real friends are the masses of the people, the people whose children constitute at least 90 percent of those attending public school."[25]

Strayer and Coffman recognized the appeal of the AFT as a threat to the ideology of professionalism; using the sense of urgency caused by the war, they hoped to convince the more conservative members of the NEA to make a genuine commitment to improving salaries and to avoiding the pauperization of the schools. "The drafting into other work of large numbers of the most capable teachers, the continual opening of new doors of opportunity to thousands of others, the utterly inadequate financial provision for the majority of the remainder—these are no longer matters for debate—these are facts. And they are facts ominous with disaster for the nation."[26] The "facts" penetrated the inner sanctum of the National Council, but the message was delivered personally by school administrators to the teachers. Haley's arguments were turned on their head: salaries, pensions, tenure, and higher school revenue were important to encourage the right kind of people into teaching. Lotus Delta Coffman had long been concerned with the allegedly inferior social composition of teachers. Poor salaries would discourage the "better teachers," and "their places are taken by men and women of less native ability, less education and culture, and less training and experience."[27]

Coffman's exaggerated pessimism about the social composition of teachers was just as blatant in 1918 as it had been when he published his survey in 1911.[28] Teachers in 1918 were already better trained than ever before. In 1925 the NEA took cognizance of this fact but still lamented that teachers did not have enough "character."[29] This had been part of the modern profes-

24. Hattie Kimbal, "Federation of Teachers," *Journal of Education,* 90 (September 1919), p. 231, as quoted in Wellington G. Fordyce, "The Origin and Development of Teachers Unions in the United States" (Ph.D. diss., Ohio State University, 1944), p. 144. See also Stecker, "First Ten Years."

25. Samuel Gompers, "Teachers' Right to Organize Affirmed," *American Federationist,* 21 (December 1914), p. 1085, as cited in Fordyce, "Origin and Development," p. 144. In the words of John P. Fry, "But there has always been a barrier that has separated the teachers from other wage earners and, in fact, has prevented the teachers from seeing their own problems clearly and from engaging in a practical solution of their problems. This barrier has been the erection of a caste, setting the teachers apart as a sort of professional group and yet leaving them without the means of self-protection, relying entirely upon 'benevolent paternalism.' " Fry, "Teachers: Freedom through Organization," *American Federationist,* 23 (June 1916), p. 477.

26. Wesley, *NEA,* p. 31; "An Educational Platform," *Supplement to the NEA Research Bulletin,* 6 (September 1918); Strayer, "Plan to Meet the Emergency."

27. *NEA Proceedings,* 1918, p. 741; Coffman, "Teachers Associations," p. 21.

28. Coffman, *Social Composition,* p. 8; Coffman, "Teachers Associations," p. 21.

29. Wesley traces the rapid growth of normal school education: "By 1925 the training of teachers was rather standardized." *NEA,* p. 91; see also *NEA Proceedings,* 1926–27.

sionals' outlook during the war as well: the impoverished schools attracted less-cultured teachers, and "the character of the schools is being lowered just at a time when it ought to be raised."[30] For this reason, the emergency commission reported, "If the American people cannot be made to see the situation and to supply an early and drastic remedy, we shall run the risk, even though we win the war, of losing much that makes the war worth winning."[31]

The real emergency was a situation caused partially by the war-induced inflation and partially by changes in school revenues. Both acted to decrease teachers' earnings. The emergency commission argued that teachers' wages had fallen "below subsistence," an exaggeration even Haley resisted. Not to be outdone by the radicals in flamboyant speech, Strayer and Coffman referred to teachers who remained in teaching as "the exploited."[32]

The war summoned forth bold language and drastic remedies. Strayer and Coffman believed that only by securing large salary advances could the NEA "hold teachers to the professional point of view and to professional methods in taking action in their own interest and in the interest of the community."[33] With this, they launched a 100-percent-enrollment plan, issuing a special certificate to principals and superintendents who enrolled all of their staff as members of the NEA. Many superintendents were successful in getting their boards of education to require it. To help them in their campaign, Strayer visited more than thirty states in 1919 and 1920. Hugh Magill, the new NEA lobbyist, spent most of his time lobbying business groups and women's clubs at the national level; he also visited state and local association meetings around the country.[34]

Because of the frenzy of the war, the 100-percent campaign, and the constant desire of superintendents to please business-dominated boards of education, the educational experts participated in, and often led in, the worst of wartime hysteria. Scott Nearing, a professor at the University of Pennsylvania who was dismissed and blacklisted during the war, wrote about the damages to academic freedom inflicted on the teaching profession by the atmosphere of war.[35] "Once dismissed," Nearing wrote, "there is perhaps no profession where the blacklist is used with greater vigor than in the field of education."[36]

30. *NEA Proceedings*, 1918, pp. 62–68, 381–87. Strayer, "Plan to Meet the Emergency," pp. 8–15; Committee on the Enlistment of the Profession, "To the Teachers of America," *NEA Research Bulletin*, 6 (April 1918), p. 12.
31. Wesley, *NEA*, p. 300; *NEA Proceedings*, 1918, pp. 62–68.
32. *NEA Proceedings*, 1918, pp. 381–87; Wesley, *NEA*, p. 282.
33. *NEA Proceedings*, 1918, p. 741; Reid, "Professionalization," p. 246.
34. *NEA Research Bulletin*, 7 (January 1919); Mildred Fenner, "The NEA, 1892–1942" (Ph.D. diss., George Washington University, 1942), p. 294.
35. "American teachers with ideas that differ radically from those of the established order, speak out at their peril." Scott Nearing, *Educational Frontiers* (New York, 1925), p. 167; see also pp. 168–218.
36. Ibid., pp. 177–78.

Fanatical patriotism served to legitimize affiliation with the NEA as the official "professional organization." In pursuit of national legislation for compulsory Americanization, lobbyist Hugh Magill came in close contact with the fledging American Legion. "The Legion was greatly concerned with the removal of illiteracy, the Americanization of aliens, and the teaching of history, citizenship, and patriotism. These objectives were also objectives of the NEA."[37] In 1921, a joint committee was established to promote cooperation between the NEA and the American Legion. As the Legion was coming into the NEA, the Department of School Patrons was leaving; in 1922 the patrons were disbanded on the grounds that a lay organization had no role in a professional organization.

The AFT Defends Academic Freedom

The AFT's defense of academic freedom was not so much a policy decision as it was the spontaneous response of the union's leaders to wartime repression of teachers' individual rights. It was also a departure to defend all teachers, regardless of their popularity, and focus instead on the principle of academic freedom and the notion that teachers deserved a right to respond to charges made against them. The American Civil Liberties Union worked with the early AFT to establish the notion that public employees had the right to free association and free speech. The efforts of the two organizations resulted in procedures and general practices that assured public workers some protections against arbitrary treatment. Anti-unionists were fond of accusing the union of defending incompetent teachers, but the teachers were convinced that in most cases competency was not the issue. The point was that teachers, like all American citizens, had inalienable rights and that the conditions of their employment had not abridged those rights. If teachers were to be charged as incompetent, then only their teaching record was relevant—not their Liberty Bond investment portfolio.

The war set into motion several reactionary forces that played havoc with teachers' basic civil liberties. During the war it was not uncommon for an ambitious politician to declare that all public employees should purchase a certain amount of Liberty Bonds. These mass contributions were enforced by local school principals who thought it their patriotic duty to report teachers who failed to purchase the requisite amount. Once reported, a teacher came under intense public scrutiny. If she failed to express enthusiasm for the war, or intimated that war was anything but glorious, she stood a good chance of dismissal. German-language teachers became special tar-

37. Wesley, *NEA*, p. 316; *NEA Research Bulletin*, 18 (May 1930), p. 126. "It is not merely by increasing productiveness that education contributes to making the state a better place in which to make a living." *NEA Research Bulletin*, 8 (September 1920), p. 217.

gets. Elementary schools in Chicago once offered German instruction, but the war ended most of this special language teaching. The teachers were then phased into high-school programs where German was taught as an elective. But the teachers often did not have the proper credentials and were therefore easily isolated from the rest of the teaching staff. Frequently German teachers were of German descent and were ridiculed for their ethnic ties.[38]

Jewish socialists were especially subject to harrassment. In New York City a number of teachers were fired because they were suspected of antiwar activity, but it was later discovered that their association with the Socialist party and their ethnicity constituted equally grievous deviance. Henry Linville protested that teachers were fired indirectly for crimes of disloyalty but were charged with "conduct unbecoming a teacher." He pointed out that although these teachers were not formally tried for disloyalty, the dismissals implied that they had been unpatriotic. "The officials may then say that the teacher is not being charged with being disloyal, and even that there is no evidence of disloyalty, but the impression of disloyalty has gone out." In fact, Linville argued, ethnicity and socialist sympathies were often the root of the problem. "If a teacher happens to be a Jew, and a Socialist, and to be personally disliked by an official, the technique of 'indirection' takes care of it all through the euphemism 'conduct unbecoming a teacher.' All three of the dismissed teachers are Jews, all are socialists, and at least one . . . was especially disliked by the Associate Superintendent."[39]

The New York firings were especially mean spirited, and I will return to them later. But first it is important to note that the extent of harrassment over the war depended on the attitude of local power elites toward the war. In Chicago, for example, Mayor Big Bill Thompson opposed the war as did most of his German and Irish constituency. Although the teaching of German was eliminated in Chicago, few teachers were harrassed, and it seems that the cutting of German instruction had more to do with budget considerations than the possible offense of perpetuating German culture through language study. In California, however, pro-war sentiment was strong, and teachers were hounded to buy bonds by an organization that called itself the Better Federation of Government. Teachers in other states were harrassed, in a few cases physically beaten and fired from their jobs.[40]

Compelling teachers to demonstrate unwavering loyalty became institutionalized after the war. Several organizations, notably the infant American Legion, directed their prime efforts at teachers and their organizations.

38. Howard K. Beale, *Are American Teachers Free? An Analysis of Restraints upon the Freedom of Teaching in American Schools* (New York, 1936).

39. Linville, January 28, 1918, Linville Collection, Box 2.

40. Samuel Gerald McLean, "Teachers, Do You Begin to Understand?" *American Teacher*, 9 (September 1920). The Better Federation of Government warned unionized teachers that "like soldiers and policemen they are wards of the state, that if they unionize they will be dismissed in favor of teachers true to the traditions of the profession." See also Beale, *Are American Teachers Free?* pp. 32–36.

Government commissions, however, lent an air of legitimacy to these small but growing efforts toward uncompromising patriotism. In New York the Lusk Commission served as a model of investigatory harrassment for contemporary states and for similar efforts on the national level twenty years later.

The Lusk Commission was organized in the wake of the red scare of 1919. Commissioned by the New York State Legislature to investigate Bolshevism in the schools, Senator Lusk called every teacher who had been accused of unpatriotic behavior during the war to Albany to testify before a widely publicized set of hearings. The impetus for the investigation grew out of a wartime incident in New York City. In April 1917 the New York Board of Education passed a loyalty oath that schoolteachers had to sign in order to receive their paychecks. Hundreds of teachers protested, but thirty teachers, most of them members of the AFT, were singled out for investigation by the Board of Education. Three schoolteachers who were pacifists became the central targets of the investigation. Eventually dismissed because of their ideas, the teachers were subjected to further attack and encouraged to name other teachers who were involved in what was labeled a conspiracy. Unwilling to cooperate by naming names, one teacher had argued that his dismissal was because of his union activity. This confession led to a full-scale investigation of the American Federation of Teachers, especially Local 5 in New York City. The Lusk Commission wanted to find out why teachers would not sign the loyalty oath.[41]

Henry Linville, the founder of New York's Local 5 and full-time editor of the *American Teacher,* the national paper, vocally defended dismissed teachers throughout those years. Linville always claimed that the teachers were intensely loyal but would also uphold the rights of their fellow teachers, who deserved an appropriate hearing. The battle against the Lusk Commission was a bitter one, costing the fledgling union energy and funds. The three dismissed teachers never gained reinstatement, and the statewide loyalty oath recommended by the Lusk Commission was not rescinded until Alfred Smith became governor of the state in 1924.[42]

The Lusk Commission hearings left a permanent imprint on the internal politics of the AFT. Linville's support of the war protesters was well advertised in the pages of the *American Teacher* and later became the beginning material for Howard K. Beale's investigation into academic freedom *Are American Teachers Free?* Between the dismissal of the teachers in 1917 and the publication of Beale's book in 1936, union teachers were harassed for their belief that all teachers needed protection against arbitrary dismissal. Beale found that even with the end of the red scare, teachers were still subject

41. New York State Legislature, *Lusk Commission* (Albany, 1923).
42. Papers (unprocessed files) in the Guild Collection, Robert Wagner Archives, New York University.

to intense scrutiny by patriotic groups. Teachers who opposed loyalty oaths, who associated with socialists, or whose behavior was less than conventional met with stern disapproval and the threat of innuendo, letter-writing campaigns, and open hostility. Reading lists were scrutinized, library lists became subject to censorship, and personal or professional associations were investigated and measured for their patriotism. If a union meeting failed to display the American flag, or if a teacher forgot to salute the flag, then these voluntary associations took action. The National Education Association's close association with the American Legion gave member teachers a shield of approval, whereas union teachers were looked on as suspect.[43]

Professionalism versus Unionism

Although the differences between the AFT and the NEA appeared immediately on the formation of the new national union and its policy toward academic freedom, the demarcation of two distinct organizations in opposition to each other remained obscure until 1920, when the NEA reorganized itself. As long as Margaret Haley and other women leaders from urban centers could attend general meetings and affect national policy, the NEA would be subject to the backyard rebellion of the teachers. The Commission on the Emergency in Education solved some of these problems by insisting on NEA membership and by adopting its own policy on salaries that would co-opt the teachers movement. Still, the fear remained that the NEA could be taken over by union-oriented teachers.

Once the emergency in education was declared and the membership campaign launched, the new school administrators had only to devise a plan by which the rank-and-file rebellion, led chiefly by Margaret Haley and the CTF, could be prevented from ruling the new organization. In 1919 the National Council presented its plan for a delegate assembly, a representative body composed of delegates from state associations, with no voice for delegations from local organizations. The plan would essentially disenfranchise the large city organizations that the Chicago Teachers' Federation had built over the years. Margaret Haley called it "a vicious scheme to choke off the voices of the rank and file." Teachers easily defeated the measure in 1919 because the meeting was held in Milwaukee, where a strong socialist presence in the city and in the teachers' federation suggested more democratic means of organization. It was also a place where teachers from Chicago and St. Paul could easily afford to attend the meeting. In the same year, however, the NEA applied to the United States Congress for a revision of its charter (originally granted by Congress in 1857), which would grant

43. Beale, *Are American Teachers Free?* pp. 32–40. See also Howard K. Beale, *A History of Freedom of Teaching in American Schools* (New York, 1941).

the controversial delegate assembly. With Congressional approval NEA leaders asked the body of voting teachers either to uphold the will of their government or to vote against it in the wake of the Red Scare. The NEA went to great lengths to gain teacher approval for this revision in the national charter.[44]

Howard R. Driggs of Utah suggested that the 1920 NEA convention be held in Salt Lake City, "in the belief that the teachers in the area would favor the reorganization plan." The *School Review* noted that it was in order to "escape the packed meetings of recent years." A. E. Winship, editor of the *Educational Review,* understood who was packing the meeting: "Salt Lake City had been selected because it would be impossible for the 'Holy Terror' [Haley] to issue an S.O.S. call to the grade teachers of any large city as was done at Milwaukee, and city and state officials had assured the panic-stricken officials that they could keep the teachers of Salt Lake City and all of Utah under control."[45] Driggs admitted he had packed the Salt Lake City meeting, although he was gracious enough to let Haley speak after she had been abruptly refused recognition by the woman chair of the meeting. Her speech was "ineffective." Thus, as the historian of the NEA noted, "proponents of the new plan used some of the same tactics to effect it that it was designed to prevent."[46] Under the new plan the city teachers' locals no longer had the power to bore from within as had been Haley's plan. The two organizations, the NEA and the AFT, were in direct competition for teacher loyalties.

The success of the NEA in these early years was not the foregone conclusion it may now seem to teachers in retrospect. Consider, for example, the membership numbers of the union-affiliated Chicago Teachers' Federation. The CFT had between 3,500 and 4,000 members in 1902, and the NEA had a nationwide total of 2,200. In 1920, however, while the AFT had 10,300 members (an impressive number considering the ravages of the war on union organizing), the NEA's 100-percent campaign had given it a total of 52,850 members. By 1925 the NEA had 150,103 members and the AFT had only 11,000. As AFT leaders pointed out, there were real reasons for the decline of the union idea. "Officers of locals were fired, or bought off, or intimidated; groups were denied contracts for the following year and scores of locals melted away. The American Federation of Teachers fell into a slump which was to cost it more than half its membership."[47]

The professionalization project continued in the NEA during the twenties, but the tone of the campaign had changed in peacetime. Joining the NEA was no longer depicted as a response to an emergency; it became simply legiti-

44. Wesley, *NEA,* p. 331.

45. A. E. Winship, in the *Journal of Education* 92 (August 1920), pp. 481–82; Wesley, *NEA,* pp. 282–332; Howard R. Driggs, "Some Closing Scenes in the Old NEA," AFT Collection, Series 13, Box 2.

46. Wesley, *NEA,* p. 332; *NEA Proceedings,* 1920, pp. 343–55.

47. Stecker, "First Ten Years."

mate professional conduct. Much of this change in the NEA can be traced back to the reorganization of schools, the shift in the teacher population, and the need of the new school superintendents to gain control over the professionalization project. On this shifting terrain the teachers' union movement sought to plant the seeds of a new consciousness for teachers. The immediate success of unionism and then the abrupt change in the NEA, followed by its success in luring teachers away from unionism, gave teachers reason to reflect on the meaning of their movement. It was not difficult to convince teachers in the twenties that membership in a teachers' union was something radical and even dangerous. Teachers in the AFT were concerned with academic freedom and teacher rights, while the NEA emphasized professionalism and "character." As one critic pointed out in the thirties, if teachers had been included under the Wagner Act, the NEA would have been in serious trouble as a company union.

CHAPTER SIX

Gadfly Union:
Outside the Mainstream

In the interwar years the AFT declined in membership and morale. Overpowered by the aggressive organizing tactics of the NEA's 100-percent campaign, teacher unionists developed the self-perception that they had become a gadfly institution loyally tending the dying embers of Progressive Era reform. The union contained two factions: a very conservative wing consisting mainly of vocational-education men who admired Gompers and bread-and-butter unionism and a decidedly radical wing of Progressive men and women who embraced municipal socialism and remained critical of Gompers's labor program. Gender issues played a role in this factionalism because, though the new woman was quite content to embrace professionalism, she was not at all enchanted with Gompers and instead favored the high idealism of the municipal socialists. These conservative and radical factions vied for control in the interwar years as the organizing strength of the union dwindled. And as the purpose of the union dimmed, its direction meandered. Only the original founders could recall the initial energy and enthusiasm that had brought them together.

The union confronted several new and formative issues in these beginning years. The first was the atmosphere of absolute conformity and teacher intimidation during the postwar Red Scare. In response the union became an aggressive defender of academic freedom. For the first time teachers who were dismissed without a procedural hearing had a national organization to appeal to for help. The union's willingness to defend teachers gave it a radical reputation, which was no doubt reinforced by hostile school administrators anxious to bolster NEA membership. This reputation started an internal dispute within the union between the first AFT president, Charles Stillman, and the editor of the union newspaper, Henry Linville. Tensions between Stillman and Linville, representing two factions in the union, revealed two opposing concepts of unionism within one house of labor.

Directly related to this internal factionalism was the question of the degree to which the union would follow Samuel Gompers's conservative leadership. The family wage was not the only issue that divided Gompers and women schoolteachers. Alice Kessler-Harris has shown that after World War I unions' attitudes toward women trade unionists shifted from the stance of admitting women as an issue of chivalry to that of protecting women because they were economically weak. Women trade union leaders who pursued issues beyond economic clout appeared to the trade unionists to be derailing the organizing project of the union. "In the new environment of the 1920s, protection would come from legislation, while trade unions would reduce competition for jobs by organizing those women who competed directly with their male members. Women inside unions would continue to be treated as 'different' but now not because they required protection, but because they lacked economic power."[1] Political community issues persuaded Gompers that the women teachers were not serious about their trade union affiliation. The AFT championed such unpopular causes as due process for the Industrial Workers of the World (IWW), the legal rights of the accused immigrants Sacco and Vanzetti, and the innocence of Tom Mooney and Warren Billings, the radical labor agitators who were jailed for life in the 1916 Preparedness Day bombing. These enthusiasms especially annoyed the AFL.

From their perspective, Kessler-Harris observes, women trade unionists did not see the trade union movement as the only avenue of social change. Because the machinery of local taxation was often structured at the state level, women schoolteachers were especially anxious to test their new political power in the state legislatures and in Washington. Furthermore, the women schoolteachers did not approve of Gompers's manipulation of Stillman in his campaign to support the country's entry into the war, Stillman's promotion of Gompers's reconstruction project, or Stillman's rubber stamp of Gomper's antistrike stance for public employees in the wake of the Boston police's strike.

Another source of tension between men and women trade unionists in the AFT was the fact that in the high schools men and women had separate unions which had to cooperate when negotiating with their boards of education. Few work sites were as gender-integrated as the high schools, where the distribution of men and women teachers was near parity. Male trade unionists were particularly sensitive to what they perceived as a contradiction between women's claim to special protection and their claims for equal pay for equal work. Indeed, historians Nancy Cott and Alice Kessler-Harris have observed the contradictions and ambiguities among feminists, especially after suffrage in 1919. With no apparent chivalrous role to play, and with the

1. Alice Kessler-Harris, "Problems of Coalition-Building: Women and Trade Unions in the 1920s," in Ruth Milkman, ed., *Women, Work, and Protest: A Century of U.S. Women's Labor History* (Boston, 1985), pp. 113–14.

threat that as women dominated in the high schools wages would fall, as they seemed to do during the inflation of the war, men high school teachers were particularly anxious to control the process of negotiations. The women high school teachers were inclined to share equally in the discussions, asserting their new political rights. They were disinclined to pay full dues, however, because they earned less than the men. These tensions were repressed during negotiations but when teachers got out of town and attended AFT conventions the conflicts became elaborately choreographed displays of local jealousy, where men and women vied for control of the national organization. The defense of academic freedom, support for unpopular radical causes, hostility toward the AFL leadership, and incessant bickering between men and women were related characteristics of a union that fit uncomfortably with the rest of organized labor.[2]

Teaching as a job was also drastically changing as urban school boards looked to junior high schools as an answer to overcrowding in upper grades. The introduction of a federal bill to support vocational education came at the right moment to help the normally strapped school districts fund these new construction projects. Unionized teachers played pivotal roles in this further restructuring of modern education.

At the same time the NEA continued to enjoy its hegemonic position as head of the educational establishment. Assuming a new national role, the association focused on educational policy rather than grass-roots organizing.

Women in both the NEA and the AFT assumed a greater leadership role in the interwar years. In the union they were especially instrumental in holding the organization together through difficult times. But they could not make effective alliances within the AFL, and they were plagued by the constant questioning of their patriotism by the American Legion.

A Divided House of Labor

When the AFT first organized on 15 April 1916, there were really only four locals at the meeting: three from Chicago and one from Gary, Indiana, which became Local 4. The New York union, henceforth known as Local 5, sent its warmest regards. Theoretically there were eight other locals to apply for a charter, but only the Washington Teachers Union, Local 8, remained in existence. The first charter that the new AFT issued was to the Armstrong-Dunbar High School Teachers' Union on 14 September 1916. This new union was a "colored" union, representing faculty in the segregated school system of the nation's capital. AFT secretary-treasurer Freeland Stecker warmly welcomed the new unionists, although he never for a moment

2. Ibid., pp. 110–33; Nancy F. Cott, *The Grounding of Modern Feminism* (New Haven, Conn., 1987), pp. 13–41.

questioned the policy of segregated locals.[3] Three new locals in Washington, D.C., Jacksonville, Indiana, and Schenectedy, New York, joined the union in 1917. Thirteen others joined in 1918, before the AFT convention where the "Pittsburgh Principles" were drawn up. (This convention was especially small because of the flu epidemic, which claimed the lives of several prominent educational leaders including Ella Flagg Young.) The "Principles" became the basis of the first AFT constitution, but they also allowed for a wide range of opinions and later caused confusion over just what stance the union had taken on, most important, the no-strike issue. The agreement at Pittsburgh had apparently been to leave mention of strikes out of the constitution altogether, a principle which the union followed. Later, however, Stillman would claim that the AFT had a no-strike provision.[4]

Within the organization a seige mentality developed that divided more conservative teachers from radical ones. The division first appeared over the direction of the *American Teacher*. Henry Linville wanted to present in it a forthright defense of academic freedom, which was part of his overall vision of unionism. He wanted teachers and all workers to develop an alternative, less submissive relationship to their work. His liberal (though not radical) slant had a deeper impact in the years of postwar hysteria. Charles Stillman consistently tried to muzzle Linville's more militant tone. Before long the editor and the president engaged in verbal combat over the direction and tone of the organization's newspaper.[5]

The first of Linville's editorials to ignite Stillman's wrath appeared in September 1918, when Linville argued that the Industrial Workers of the World had much in common with the AFL and had a legitimate claim on AFT members' sympathies. Given the climate of hysteria, Linville doubted that the Wobblies could get a fair trial in this country. Stillman was furious with the editorial and suppressed the issue in which it appeared; instead of becoming the organizing tool that Stillman had wanted, it was consigned to Stillman's basement. Linville then began sending galleys to Stillman, who took this as a signal to edit freely. Linville resented the intrusion and often ignored Stillman's blue pencil marks. Linville later admitted that the IWW editorial may have been a blunder. He discovered to his dismay that even the teachers who agreed with his sympathy for the Wobblies thought that Still-

3. Freeland G. Stecker, "Report of the Financial Secretary of the AFT: Pittsburgh, July 5–6, 1918," *American Teacher,* 7 (September 1918), pp. 148–50.

4. Charles B. Stillman, "Four Months of Progress," *American Teacher,* 8 (January 1919), pp. 12–16.

5. "Beginning with the IWW editorial, and passing to the reference to Dr. Anna Howard Shaw, to the implied criticism of the Southern Senators, to the editorial in the December number relative to the strike, it has been one continuous nightmare of bickering criticism." Linville to Wilcox, 5 January 1919. Linville Collection, Box 2. Clara K. Stutz to Linville: "I have just received a letter from Mr. Stillman relative to the *American Teacher.* I take it you have been behaving *very* badly." Linville Collection, Box 3.

man was right—for organizing purposes it was best left out of the official newspaper.[6]

Stillman felt his conservative perspective was confirmed by his constant contact with teachers in all sections of the country, who, he argued, were basically timid. From his work organizing new AFT locals he concluded that the teachers' union should address only very narrow economic issues. He felt that all teachers were conservative "scared rabbits" and incapable of embracing radical policies. Often Stillman's assessments of the teachers' relationships with other workers were colored by his fear of radical tendencies. During the 1919 steel strike, for example, he advised Gary, Indiana, teachers not to support the strike because their sympathetic walkout would scare teachers elsewhere. The strike was organized by John Fitzpatrick and William Z. Foster within the Chicago Federation of Labor. Their hope was to organize an industrially based union. After defeated steelworkers returned to their jobs, the Gary teachers' local, one of the original AFT charter unions, suffered with the subsequent demise of the steelworkers' union and eventually collapsed in what became a nonunion company town.[7]

To support his views, Stillman was not above drawing on conservative trade unionists as authorities on any labor issue and using them as evidence that Linville had gone against the labor movement. In February of 1919 Stillman demanded that Linville delete a reference to the Seattle general strike. Stillman said, "It is of course an illegal strike, called in defiance of the constitution and of the resolutions of the A.F. of L. and of the international unions concerned, and failed for that reason. . . . Of course it is not up to us to condemn our fellow workers in Seattle, even if we think they are mistaken, but I know you agree it is not incumbent upon us to praise labor's mistakes. Why not be silent on that point, until someone forces it on us at any rate."[8] Unwilling to venture an opinion outside of official AFL circles, Stillman considered the strike a setback to teacher unionization. "Even if you think my interpretation wrong (and I have talked with many labor men in close touch with the situation), you will probably agree that the Seattle teachers would be more likely to have my view, and that your sentence in that editorial would make organization much more difficult."[9] If Seattle teachers did not already share Stillman's ideas he could pass the word out to the local

6. *American Teacher*, 7 (September 1918); "The I.W.W. editorial has been a fatal handicap in using the Sept. number for propaganda purposes. I took a quantity of them into Indiana with me last week, and had to bring all but a dozen back." Stillman to Linville, 30 September 1918, Linville Collection, Box 2.

7. Stillman to Linville, 10 November 1918, Linville Collection, Box 3.

8. Stillman to Linville, 20 March 1919, Linville Collection, Box 3; *American Teacher*, 8 (February 1919).

9. "Stillman and Balmson [sic] have been expressing what seem to me to be the most reactionary views, so far as concerns the matter of forging a character for the AFT." Linville to Ethel Beers, 9 February 1919, Linville Collection, Box 2.

AFL contact and make organization more difficult by alienating local teachers from the central trade council. He was simply in a better position than Linville to control these events, and he wanted nothing more than to have a newspaper that reflected his economic unionism. He worked in vain to draw other unionists to his position. For his part, Linville was not as forgiving on the question of the Seattle strike and wanted these issues and others of editorial control raised at the next convention.[10]

Linville wanted to be a Max Eastman for the nation's teachers. He wanted a journal with the iconoclastic vision of *The Masses,* one daring to take on controversial issues. A Harvard graduate and respected member of the DeWitt High School faculty, Linville was insulted by Stillman's petty corrections and accused him of misreading his editorials. He was highly critical of Stillman's plan to use the *American Teacher* as a propaganda device to "sell" trade unionism to schoolteachers. "Lampson and Stillman are like good commercial travelers who feel obliged to remove all possible obstacles to success. This they can never do, because *they are not selling anything.* They are bringing a new vision of life, and they ought not to imitate the drummers."[11] This new vision of life, Linville hoped, would unite teachers around the single organization of the AFT. This was quite a contrast to Stillman's impression that all teachers were scared rabbits who wanted a basically conservative organization.[12]

The differences between Linville and Stillman represented deeper antagonisms within the union. The most impressive difference came over what type of organization the union would be. Linville wanted an organization of professionally prepared teachers taking the reins of progressive educational leadership. Stillman wanted an organization of devoted trade unionists who shared a humble yet dignified program of economic advancement. Although not a vocational education teacher himself, Stillman taught at Lane Technical High School. His union was one of the early vocational education locals to join the AFL. It was a model of teacher trade unionism for Stillman. In New York Linville had done little to organize vocational education teachers. When mechanics at a local high school wanted to join the union through their own local, he agreed, granting a charter to a separate local within his own jurisdiction but separate from "regular" teachers. Stillman, on the other hand, was a crusader for vocational education and its teachers.[13]

Both men sought to draw women leaders into the feud. Linville wrote of "the continuous nightmare of bickering criticism" to Jennie Wilcox, a high school teacher in Chicago. He wrote to Clara Stutz, a teacher in Washington, D.C., and invited her to show his letter to Stillman and Lampson, the AFT

10. Linville to Wilcox, 5 January 1919, Linville Collection, Box 3.

11. Linville to Stutz, 8 January 1919, Linville Collection, Box 2.

12. "Files of a Historical Nature," AFT Collection, Series 13, Box 1–3.

13. Guild Collection (unprocessed files), Robert Wagner Archives, New York University; Linville Collection, Box 2.

organizer. "I feel sure it will not anger them and may serve to clear the air for further and intelligent progress."[14] Linville's gestures of conciliation were consistently met by rebuff from Stillman, who had the full backing of his local but needed the support of women, who seemed to lean in Linville's direction, especially after the war issue.

Stillman may have thought that he had Linville nailed when an article appeared in the *American Teacher* entitled "As the Worm Turns," which criticized Anna Howard Shaw. Whatever Shaw's latest transgressions had been (the article is obscure and it is difficult to decipher what the issue was about), they had certainly not been against schoolteachers, in whose support Shaw had mobilized many women's clubs. Hoping to elicit general condemnation from the feminists, Stillman quickly showed the piece to Margaret Haley and Lydia Trowbridge of the Chicago Women High School Teachers. Neither gave Stillman a properly indignant response, which is more indicative of the women's negative opinion of Stillman than it is of their ability to defend feminists. The most Stillman could get out of the incident was to let Linville know that he had shown it to the feminist leaders in the movement and to tell him again that the paper ought not to take unpopular stands.[15]

The women may have been concerned that the union was headed for a sectarian division, and there is some evidence to indicate that they tried to reconcile the two men. They agreed with Linville that Stillman was a reactionary. Some went so far as to say they did not want him to represent them. But they thought that he might appeal to conservative teachers, and in order to capture a majority of teachers his conservative appeal was a useful talent. "Some of us have long been of the opinion that Mr. Stillman was in favor of a reactionary policy for the AFT. Still for that very reason he may be a better organizer and able to reach more teachers," socialist Ethel Beers wrote from Chicago.[16] "The radicals here in Chicago are greatly exasperated, at times, by Mr. Stillman's attitude," Jennie Wilcox wrote. She responded to Linville's threat to sever ties to the national as a natural response that would not be resented by the Chicago people.[17] But Linville did not want to secede from the union; his purpose was to steer the course of the union into a more radical direction.

Despite the bickering in the immediate postwar period within the male leadership, the union flourished in its first three years. By 1919 the union claimed in excess of 10,000 members and hoped to win back the Chicago Teachers' Federation with its 3,000 members. These hopes were shortlived. After the spring of 1919 membership growth fell off as the red scare intensified. The following year membership fell by more than half to 4,237. Another 1,000 teachers left the union in 1921, and when Gompers suddenly

14. Linville to Stutz, 8 January 1919, Linville Collection, Box 2.
15. Stillman to Linville, 11 October 1918, Linville Collection, Box 2.
16. Beers to Linville, 14 February 1919, Linville Collection, Box 3.
17. Wilcox to Linville, 19 January 1919, Linville Collection, Box 3.

axed all five AFT organizers that year, the union went into a tailspin of depression. The teacher organizers were shocked by their sudden dismissal; they could not simply find jobs in their "trade," as Gompers may have presumed. The union boldly borrowed money and worked to get the leaders back into unfriendly school districts. Only Stillman remained on the payroll.[18]

Gompers's sudden cutoff of the AFT subsidy marked the end of a very brief episode in the AFL's relation to public-employee unionism. It was an episode in which Gompers's primary motive was to head off a radical surge within the AFL. He had shown little interest in the teachers' union until 1919, when he offered a reconstruction program that for the first time mentioned the right of public employees to unionize. Gompers's sudden interest can be easily explained. In the same year John Fitzpatrick, president of the Chicago Central Labor Union, was running for mayor of the city. His third-party candidacy stirred a lot of excitement in the city, as nearly every teacher voted for him, though he received barely over 10 percent of the total vote. Fitzpatrick was promoting a national labor party, like the one that had been established in England, and he was attracting large segments of miners in Illinois to support the idea. Gompers was adamantly against third-party movements and wanted to get labor's firm pledge for the Democratic party in 1920. He could not afford to have the American Federation of Teachers or any AFL affiliate endorse a labor-party candidate. Still, talk of a labor party was in the air, and Gompers, Matt Woll, and John Frey denounced it constantly in the pages of the *American Federationist*. Gompers's reconstruction program of February 1919 was supposed to placate radicals in the AFL. At the June AFL convention Gompers gave Fitzpatrick the green light on his favorite project, to organize steelworkers in South Chicago along industrial lines. Labor-party proponents quieted down, and the convention endorsed the Democratic party for the first time in its history, much to Gompers's pleasure. In a quieter debate, the AFL welcomed hundreds of public worker unions into its ranks, including Boston's policemen.[19]

It seemed in the summer of 1919 that public employees would get the attention of the AFL leadership that they had been begging for since the turn of the century. Phone workers whose companies had been nationalized and who thereby became "public servants" were breaking the prohibitions against strikes by public workers and winning substantial victories. Policemen in Kansas City went on strike and successfully won a wage settlement. Other public workers whose salaries suffered in the wartime inflation took heed, and the AFL was flooded with charter applications. Then the setback came.

18. Report of the Secretary-Treasurer to the Executive Council, 18 October 1920, AFT Collection, Box 67; Lucie Allen to Freeland G. Stecker, AFT Collection, Series 1, Box 1.

19. Marjorie Murphy, "The Aristocracy of Women's Labor in America," *History Workshop Journal,* 22 (Autumn 1986), pp. 56–69; *American Federationist,* April 1920, p. 332; May 1920, p. 436; February 1919, p. 322.

In August, fourteen hundred Boston policemen were locked out of their jobs in a basic struggle over union recognition. Although Gompers fought for the reinstatement of the policemen, he was quick to accept the premise that public workers were different from private sector workers and did not have the same rights as private-sector workers. To set an example for other unions, Gompers leaned heavily on the compliant Stillman to cast the AFT constitution with a no-strike clause. Shaken by the disaster of the Boston police, schoolteachers debated the issue and decided to include the no-strike position in their statement of principles,—the Pittsburgh Principles—not in the constitution. In the spring of 1920, Gompers returned to Boston and argued with a local chamber of commerce that no public employee unions in the AFL could apply for affiliation without the no-strike clause. Ignoring the teachers' reluctance to renounce the strike option completely, he waved before his audience a draft of the AFT "Pittsburgh Principles." As for the procedure of requiring public employee unions to have no-strike clauses, no AFL convention debated the issue.[20] Yet the practice became so ingrained in the AFL that when in 1934 the American Federation of State County and Municipal Employees (AFSCME) formed, it automatically included a no-strike clause in its constitution, not because AFL president William Green insisted on it but because the members assumed that it was policy. Gompers's sudden cutoff of AFT funds in 1921 made it clear that the emergency over the labor party was over, that the police strike had decided against public employee unions, and that in the broader picture of trade-union goals, teachers were expendable.[21]

Stillman's method of getting the AFT convention to support the no-strike clause demonstrated the way that factionalism between socialists and conservatives often served the interest of the most astute politician. Apparently socialists thought the issue was irrelevant because the labor party would supersede the AFL, while conservatives thought the AFL would defeat the labor-party idea and the AFT would benefit by helping Gompers along the way. The strike issue had been debated by the teachers long before Gompers's needs became clear. Some locals had no-strike clauses, but the majority of teachers were content not to mention the issue. Margaret Haley's CTF considered striking on many occasions and may have collaborated with a student boycott in 1905 but never publicly raised the issue for debate. In September 1918 Linville ran an article in the *American Teacher* that explained that the New York AFT constitution had no reference to strikes in it. Stillman and Lampson apparently read the article to mean that the New York local had a strike clause. Several months later, Linville tried to correct the

20. See the debate over the strike clause in the *AFT Proceedings,* 1947, AFT Collection, Series 13; Florence Curtis Hanson, "The American Federation of Teachers and Strikes," *School and Society,* 25 (January 1927), pp. 52–53. For more on Stillman's position, see Charles B. Stillman, "The AFT," *American Teacher,* 9 (November 1920), pp. 182–86.

21. *AFT Proceedings,* AFT Collection, Series 13, Box 2.

impression in an editorial in which he said that probably very few AFT constitutions had no prohibition against strikes. Stillman objected to Linville's vagueness. He wanted certainty: no AFT unions had strike clauses. Linville replied that he could not attest to such a statement, since at least his own local had no such prohibition. The national convention had to decide the issue, and it took considerable prodding by Stillman to get the convention to support the "Pittsburgh Principles."[22]

Time and again the teachers went along with Stillman, even though they were aware that he was ambitious within the AFL. "He evidently desires to hold an influential place with the powers that be in the labor organization of the present," Jennie Wilcox explained to Linville. It came as no surprise to the women, and as a bitter pill to the men in the union, that Stillman eventually became a principal at a prestigious Chicago high school. His old buddy in the union, Freeland Stecker, recalled pointedly that in the course of the first ten years of AFT history some unnamed leaders had been "bought off." The women were neither surprised nor bitter. Wilcox placed her faith in the labor party idea and informed Linville that he should do the same. She seemed to be telling Linville to let Stillman have his way with the union because the AFL was not that important; it was the labor party that would be the vehicle for the teachers.[23] As long as Stillman brought in money and organizers, the women let him lead unchallenged. When the money stopped, Stillman became a token president and looked for jobs outside the union.

A clear illustration of the AFT's discontent with the AFL came in the teachers' 1922 convention, which advised Gompers to set his own strike policy by studying the relationship between business cycles and strikes. Without referring to their own no-strike policy, the teachers urged Gompers to make a "scientific" use of the strike. Perhaps more directly referring to their own predicament, the union voted not to accept any funds from the AFL unless they were "free of all conditions."[24]

Changes in the Schools: Junior High Schools and Vocationalism

While the AFT concerned itself with the philosophic stance of the new unionism for teachers, public schools were changing the meaning of the job of teaching. Centralization moved onward, schools were reorganized, state legislators created laws to assure a more streamlined administration of urban education, and educational "experts" were drawn into debates where they inevitably followed the pattern of good business practices. In his almost yearly studies of schools, George Strayer paid little attention to the expan-

22. Stillman to Linville, 31 December 1931, Linville Collection, Box 3.
23. Wilcox to Linville, 19 January 1919, Linville Collection, Box 3.
24. Proceedings of the 1922 Convention, AFT Collection, Series 13, Box 2.

sion of the physical structure of schools but examined closely school administration and finance. One thing became clear: as more and more working
people sent their children to school longer, there was pressure on school
districts to build high schools, which were extremely expensive to construct
and to staff. Although vocational education plans had been suggested in the
early 1890s, in most city systems it was not until the Progressive Era that the
idea of special junior high schools with a vocational education component
came into vogue.[25]

The AFL's embrace of vocational education tended to exacerbate the
divisions within the union. Until the time of the passage of the Smith
Vocational Education Act of 1917, union reaction to state-sponsored training
programs was at best mixed. Samuel Gompers and most labor leaders were
strongly opposed to vocational education as it was originally proposed, that
is, as an alternative to high school for working-class children. In Chicago a
1912 vocational education bill proposing this plan was quickly defeated by
Gompers and Margaret Haley. Haley called the new schools "scab hatch-
eries." Indeed the idea was borrowed from experiments in Germany that
aimed to help form the "character" of working-class children. The Cooley
plan, as this proposal came to be called, gave vocational education a bad
reputation in labor circles and stymied the growth of vocational education on
a national level.[26]

School systems still struggled with the problem of overcrowding and
looked for various solutions. One plan, called the Gary plan or the platoon
system, rotated children from class to class on various schedules. Others
built large vocational high schols devoted to the commercial and industrial
arts. But the schools were too quickly overcrowded, and the notion of junior
high schools came as a godsend to school boards. As early as 1905 New York
City had begun to plan a system of junior high schools that would extensively
alter the system of education. Chicago did not begin to consider the idea until
1923, but schools were built rapidly, and the city soon caught up to New
York in its commitment to these new schools.[27]

The popularity of the large vocational high schools helped convince
Gompers to support national legislation for vocational education. Stillman
and Freeland Stecker considered vocational education teachers to be the
backbone of the future teacher movement. These teachers, often with shop
experience and sometimes without college degrees, gave teacher unionism a
degree of legitimacy in the labor movement. If vocational education would

25. David J. Hogan, *Class and Reform: School and Society in Chicago, 1880–1930* (Philadelphia, 1985), pp. 157–92; Julia Wrigley, *Class Politics and Public Schools: Chicago, 1900–1950*
(Urbana, Ill., 1982), pp. 62–90. See also the Victor A. Olander Collection, Chicago Historical
Society.
26. Margaret Haley's autobiography, pt. 3; G. M. A. Kerchensteiner, *Three Lectures on Vocational Education* (Chicago, 1911).
27. Diane Ravitch, *The Great School Wars: New York City, 1805–1973* (New York, 1974),
pp. 197–233; Hogan, *Class and Reform*, pp. 138–93.

teach values of work, Stillman argued to Gompers, then it was important to have these teachers in the union movement. The passage of the Smith Vocational Education Act in 1917 was the culmination of this educational effort.[28]

The Smith Vocational Education Act made it possible for schools to add a vocational education component to junior high schools to help defray the expenses of the new schools. The growth of the junior high schools in response to working-class demands for more education and the equally forceful demands for vocational education created a new breed of schoolteacher. They were not stigmatized like the lowly paid elementary school teachers, nor did they suffer the status anxiety of highly paid high school teachers. Many of them responded readily to the appeals of the union.

At the same time, the enthusiasm that working people showed for vocational high schools did not carry over to junior high schools. Local labor leaders were quick to point out that junior high schools provided less than a high school education. Junior high schools meant tracking and the worst sort of class-oriented education. It was obvious that the junior high schools were a cost-cutting device made possible by the enhanced prestige of the superintendent. In Chicago the campaign against junior high schools, led by John Fitzpatrick and Margaret Haley, also fed a movement against the use of intelligence testing as a means of tracking. Despite mass meetings and wide labor opposition, the schools were built. And teachers were found to staff the schools.[29]

Some teachers (and administrators) were adamantly against the junior high schools, but others embraced them. While the new schools meant fewer jobs for high school teachers, for elementary school teachers it was a means of advancement. Both the NEA and the AFT discussed the issue, but educators were so divided over the issue that they could only decide to wait and see and assure that all schools met the same standards of quality. Margaret Haley and her CTF opened opposed junior high schools and then found that the high school teachers group had launched a new union in 1927, AFT Local 199, which organized junior high school teachers into an effective union. The lesson for union teachers was quite clear—they could embrace these new teachers for the movement.[30]

The decision to build junior high schools with a strong vocational education component was never really debated as fully as the centralization project had been fifteen years before. There were parent protests in New York, Gary,

28. Stillman, "Four Months of Progress."

29. Mary J. Herrick, *The Chicago Schools: A Social and Political History* (Beverly Hills, Calif., 1971), pp. 145–47; *New Majority,* 31 May and 7 June 1924; Olander Collection, Box 2; George S. Counts, *School and Society in Chicago* (New York, 1928), pp. 170–72, 194, 198.

30. Florence Hanson to Mary Abbe, 10 May 1929, CTF Collection, Box 54; "Stenographic Report of Dinner Meeting," 2 March 1928, CTF Collection, Box 55; interview with Mary J. Herrick, Chicago Loop City College, January 1972.

and Chicago. But teachers and parents were not as united on this issue as they had been on centralization, and even within the professionalization movement there was surprisingly little debate. Education experts seemed to embrace the idea, and in the fiscally conservative climate of the twenties, these schools made financial sense. In comparing the two debates, however, we can see how far the education experts had moved from the community. Teachers in both the NEA and the AFT were preoccupied with their own internal concerns, not with community reaction.

Legislative Lobbying in the NEA, AFT, and AFL

Gender divisions rarely entered into NEA deliberations although the feminist leadership of Charl Williams lent a progressive air to the association's more conservative program. The serious, ambitious restructuring of education continued at Columbia's Teachers College under the leadership of George Strayer, Lotus Coffman, and, in the late twenties, George Counts. At the same time Williams created a powerful alliance of women and labor leaders to implement the program under Crabtree's critical eye. Williams hoped to join society women, women reformers, and former suffrage advocates into a legislative council that would endorse the "emergency in education" program while pursuing broader social and protective legislative agendas including child labor legislation, protective legislation for women factory workers, and legislation to protect mothers and newborn infants. A series of educational reforms—known as the Smith-Towner acts—supported more vocational educational aid. The NEA added to this the idea of creating a national cabinet office for the secretary of education.[31]

The issue of gaining a cabinet position for a secretary of education had been the goal of both the NEA and the AFT earlier in the Wilson administration. In the 1918 statement of principles by the AFT, the union committed itself to the idea. But the NEA had its national headquarters in Washington and Charl Williams to push the issue. Williams was able to form a national network in support of the idea, which included Matthew Woll of the AFL. The AFT meanwhile had no national representative in Washington. L. V. Lampson was a Washington-based organizer but he stopped his union work when Gompers cut the AFL grant in 1920. By 1924, when high school teacher Selma Borchardt began working as AFT national lobbyist in her spare time, Charl Williams had absolute control of the national network plus the NEA National Council, which consisted of 48 state superintendents of schools, 25 citizens, and 25 educators. (One AFT member said this formula meant "48 superintendents and 50 members of the Chamber of Commerce.") Williams's power over the congressional committees on labor and

31. Charl Williams Papers, NEA Headquarters, Washington, D.C.

education was formidable, and Woll was more than willing to support Williams on educational issues in return for the support she readily gave on labor issues. This arrangement effectively kept the AFT on the margins. In 1924 the AFT called for a new strategy for proposing legislation. Rather than support the idea of a secretary of education and hope the prestige of a cabinet position would automatically fund education nationally, the AFT wanted to drop the issue of the cabinet position and legislate directly for federal funds. The NEA disagreed and continued with its program while the AFL endorsed the NEA line, supporting Charl Williams at every turn.[32]

Williams benefited from the support of several key Republican women who hoped the cabinet position in education would be awarded to a woman in education. Grace Bagley of Boston, who worked on the national network, told Williams that she secretly hoped Charl Williams would get the nod. Several Boston women claimed to have powerful connections with President Coolidge and nearly abandoned the congressional route for lobbying with the executive branch. This ploy proved ineffective but it did not stop the ambitions of the women's group. Williams was also a successful organizer in the Joint Women's Congressional Union, which was a loose federation of women's organizations working for various legislative changes to benefit women. Williams saw to it that educational issues were high on this agenda. AFT lobbyists had little more to do than to register a protest occasionally and point to the ineffectiveness of the NEA campaign.[33]

It was not for lack of trying that the NEA failed to get a national bill for funding education. George Strayer was an especially effective witness in a series of hearings on the various NEA funding bills. The only area where the NEA managed to expand the budget was in the area of vocational education. Both the Chamber of Commerce and the AFL agreed that vocational education needed further funding. The Smith-Towner Act of 1917 had established vocational education as a national concern, and federal funds were directed to that purpose.

Although there was little more that Williams could do in a fiscally conservative environment, she had managed to organize the first long-term educational lobby in Washington. She also had the tremendous resources of the now wealthy NEA. New membership had brought the NEA the ability to establish a research center, which began to collect regularly statistics on teachers' salaries, tenure laws, and pensions. Coordinating activities with the efforts of students at Teachers College at Columbia, the NEA was able to give teachers an informed profile of educational change. In this regard it was able to supplant the work of the Office of Education, a small agency that published a biannual report and housed the United States Commissioner of Education. This presidential appointee did little more than advise the president, address major educational conferences nationally, and collect statis-

32. Linville to Wilcox, 21 February 1921, AFT Collection, Series 6, Box 1.
33. Charl Williams Papers.

tics. The new professional NEA worked through the Office of Education but because of its superior resources was able to collect the publications of most urban schools and generate its own ambitious publishing plans. The resources of the office of research in the NEA far outstripped those of the U.S. Commissioner of Education. NEA leaders took great interest in the appointment of the commissioner, though it reserved its energies for the lobbying efforts and the press for a new cabinet post.

AFT Women and the AFL

While Charl Williams was given free rein within the NEA, the women in the AFT were stifled by the AFL's hostility toward women and white-collar workers. Alice Kessler-Harris has found that in the twenties labor leaders "often insisted that women accede to the prevailing male methods and goals, and interpreted women's attempts to find new paths to loyalty and participation as subversive." Often, women trade-union officials, in an attempt to accommodate the demands of male labor leaders, ceased to speak for women or their issues and therefore lost the following of rank-and-file women. For the teachers such accommodation was impossible. The pursuit of suffrage had produced a powerful sense of a women's culture to which the teachers especially subscribed. Prejudice against what Gompers called "brain workers" compounded the underlying tensions between men and women in the AFT. Further, the women school teachers were simply less willing to display deference to the AFL leadership. The women complained of the high salaries AFL organizers received, and they were unwilling to have men in their own union imitate the style of the AFL organizers at their expense. Finally, the women were in fact more middle-class than most members of the AFL; they had no class credentials (as Matthew Woll liked to remind them), and their socialism was being roundly denounced in AFL circles. The women teachers' hostility toward Gompers and the decidedly male leadership of the labor movement was felt throughout the new union as the women prepared to oust Gompers's men, Charles Stillman and Freeland Stecker.[34]

34. Alice Kessler-Harris, "Problems of Coalition-Building: Women and Trade Unions in the 1920s," in *Women, Work, and Protest: A Century of U.S. Women's Labor History,* ed. Alice Kessler-Harris and Ruth Milkman (Boston, 1985), p. 123. Kessler-Harris argues that by the twenties the AFL perceived women as a source of weakness and that their concerns were best taken care of by the state, not by the unions. Nancy F. Cott discusses the difficulties women encountered in trade unions and argues that the difficulties were similar to those faced in the professions, especially education and social work. She argues that feminized professions were a source of leadership for women but that the professional ethos caused women to see other women as clients rather than as comrades in a common endeavor. In the unions, she argues, there was no incentive for women to choose women leaders because male priorities dominated and women leaders had to accommodate them. Cott, *The Grounding of Modern Feminism* (New Haven, 1987), pp. 235–37. In the AFT the hostility between men and women can be traced to the question of following Gompers. See Lucie Allen to Freeland G. Stecker, 19 September 1920, AFT Collection, Series 6, Box 1: "Frankly, we have questioned the wisdom of the National going ahead faster than the funds were coming in and then asking the locals to make up the deficit."

Stillman faced the first challenge to his leadership at the 1923 convention. With the AFT facing a debt of more than $3,360, more than a yearly salary for most teachers, the opposition to Stillman at last publicly aired its grievances. Women teachers generally earned less than men in the union, yet they paid the same dues. They resented dues increases to pay for salaries they felt were too high to begin with, and they resented having to pay as much as the men paid for these special assessments. Lucy Allen of the Chicago Federation of Women Teachers accused the men of traveling throughout the country first class to keep up with the AFL organizers rather than living as the rest of the teachers had to live—very frugally. Others felt that the resources of the union had been squandered while the organizing opportunity had been lost. Discouraged by the results, they felt that the leadership had badly blundered in its cautious and unpopular policies. Stillman tried to urge more optimism, arguing that this had to be the "low point" and although there was "a hard road ahead" he insisted that it was "upgrade." Few of the teachers were convinced.[35]

A comparison of the 1918 convention with the 1923 convention illustrates how much the Gompers/Stillman stock had declined in the union. In 1918 the union voted its "firm loyalty in the Great War," whereas in 1923 it voted to "outlaw war." Even the tone of the resolutions changed. Stillman was resigned to introducing the favorite resolutions calling for a new trial for Sacco and Vanzetti and the pardon of Mooney and Billings, but he was always topped by Linville, who called for the pardon of all political prisoners. The real shift came in 1924 when Stillman, ill and discouraged, resigned from office. He was replaced by the more liberal Florence Rood, whose leadership in the St. Paul women's union was unquestioned. Rood was the equal of Margaret Haley and headed one of the more successful unions in the federation.[36]

Without Stillman the small, stagnant union grew more radical. In 1924 Linville was not alone in moving the union further left; his colleague Abraham Lefkowitz, a New York high school teacher, introduced resolutions condemning the Ku Klux Klan, calling for an end to anti-Negro discrimination, and the freeing of political prisoners. New York's Local 5 sponsored a resolution for the immediate recognition of the Soviet Union, and Chicago wanted everyone to vote for the Farmer-Labor party. Stillman's neighbor and co-worker Freeland Stecker fought the new radical tendencies. The secretary-treasurer objected to the resolution on the platoon system of

35. Freeland G. Stecker to Selma Borchardt, 11 January 1926, Borchardt Collection, Box 88, Walter Reuther Archives, Detroit. The issue of equal pay for equal work was also part of this debate. See "The Single Schedule for Those Having Equal Experience, and Other Qualifications," *American Teacher,* 11 (January 1927), pp. 14–15.

36. *AFT Proceedings,* 1918 and 1923, AFT Collection, Series 13, Box 2. For more on the work of Rood, see her "It's the First Step That Counts," *American Teacher,* 13 (October 1928), pp. 28–29.

rotating classes because the resolution said it perpetuated wage slavery and class privilege. "There are no classes in America," protested a Stecker ally. Despite the protest, the resolution with its radical language passed the convention. From the ashes of Stillman's addministration a new union emerged that was more activist and less willing to trust AFL leadership. Instead of just condemning war, this year the union affiliated with the National Council for the Prevention of War.[37]

The AFT was not the only house of labor changing in 1924. Teachers looked anxiously to the AFL after the death of Samuel Gompers to see if William Green's new leadership would bring more cooperation with labor. In the same year the Farmer-Labor party seemed to fall apart, the Communist party had attempted to take over its leadership and the coalition dissolved, despite the efforts of Senator LaFollette to hold it together. Women teachers had hoped the labor party would be the vehicle for political change, whereas men in the Chicago men's local (the organization of Stillman and Stecker) thought support of the third party was foolish. New leadership in the AFL might change things for the teachers' union and bring them unity.

The teachers hoped that under William Green's presidency of the AFL relations with the national body would thaw. Green sent greetings of welcome to the AFT convention that year, the first time the president of the AFL had ever addressed the convention. He also sent Matthew Woll, as head of the AFL's committee on education, to address the teachers. Unfortunately, Woll managed to insult most of the delegates by denigrating their economic needs and calling into question their judgment in labor affairs. The anti-intellectualism and general tone of Woll's address left a stunned audience. He accused the delegates of talking down to other trade unionists when teachers ought to be silent and listen to their brother trade unionists. Sister trade unionists were notably silent in the wake of Woll's address, although a few clearly embarrassed male delegates rose to agree that some of them had talked too much at AFL conventions. Serious talk of seceding from the AFL followed the convention, although the power of local central labor bodies forced a more realistic assessment in the next AFT convention. Nevertheless, Green's administration had not begun well with the teachers, especially the women teachers.[38]

The Revolt of the Women Teachers

The revolt of the women teachers began in 1926 with the election of Florence Hanson to replace Freeland Stecker as secretary-treasurer. Stecker represented the last of Stillman's influence at the national level. Stecker had

37. *AFT Proceedings*, AFT Collection, Series 13, Box 3.
38. Mary Barker to Florence Hanson, 17 January 1929, AFT Collection, Series 1, Box 1.

been a conscientious worker, supplying the teachers with a bulletin in 1923, when the *American Teacher* was suspended for lack of funds. For all of his editorial efforts, however, Stecker was no Henry Linville, and many teachers resented the shutdown of the paper. The move had been expedient, nevertheless: it forced Linville back into the classroom, while revenues left from the old *American Teacher* kept Stecker on as an employee of the union. Moreover, the union news clearly shifted in focus from broad social commentary to bits and pieces on the AFL, the Chicago local, and the condition of the treasury.[39]

The attack on Stecker was indirect. Rumors passed in the halls of the New York convention to the effect that Stecker was being forced back into the classroom or he would lose his teaching pension. Another secretary-treasurer would therefore have to be nominated. On the day of the nominations the women members of Local 3, Chicago, nominated their local president, Florence Hanson. Men of Local 2, Chicago, angrily nominated Stecker, and a confused convention retired to vote. The issues were not simply gender disputes but in part arguments about why the union was not growing. Stecker was accused of being lazy because he refused to leave Chicago to do any organizing work. Margaret Haley, the first AFT organizer, had been fired ostensibly because she had rarely left Chicago to organize for the national. Stecker's men defended him, saying that the secretary-treasurer was not supposed to organize. Yet if the teachers were to pay a special assessment to keep the secretary-treasurer in office, which they would have to do in order to have Stecker continue, then as the only union employee, he would have to organize new locals. Mrs. Hanson, on the other hand, was retiring from the Chicago school system and would have her pension to live on. She volunteered that she would be willing to travel for organizational purposes. Stecker was stunned by the attack and silently accepted his defeat by Mrs. Hanson, but he retained his bitterness toward the women in Local 3, and in Chicago there was very little peace between the two locals.[40]

Florence Hanson and the new president of the AFT, Mary Barker, became close associates who kept the union operating between 1926 and 1931. Their reign marked a high point for women in education politics in the twenties. In both the AFT and the NEA it seemed that women were gaining recognition for their political abilities. Mary Cornelius Barker was a graduate of Agnes Scott College in Georgia and supported her widowed mother and two sisters as an elementary school teacher and later as principal in the Atlanta school system. Although initially opposed to union affiliation, she was part of a committee that unanimously supported affiliation after the union's no-strike

39. See Stecker's reports in the Secretary-Treasurer's Collection, AFT Collection, Box 3. On the overthrow of Stillman and Stecker, see Abraham Lefkowitz, "Impressions of the Thirteenth Annual Convention of the AFT," *American Teacher*, 14 (November 1929), pp. 12–13.
40. Stecker to Borchardt, 11 January 1926, Borchardt Collection, Box 88.

policy was made clear in a presentation by L. V. Lampson, Margaret Haley's successor as AFT organizer and a close associate of Charles Stillman.[41]

Barker was a strong advocate of racial tolerance and professionalism and brought both ideals with her to the national organization. "Unless we ourselves consider our services valuable and show what we can do no one else will so recognize us." Autonomy was an important part of Barker's definition of professionalism, yet she wanted a union that also balanced pedagogy and bread-and-butter unionism. She even once tried to get her superintendent of schools to sign a contract with Atlanta Local 89 guaranteeing teachers certain rights concerning overall school policy. Although Barker may have seemed conservative to socialist Florence Hanson, the two women engaged in a long and friendly correspondence during Barker's presidency. Hanson was also a college graduate and an accomplished high school teacher before she became president of the Chicago Federation of Women Teachers in the early 1920s.[42]

Barker and Hanson also worked closely with Selma Borchardt, who was much younger than Barker and Hanson but who had entered the AFT in the early twenties and impressed everyone with her cold competence. Borchardt had taught briefly in Washington public high schools before getting a law degree. She worked together with Barker on national child-labor legislation and the Joint Women's Congressional Union. Borchardt complained bitterly that Charl Williams refused even to recognize the AFT legislative representative at Joint Women's Congressional Union meetings. Williams was sponsoring the NEA's legislative proposal for a cabinet post devoted to education. The AFT supported the idea under Stillman but reversed itself when the women took over leadership. Williams was furious, for she had her own ambitions tied to the bill. The significance of the whole deal was just how important these women in education had become. They had hoped in the twenties that their new-found electoral strength would mean more funding for education and more recognition for women in the leadership of education. No such rewards were forthcoming.[43]

The rivalry between Borchardt and Williams, although predominantly a fight between the AFT and the NEA, was also representative of a rift between older women leaders in the movement—Hanson, Barker, and Williams—and younger women such as Borchardt, Mary Herrick of the Chicago women's high school local, and Allie Mann of the Atlanta Teachers' Federation. Although all the women in the union had supported the ouster of

41. Joseph Whitworth Newman, "A History of the Atlanta Public School Teachers' Association, Local 89 of the American Federation of Teachers, 1919–1956" (Ph.D. diss., Georgia State University, 1978), pp. 95–106; Wayne J. Urban, *Why Teachers Organized* (Detroit, 1982).

42. Newman, "Atlanta Public School Teachers' Association," pp. 102–4; Urban, *Why Teachers Organized.* See also the correspondence between Barker and Hanson in the AFT Collection, Series 1, Box 1.

43. Borchardt Collection; Charl Williams Papers.

Stillman and the men leaders, they seemed to divide immediately into factions of older- and younger-generation feminists. The older women were more willing to condemn the men, more open in their hostility toward the AFL, more strident in their push to get women into positions of leadership. The younger generation seemed to want to work with the men. They assumed that leadership positions would come to them, but they wanted to pick women candidates according to principles they thought were right. Older women were for peace and had fought against entry into the war; younger women joined international organizations and traveled to European conferences to discuss peace. The younger women also considered the older women old-fashioned, and when in 1934 they ousted Florence Hanson from her position as national secretary-treasurer, they argued that she was simply too old to hold the post. In the Atlanta local Barker was pushed aside by Mann in much the same way. The older women took their college degrees as signs of progress, as trusts in a community of professional values, whereas the younger women sought higher degrees and talked a tougher bread-and-butter union line. Both generations represent a remarkable group of women who led the educational world for a very brief period of time. They were women of ability and independence whose devotion to teacher unionism was a tribute to the federation movement that Haley and Goggin had begun twenty-five years earlier.[44]

AFL-AFT Relations, 1926–1932

During the tenure of office of Barker and Hanson in the AFT, relations between the AFT and the AFL went from bad to worse. Referring to Matthew Woll's address to the convention in 1925, Mary Barker declared, "I do not believe our program is the root of the trouble. That is just to replenish the fire. Mr. Woll revealed some of his own personal feelings in 1925 and at the same time a class feeling."[45] AFL leaders insisted that the AFT program was the center of AFL discontent with the teachers. AFL president Green pointed to the lack of growth in the union, the radical nature of AFT resolutions, and the threat of communism in the locals. The union in turn complained that the AFL had not appointed a teacher to the education committee since Stillman's retirement and that the AFL refused to follow the legislative lead of the AFT in national education legislation, preferring instead to go along with their rival organization, the National Education Association. Although Green conceded that a teacher ought to be on the education committee and appointed Florence Hanson to it, he was reluctant to follow the legislative initiative of the union teachers because it seemed that the AFT had changed its goals in national legislation too many times for

44. Florence Curtis Hanson to Mary Barker, 30 January 1931, AFT Collection, Series 1, Box 1; Cott, *Grounding of Modern Feminism*, pp. 276–83.
45. Barker to Hanson, 17 January 1929, AFT Collection, Series 1, Box 1.

the tastes of the AFL. The men in the union claimed that it was the switch over the secretary-of-education issue that had alienated the AFL, but the women dismissed this criticism as another case of sour grapes on the part of the men. The men suspected that the AFT was being drawn into some Joint Women's Congressional Union dispute or a Borchardt-versus-Williams rivalry that had all the marks, one unionist recalled, of "a cat fight." Whatever the reasons why the AFL was so blatantly supporting the NEA to the embarrassment of the AFT on educational issues, its support provided the background for an incident in which the union defied the AFL for the first time.[46]

The issue that drew the most fire between the AFT and the AFL in the twenties was over national autonomy. Green wanted the AFT to oust socialist A. J. Muste and the Brookwood Labor College from the union. Muste had been outspoken in campaigns for child-labor legislation in the South and had criticized the AFL for not successfully unionizing southern textile workers. His criticisms were heard both by Green and Woll, who vowed to get Muste out of the labor movement. The teachers were directly asked in 1929 to oust the local, but they refused to do so. Selma Borchardt, the legislative representative in Washington, tried to have Green come to the 1929 convention to present his case, but the AFL president refused, explaining that he was addressing the NEA convention at the same time. This engagement with the rival institution infuriated Barker. "The affinity between the AFL and the NEA has finally dawned on me. As much alike as two peas in a pod. Autocratic, complaisant, monopolistic—antisocial, fear ridden, illiberal inherently."[47] Later, when Hanson approached Barker over issues the AFT wanted to submit to the AFL convention, Barker responded, "No, at present I am not in favor of offering the AFL any resolutions. I have so completely lost confidence in that Woll-ridden machine that I fear I am not a good barometer."[48] Barker easily defeated Green's attempt to oust Muste and the Brookwood local, not so much because she controlled the convention of between twenty and thirty delegates but because Muste had been a loyal member since 1922. He befriended many of the old-timers, and Green, for his part, seemed to do everything to alienate the teachers.[49]

The minority of teachers who defended Green in convention were certainly mortified to learn in 1930 that he had invited the president of the American Legion to address the AFL convention. Public school teachers had been targets of the American Legion since its inception. In 1921 representatives of the Legion appeared before the NEA to berate teachers for not

46. Proceedings of the Executive Council, 1930, AFT Collection, Series 3, Box 21, pp. 167–75.
47. Barker to Hanson, 23 June 1929. AFT Collection, Series 1, Box 1.
48. Ibid., 30 September 1929.
49. *AFT Proceedings,* 1929, AFT Collection, Series 13, Box 2; Abraham Lefkowitz, "Shall Brookwood and Academic Freedom Die?" *American Teacher,* 13 (October 1928), pp. 25–26; "What Brookwood Means," *Nation,* 12 September 1928, p. 241; "Brookwood Asks Hearing of AFL Charges," *American Teacher,* 13 (September 1928), p. 8; James O. Morris, *Conflict within the AFL: A Study of Craft versus Industrial Unionism, 1901–1938* (Ithaca, N.Y., 1958), pp. 111–16.

instilling the proper loyalty into American children. In the following year the Legion endorsed the activities of the Lusk Commission, and in 1926 it launched its own investigation of the AFT, which produced a nine-page, single-spaced typed letter indicting one issue of the *American Teacher* and Mrs. Hanson. It was an open letter to all of Chicago's high school teachers aimed to expose Hanson as a socialist. "After my visit to your office last Friday, I appreciated more than ever before why you take this un-American, socialistic stand that you do, for as I looked about your office I noticed all the books in your library were on the subjects of socialism and the controversy between labor and capital. I also noticed that in place of a picture of George Washington, Abraham Lincoln, or some other outstanding American, the only picture on the wall was that of President Calles of Mexico, which explains your being affiliated with the radical movement."[50]

The American Legion attack was calculated to put fear into the teachers, who would realize that the American Legion had walked into the union office and inspected Hanson's library—had they seen the membership lists as well? The men high school teachers predicted that the letter would destroy the union local and hinted that Hanson's politics were at fault. Others were not so anxious to allow the Legion to divide their ranks.[51]

Still, in the months to come there was little that the union could do to prevent the Legion from introducing loyalty oaths to state legislatures across the country. At first AFT legislative committees, often consisting of women, fought successfully against the all-male Legion until the Daughters of the American Revolution joined the attack in the late twenties to make a successful program of promoting "red" riders to school-appropriations committees. These riders were attached to school-funding bills and proved highly successful. By the midthirties two-thirds of the states had some form of loyalty oath. The invitation by Green to the Legion at the height of this campaign came as a stinging reminder of how peripheral the teachers were in the labor movement. From Green's perspective, the teachers had simply lost the sensible leadership of Charles Stillman and had turned into a social reform organization run by two women and a coterie of socialist men.[52]

Loyalty, after all, had hardly been an issue in the early years of the union. Yet, for Linville and the New York City teachers, the issue was formative in the experience of the union. Stillman had ignored the issue because the war itself was not promoted in Chicago as it had been in New York. Later in the thirties Chicago teachers were not aggressively opposed to loyalty oaths. One union leader from the men's local, Jack Fewkes, actually wished to endorse the loyalty oath when it appeared in the Illinois State Legislature in 1933. He felt it was an easy concession that would gain the goodwill of the community.[53]

50. Fred E. Busby to Florence Hanson, 9 April 1927, CTF Collection, Box 54.
51. CTU Collection, Minutes of the Men's Local, 1929–34, Box 2.
52. Howard K. Beale, *Are American Teachers Free?* (New York, 1936).
53. Jack Fewkes to Mary Abbe, 15 May 1935, CTU Collection, Box 67.

Margaret Haley, who was becoming less and less active in school politics, made it a point to defeat the legislation as one of her last lobbying performances for the teachers. She was supported by the women high school teachers and her own independent teachers' union. She surprised her detractors when she gathered considerable support from unorganized teachers in the city. She told legislative representatives that nothing done in Russia could be so bad that she could not tell American children about it, and she refused to believe that the legislature would want to dictate what teachers could think. Her arguments were persuasive, and Illinois was one of the few states that did not institute a red rider. The issue, however, remained divisive in the union, with the more progressive, antiwar women leaning against loyalty oaths and conservative men tending to accept them as necessary safeguards. Others, outside the union, had been targets of Attorney General A. Mitchell Palmer in his 1919 Red Scare and fought bitterly against it, presenting their cogent arguments of civil liberties to vulnerable schoolteachers.[54]

The red riders, the question of relations with the AFL, the ouster of Stecker, and the demise of Stillman set the stage for a long-awaited debate over the future and direction of the union. The debate took place at the 1931 convention when Henry Linville put in his successful bid to become president of the AFT. The occasion seemed to recall all the wounds and slights experienced in fourteen years of organizing. It also provided the opportunity for union members to articulate frustrations over the lack of success in reaching the majority of American teachers.

The depression years, then, were key to the transformation of the AFT from a feminist and gadfly union to the bread-and-butter union that emerged in the early sixties. Even in the twenties the union had moved away from its origins in the federation movement inspired by Goggin and Haley. The new women leaders were more professional and were college educated; more important, as the twenties progressed, they had less and less of a feminist movement behind them. After Mary Barker retired in the early thirties there were at least a half dozen younger women ready—in terms of experience, ability, and national recognition—to assume the presidency of the AFT, and several of them tried to get elected, but the times had changed. The economic emergency at the time seemed to call for male leadership. The union's difficulties in the depression era were rooted in the disagreements of the twenties. The fight with the AFL, the internal bickering between the New York socialist men and the Chicago conservative men, the women's revolt, and then their own generational differences set up the organization for continuing conflict. The catalyst in this maelstrom was the economic collapse of the cities and the subsequent fiscal crisis in education.

54. Margaret Haley to Frank Walsh, 12 September 1936, CTU Collection, Box 69.

Student strikers at Chicago's Tilden School, November 1902. Chicago Historical Society.

Delegates at the AFT convention in St. Paul, December 1920. The Archives of Labor and Urban Affairs, Wayne State University.

A display of NEA faith in the federal government's commitment to education, 1923. From the *NEA Research Bulletin*.

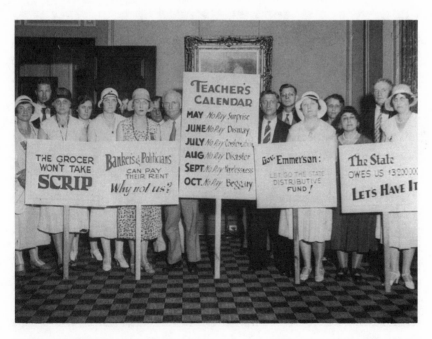

Chicago Teachers' Union protesting payless paydays, 1933. Chicago Teachers' Union Collection, Chicago Historical Society.

Chicago Teachers' Union demonstration against banks, early 1930s. Chicago Teachers' Union Collection, Chicago Historical Society.

Chicago teachers signing for scrip payments on a payless payday in 1934. Chicago Teachers' Union Collection, Chicago Historical Society.

An AFT convention in Chicago during the 1930s. Chicago Historical Society.

Overcrowded Detroit classroom, late 1940s. The Archives of Labor and Urban Affairs, Wayne State University.

Chicago teachers taking a strike vote, 1948. Chicago Teachers' Union Collection, Chicago Historical Society.

"You Read Books, Eh?"

A look at witch-hunting
in the schools.
Copyright © 1949 by
Herbert Block;
reproduced by permission.

Anonymous anti-Semitic postcard sent to a New York City teacher in 1950. Teachers Union Archives, School of Industrial and Labor Relations, Cornell University.

A prize-winning float entered by the Detroit Federation of Teachers in the 1953 Detroit Labor Day parade. The Archives of Labor and Urban Affairs, Wayne State University.

Carole Graves, president of Local 48, and David Selden, AFT president, during a teachers' strike in Newark, N.J., in February 1970. The Archives of Labor and Urban Affairs, Wayne State University.

Raoul Teilhet, the organization's president, greets Albert Shanker at the California Federation of Teachers convention in 1974. Photo: Kenneth S. Lane.

CHAPTER SEVEN /

The Crash and
Its Effects on Schools

In the twenties, school districts throughout the country built impressive high schools—palaces of learning with Greek columns and a liberal arts curriculum. They appeared with the evident wealth of the decade, but when the depression hit, the buildings and the debts that went with them were an albatross around the taxpayers' necks. Just as people sought new styles of clothing, new forms of art, and new music to convey the sense of loss and hopelessness brought on by unemployment, they looked with disdain at the excesses of the twenties—short skirts, art deco, and "putting on the Ritz." New high schools, junior high schools, and highly paid professional teachers, whether real achievements or just well-articulated goals, grew equally unfashionable in hard times. Schools were too lavish, teachers' salaries were extravagant, the curriculum seemed irrelevant.

Conditions in the schools brought on by the depression greatly transformed teaching as a job. Distinctions in class size and teaching load between elementary and secondary school teachers began to erode. Schools were tied to the local economy, and despite great unevenness among regions and among industries, no local economies were thriving. Those fortunate few teachers whose school districts did not force a pay cut, or close schools early or close schools altogether, still confronted daily the long-term effects of the depression. They observed the deterioration of school programs they had spent years investing their energies to improve. They had to direct their sights instead on poorly fed children whose families had been devastated by unemployment. This incessant confrontation with the failures of capitalism had a radicalizing effect on teachers. They responded through their representative organizations, demanding more funds for education and more attention to the needs of children. These appeals, however, went virtually ignored.

Neither the AFT nor the NEA came to the New Deal with new ideas and

131

programs for attacking the conditions caused by the depression, but in time the demands of constituents and the administrative leadership of New Dealers led both organizations to abandon their organizational personas of the twenties. The AFT, after a decade of debate, moved itself into the bosom of the AFL, leaving behind its former identity as a more radical, gadfly institution. The NEA, which was less successful in moving on to a new persona, nevertheless shed its former associations with lay organizations and shifted its legislative focus from the single purpose of gaining a cabinet-level secretary of education to passing a multipurpose public finance bill that would directly supplement local property taxes in school financing. The remarkable aspect of these changes is that they took most of the depression decade to accomplish. They required new leadership in both organizations, and they essentially resolved contradictions that had remained stubbornly unresolved a decade earlier.[1]

Women continued to dominate the lobbying efforts of both the NEA and the AFT. The question of federal aid to education grew to primary significance for both organizations while women lobbyists attempted to draw together a coalition to support federal funding. Behind the failure of this attempt was the issue of segregated schools. The problem was that any federally sponsored bill would have either to condone segregated schools or to condemn them. Despite the efforts of a coalition of union teachers, association teachers, and the National Association for the Advancement of Colored People (NAACP), this roadblock held firm throughout the years of the New Deal. Having abandoned their claims to moral superiority and moral suasion, the women were left to make political compromises that weakened their own collective impact and the programs they hoped to foster. Even those who had joined the Roosevelt bandwagon as part of the factory reform system, most notably Frances Perkins, refused to see schoolteachers, especially women teachers, as workers. For their part the lobbyists most often took the line that they were keeping schools open for the sake of children, not for the sake of saving the jobs and livelihoods of hundreds of schoolteachers. Even when they were arguing for federal funds that would be used to keep African-American children in school, the issue was always focused on helping a minority—not on helping minority teachers hold their jobs. A steady job in the depression was a precious commodity. Women teachers seemed to softpedal their own self-interest at this time and argue that for the good of the community, and the children, education ought to be federally supported.

1. For a good overview of the depression's effect on teachers, see the *American Teacher,* especially for 1933–34. See also Wellington G. Fordyce, "The Origin and Development of Teachers Unions in the United States" (Ph.D. diss., Ohio State University, 1944); *NEA Proceedings,* 1936, p. 887; Charl Williams Papers, NEA Headquarters, Washington, D.C.

The Fiscal Crisis

School closings came at the end of a four- to ten-year period of high expenditures to meet the rising demand for free secondary schooling. By the time of the depression, schools were paying larger proportions of their budgets to debt financing. These costs remained constant as the tax base shrank after the stock-market crash. By the depth of the depression, 1933–34, in some school districts income had fallen by 30 to 50 percent. In 1934–35, according to the AFT, forty-two thousand schools had insufficient funds to keep operating, and nearly forty thousand other schools operated for less than six months of the year.[2]

Chicago had by far the most distressed of the city school systems during the depression. Back in 1929, when Chicago teachers were still campaigning for a salary raise that would regain income lost to inflation during the war, Margaret Haley and the Chicago Teachers' Federation had pressed for a new tax evaluation.[3] Haley's vision was that the wealthy and powerful Loop businesses should take on a greater share of the tax burden. Her plan backfired when a reassessment in 1929 was declared illegal and Loop businesses refused to pay taxes until a new assessment was produced. Hence taxes for 1929 and 1930 remained uncollected, and in January 1931 teachers were offered their first scrip payment. All of the teachers' unions in Chicago opposed scrip, but there was little the Board of Education could offer them until the county's tax machinery began operating again, and even then banks holding bonds on school buildings were demanding that schools pay interest and outstanding debts before paying teachers. This political roadblock was further complicated in 1932 by the sudden demise of Samuel Insull, the utilities magnate whose financial empire built on the securities of many Chicago banks. Under pressure because of the Insull failure, banks leaned more heavily on the city government, while the tax-collecting machinery limped along through the deflated tax rolls of 1929–32. Unwilling to accept scrip, teachers were paid nothing at all.[4]

2. David B. Tyack, Robert Lowe, and Elisabeth Howe have written most extensively on the depression in public schools in *Hard Times: The Great Depression and Recent Years* (Cambridge, 1984), especially pp. 32–39. See also Studs Terkel, *Hard Times: An Oral History of the Great Depression* (New York, 1978); and David Shannon, ed., *The Great Depression* (Englewood Cliffs, N.J., 1960). In addition, see Clarence E. Ridley and Orin Nolting, *The Municipal Yearbook: An Authoritative Resume of Activities and Statistical Data of American Cities* (Chicago, 1934); W. S. Deffenbaugh, "Effects of the Depression upon Public Elementary and Secondary Schools and upon Colleges and Universities," in *Biennial Survey of Education in the United States: 1934–1936*, comp. Bess Goddy Koontz (Washington, D.C., 1938); NEA Research Division, "Studies in State Educational Administration" (January 1931), pp. 2–3; "Current Conditions in the Nation's Schools," *NEA Research Bulletin*, 4 (November 1933).

3. Marjorie Murphy, "Taxation and Social Conflict: Teacher Unionism and Public School Finance in Chicago, 1898–1934," *Journal of the Illinois Historical Society*, 74 (1981), pp. 242–49.

4. Mary J. Herrick, *The Chicago Schools: A Social and Political History* (Beverly Hills, Calif., 1971); pp. 184–88; Alexander Gottfried, *Boss Cermak of Chicago: A Study in Political Leadership*

Even when taxes on the reduced base were collected, most local governments were pressured to reduce their rates further. Schools became special targets for tax reformers. The Office of Education reported: "Considering only 60 cities between 30,000 and 100,000 population, 56 per cent decreased tax rates for schools while only 41 per cent decreased the rate for other purposes."[5] Some states were able to reform their tax codes. In Michigan a sales-tax bill raised between fourteen and fifteen million dollars for schools, but this was a state where the local economy had literally collapsed, and teachers in major cities, including Detroit, were simply not being paid.

In rural districts where the agrarian slump had progressed slowly in the twenties, schools had added very few new services that could be cut in the depression. The only way to cut taxes was to close the schools. Dust bowl schools in Arkansas closed their doors after sixty days of instruction in three hundred schools. In Alabama half the schools were closed. Many teachers continued to teach, and in some rural states teachers were offered free room and board but no pay in exchange for their services.[6]

Various ingenious methods for reducing teacher salaries appeared in the distressed cities. For teachers in Chicago, three years of intermittent pay and occasional scrip made a 10-percent pay cut with the promise of regular payment a relief. Other cities preferred a more "voluntary" approach. In Philadelphia, unless a teacher could demonstrate extreme hardship, the teacher took a "voluntary" 10-percent pay cut. Denver teachers "volunteered" 20-percent pay cuts.[7] Another means of lowering school costs through wage cuts became prevalent in New York, where substitute teachers were hired as replacements for regular teachers. This tactic was used primarily to reduce the high cost of high school teachers. Because of a decline in birth rates, school boards could cut budgets by not hiring elementary school teachers; this tactic was less successful in the high schools, where the student population continued to grow, partly because of New Deal restrictions on child labor. Administrators began hiring substitute teachers on a temporary basis because substitutes earned no more than two-thirds of a full-time teacher's pay. In New York, for example, a regular teacher earned $2,148 a year, whereas a substitute teacher could earn only $1,425.[8]

(Seattle, 1962), pp. 249–50, 295; Citizens Schools Committee Collection, Chicago Historical Society, Boxes 1–2; Robert Reid, ed., *Battleground: The Autobiography of Margaret A. Haley* (Urbana, Ill., 1982), pp. 227–69.

5. U.S. Office of Education, *Circular No. 79* (February 1933).

6. *American Teacher,* 19 (November–December 1934); Haym Jaffee, "Children Strike for Teachers," *American Teacher,* 21 (November–December 1936), pp. 11–13.

7. U.S. Congress, Committee on Education, "Federal Aid to Education," Hearings before Committee, 73rd Congress, 2nd sess., 23 February–1 March 1934 (Washington, D.C., 1934); *School and Society* 42 (December 1935), pp. 781–82.

8. David Paul Higgins, Commissioner of Education, "A Survey of the Substitute Teacher in the City of New York" (Board of Education, 1938), pp. 18–48; "Statistical Report on New York Schools," New York City Board of Education Records, both in the Special Collections, Millbank Library, Teachers College; Tyack, Lowe, and Howe, *Hard Times,* pp. 144–50.

While the number of teachers who were qualified to teach in the New York system but were unplaced grew to 12,000, the Board of Education hired the often less-qualified substitute teachers. Enrollment in training school classes decreased from 1,200 yearly to 179 in 1932 because of the unavailability of jobs. The school system regularly needed 1,200 substitute teachers and 2,000 new replacements yearly, but instead of hiring new teachers the board allowed the substitute teachers' rolls to grow to an unwieldy 20,000 names.[9]

Hard-pressed administrators balanced their budgets by reducing teachers' pay, but they could never satisfy the demands of local tax organizations. Teachers' wages were the largest daily operating expense of the schools, and they were a leading target of tax-reduction movements. Even before the stock-market crash, as business slowed in the late twenties, there was a growing business-community movement to cut taxes at all levels of government. Tax-cutting organizations first appeared locally in 1915 in large cities like Chicago and New York, just two years after the income-tax amendment was added to the U.S. Constitution. These organizations, variously known as "public efficiency leagues" or "better government federations," aimed their investigations at local government waste and frequently demanded better accounting systems in public agencies. Under Herbert Hoover's administration, from 1929 to 1933, these watchdog agencies became national organizations. Hoover himself helped launch the National Economic League in 1932; it targeted veterans' appropriations on a national level and school expenditures on the local level. In the Midwest the National Organization to Reduce Public Expenditure formed by networking among the Chicago Chamber of Commerce, the Illinois Manufacturers' Association, and 648 other similar organizations. Inspired by this example, the National Association of Manufacturers organized the National Committee for Economy in Government in the summer of 1932. Most of these organizations had programs that would hit government expenditures at the federal, state, and local levels. And predictably, education was a prime target at the local level.[10]

Older business organizations that had once generously contributed to the

9. Finally in 1935 the state commissioner of education ruled against the New York City system of substitute teachers, demanding that the schools hire regular employees. The transition to regular teaching, however, was difficult because many eligible teachers had applied as substitutes and had gotten regular substitute positions that constituted up to 80 percent of some high school faculties in the city. To fire these teachers and set up a new procedure for hiring would prove disruptive to the schools, not to speak of the hardship to qualified teachers who had accepted the board's substitute policy because it was the only way to work. Moreover, the teachers' union had secured legislation granting these substitute teachers better pay and some job security, making reform of the system all the more imperative. Higgins, "Survey of the Substitute Teacher," pp. 4–39; Teachers Union Collection, Reports of the Legislative Representative, Bella Dodd, Mimeographed Bulletin, Accession 5015, Box 10, Labor Documentation Center, Martin P. Catherwood Library, Cornell University; Tyack, Lowe, and Howe, *Hard Times,* pp. 64–67; Eunice Langdon, "The Teacher Faces the Depression," *Nation,* 16 August 1933, pp. 182–85.

10. S. Alexander Rippa, "Retrenchment in a Period of Defensive Opposition to the New Deal: The Business Community and the New Deal 1932–34," *History of Education Quarterly,* 2 (June 1962), pp. 76–82; Harry L. Tate, "Educational Breakdown," *American Teacher,* 17 (October 1932), pp. 8–9.

expansion of education responded to this new national networking by adopting a hard line against further educational expenditures. The United States Chamber of Commerce was the most prominent of them. Once the darling of the National Education Association, the Chamber of Commerce published a list of ten areas that local school boards might address in making economy cuts that chamber leaders thought necessary. The most important of these cuts included shortening the school day, increasing class size, reducing school hours, shortening the school year 12 percent, reducing teachers' salaries 10 percent, discontinuing kindergartens and evening classes, charging a fee for high school students, charging for textbooks.[11]

The image offered by the budget cutters was that schools had spent money extravagantly and that teachers were basically overpaid. And many teachers bought the notion that they had a relatively privileged position in the work force. Indeed, school continued in most areas and teachers taught in them. Wages declined, but more slowly than in the private sector, and deflation gave many teachers their first real raises in decades. Appearances thus suggested that schoolteachers did relatively well in the depression, but this is an illusion of the time, one that teachers themselves thought divided them from the bulk of American workers and kept them in a privileged position.[12]

Teachers could not fail to notice that the size of their classes was doubling, that no new teachers were being hired, that substitutes were hired while eligible normal school graduates waited by the thousands to be called by the district. All teachers were haunted by the spectre of Chicago teachers, whose situation grew steadily worse in the depression: "Homes have been lost, families have suffered undernourishment, even actual hunger. Their life insurance cashed in, their savings gone, some teachers have been driven to panhandling after school hours to get food."[13]

11. Tyack, Lowe, and Howe, *Hard Times,* pp. 74–78.

12. The question of how high teacher salaries actually were provides an important point of departure for this discussion. Teacher salaries did rise in the years from 1913 to 1929, and yet wartime inflation had canceled prewar gains, forcing schools to raise teacher salaries again in the mid-twenties after a seven-year campaign on the part of both NEA and AFT teachers. On the average, teachers appeared then to have wages slightly above the national average wage in 1929, and these wages were maintained as deflation hit in the next four years. The values of the teachers' salaries rose with the deepening of the depression. It is important to remember that the statistics give us the average official salary of schoolteachers, which is an average that includes the salaries of the superintendent and administrative personnel. Also they give average salaries for full-time employees. By taking into account the administrators' higher salaries and subtracting two or three hundred dollars from the teacher average, one would find that the teachers' salaries were about equal to the average salary of the time. Getting closer to median incomes, in 1929, 65 percent of families and individuals earned less than $2,000 a year; in 1937, 77 percent of families earned less than $2,000 a year. Teachers' salaries in 1929 averaged $1,420 a year, and by 1937 they averaged $1,374 a year, well within the range of the majority of Americans. These salaries do not include the 10 to 20 percent "voluntary" wage cuts in two-thirds of the cities, nor do they include the instances where teachers were not paid at all. *American Teacher,* 21 (November–December 1934); W. Vance Grant and Thomas D. Snyder, *Digest of Education Statistics, 1985–86,* Office of Educational Research and Improvement, Department of Education (Washington, D.C.), p. 57.

13. *Nation,* 10 May 1933.

The impression that teachers were not doing so badly during the depression may simply have been the perspective of a sexist society that did not value women's work and thought of their wages as "pin money" and extra income. Very little has been written about women workers in the depression. The crisis seemed to focus on families, especially the unemployment of male heads of households. Frances Donovan found, however, that many women schoolteachers already had family burdens before the depression and that these responsibilities were heightened during the depression.[14]

Patriotism and School Finance

The struggle between the pressed and often unpaid teachers and a demoralized business community bent on tax reduction occurred while a revitalized patriotic front advanced on many state legislatures to propose new loyalty oaths for public school teachers. The American Legion, which was ten years old in 1931, had a half million dollars in its treasury, one million members, 16 members in the U.S. Senate, and 130 members in the House of Representatives. The Legion sought to redirect the tax revolt, which often focused on veterans' programs, toward public school teachers. By focusing on educational programs and loyalty oaths in state legislatures, the Legion drew attention to local tax-cutting issues and away from the national veterans' payments issues. Along with the Daughters of the American Revolution, the Legion began to renew old loyalty-oath legislation with some success in the early thirties. Teachers easily divided over the issue of loyalty oaths.[15] In Chicago, for example, John Fewkes, who had led the teacher parades against the banks, saw no reason to oppose the oath in the Illinois legislature, even as Margaret Haley told a legislative committee that the purpose of the oaths was "to keep teachers silent and afraid. Keep them from finding and revealing the rottenness of the system." Haley added, "I wish to state definitely that I am not in opposition to the Russians' Soviet Government. They have the right to any sort of government they wish in Russia."[16] Desperate for allies in the fight for more school funding, teachers' unions and associations were often tempted to forego the battle against the oath in order to gain lobbying

14. Frances R. Donovan, *The Schoolma'am* (New York, 1938).

15. Richard Seelye Jones, *A History of the American Legion* (New York, 1949), pp. 45–59; Laurence W. Chamberlain, *Loyalty and Legislative Action: A Survey by the New York State Legislature, 1919–1949* (Ithaca, N.Y., 1951), pp. 18, 45–55.

16. The American Coalition of Patriotic Societies made teacher oaths their prime target as this coalition of the Betsy Ross Corps, the Anglo-Saxon Federation, the Immigration Restriction Society, and the Junior American Vigilante Intelligence Federation made its way into legislative subcommittees on education. In most cases, however, these ultrapatriotic groups were strongly nativist and insisted that all educational funding be strictly limited to public programs, a stricture that alienated the large number of Catholics among public school lobbyists sent from teacher organizations. Margaret Haley to Frank Walsh, 12 September 1936, CTF Collection, Box 69/3.

strength on educational funding issues. By 1936 twenty-two state legislatures had passed a "red rider," usually a loyalty oath attached to some fiscal relief bill for schools.

The National Education Association and the American Legion cosponsored National Education Week in the midtwenties. Well into the fiscal crisis, the NEA continued to feature Legion leaders prominently on its programs. (Teachers in the NEA Department of Classroom Teachers, however, passed motions opposing the loyalty-oath campaign.) The Legion made it clear that its favorite teacher target was membership in the American Federation of Teachers. A Legion pamphlet, *The ABC's of the Fifth Column,* asserted that 80 percent of the members of the AFT were Communists and that the rest were fellow travelers. A report on the 1936 AFT convention by a Legion commander pointed to the lack of an American flag in the auditorium as a clear indication of Soviet domination.[17]

The ability of the Legion to connect its lobbying efforts to the fiscal crisis in education led to some powerful coalitions against public school teachers. A case in point was the friendship between William Randolph Hearst (who had become a bitter foe of the national income tax) and the American Legion. In 1935 the Hearst newspaper chain ran a series of articles by Commander Joseph V. McCabe of the Legion, attacking progressive schoolteachers who attempted to explain the economic crisis in terms of market failure. Teachers were warned to stay away from issues of social change and leave the financial crisis in the able hands of business-community leaders.[18]

The New Deal and Teachers' Salaries

Though Chicago's situation was extreme, it was not an alien experience for cities with large debts and a collapsed or only partially functioning tax system. Still, in order to get emergency funding from the federal government, city officials made the case that their situation was an exception caused by tax revolt and the collapse of the Insull empire. In February of 1933 Mayor Anton Cermak paid a visit to President-elect Roosevelt, who was vacationing in Florida, to get a Reconstruction Finance Loan to bail out the city's schools. While he pleaded his case, an assassin's bullet hit him and spared the president, leaving a martyr to the cause of the Chicago teachers to linger in a Florida hospital and say with his last breath that the president would not let the teachers down. Roosevelt, however, approached the issue

17. Mildred Sandison Fenner, "NEA History: The NEA, Its Development, and Program" (Ph.D. diss., George Washington University, 1942), p. 46.
18. S. Alexander Rippa, *Education in a Free Society* (New York, 1967), pp. 266–74; Chamberlain, *Loyalty and Legislative Action;* Lt. Col. Orvel Johnson, "Red Mist over Philadelphia," *National Republic,* 4 (October 1936), pp. 1–2; Eaton, "AFT," pp. 131–32. See also *NEA Proceedings,* 1921; *AFT Proceedings,* 1936.

as a fiscal conservative. He was loath to use Hoover's Reconstruction Finance Corporation (RFC) to bail out a Democratic city. But he was equally reluctant to jump into the business of giving money to a city whose reputation for fiscal responsibility had been less than laudable.[19]

Because of Roosevelt's unwillingness to act immediately, the antagonism between teachers and bankers rapidly deteriorated into a series of street brawls. Pressure on Cermak's successor mounted, Edward Kelly, while parade permits stalled in the city police department and threats and counter-threats were hurled between teachers and businessmen. Finally the teachers rioted. Thousands of teachers marched in the downtown Loop business area, breaking windows, entering banks and confronting bank president Charles Dawes, who responded by declaring, "I don't talk to troublemakers." In an attempt to cool tempers, Mayor Kelly heard delegations of hundreds of teachers who threatened to picket the opening of the Chicago World's Fair. Business leaders responded by saying that they would prevent the purchase of anticipated tax warrants, thus holding up teachers' salaries for another four months. Finally, on the eve of opening the fair, a compromise was reached that called off the mass demonstrations of unpaid teachers. Soon afterwards, however, the bankers announced that they could not sell the tax warrants because teachers were "uncontrollable."[20]

Roosevelt preferred to see the Chicago situation as a local affair complicated by the divisiveness of the community. He would approve no government money until the banks and business agreed to carry the loan for the teachers. Business then would determine the conditions under which teachers would be paid.

The compromise between businessmen and teachers in Chicago occurred in a small hotel room in downtown Chicago, with representatives of the Men's Federation of Teachers acting to represent the city's teachers. Women teacher unionists resented the secretive way in which the negotiations were conducted. "They were all men," Margaret Haley remarked as if to summarize the situation. "It is a Committee that is our enemy—made up of bank presidents, packers and directors generally representative of the wealth of the second largest city of the United States. There is no doubt of their intention; they are attempting to starve the teaching force into submission to their program and to cripple the city's educational system."[21] Fred Sargeant,

19. Gottfried, *Boss Cermak of Chicago*, p. 326: "Even in delirium he babbled about teachers. FDR commented, 'It seemed the one thing that was puzzling him.' "

20. "The Chicago Riots," *American Teacher*, 18 (June 1933); *CT*, April 1933; CTF Collection, Box 60; and scrapbooks in the CTU Collection. See also Sterling D. Spero, *Government as Employer* (New York, 1948), pp. 323–24; Leslie Hughes Browder, "Teacher Unionism in America: A Descriptive Analysis of the Structure, Force, and Membership of the AFT" (Ed.D. diss., Cornell University, 1965); "Spasmodic Diary of a Chicago School Teacher," *Atlantic Monthly*, 152 (November 1933), p. 517; Herrick, *Chicago Schools*, pp. 210–13; Tyack, Lowe, and Howe, *Hard Times*, p. 107.

21. CTF Collection, Box 67/1.

president of the Northern Railroad, emerged as head of the committee and elicited the cooperation of the teachers in a program that would fire fourteen hundred teachers, reduce salaries and curtail the educational program. Bankers would gain an RFC loan, a program continued through the National Industrial Recovery Act (NIRA), and lend money to the city for school purposes. The federal government through the RFC and the city's banks and railroads accepted thirty-five million dollars in collateral from the schools and lent twenty-five million dollars for operating expenses, thus ending Chicago's fiscal crisis. Although the announcement of the cutbacks in the city raised a storm of protest among teachers, the promise of regular pay kept them from further action.[22]

The "Educational Establishment" in Crisis

The financial pressures coupled with the tax revolt and the wave of patriotism tended to excite the interests of teachers who looked to their organizations for moral support, legal advice, and legislative remedies. The National Education Association, which had spent much of the decade of the twenties working to raise teachers' salaries as part of its general program of raising standards, spent much of the thirties trying to preserve principles of educational standards, even when they were fiscally impossible to keep. Internally the organization was plagued with problems. In 1934 Executive Secretary Crabtree retired from office, and many wondered if the organization faced a big change. The Department of Superintendence had grown in strength and numbers and seemed to want to break off from the large, unwieldy summer meetings.[23]

For their part, schoolteachers in the rank and file of the NEA found the organizational meetings less compelling and more difficult to attend under their current financial strain. In 1934 the national meeting had its lowest attendance since the early twenties, and it was rumored that when Crabtree resigned the superintendents would break off and the organization would become a National Teachers' Association. The prospect was alarming for many: after all, the NEA had prided itself on representing all of education, not just the interest of the teachers. The doomsayers were proved wrong, however, when the dynamic school administrator William Givens took over as executive secretary in 1935 and rebuilt the organization. Despite the

---

22. In other cities similar settlements were made with or without the teachers' cooperation. In New York City, when Abraham Lefkowitz and Henry Linville emerged from a similar meeting with city officials, they were met by a waiting and hostile crowd of teachers. Abraham Lefkowitz, "The Depression and Educational Statesmanship," *American Teacher*, 16 (November 1931), p. 10; Teachers Guild Collection, Box 1/7, Robert Wagner Archives, New York University.

23. *NEA Proceedings*, 1933, p. 26; Edgar G. Wesley, *NEA, The First One Hundred Years: The Building of the Teaching Profession* (New York, 1957).

NEA's internal turmoil, the period of transition was very quiet compared with the internal upheaval of the AFT, discussed in the next chapter.[24]

Roosevelt and Emergency Relief

Immediately on taking office in 1933, President Roosevelt's first commissioner of education, George Zook, convened an advisory committee on educational proposals. It purportedly represented a broad cross-section of the education industry but was in fact very heavily loaded with active NEA superintendents and members of the educational establishment. Zook established a legislative subcommittee and appointed Sidney Hall, the head of the NEA legislative commission, as chair.[25]

Beyond creating this advisory committee to discuss possible legislative solutions to the problems of school finance, the new commissioner devoted time and energy toward getting relief funds in the hands of teachers. Zook worked with Harry Hopkins in disbursing sixteen million dollars in relief funds from February through June 1934 for schools in thirty-three states that would otherwise have to close early. Under this program, Chicago schoolteachers were beneficiaries, receiving an average of fourteen hundred dollars per teacher. But the point of the program under Hopkins was that the funding was relief, a temporary measure to bridge, not to correct, the shortfall in local tax funding.[26]

Other educational relief funds operated in much the same way. Under the NIRA seventy-five million dollars in loans were made for rehabilitation of the nation's more than 245,000 one-room schoolhouses that were in disrepair. This emphasis on relief, as opposed to ongoing federal aid to education, reflected the strong preference of President Roosevelt. Trained exclusively in private schools, he distrusted "the school crowd," as he called the traditional leadership of public education. New Dealers sometimes accused the educational establishment of racial and class bias, but this charge had a certain hypocrisy to it. Within the administration it was Commissioner George Zook—tied to "the school crowd"—who persistently tried to raise issues of educational equality. Zook sponsored a major conference in 1934 devoted to problems of black rural education. He managed to gather statistics and testimony indicating the discouraging effects of black illiteracy in the South. With Mary McLeod Bethune organizing the event, Zook had man-

24. William Dow Boutwell, "The Washington Meeting of the NEA," *School and Society,* 11 August 1934, pp. 48–53.

25. George F. Zook, "Federal Aid to Education," *School and Society,* 14 July 1934, pp. 41–48; Charl Williams Papers. See also Harry Zeitlin, "Federal Relations in American Education, 1933–43: A Study of New Deal Reports and Innovations" (Ed.D. diss., Columbia University, 1958); Tyack, Lowe, and Howe, *Hard Times,* pp. 103–6, 134.

26. George F. Zook, "Education Program for Relief and Reconstruction," *School and Society,* 23 December 1933, pp. 813–18; U.S. Congress, Hearings (26 February–1 March 1933).

aged to attract Eleanor Roosevelt to the event, which publicized the sorry situation of black education.[27]

In helping Hopkins distribute the relief funds, Zook pointed out that the administration had in fact done nothing to get at the problem of equalization: "There was no attempt at equalization of any kind. If the normal school term of a Negro school was four months as against seven months for whites, it was assumed that the states should be helped to maintain their own chosen situation."[28] This issues became a central point of contention between the commissioner of education and the president, until Zook resigned immediately after his conference on Negro education. In an article defending his year in office, Zook pointed out that under the same legislation, the government had given $400 million for road repairs while schools had to settle for much more meager fare. He argued that these "small handouts" were not enough to address the problems of inequity in public education. Zook wanted a large appropriation for education under the direction of the Office of Education; his resignation from the administration marked the depths of his disappointment.[29]

It also marked a victory for Hopkins and his relief approach to school aid. All subsequent educational funding was administered by the Federal Emergency Relief Administration (FERA), the Civilian Conservation Corps (CCC), and the National Youth Administration (NYA), agencies that studiously avoided the Office of Education.[30] Zook's replacement was John W. Studebaker, a superintendent from Iowa. He lacked Zook's passionate concern for educational equity, but he fought a protracted struggle in the bureaucratic trenches to have education-related aid administered through his office. He was unsuccessful, and his isolation emphasized the degree to which "the school crowd" was scorned by the New Deal.[31]

"Always there has been the element of relief," Roosevelt wrote; "In fact it has been the relief feature which has justified the federal government's supplying funds for programs so largely educational."[32] Temporary relief, educators retorted, could not possibly solve the crisis in education. This argument irked Roosevelt. His response was to point to the NEA's persistent reference to the "emergency" in education, a condition that implied temporary solutions. School shutdowns and layoffs were temporary; low salaries for teachers and inadequate tax revenues were local problems. In answer to temporary problems, the Works Progress Administration (WPA) hired over

27. Zook, "Federal Aid to Education"; *NEA Proceedings,* 1934, pp. 37–43.
28. Tyack, Lowe, and Howe, *Hard Times,* pp. 95–100; Zeitlin, "Federal Relations," pp. 125, 207.
29. Tyack, Lowe, and Howe, *Hard Times,* pp. 95–100; *New York Times* (hereafter cited as *NYT*), 6 July 1934, p. 12.
30. Zook, "Federal Aid to Education"; Doxey Wilkerson, *Special Problems of Negro Education* (Washington, D.C., 1935), pp. 35–41.
31. Tyack, Lowe, and Howe, *Hard Times,* p. 108.
32. Zeitlin, "Federal Relations," pp. 50–127.

one hundred thousand professional and technical workers for its programs, including 36,059 teachers, all of whom had to be on relief to qualify for the program.[33] When asked if he would ever support federal funds for education, Roosevelt replied, "I don't like to say yes or no to that question. . . . There are certain sections of the United States that are so poor that their tax valuations, their assessments are necessarily insufficient to bring in the revenue to run modern and adequate schools."[34] But while admitting to the need for some equalization the president stood firm against sending aid out to all states or altering in any way the tax basis of education. Only the "poorest schools," he argued, deserved aid. "Certainly the richer states do not need any money." He continued to support his relief program, leaving Congress with the thorny problem of equity in education.[35]

Roosevelt's reluctance to provide general school aid appears to contradict the take-charge attitude displayed in his first few years in office. It is more puzzling when one considers the many ways in which the New Deal carried forth the programs and proposals of the Progressive Era. Certainly the expansion of education, the improvement in the quality and extent of schooling, stands as one of the major reforms of the Progressives and yet, in this particular area, the new administration seemed to distance itself from that reform impulse. As a public works project, education had served in the late nineteenth century to provide employment for thousands of construction workers. It reached to the grass roots of society and purportedly served all classes of society. Yet Roosevelt preferred to see education as a local affair.

Federal Legislation

The NEA's disappointment with the Roosevelt administration set in very slowly in the years between 1933 and 1935; it was an instructive preamble to the final fight for federal aid in 1937. Despite Roosevelt's apparent sidestepping of the Chicago situation, the head of the NEA legislative commission, Sidney Hall, continued his optimism in the 1933–34 school year, hopeful that some form of financial aid would be passed soon. Hall reported enthusiastically that the House of Representatives seemed to encourage the NEA lobbyists: "At first the committee was cold but courteous. A change in their attitude was noticeable as facts were brought before them. You could see them melt." Hall asked for $100 million and the committee counteroffered $75 million. To secure passage for the aid bill Hall visited Roosevelt at the White House in May and was granted a five-minute interview, which expanded to fifteen minutes. "I told him the story. In Georgia, I pointed out the

33. Works Progress Administration, Papers, National Archives; *Inventory: An Appraisal of the Results of the WPA* (Washington, D.C., 1938), p. 40; Tyack, Lowe, and Howe, *Hard Times,* p. 129.
34. Zeitlin, "Federal Relations," p. 204; Tyack, Lowe, and Howe, *Hard Times,* pp. 129–32.
35. Zeitlin, "Federal Relations," pp. 201–7.

average salary of teachers is $450 a month while in my state [Kentucky] it is $390 and furthermore that there are over 1,000 teachers in Kentucky getting $30 for six months which is one half what is paid relief workers in the state."[36]

Despite the apparently sympathetic reception, the bottom line was that the president directed Hall to speak to Harry Hopkins, a clear indication that he refused to consider school aid outside the context of relief. When the summer NEA meeting convened several blocks from the White House (it was scheduled for Washington in an effort to focus national attention on education and the New Deal), Roosevelt failed to send his greetings. He pointedly left town in the course of the meetings. The teachers, sitting at the mercy of a midsummer swelter, were miffed by Roosevelt's indifference. This apparent snub combined with the internal problems of the organization and the difficulties teachers were themselves experiencing in their own districts to set a tone of mild gloom throughout the organization. The new legislative program the NEA formulated included $100 million in economic aid, funds for rehabilitation of rural schools on the same basis as federal aid for road improvement, the devotion of between 3 and 7 percent of Public Works Administration [PWA] funds to school construction, $100 thousand dollars for school maintenance, provisions for loans to districts to cover losses, and aid to college students on the same model as the Civilian Conservation Corps. Once brought before the legislative commission of the NEA this program was extended to place all funds under a newly created cabinet appointment of secretary of education. Hall was assured by leaders of Congress that he had support in both houses, but word from the White House killed the bill in the House Rules Committee over the issue of whether the bill would be a relief measure or an educational measure. The problem with disbursing funds through the Office of Education was that Congress would have to lay down specific guidelines for use of the funds by the states. This was precisely the political problem, the issue of equity, that Roosevelt wished to avoid.[37]

In subsequent legislative maneuvers with Congress it became even clearer that Roosevelt wished to distance himself and his administration from these proposals and from the "school crowd." Commissioner Studebaker's close association with the NEA continued a tradition of the office, which in previous years had assured but now precluded the NEA from a friendly relationship with the president. Unaccustomed to being ignored, NEA leaders bristled at new programs with educational content such as the CCC and the NYA. Williams Givens, the new executive secretary of the NEA, gave expression to this exasperation in an article blasting Roosevelt and his "Raw

36. Legislative Council papers, NEA Headquarters; *NEA Proceedings,* 1934, pp. 30–37; *NYT,* 6 July 1934; Zeitlin, "Federal Relations," p. 293.
37. Zeitlin, "Federal Relations," pp. 131–36, 153–55.

Deal" for schools. He lashed out at the "innovative education," arguing that students were being taught harmonica playing, fancy lariat throwing, and boondoggling while schools and qualified teachers were becoming "the untouchables of the present depression." He argued that loyalty to the New Deal had become more important than professional expertise. He quoted William Carr, the NEA research director, as estimating that depression-ridden schools needed $500 million in order to save the programs that had been struck down by retrenchment. Givens pointed out that Roosevelt's policy of relief would never adequately meet these needs.[38]

Although the article was a departure from NEA-style politics, for Givens it was the only appropriate response to a president who seemed to have no appreciation for the problems of public education. Givens's intemperate remarks signaled a new era in educational policy when the NEA could no longer claim, as it had, close contact with the president. Old allies like the Chamber of Commerce and the American Legion seemed less reliable, while the AFL waited to find out what the AFT line would be. Nevertheless, the NEA still led the fight for federal aid. In 1937, without regard to shifting alliances, the association wrote its own bill to present to Congress, a bill that promised to answer the desperate needs of educators nationwide.[39]

The bill was introduced on 9 February 1937 by Senator Pat Harrison of Mississippi, who wrote it with Senator Hugo Black of Alabama, chair of the Senate Committee on Labor and Education, and Representative Brooks Fletcher of Ohio. All were Democrats. Compared with NEA estimates of the needs of education, it was a relatively modest proposal, providing $100 million in federal aid in the first year and $300 million after five years. Each state would receive a flat grant based on the population of schoolchildren. As the bill was written it answered none of the problems of equity and invited three long months of negotiations.[40]

Congress had been relatively sympathetic to an appropriations bill in 1934, and members of Congress who had served during the Smith-Towner years remained on record in support of federal aid to education. Four important lobbying groups had to unite behind a single bill, however, before Democrats would support a measure in the face of the president's opposition. The groups were the NAACP, which was becoming more important in its lobbying efforts; the AFL, which was very powerful; the Catholic lobby, which had a conservative and liberal wing; and finally the teacher-advocacy groups including the AFT and the NEA.

The NAACP had opposed segregated schools ever since its founding in

38. Zook, "Federal Aid to Education"; *NEA Proceedings,* 1934, pp. 37–43; Willard E. Givens, "New Deal a Raw Deal for Public Schools," *NEA Journal,* 24 (September 1935), p. 198.

39. Gilbert E. Smith, *The Limits of Reform: Politics and Federal Aid to Education, 1937–1950* (New York, 1982), pp. 40–47.

40. Ibid., pp. 56–65; William Givens, "The Harrison-Black-Fletcher Bill," *NEA Journal,* 26 (May 1937), p. 133.

1909, but black schools had suffered so badly in the depression that in 1935 its executive board urged branches to focus on securing equal rights and accommodations in areas where segregation seemed immovable. Catholic organizations underwent a similar change in response to depression conditions, albeit over different issues. Long opposed to federal aid to education, Catholic representatives argued it amount to a double tax on parents who paid tuition fees as well as school taxes and would support a predominantly secular, if not Protestant, form of education. But the National Catholic Welfare Council, founded in 1919, warmed to the overtures of the Roosevelt administration as Catholics took prominent positions in the New Deal. When the NYA applied its programs to both public and parochial schools in 1935, it seemed inevitable that Catholic lobbyists would ease their opposition to federal funding.[41]

The situation for the education groups was far more complicated. The AFT had been in the forefront of the vocational education movement and had the full support of the AFL in 1917, but relations between the AFT and the AFL worsened in the twenties when the NEA with its new base in Washington took the reins of leadership. As previously noted, the NEA's struggle for a secretary of education, gained the full support of Matthew Woll, head of the AFL education committee, despite the AFT's considered opposition to the proposal. NEA leaders looked at the AFT as one of their least important allies on Capitol Hill. In 1935, however, the situation was different. The AFL paid greater heed to its teachers' union affiliate, not out of a suddenly enhanced respect but out of concern that the AFT might secede and join the newly formed Congress of Industrial Organizations (CIO). As for the NEA, estranged from the Roosevelt administration, it was quick to see the advantages of working with the AFT in support of an education bill.

Race and Coalition Politics

The AFT legislative lobbyist, Mary Grossman, and AFT vice-president Doxey Wilkerson were determined to make a successful attempt at revising and pushing a compromise bill. They had to convince the NAACP and other minority groups to support it, and they had to get southern members of Congress to pledge money to black schoolchildren. The problem of educational inequality was intimately bound to the institution of segregation, which prevailed in schools, unions, and educational associations. New Dealers, provoked by the incessant lobbying of educators, were quick to point to shortcomings in this regard. The alliance between the NEA and Senator Harrison, a strong opponent of antilynching legislation, would

41. Smith, *Limits of Reform,* pp. 20–26.

hardly suggest an educational establishment poised to battle the problems of educational inequality.[42]

With its state-by-state association structure, the NEA had many state affiliates that simply refused to admit black members, although they could join the national organization. Most active black educators in the South preferred to join the very small American Association of Colored Teachers (AACT), which was quite independent of the NEA. Organized by prominent black educators from Tuskegee and Hampton Institute, the AACT approached the NEA in 1926 for formal affiliation but was welcomed only to confer on issues regarding Southern black education. In 1933 there were some signs that the AACT sought more national recognition, but the NEA was still slow and unresponsive to the overtures of black teachers. In the late thirties and again in the early forties, William Givens proposed a confidential report on merger of the two organizations, but this preliminary investigation produced futile discussions that led nowhere. Unable to face the challenge of integrating black educators into the structure of the organization, the NEA proved incapable of compromising its legislative proposals to include the wishes of educators outside the NEA. In the course of insisting that the NEA had black support for the 1937 legislative bill, one black educator from Virginia testified against proportional distribution and for the NEA proposal, but it was discovered by the black press that his boss was Sidney B. Hall, chair of the NEA legislative commission.[43]

In 1937 the AFT, after years of relative invisibility on national legislation, found itself in a pivotal position to help black educators persuade the NEA to compromise. The AFT had admitted segregated locals, but most of its locals were integrated. As the depression deepened and federal funds reached rural black educators through the WPA, new AFT locals formed that brought in new black teachers. The AFT gained black members in urban areas as well, so that by the midthirties the AFT was careful to choose its convention sites so as to avoid incidents of discrimination. At one session the entire convention was moved from one hotel to another; at another the hotel was asked to apologize for incidents of discrimination; and at another a hotel worker was called forth to apologize for behavior incommensurate with the ideals of the union and taken as an insult by the body.[44]

These rather dramatic events failed to move the union to insist that its locals integrate immediately, nor did they carry the school-segregation issue back into the classroom. But they were important formative steps in chang-

42. Mary Grossman, "Legislative Report, 1937," Mary Grossman Papers, Urban History Archives, Temple University, Philadelphia; *AFT Proceedings,* 1937, AFT Collection Series 13, Box 22.

43. Allan M. West, *The NEA: The Power Base for Education* (Washington, D.C., 1980); Ronald Lloyd Dewing, "Organizations and Desegregation, 1954–64" (Ph.D. diss., Ball State University, 1967).

44. Smith, *Limits of Reform,* pp. 52–55; Mary Grossman Papers.

ing social practices that few other organizations would challenge at the time. The AFT quickly began to promote black members to leadership positions in the union, especially as regional vice presidents. Best known was Doxey Wilkerson, a professor at Howard University, whose studies on the problems of black education had broken new ground and exposed the economic and political realities of educational reform. In 1937 Layle Lane, another prominent black teacher in the union, devoted a sabbatical leave to organizing black teachers in the South for the union. Perhaps fifteen years of gadfly existence had better prepared the AFT to take the first steps toward integration. The low average annual wage of black teachers in the depression provided more economic reasons why the union, more than the association, could more gracefully bend to the winds of change. These changes brought the AFT closer to the NAACP, but it was the AFT's enhanced relationship with the AFL that brought the NEA around on the equalization issue.[45]

Membership in the AFT grew rapidly in the early thirties because of the influx of WPA teachers who brought with them militancy and a strong identification with workers generally. There were thirty-six thousand WPA teachers, many of whom were regularly trained professionals thrown out of work because of the depression. The policies of Roosevelt and Hopkins required that a teacher seek relief before applying to the WPA for work. Many of these teachers worked in adult-education courses and felt a great mission in the literacy work they accomplished in cities among the unemployed poor and in the country among destitute sharecropper families. Others worked for unions as worker-education personnel and were responsible for gathering and teaching the history of labor unions and the struggle for labor recognition. These new recruits in the AFT were militant enough to strike in several instances, provoking Roosevelt's famous interdiction against striking public employees in 1937. The AFT, for its part, welcomed the WPA workers' militant spirit. The AFT's new lobbyist, Mary Foley Grossman, was able to mobilize these and other teachers to pressure public officials. Her work was enhanced by the split in the AFL and the rise of the CIO, with both federations courting the teachers' union. In the temporary thaw in AFT/AFL relations, Grossman, who was associated with the AFT's left wing but was widely respected as a lobbyist, was able to command some support for AFT issues in making legislative policy.[46]

The Defeat of Federal Aid

Despite the strength of the coalition pushing for the Harrison-Fletcher bill, President Roosevelt's opposition could not be overcome. On 19 April 1937 Roosevelt met with congressional leaders to outline his plans to cut relief programs, pointedly asking that Congress avoid passing programs with large

45. James Earl Clard, "The AFT: Origins and History, 1870–1952" (Ph.D. diss., Cornell University, 1966), pp. 60–67.
46. Mary Grossman Papers.

appropriations. Harrison did not immediately capitulate, but the president again pressed the issue in remarks to reporters the following day. He finally closed the issue by announcing his creation of a new Educational Advisory Committee, headed by Floyd Reeves of the University of Chicago. Roosevelt's negative signals toward the Harrison-Fletcher bill, combined with the confusions caused by the appearance of his new committee, meant that the legislation was temporarily halted.[47]

Roosevelt's new advisory committee proved controversial enough to split the momentary unity in education. The NEA would continue to see the Catholic lobby and southern Congressman as their chief obstacles and ignore the importance of alliance building. Perhaps the most enduring contribution of the committee came in the form of a series of studies on black youth produced in part by Doxey Wilkerson. On the whole, however, the committee's report left the coalition of educators divided and made future cooperation at best difficult.[48]

The fragility of the 1937 coalition cannot be exaggerated. Given the historical divisions between Protestants and Catholics, blacks and whites, northern liberals and southern conservatives, it was a remarkable moment of cooperation. The tragedy was that Roosevelt was too tied up in his own Court-packing war to appreciate the significance of this accomplishment. By 1941 all semblance of cooperation between the NEA and the AFT ended as new legislation raised the issue of religion which would stymie any discussion of funds for the duration of the war. The NEA remained firmly against what was considered the "Catholic oligarchy," while the AFT fought to allow some discretion on disbursement of funds, especially in urban areas where parochial schools carried the burdens of education as partners with public institutions. Federal funds for education served specific wartime purposes on an emergency basis, which was quite in keeping with Roosevelt's policy.

The depression changed both the AFT and the NEA in fundamental ways. For the NEA it was a time of disillusionment, for the formulas derived from the experience of World War I proved inadequate in the face of economic collapse; for the AFT it was a time of exhilarating growth accompanied by overwhelming dissension internally. Both organizations, however, refashioned a policy that they thought would bring educational issues to national attention and gain the same support and recognition that the New Deal administrators seemed to be lavishing on other victims of the depression. In 1954 the realization finally sank in that education would never become a national priority but rather would remain at the mercy of tax revolters and an often parsimonious public. The days of glory and growth were over.

47. William Edward Eaton, *The American Federation of Teachers, 1916–1961: A History of the Movement* (Carbondale, Ill., 1975), pp. 192–215; Smith, *Limits of Reform,* pp. 64–65.

48. Smith, *Limits of Reform,* pp. 68–72; Tyack, Lowe, and Howe, *Hard Times,* p. 102; Advisory Committee on Education, *Report of the Committee* (Washington, D.C., 1938).

Chapter Eight

Warfare in the AFT

The effects of the depression on the AFT had been immediate and dramatic. The sudden falloff in dues from the Chicago locals and other hard-hit areas had noticeably impoverished the union. The national office was in Chicago, a city hit hard by unemployment, and when other local unions stopped paying rent in the AFT office, the secretary-treasurer, Florence Hanson, announced that the union had no money to pay for the 1932 convention. By trimming the expenses of outside speakers, locating free housing for visiting teachers, finding rent-free halls for speakers, and cutting back on the travel expenses for Executive Council members, Hanson was able to host the 1932 convention and keep the union functioning. Holding the national conventions in Chicago in the early thirties exposed teachers from all parts of the country to the impoverishing effects for teachers of the "payless paydays" in the city. At the same time the union experienced a surge of growth that began slowly in 1931 and 1932 and picked up pace until middecade, when some locals were doubling their membership. In 1934 the union had 7,500 members; by 1940 it had 32,000.[1]

It was an exciting time in the union. The listless sense of marginality lifted as the economic crisis hit teachers. New members joined and organized in new patterns, promoted new ideas, and expanded on the old Progressive program. They were impatient with tired arguments between men's and women's locals, between New York socialists and Chicago conservatives, between one faction of women and another. This new blood revitalized the movement at the same time that it brought new lines of cleavage.

Most histories of the union at this stage focus on the rise to prominence of a small fraction of Communist party teachers whose presence on the Executive Council of the national brought about complete censure by the AFL,

1. AFT membership rolls, part of the AFT Collection.

near reaffiliation with the CIO, and a final bloody battle in which the union ousted three of its largest locals to rid itself of Communist "domination." The civil war within the union was profoundly ideological. What these interpretations miss is that the sound and fury reflected a deep division over the definition of unionism for public school teachers. The time had come for the union to decide if it was indeed a trade union or a pale professional reflection of the NEA. Old-timers in the union had uncomfortably clung to professionalism in asserting the meaning of teacher autonomy, while the younger generation cared little for the promised rewards of professionalism in a time of few jobs, little money, and the threat of no future. Over the course of the thirties the teachers' union gained a sense of definition, a place in the labor movement, and a firm grasp of the importance of trade unionism to their particular job.[2]

The depression decade was also one of the most personally costly journeys for union teachers in the AFT's history. In the old union convention delegates not only knew one another but they knew the school districts, the local and regional problems, and the particular foibles of the other delegates. All that changed rather suddenly. Old-timers gave dramatic retirement speeches at conventions, announcing that they knew they would never again be elected to attend the convention because a new faction was gaining control of the local they had founded. Late-night meetings, secret caucuses, and tricky parliamentary maneuvers replaced the old familiar letter-writing campaigns. It is important to keep in mind that the battle in the union ran from the locals, especially Local 5 in New York City, to the national level. In New York the old guard meant Henry Linville, his longtime friend Abraham Lefkowitz, and the younger Jacob Jablonower.

The substance of the dispute was ideological, but its language, impersonal style, and often brutal, always bitter, form of engagement grew out of an intense generational conflict.

Perhaps the most interesting aspect of the ideological and generational confrontations was that the former battles over gender receded in importance. Without disappearing, gender issues were marginalized by new divisions. Contradictions among the membership along these fissures meant that women could integrate themselves more readily into the debates, but the

2. Several books contain parts of the story of the AFT in this period. Robert W. Iverson, *The Communists and the Schools* (New York, 1959) is perhaps the most comprehensive, although it was part of a series on subversion, not on the teachers' union itself. There are two dissertations on the subject: William Edward Eaton, "The Social and Educational Position of the AFT, 1929–1941" (Ph.D. diss., Washington University, 1971), is perhaps the best (it was published in 1975 by Southern Illinois University Press); and C. W. Miller, "Democracy in Education: A Study of How the AFT Met the Threat of Communist Subversion through the Democratic Process" (Ed.D. diss., Northwestern University, 1967). See also Celia Zitron, *New York City Teachers Union, 1916–1964: A Story of Educational and Social Commitment* (New York, 1969); and William W. Wattenberg, *On the Educational Front: The Reactions of Teachers Associations in New York and Chicago* (New York, 1936).

styles of the debates were still masculine. The ability to shout down an opponent, out-maneuver a chair, or simply stay latest at the meetings divided the men and women on purely practical grounds.

The Generation Gap in the New York Union

The generational conflict affected questions such as whether to admit WPA teachers, how to handle school finance, what aspects of the union's program to protect, and how broadly or narrowly progressive issues were conceived. It was also and most profoundly a question of style. New men and women entered the union as teachers who had waited much longer than older members to get teaching jobs. They had not been hired in the regular, long-accepted pattern. Most had spent time unemployed on the eligibility lists and then moved to substitute lists and then to permanent substitute status. Others had found teaching jobs but their schools were suddenly closed; they were unemployed and on charity when the WPA came in and started giving them paychecks.

These teachers were better educated because many had marked time in graduate school, waiting for a job. They were young but their experiences had been hard, disappointing, and often bitter. Old debates between municipal reformers, mild-mannered socialists, and AFL conservatives seemed senseless and silly to them. They would embrace Marxism in a variety of forms: communism, Trotskyism, and left socialism. The young radicals were fond of reminding the old guard that they were over the hill. In one tense moment the twenty-eight-year-old Isidore Begin told the union that Henry Linville's radical days were long behind him. "I will grant you that in 1917 and 1918 Dr. Lefkowitz was a dangerous agitator and Dr. Linville was a red Bolshevik. I will grant you that, . . . but that was twenty years ago. . . . It is not impolite to suggest that life goes right on and sometimes leaves people behind."[3]

John Dewey was appointed by Linville and Lefkowitz to investigate the left-wing presence in the union; in his report to the union he turned to the generational problem: "There is a certain amount of cleavage between older and young teachers, the former feeling that they have the wisdom of maturity and the latter feeling that age tends to become conservative and that youth brings in new vigor and fresh blood for more energetic and vital activity."[4] Dewey could not resist reprimanding Isidore Begin, his old student and a

3. Proceedings of the 29 April 1933 meeting of Local 5, New York City, pp. 17–41, in the Teachers' Union Collection, Series 5051, Cornell Labor School Archives, Cornell University, Ithaca, New York. See also the collection of the Teachers' Guild, unprocessed files, Robert Wagner Archives, New York University.

4. "Report of the Dewey Committee," p. 1, Guild Collection (unprocessed files), Robert Wagner Archives, New York University.

leading spokesman for the young radicals: "I have no desire to add to any of the personal element in the situation but I do regret that I was not more successful with my pupil." The admonition was too tempting for the fiery Begin to resist. He told the union audience that he too was disappointed that the professor who had taught him about liberalism had failed to live up to his classroom ideals. "It is with great regret that I see a former teacher of mine, who taught me about democracy in education and liberalism, signing this report." The generational animus kept pace with the ideological disputes.[5]

The old guard, or "the administration" as younger members called Linville and Lefkowitz, were chiefly concerned with protecting professional prerogatives, especially the established certification program. As noted in the last chapter, New York City was only hiring substitute teachers and paying them little more than half the salary of regular teachers. Substitutes were hired casually without reference checks and without having to take the standard examinations. In some of the larger high schools, substitutes made up more than half of the teaching force. How should the union deal with them? Linville and Lefkowitz argued with city and state officials that only properly credentialed teachers should be employed. Younger activists, however, wanted substitute teachers to be declared permanent substitutes with all the rights to sick leave, pensions, and retirement that regular teachers had. They also wanted the substitute teachers in the union as regular voting members, a practice that had been avoided in most local unions. The issue of substitute teachers became a constant wrangle until the "administration" finally relented and tried to distinguish between permanent substitute teachers and casual substitutes, a practice that opened the door for legislative change. Substitute teachers came into the union and chose factions, usually opposed to the old guard.[6]

There was a similar divergence over WPA teachers, who were mostly young teachers with little experience in the system. WPA teachers were largely adult-education teachers, although some taught kindergarten and special education. According to Harry Hopkins these teachers were not expected to teach classes in the regular school curriculum, but distinguishing between classes was difficult. Like substitute teachers, WPA teachers were not subject to certification requirements. Linville and Lefkowitz tried in vain to have the WPA put under the administrative control of the city's Board of Examiners. They were loathe to allow the new teachers into their union, but again younger members pointed out that WPA teachers were often unemployed teachers on the school eligibility list. Soon both Linville and Lefkowitz were urging school administrators to hire eligibility-list teachers, and by

5. Proceedings of the 29 April 1933 meeting, Teachers' Union Collection, Series 5051.

6. Daniel Paul Higgins, Commissioner, Board of Education, "Report on Substitute Teachers," New York City Board of Education, Millbank Library, Special Collections, Columbia University; also Minutes of Local 5, September 1934, Teachers' Union Collection, Series 5051; Oral History of Jacob Jablonower, Walter Reuther Archives, Detroit.

that argument they opened the doors of the union again to a young and militant constituency. WPA teachers swelled the union's ranks with young people who, like the substitute teachers, mostly opposed the leadership of the "administration."[7]

Although both Linville and Lefkowitz won office by a sizable majority, the newer generation was soon running for office and gaining a foothold on the union's executive board. Exasperated by bitter arguments, wrangling over leadership and policy questions, and long meetings, Lefkowitz proposed in 1934 that the union not accept any new members. The desire to hold off growth at a moment when teachers were joining in record numbers appeared to the young and ambitious new members a foolish and self-destructive policy. To the older members it was a precaution. In the old days membership growth was slow; prospective members were nominated by insiders, and individual cases were discussed: where did the teacher teach, was he/she permanent or temporary, what kind of certificate did he/she hold? In the early thirties there were thirty to forty new members per meeting, and it became impossibly time-consuming to check each one. Lefkowitz and Linville argued that they had to maintain professional standards; the young left accused them of foot-dragging.[8]

Younger teachers also maintained that the economic situation called for reforms in teaching methods. Rejecting the division between the community and professional, an idea that the young Columbia Teachers College professor George Counts was developing, the new generation found that more and more working-class children attended high schools looking for an education that addressed their job needs. The high schools were either teaching redundant skills in areas where students knew there were no jobs or college preparatory courses.

Few cities had had community colleges or junior colleges, and in the depression these rare programs were discontinued as "luxury" items in city school budgets. The children of the depression, characterized by hopelessness and anxiety, evoked sympathy among younger teachers whose own recent experiences in the job market had proved disappointing. Progressive education as embraced by the prewar generation contained the liberal promise of social mobility and progress. For these younger teachers, however, it was difficult to embrace fully John Dewey's Progressive Era optimism. Instead, they added to Dewey's educational idealism a Marxist class analysis, which they learned at the unemployment rallies, study groups, and parties sponsored by the Communist party. The focus of the new teacher in the thirties was the community and the teacher as an empowering agent,

7. Adult Education, Board of Education Archives, Millbank Library, Columbia University; "Minutes," Teachers' Guild Collection (unprocessed files), Robert Wagner Archives, New York University.

8. Minutes of Local 5, Teachers' Union Collection, Series 5051; see also Henry Linville, "Communists at Work," mimeographed, Henry Linville Collection, Boxes 1, 14.

bringing to the masses, including students and parents, class analysis of education which rejected the potentially elitist characteristic of professionalism.

With the enthusiasm of beginners, the new teachers sought solutions in the union and were often rebuffed by what seemed to them the narrow trade union interests of the old guard or the "administration." Communist teachers, who long stood on the fringes of the union, recognized an organizing potential. Originally the Communist party viewed students as the primary target for organization and saw the professional goals of the union as largely irrelevant to the class struggle. The influx of new recruits and new unionists promised a change in party policy and, in part because of the changes in the trade union movement generally during the Roosevelt years, the party began to view the teachers' union as an important aspect of its program.

The generational split also affected questions of what concessions to make to budget-conscious school authorities. Old-guard teachers had fought hard for pensions, tenure laws, and professional standards, and they were ready to fight to keep them. To the younger teachers the overriding issues were salary and the number of jobs. The two groups seemed to be speaking different languages.[9]

The Radical Attraction of the AFT

The AFT was attractive to young idealists precisely because of its old gadfly reputation and its positions on a broad range of social issues. The issues were changing but the union had already built a foundation for furthering social justice. For example, the union had opposed an Office of Education bill because it had provisions for military training in the schools. The union affiliated with international peace groups and sent regular delegates to international conferences concerned with disarmament and world peace. To many it seemed a small step from the old union program to the new radicalism of the depression era. Some of the old-old guard even welcomed these newcomers for their spirit and fight. Mary Barker, at her last convention, took a brave stand in favor of a resolution defending the Scottsboro boys. Margaret Haley, who was slowly dying of heart disease, expressed her approval of the young Communists. "Class consciousness is what we missed in our organizing work," she concluded.[10]

Although the voice of youth may have seemed sweet and daring to Margaret Haley in Chicago and Mary Barker in Atlanta, it was a deafening roar in the ears of Linville and Lefkowitz. The old guard had grown ac-

---

9. Linville, "Communists at Work," pp. 266–68.

10. Margaret Haley's autobiography; Mary Barker to Florence Hanson, 23 May 1934, Correspondence of the Financial Secretary, AFT Collection.

customed to reporting legislative victories and bargaining gains at general membership meetings, but young members wanted mass demonstrations, mass rallies, and open-air meetings to dramatize, publicize, and mobilize for further action. One mass demonstration called at City Hall was disrupted when Linville and Lefkowitz came out of the mayor's office to announce cuts that the Board of Education was imposing on teachers. Instead of denouncing the city for the 8.3 percent pay cut proposed by the mayor, the crowd turned on Linville and Lefkowitz and blamed them for participating in a sellout.[11]

The same issue arose in Chicago, but the factionalism there was much more blatantly a generational issue and not ideological. Young John Fewkes had organized an extra-union organization consisting of teachers from various unions, and he had promoted parades in the downtown Loop area. Fewkes's Volunteer Emergency Committee drew several thousand teachers to dramatize the city's payless paydays. Fewkes lost badly when he ran for office in the Chicago Men's High School Local at the time of the parades, but his presence was felt by the old guard; for all of their distaste for his tactics, he was a man who commanded thousands of teachers. Older men in the local—Charles Stillman, Freeland Stecker, and James Meade—met with city officials to discuss pay and had the unhappy job of reporting the bad news to the teachers. Their dull-sounding reports culminated in the depressing news that teachers would not get paid; Fewkes had few concrete answers, but, Margaret Haley reported, he could lead a parade in evangelical prayer and arouse members' hatred toward the banking interests that held all the cards. He appealed to the younger teachers whose anger could not be assuaged by Charles Stillman's reasoned pronouncements.[12]

Key Players in the Left Revolt

The generational split was complicated by the fact that the new left-wingers were not all of a piece. At the time that Linville was first noticing the presence of Communists in his local in 1927, the American Communist party was undergoing an upheaval in which two separate factions in the leadership would be expelled. James P. Cannon and other followers of the purged Soviet leader Leon Trotsky were expelled in 1928. Six months later the party expelled its former national leader Jay Lovestone, whose influence in New York was potent. Linville and Lefkowitz then faced not one group of "reds" but four: the regular Communist party faction; the Lovestonite faction, which was led in the union by its major theorist, Bertram Wolfe; the Trots-

11. Guild Papers, unprocessed files, Robert Wagner Archives, New York University; Teachers' Union Collection, Series 5051.
12. CTF Collection, Box 67.

kyites, who were only a handful in the early thirties but led a militant attack on the Communists in 1937 and again after Trotsky's murder in 1940; and the Musteites, a left-socialist grouping led by A. J. Muste, an ex-minister. Not knowing who was in which faction or even understanding that the factions were bitter enemies, Linville and Lefkowitz pitted their mild-mannered municipal socialism against sophisticated Marxist arguments and often lost. What was more disturbing was that often the response to the Communist party line by other factions was to bid up the level of militancy and thereby increase the pressure on the "administration." The Communist party had its own Rank and File Caucus, which included Williana Burroughs, Isidore Begin, and, much later, Bella Dodd and Dale Zysman. A Lovestonite faction split off from the Communist faction and included Bertrand Wolfe and Simon Beagle. Other groups amalgamated into the Progressive Caucus. Each faction organized an unemployed teachers group, each faction demanded more militancy for teachers, and each faction denounced the others at meetings.[13]

Although these factions caused a certain disruption in the union, they were responsible for some positive changes as well. They brought in new energy, new militancy, and a broadened social consciousness. The Communist party, indifferent to the largely professional goals of the teachers' union leadership, was most active in pursuing alliances with parent and community groups. Projects in Bedford-Stuyvesant and Harlem were particularly successful. In 1935 the Communist party successfully launched the Harlem Committee for Better Schools, a coalition of parents' associations, churches, community groups, and teacher-union members. The committee had access to the mayor's office through the Reverend John W. Robinson of the Mayor's Commission on Conditions in Harlem and began to agitate for better schools independently of Local 5. The committee succeeded in getting two new schools built in Harlem in 1938, a remarkable achievement at that time. In Chicago, by way of contrast, angry black students in the Lilydale community burned the temporary buildings they attended when more peaceful protests were ignored.[14]

Left-wing teacher-union activists were also concerned with the content of educational materials in the schools and accomplished a great deal in broadening the narrowly racist curriculum of the time. Communist party teachers worked with the Committee on Better Schools in Harlem to remove racist books from the schools. Alice Citron was a pioneer in this work, writing plays dramatizing themes in black history, compiling bibliographies on black history, and agitating for the celebration of Negro History Week in the schools. Langston Hughes, Richard Wright, and others worked closely with

13. Harvey Klehr, *The Heyday of American Communism: The Depression Decade* (New York, 1984), pp. 15–21; interview with Simon Beagle, summer 1974.
14. Mark Naison, *Communists in Harlem during the Depression* (New York, 1983), pp. 214–16; Michael W. Homel, *Down from Equality: Black Chicagoans and the Public Schools, 1920–1941* (Urbana, Ill., 1984), pp. 65–78.

teacher-union activists in providing material and speakers for the project. In the Bedford-Stuyvesant community a similar project pushed for reduction of class size, better school buildings, and an end to the system of permanent substitutes.[15]

Teachers in both projects expressed frustration with the union leadership, which seemed to focus on the city's most elite high schools. They were sympathetic to black and ethnic frustrations over declining educational services, many of them having experienced ethnic harrassment in their own educational history. Allying with black teachers, they impressed community workers with their dedication to the children and the community. Frustrated with the slowness of Henry Linville's leadership, the activist teachers thought nothing of creating their own union within the union and conducting separate negotiations on affairs for their community. With the teachers' union in their control, after 1935, teachers in both projects were able to welcome in WPA teachers, whose community projects in adult education enhanced the two community projects. "When Henry Linville left," Mildred Flacks, a Bedford-Stuyvesant teacher recalled, "we had our own union."[16]

Although Communist party teachers would remain active in school and community affairs until the fifties, the investigation of teachers by the Rapp-Coudert Committee in 1940, the 1940–41 crisis in the AFT, and finally the Communist party's growing preoccupation with foreign affairs in the forties weakened its community alliance. The demise of the WPA further weakened the union's base in the community. The perspective of community organizing never died for a few dedicated teachers who maintained their contacts until they were kicked out of teaching in the fifties. As one community member recalled, "Most of the teachers who they said were Communists and kicked out of the school system were much more dedicated to teaching black children the way out of the crucible of American life than the teachers we now have. When they left, Harlem became a worse place. They stayed after school with the children and gave them extra curricular attention to bring them up to level. You didn't have these reading problems like you have today. These people were dedicated to their craft." Seeking an alternative vision in the direction of teacher unionism, these teachers revived the original vision of unionism as Jennie McKeon saw it. They ignored, however, the powerful influence of professionalism in this vision.[17]

The negative side was that the policy of the Communist party often had nothing to do with the welfare of teachers or of the AFT but rather with the

15. Klehr, *Heyday of American Communism*, pp. 238–51; leaflet by the Rank and File Caucus, January 1934, 9 April and 14 June 1934, in the Teachers' Union Collection, Series 5051. See also minutes of Local 5 meeting, 23 April 1934, and leaflets in the Teachers' Union Collection, 74/4A, Series 5051; Linville "Communists at Work," pp. 259–75 (pages variously renumbered); Naison, *Communists in Harlem*, pp. 214–17.

16. Interview with Mildred and David Flacks, summer 1988; "Undemocratic Rulings and Restrictive Regulations," Teachers' Union Collection, 74/4a, Series 5051.

17. Naison, *Communists in Harlem*, p. 216; Zitron, *New York City Teachers Union*.

working class as the Communist party leadership saw it. For example, in 1936, when a great many teacher unionists wanted to join the CIO, the party opposed the idea because the leadership felt the party needed a foot in the door of the AFL, and the AFT would be that entree.

In fact the real issue for teachers in the controversy between the CIO and the AFL was the question of local support. For years, citywide federations, or labor councils, provided teachers' unions with support in both legislative and school-board matters. Often a well-placed labor representative on the board of education could save teachers' jobs and protect their rights. CIO councils were too new and too weak to provide such protection. Nevertheless, the energy of the CIO and its vocal support of teacher unionism was certainly an attractive alternative to the bitter past of union affiliation. None of these considerations entered into the Communist party formulation of the problem, for the party wanted an overall strategy for workers and tended, like William Green, to dismiss teacher needs lightly. Such calculations ignored the welfare of the teachers as workers.[18]

From Local 5 to the National

In the fall of 1932 Linville, Lefkowitz, and Jablonower appointed a commission headed by Linville's friend John Dewey to assess the causes of, and cure for, factionalism within the union. Dewey offered his report at a raucous meeting in April 1933 at which he tangled with his young former student Isidore Begin. Linville had two objectives for this meeting. He wanted Begin and Bertram Wolfe out of the union, and he wanted a delegate assembly, a representative body of teachers instead of the freewheeling bring-out-the-vote-and-pack-the-meeting style he was currently directing. The meeting was an intense affair with a two-hour wrangle over the agenda. Begin, whom Jablonower described as "a very dynamic person, a very able speaker and one very quick to see the vulnerable points in the position that you took or the course you espoused," and Wolfe, whom Jablonower called "a man who is as well read as anyone I've ever met, a man who has achieved high standing as a writer and a scholar," took to the floor to defend themselves and the militant tactics they espoused. Linville said at the time that he was glad Dewey was there because he knew the young militants had angered the philosopher as much as they had exasperated the union president. But despite their years of trade-union experience, Lefkowitz and Linville were no match for the young Communists. After the union voted for the suspen-

18. Proceedings of 29 April 1933, Teachers' Union Collection, 74/12, Series 5051; Celia Lewis and William J. McCoy, "Shall We Affiliate with the CIO—A Forum for Union Members," *American Teacher*, 22 (September–October 1937), pp. 12–14; responses in *American Teacher*, 22 (November–December 1937), p. 12; 22 (January–February 1938), pp. 14–15; 22 (March–April 1938), pp. 26–27; 22 (May–June 1938), pp. 24–28.

sions, Linville wanted to call the question of the delegate assembly, but the Communists quickly fielded a motion to adjourn, which the confused Lefkowitz seconded. A motion to adjourn always takes precedence over ordinary business. The angry Linville then called the delegate-assembly question, and of course there was great confusion about which motion had been called, but Linville went ahead and declared that the delegate-assembly motion had passed despite the fact that some unionists thought the meeting had adjourned. Calls of "point of order!" ended the stenographic report on this chapter in the union's history.[19]

Never before had Henry Linville sacrificed democratic procedure to gain a programmatic change, but this time he seemed to have moved beyond reason. Years later when the national union ousted the young, radical leadership, similar breaches in union democracy were committed for the sake of what was thought to be the best interest of the union. Linville was a changed man as a result of the fight against communism in his union. In his mind, it became the most important aspect of his union career, completely overshadowing his earlier radical dreams expressed in the *American Teacher*. In the next year, when the factionalism continued and when he lost the presidency of the AFT to new leadership, he became convinced that the only way to rid his local of his enemies was to call on the national to oust the Communists.[20]

Politics in the national organization had changed so rapidly in the early thirties that when Linville called for help from the national his only wholehearted ally was Selma Borchardt, the AFT's lobbyist in Washington, who was regarded within the union as ineffective. Florence Hanson was strongly opposed to any efforts to purge the left within the union and was a factional opponent of Linville and Borchardt. Younger women in Chicago like Mary Herrick were not impressed with Borchardt's record and remained distant from Linville. These relationships would greatly retard the opposition to the radical faction in years to come.[21]

Hanson was ill and tired, but she was moving further to the left in her last years. Having taught in Chicago and come to leadership in the feminist and somewhat socialist women high school teachers' local, Hanson wanted to reshape the union into a progressive force that would attract young, idealistic socialists to the movement to reenergize it. She recruited University of Chicago socialist Mayard Krueger and through his influence was able to organize a number of active socialist unions in the Ohio Valley region. These young leaders seemed to put new energy into the old municipal socialist

19. Linville, "Communists at Work," pp. 260–75; "Minutes, April 19 Meeting," Guild Papers (unprocessed files), Robert Wagner Archives, New York University.

20. Henry R. Linville to Selma Borchardt, 30 October 1939, and Selma Borchardt to Henry R. Linville, 16 November 1939, Borchardt Collection, 125/9, Walter Reuther Archives, Detroit (see also various letters in Box 88).

21. *AFT Proceedings*, 1933, AFT Collection, Series 13 7/2, pp. 98–108.

ideas of the early federation movement. Raymond Lowry of Toledo was the chief proponent of this new unionism and explained his strategy for success-fully organizing several thousand Ohio teachers in one year. "We thought that perhaps making a quiet program of search into the tax books might help a bit to let them know who in the city of Toledo paid their taxes," the young Lowry explained to the 1934 convention. He found that the poorer families had paid up, but it was the wealthy and corporate "tax owners" who were holding out 13.5 million dollars in unpaid taxes. The Toledo local broadcast this information on a friendly radio station and in editorials and found that in the first week seven hundred thousand dollars in delinquent taxes were turned in at the county courthouse. Lowry's story captivated the convention as did the story of the rural Arkansas teachers who said they had been inspired to unionize when they saw that their schools were closed while firehouses remained open because the firemen had a union. Linville and Borchardt very much resented Hanson's new recruits to the union, but they could not stem the tide of enthusiasm that carried Lowry into office as the next union president.[22]

With Hanson about to retire, Linville attended the 1935 convention with the firm intention of getting the Executive Council and the convention to oust the Communists from his local. He might have succeeded except that before Lowry brought up the question he read a telegram from AFL president William Green that urged the convention to act immediately to oust the Communists from New York's Local 5.[23] A rumor spread that the AFL would revoke the AFT's charter unless the convention voted to expel the Communists. Green's intervention, however, had the opposite effect. The old union dug in its heels and refused to accommodate labor's chief. Linville was beside himself in fury and stalked out of the convention hall with the Chicago, Washington, and Seattle locals in tow.[24] Linville immediately began planning a mass resignation of officers of Local 5 and the creation of a totally unaffiliated organization, the New York City Teachers' Guild.[25]

The Radicalization of the AFT

Discussion of the CIO and its meaning for labor, especially for the American Federation of Teachers, encouraged more progressive teachers to seek out the union and build its organization. The 1936 convention brought a

22. *AFT Proceedings,* 1935, AFT Collection, Series 13 8/1, pp. 213–48.
23. Ibid., p. 535.
24. Papers of the New York Teachers Guild (unprocessed files), Robert Wagner Archives, New York University; see also the correspondence between Linville and Borchardt in the same collection.
25. "Report on the 1936 AFL Convention," Mary Grossman Papers, Urban History Archives, Temple University Philadelphia; Guild Papers (unprocessed files), Robert Wagner Archives, New York University.

whole new contingent of WPA teachers, who participated actively in the convention and brought new leaders into the Executive Council. These teachers were excited about CIO-style industrial unionism and pressed the convention to investigate the possibility of joining with the industrial unionists in a new trade-union movement. Even old-time delegates pointed to the disappointing results the AFT had achieved with the AFL in federal aid legislation. It seemed that new labor legislation systematically discriminated against public employees. Teachers declared that they wanted to be included under the Wagner Act, a move they thought would disenfranchise the NEA as a company union. They also wanted to be under Social Security, provided they could have their city and state pensions protected and extend the protection to rural teachers who had no protections. To this end they elected Mary Foley Grossman as the new legislative representative and booted Selma Borchardt.[26]

Relations between the AFT and the AFL reached an all-time low in 1936. The AFL had refused to hire new organizers for the AFT, had refused to send out women organizers, and had not helped teachers who were unemployed. Instead, Green, following Selma Borchardt's scenario, appointed a three-member investigating committee to look into Local 5 in the spring of 1936. As expected, the committee recommended that the AFT oust the local and put in new leadership in New York. But, keeping the CIO split in mind, the committee held back from recommending that the AFL step in if the AFT union failed to act. "We've been double-crossed," Borchardt declared, but she was only thinking of her own internal struggle, not of the entire labor picture at the time.[27]

Green intensified his pressure on the union in 1937 to rid itself of "reds" and openly expressed his contempt for Jerome Davis, the Yale University theology professor who succeeded Lowry as AFT president in 1936 and who had the forlorn hope of patching the split between the AFL and the CIO. Finally, in 1939 Matthew Woll issued a statement from the AFL Executive Committee declaring that the AFL believed the AFT was Communist-led and hinting that the charter would be withdrawn. Again, AFT conservatives and radicals reacted in uniform anger. John Fewkes demanded an apology from Woll and a clarification from Green stating that the AFT was not under investigation and that it was a legitimate organization. Green publicly said the statement was incorrect and no investigation was underway, but he reminded the union that if it had kept its own house in order such a misstatement would not have occurred. Perhaps the reason conservatives in the union responded so angrily was that they had launched a secret movement to unseat the radicals, and it was in a very delicate early stage. Green's interference threatened a repeat of the 1935 fiasco.[28]

26. Borchardt to John Frey, 29 April 1936, Borchardt Collection, 88/16.
27. Telegram, John Fewkes to Matthew Woll, 8 February 1939, CTU Collection, 6/8; Guild Papers, Robert Wagner Library.
28. Guild Papers (unprocessed files), Robert Wagner Archives, New York University.

Secret negotiations had begun as early as 1935 when Henry Linville left the union, but the CIO split and the cold response of AFL unions toward Linville's Teachers' Guild had slowed any action within the union. Linville and Lefkowitz, helped along by the New York State Federation of Labor president, George Meany, were able to get a new labor affiliation for the Teachers' Guild. Even though they could not themselves oust New York's Local 5 they could continue to encourage others inside the union who would.[29]

Selma Borchardt was one of the main leaders in the ouster of Local 5, although she did not have the temperament to think out a national plan. Borchardt was angry at being replaced by Mary Foley Grossman, whom she accused of following the NEA and its racist approach to a federal aid bill. In 1936, she wanted to oppose the election of Davis because he clearly represented the radical faction, but she could not bring herself to support Davis's opponent, Allie Mann, the young activist who had replaced Mary Barker in Atlanta. Borchardt charged that Mann was a racist and reactionary and was using the Communist leadership issue as a way to gain office. She said that Mann had prevented Mary Barker from becoming a delegate for the Atlanta local because Mann disapproved of her brave defense of the Scottsboro case and her fight against racism. Mann, Borchardt insisted, had played to the lowest form of racism on these questions. Borchardt voted for Davis, as did many municipal socialists, and the new radical group gained leadership.[30]

Davis's CIO-leaning leadership did not please the pro-AFL Chicago locals, however, and in 1937 Chicago women and men joined forces to produce a new amalgamated local consisting of high school and elementary teachers, women and men. The new organization had 5,000 members and quickly gained 2,000 more with amalgamation; it had 8,500 members by 1940. By surpassing the membership of Local 5, which had 6,500 but was losing members in the WPA locals, Chicago teachers expected to be able to name the new AFT president in 1938. Having taken on the local designation of Margaret Haley's old CTF, Chicago Teachers' Union Local 1 elected Jack Fewkes as its first president. On the national level the local prepared the way to elect Lillian Hernstein as president of the AFT. Hernstein represented much of what the old union had to offer with respect to social justice and the limits of reform.[31]

Although Hernstein's candidacy was fielded as a distinct alternative to Davis and the radicals, she was also to symbolize the modern spirit of growth that the Chicago local felt it had attained by following a conservative leadership and sticking with the AFL. But the New York City local was hardly cowed by the success of the Chicagoans. Local 5 was still growing

29. See letters from Selma M. Borchardt to Frederick Ringdahl, 21 July 1938 and 22 November 1938, and Mary Herrick to Selma Borchardt, 1 July 1938, Borchardt Collection, 89/1.
30. Selma M. Borchardt to Florence (unknown), 18 September 1938, Borchardt Collection, 88/18.
31. *AFT Proceedings*, 1938, AFT Collection, Series 13, pp. 638–660, 733.

and it had gained substantial victories in the state legislature, notably passage of a bill that gave substitute teachers tenure rights and limited their numbers. At the convention, the young Italian-born lobbyist Bella Dodd exuded the sophistication of a Hunter College professor and the sincere compassion of a determined Communist organizer. As the legislative representative of Local 5, she dramatically led floor fights for progressive legislation. She was young, smart, successful, and dynamic. It seemed that Hernstein would not measure up to the younger Dodd. Hernstein's defeat was not a surprise. In her concession speech she made an eloquent plea for unity, declared that the convention had operated with some degree of harmony despite disagreements, and congratulated Davis on his success.[32]

The Triumph of the Conservatives

Although Local 5 appeared to have met the Chicago challenge at the national convention, all was not well within the politics of the local. Local 5 was kicked out of the New York City Trades Council in 1938 for participating in a CIO conference in the city and for charges, brought by Local 24, of raiding. Disaffiliation with the state organization followed, and in Albany a legislative committee was formed—ostensibly to investigate the finances of the New York City school system but, in actuality, to investigate communism in New York City public schools. The Rapp-Coudert Committee hearings consumed the time and energy of Local 5 and turned its attention away from national politics. The national opponents of Local 5 were then free to organize a comeback in 1939.[33]

The 1939 convention was scheduled to be held in Buffalo for the sole reason that the AFT insisted on having fully integrated facilities for its delegates and would not tolerate the least suggestion of special treatment of minority members. Buffalo, everyone agreed, was a city that was relatively inexpensive and open to all delegates. Although these issues were symbolic gestures of defiance against segregation, they were still costly and indicative of the generally progressive tenor of the entire convention. The issues in the 1939 convention were not as progressive. In the battle to gain a new seat on the Executive Council, conservatives ran a new black candidate for the delegate-at-large position, a seat generally regarded as the minority seat since 1936. Doxey Wilkerson, a Howard University professor, was being challenged by Layle Lane, a New York City high school teacher. In Harlem, Socialist Layle Lane, along with A. Philip Randolph and Frank Crosswaithe, were working toward the complete exclusion of Communists in civil rights

32. Bella Dodd, *School of Darkness* (New York, 1954), pp. 75–78; Teachers' Union Collection, 58, Series 5051; Iverson, *Communists,* pp. 38–41.
33. *AFT Proceedings,* 1939, AFT Collection, Series 13, pp. 470–529; Naison, *Communists in Harlem,* p. 287.

activities. At the convention, the Communists did not attack Lane directly but charged that her challenge was an old tactic to pit one black against another, but Lane managed to be recognized and pointedly told the audience that she hoped people would not vote for either herself or Doxey Wilkerson because they were black but because they were ideologically on two sides of the issues. In this debate the issues were clearly drawn, and it seemed at the time that Wilkerson had the support of a majority of the black delegates at the convention. But Wilkerson's strength tended to conceal the weakness of the radicals.[34]

The issue of fascism and the treatment of European Jews seemed to divide the radicals while it oddly played into the hands of the conservatives. The year before, Lillian Hernstein's loss to Jerome Davis had been largely attributed to the anti-Semitism of Atlanta Local 189 and the leadership of Allie Mann. Selma Borchardt claimed that the Communists had allied with the bigots in the union to defeat Hernstein. Perhaps it was for this reason that Jerome Davis planned his opening speech to address the growing threat of anti-Semitism to European Jews and express his dismay that the same reactionary forces seemed to be gaining momentum in the United States. It was perhaps indicative of Davis's bad timing throughout his tenure of office that on the eve of the 1939 convention the Stalin-Hitler pact was announced. It threw the entire convention into an uproar. Communist delegates did not know how to respond, while their enemies were quick to argue that they were not thinking for themselves. Layle Lane pointed out that the Soviet alliance was evidence that communism was an evil that needed to be purged from black life. The large number of Jewish delegates were appalled by the breakup of the antifascist alliance and the Communist party's sudden switch to the peace issue. Davis went ahead and made his address, which pointed to world fascism as the greatest threat to democracy the world over.[35]

Meanwhile, conservatives in the union were ready to make a new counteroffensive against the radicals by proposing George Counts for president. Counts was a Teachers College professor, founding member of the New York City College Teachers' local, and one of the stalwart unionists who refused to leave the AFT with Linville but resented the rise to leadership of the Communist party in Local 5. Counts had completed a study of education in the Soviet Union during the era of the Stalin purges and had become somewhat of an expert on the disappointments of communism. His firm leadership of the union represented a new force, one that could match Jerome Davis's Ivy League image, project the old liberalism of the union, and yet renounce strongly the Communist party. He was thoroughly versed in the practical problems of the union and promised nothing on the question of communism in the union but focused instead on organization. He also

---

34. Interview with Beagle; Naison, *Communists in Harlem*, p. 292.
35. *AFT Proceedings*, 1939, AFT Collection, Series 13 12/7, pp. 506–29.

claimed that he could work with all factions as he had in New York and that Davis was incapable of getting any cooperation from the Chicago or Washington locals. Selma Borchardt had sabotaged a national conference Davis had called, and largely because of her efforts he was not able to get much cooperation from the AFL. Counts was given pledges of cooperation from most sections of the country, and he seemed conciliatory toward the radicals.[36] As it turned out, the news of the Stalin-Hitler Pact provided a sufficient backlash vote to unseat Jerome Davis. But Counts's margin was narrow, and the radicals were still very much in charge of the Executive Board.[37]

The Communist party did not see Davis's defeat as a major setback. Davis was proving to be a liability, and although the Communists had no respect for Counts, they had reason to believe changes to the AFT constitution would prevent any offensive Counts and the AFL might attempt against them. Two amendments, which passed by a two-thousand-vote margin, seemed to make it impossible to discriminate against radicals. In the first, Article III Section 9, the convention ratified the idea that no discrimination could ever be shown individual members because of race, religious faith, or political activities or beliefs. The second required a two-thirds ratification by the convention to suspend or revoke the charter of any local except for nonpayment of dues. These constitutional guarantees, the mutual sense that Davis had little more to give the union, and the general distractions of the Dies Committee (House Un-American Activities Committee, founded in 1938) in Washington and the Rapp-Coudert Committee in New York caused the radicals to ignore the growing movement against them.[38]

In the next year, however, Counts moved to organize the opposition to Local 5. He succeeded in secretly negotiating with the Progressive Caucus within the local and arranged for their affiliation with the Teachers' Guild in New York. He spoke with William Green about getting national organizers, the financial resources and full support of the AFL for an ouster of Local 5. Selma Borchardt had Green appoint two AFL organizers specifically under Counts's direction to help organize against the Communists. The organizers worked to bring in new small locals from the South and West pledged to opposing Communists in the union. The tactic was similar to the charge made against Florence Hanson in 1935 by Linville, who said she packed the meeting to prevent the ouster of Communists from his local. Counts also wanted to revise the constitution to block the inroads made by the left. Mary Herrick and others had failed to alter the constitution in 1939, but by 1940 they had gained considerable experience in getting amendments through the

36. Ibid., pp. 727–34; Jerome Davis Papers, University of Oregon.
37. *AFT Proceedings*, 1939, AFT Collection, Series 13 12/7, p. 723.
38. Ibid., pp. 723–24.

convention. They were aiming at endorsing a pledge that the union would exclude "communists and fascists" from the membership and that the Executive Council could recommend the ouster of locals. At first this work began clandestinely, but by 1940 the conservatives were operating quite openly and confidently.[39]

Rebirth of the Red Scare and Defeat of the Radicals

The secrecy of the campaign against the radicals in the union was a big issue dividing the more conservative forces. Mary Herrick, a regional vice-president from Chicago Teachers' Union Local 1, had supported Mary Foley Grossman against Selma Borchardt in 1936 because she liked the progressive politics that Grossman promoted and she was suspicious of Borchardt's rabid anticommunism. This was a sentiment shared by many in the union who felt that Borchardt's views encouraged the antiteacher, anti-union sentiments of the right. Several events seemed to support this argument. First, Representative Martin Dies of Texas began his committee (HUAC) to investigate both right and left movements in the United States by specifically aiming at the AFT and calling Henry Linville in 1939 to testify about communism in the teachers' union. Many unionists were in an uproar over the unfavorable publicity Linville's testimony gave the union.

The investigation had itself been encouraged by an announcement of the AFL executive committee through Matthew Woll in February 1939 that the AFL was considering ousting the AFT unless the union cleaned house of all Communists. Green later clarified the statement, but even the most conservative John Fewkes of the Chicago Teachers' Union sent strong letters of protest to Green in which he wrote that these attacks were having some effect on the union. Finally, in the autumn of 1939 an article in the *Saturday Evening Post* informed the magazine's three million subscribers that the AFT was a "red" union. In this atmosphere many AFT conservatives, especially the old socialists, were afraid to engage in an open battle with the Communists. Others like Selma Borchardt and John Fewkes proposed to assail the Communists openly, and called in the AFL and the press to witness their fight against evil. The split in strategy meant that at first the campaign was launched secretly and was not thoroughly successful. The election of Counts, however, seemed to unite all factions. Counts wrote secretly to every "safe" local officer to encourage them to send delegates to the 1940 convention or send proxies to other "safe" leaders with open instructions to fight the

39. Ben Stolberg, "Communist Wreckers in American Labor," *Saturday Evening Post*, 2 September 1939; Borchardt Collection, 125/9. See also George Counts to Jack Fewkes, 7 September 1939; Fewkes to William Green, 26 June 1939; Green to Fewkes, 8 August 1939; Matthew Woll to Fewkes, 9 February 1939; Green to Fewkes, 9 February 1939; all in the CTU Collection, 6/8.

Communists. Borchardt's own Local 8 came with such instructions, as did hundreds of other small locals or their proxies.[40]

The leaders in Local 5 were under increasing fire at the same time to turn over membership lists to the Rapp-Coudert Committee. Over thirty college teachers were suspended from their jobs as a result of the hearings; membership was down, and it looked as if a national investigation of communism in the schools would soon be under way. The country had moved in a conservative direction, and Local 5 was able to accomplish very little either nationally or locally.[41]

In 1940, AFT secretary-treasurer Irvin Kuenzli reported that despite the *Post* article, despite the Dies Committee headlines, and despite the various right-wing attacks against the union, the AFT had maintained its membership during the year. The WPA locals had declined dramatically from forty-six chartered since 1936 to the dwindling dozen that remained in 1940; membership in the WPA section went from two thousand to five hundred in a year. But regular classroom teachers joined the union, bringing the total membership up to thirty-five thousand.[42]

The tone and direction of the 1940 AFT convention, known to old-timers as the second battle of Buffalo, was set early by a major address from AFL president William Green. "I urge you to put your house in order. If there is one union that ought to make a declaration on Americanism, that is susceptible of but one interpretation, and that is loyalty and devotion to our public schools, to our free democratic institutions, to the Declaration of Independence, and to our own country against all others, it is this union here."[43] He went on to argue that the union would never become as large as it ought to become unless it shed its reputation for being interested in "-isms"; the only kind of -ism the American people wanted from schoolteachers, he said, was "Americanism."

Boos and hisses greeted most of the AFL leader's comments, but he had the upper hand in his address to the money-starved union. "We have been asked repeatedly by your leaders to help and assist in launching organizing drives. We have helped to some extent, but it is the opinion of our executive council and the leaders of our movement that it will be only a waste of effort and a waste of money to try until you first make it clear to the nation that you are an American institution."[44] There would be no money without the

40. Dale Zysman to John Fewkes, 7 February 1939: "All this year we've been sawing wood, minding our own business and working in the interests of the teachers and the schools. . . . You'll note that the all of the disturbances which confront us from time to time come from the outside." CTU Collection.

41. "Report of the Secretary Treasurer," *AFT Proceedings,* 1940, AFT Collection, Series 13 14/2, pp. 136–82.

42. *AFT Proceedings,* 1940, AFT Collection, Series 13 14/1, pp. 27–35.

43. Ibid.

44. "Redbaiting Hit by Teachers at Convention," *Daily Worker,* 21 August 1940; "Redbaiting Marks Proceedings in AFL Teachers Convention," *Daily Worker,* 23 August 1940; Selma M. Borchardt to Harry Ferlinger, 9 September 1940, 19 September 1940, Borchardt Collection, 125/10;

revocation of Local 5's charter. Although some delegates responded with traditional AFT hostility, others were taken by Green's promises, the enthusiasm Counts demonstrated for the AFL, and the prospects of real power and real growth. These were the directions in which many in the AFT wanted to go; the days of gadfly existence were numbered.[45]

The elections demonstrated that Counts's year of patient organizing had paid off. John DeBoer, a classroom teacher from Chicago, was chosen to challenge George Counts. Affable where Counts was formal and cold, DeBoer was well liked in his local but not well known nationally. His speech was aimed at peace, an issue that was so obviously taken from the recent Communist party line that even the unsophisticated were tipped off. Opponents circulated leaflets illustrating the parallels between the Communist party's *Daily Worker* and the *American Teacher* in an effort to unseat the current editor and to point out DeBoer's sympathies. Other teachers were assailed by petitions demanding to know, "Are you a member of the Communist Party? If not then you will not mind signing this petition of support for the election of George Counts."[46] Counts was reelected.

The Executive Council election was a rout: Charles Hendley of Local 5 was defeated by a little-known candidate from the much smaller New Rochelle local; the Seattle local finally elected their old star, Lila Hunter; Mary Grossman was not returned to office; and Mark Starr defeated the old WPA organizer Ned Dearborn. Even Doxey Wilkerson lost. Counts tried to put up Ralph Bunche from Howard University, fearing that Wilkerson simply had too much support from black delegates to be defeated. But Bunche had failed to pay his dues, and Counts settled for Layle Lane, who won this time. The second battle of Buffalo completely unseated the radicals from the AFT Executive Council.[47]

The radicals at this point could surmise what was in store for Local 5. Charles Hendley, president of Local 5, announced in his summary of the meeting, "We may expect some sinister move against us from some source," and if this was not specific enough he said in private, "Green has an executive council that will now do his bidding." In the galleries above the delegates, members of the Rapp-Coudert Committee took notes on the existence of Communist teachers at the convention, while New York City Teachers' Guild members jubilantly greeted the election of Counts. In the end it was evident to everyone that the union was changing in a new direction. The old gadfly union was dead and a new, practical organization, strongly loyal to the AFL, rose from its ashes.[48]

"Memorandum to Fill in the Gaps in the Discussion of the Meeting of the Executive Board of the Chicago Teachers' Union," 30 January 1940, Mary Herrick Collection, 1/3, Walter Reuther Archives, Detroit.

45. *AFT Proceedings,* 1940, AFT Collection, Series 13 14/1, pp. 416–18.
46. Ibid., pp. 485–99.
47. Investigation of Local 5, 31 December 1940–2 January 1941, AFT Collection, Series 3 24/3.
48. Ferlinger to Borchardt, 9 September 1940; Borchardt to Ferlinger, 19 September 1940;

In the fall of 1940 Counts appointed a committee of Mark Starr, Layle Lane, and himself to investigate ways of reforming Local 5 and getting it back into the AFL. But attempts to set up negotiations between the local and the Teachers' Guild met resistance on both sides. As tensions escalated, about two hundred members of Local 5 resigned in a bloc and set up a Committee for Free Teacher Unionism. They urged the AFT Executive Council to step in directly.[49] Matters moved to a head over the winter. The Executive Council announced a hearing on charges against Local 5, along with the New York College Teachers' Union Local 537 and Mary Grossman's Local 192 in Philadelphia. The official charges were that Local 5 was "not in harmony with the principles of the American Federation of Teachers and tended to bring the AFT into disrepute and because its existence is detrimental to the development of democracy in education."[50] The two-day hearing resembled a debate over the nature of teacher unionism. Issues ranged from the importance of working with industrial unions, not just AFL-affiliated unions, to the significance of working on community projects. Local 5 representatives said they were being attacked for their brash tactics or their scattered loyalties but not for results in terms of new members, new legislation, and administrative changes.

The discussion also shifted to a debate over what Counts and Linville described as "spurious advocates of socialized democracy" who disrupted professional activities of teacher unionists. Charles Hendley replied: "These discussions reveal some of the difficulties of operation of a real union in the academic world. The whole conception of a teachers' union still seems incongruous to 'professionally' minded teachers and educators. The traditional canons of behavior among professors do not permit the lusty give-and-take between mere teachers and the administrators of educational institutions which is involved in union activity."[51]

The attack on the "professionalism" of Linville and Counts continued the long debate over the Communists' tactics and activities, which pushed the union toward a more working-class language and identity. Linville and Counts were promoting a more consensual politics, one where teachers were in trade unions because of their professionalism, not in spite of it. The community-based organizing style of the communists was anathema to the professional ethics of the Counts school, and as the depression had kept potential teachers in college longer, the professionalization project had taken firmer root. The debate behind closed doors focused narrowly on old griev-

---

Borchardt Collection, 125/10. "Hearing of Local 5, The Teachers' Union of the City of New York, on Charges by the Executive Council and Order to Show Cause Why Its Charter Should Not Be Revoked," 15 and 16 February 1941, CTU Collection, 11/3.

49. "Hearing of Local 5," CTU Collection, 11/3.
50. CTU Collection, 11/4.
51. *American Teacher,* 26 (April 1941).

ances, but the line of struggle between the Communist teachers and the new unionists over what they considered the best direction for teacher unionism was firmly drawn.

After the two days of exhausting hearings, the proponents of the charged locals retired, and the Executive Council voted to recommend revocation of their charters in a national referendum. The referendum, which was scheduled for early April, would precede ratification at the convention by several months. Counts had no intention of allowing the three locals to return to the national convention, which he feared they might be able to pack.[52]

The April 1941 issue of the *American Teacher* was devoted to the referendum on Locals 5, 537, and 192. Again the charges and countercharges were laid out clearly by both sides. On the issue of the Stalin-Hitler Pact, Local 5 president Hendley pointed out that other trade unions had followed a peace position all through the late thirties, and he argued that the sudden shift of the Soviet Union had prompted the local to look more closely at the issue. The vote in the referendum overwhelmingly favored revoking the charters of the locals.[53] The AFT convention, despite a challenge led by Doxey Wilkerson, upheld the membership's verdict with only a handful of delegates in opposition. The issue was settled. The teachers had ousted the locals and the decision was final.[54]

There were two aspects of the 1941 convention that further illustrated the close of an era in the union. First, President Counts delivered a long speech on the threat of totalitarianism, the rise of Hitler, and the likely coming of war. Counts was dramatic, but he hoped to convey the sense that the teachers did have their house in order, as William Green had put it, and they could take a more patriotic stand in the struggles to come.

Perhaps because it looked to the past rather than the future, the second event was more nostalgic than it was dramatic. The AFT celebrated its twenty-fifth anniversary in 1941 and honored Florence Hanson, Charles Stillman, and Henry Linville. Linville spoke bitterly of the days when John Dewey was assailed by radicals in his own local, but Hanson spoke sentimentally of the old, small union. "The spirit in those days was strong; the devotion was illimitable. The organization pulsed with one great heart and soul. And what we must see to is that numbers do not cause any loss of that spirit. We worked hard to have full representation at a convention. . . . In the American Federation of Teachers there is room, I believe, for everyone."[55] Hanson's comments were met with applause, but it was approval of sentiment not substance. The union had taken a new direction and was firmly in the hands of new leadership.

52. *AFT Proceedings,* 1941, AFT Collection, Series 13 15/10, pp. 142–64.
53. Ibid., pp. 256–64.
54. Frances R. Donovan, *Schoolma'am* (New York, 1938), pp. 34–35, 74.
55. *AFT Proceedings,* 1941, AFT Collection, Series 13 15/10.

Gender Issues in the Depression

The Communist issue then was more than a question of absorbing a new generation of radicals. The peculiar circumstances that brought this new generation into the union, had to do with redefining professionalism within unionism. Professionalism, however, evoked male leadership and invariably excluded women. Although the NEA revolt of the professionals in the Progressive Era had lured women leaders into the new professionalism, by the twenties only men fit the proper image. There were no more Ella Flagg Youngs to lead women. A woman was elected president routinely every other year in the NEA, but no woman sat in the powerful seat of executive director. Charl Williams had been NEA president and worked on the NEA staff, but no women followed her. When the AFT chose a college man over a woman classroom teacher, as it did in 1938 with Davis over Hernstein and again in 1939 when it chose Counts to battle communism, the concept of union leadership shifted. Although Hernstein, Herrick, Borchardt, and Layle Lane would remain highly regarded leaders in the AFT, few women leaders continued the traditions begun by Haley, Barker, and Rood. In the decade of the depression, tensions between men's and women's locals became submerged in the ideological and fiscal problems confronting the union. The union oriented itself more toward the married male leader than toward the dynamic, single schoolteacher. In Chicago this shift was evident in the unification of the three locals—high school men, high school women, and elementary school teachers.

Although there were more women than men in the proposed merger and even though there were strong women leaders in two of the three locals, the head of the men's local, Jack Fewkes, was elected head of the new union. In part his election was a compromise because the women's locals were impoverished and would enter the new union in debt. But it also marked the eclipse of the Chicago women who, up until 1937, had played a leading role in the union. Later, after World War II, fewer women ran the union headquarters, as the new secretary-treasurer, Irving Kuenzli, took firm control of the office. Counts and the male leaders that followed felt no need to encourage the presence of more women in leadership positions. Still, on the local level, in committees and at the vice-presidential level, the older women leaders maintained their positions.

The absence of a new generation of women union leaders raises the point that during the depression and the New Deal the focus was always on the head of household, usually thought to be male, as the key figure for rehabilitation and relief. In part, this attitude arose from the Progressive Era emphasis on the family wage, professional motherhood, and the family economy. Such terms were part of the language of reformers like Frances Perkins, who carried these ideas into the Department of Labor. The biggest issue for women workers during the depression, as we shall see, was the attempt by both public and private industry to lay off married women from the best white-collar positions and replace them with men (whether heads of households or not).

The fixation on sex-segregated job classification and the need to preserve the male position as family head persisted in the labor movement as well. The iconography of the labor movement in the thirties, as Elizabeth Faure has pointed out, suggests that the emphasis on male leadership and empowerment became an avenue for restoring male dignity lost in the depression. Joblessness desexed men. The teachers' union, however, always had a feminine image even though its leadership was becoming increasingly male. A cartoon appeared in the *Chicago Tribune* depicting John Fitzpatrick, head of the Chicago Federation of Labor, chasing Harold Gibbons of the AFT/WPA local out of the house as Gibbons carried a screaming baby CIO, John L. Lewis. Gibbons was drawn in drag because he headed the schoolteachers' (read female) union.

The AFT switch to male leaders, especially in the face of the Communist party, may also have been a way of getting back in touch with AFL men. As for the Communists, their clear alternative was the dynamic Bella Dodd, a woman of considerable skill and a member of a younger generation than Mary Herrick or Lillian Hernstein. Jerome Davis may have been unacceptable as a leader not because of his leftist tendencies but because of his apparently effeminate nature. Counts, on the other hand, liked to present a strong case, speak in a booming voice, and deal "firmly" with issues. This was all imagery, to be sure, but it was the kind of imagery that became important in the late thirties and early forties. By 1940, the critical year for the union, the pacifist movement, largely led by women, had become discredited, and Americans were defining the word "appeasement" to mean costly cowardice. All these elements added to the expectation that female leadership would not be strong enough to carry the union back into the fold of traditional labor. Men and women in the union agreed that what was needed was a strong hand. The strong hand, by their definition, would be male.

The emphasis on male leadership would with the coming of the war become further reinforced. The union did well during the war, and many felt it was because it had changed leadership so dramatically at its inception. Teachers, on the other hand, did poorly because wartime inflation destroyed wage levels. The general consensus from those who remained in the union, however, was that the crisis of the thirties was over.

The repercussions of the expulsion of "Communist" locals were not always as rewarding as some leaders might have hoped. The AFL did not suddenly begin listening more carefully to the AFT's legislative agenda, teachers did not sign up by the thousands, and conventions were still plagued with serious debates over issues of social justice. After World War II, however, as teacher militancy rose, there was no major debate over inappropriate tactics; teachers were even striking without much comment from the national. The teacher-union movement had finally come to terms with professionalism. As the CIO faced an anticommunist drive in the late forties, the AFT stood as an experienced union in such affairs; perhaps for the first time the union could honestly say it had faced problems similar to those of private sector workers. Finally, the union had benefited from its strong support for minorities, and after the war it enjoyed a reputation for having taken early stands on issues that became difficult for other unions. In short, the union had matured, gained experience, and grown in size.

The biggest problem facing the union, however, was shaking its image as a red organization. Despite George Counts's sterling reputation among schoolteachers, his association with the union and his many visits to the Soviet Union branded him as a Communist. John Dewey's ideas on progressive education, his participation in a panel to look into the murder of Leon Trotsky, and his open association with the union again left him on the list of suspected fellow travelers. Even within the AFL neither Matt Woll nor William Green acted to bring the labor movement closer to the teachers. The campaign against the AFT in the late thirties that led to the ouster of Communists in 1941 was not forgotten by the public. Even after they had cleaned house and rid themselves of Local 5 and two other locals for good measure, members were still pinned with the image of the red schoolteacher. It was not an image that would serve them well in the postwar red scare.

CHAPTER NINE /

Iron Curtain in the Classroom

Shaken a bit by the turmoil over the ouster of the Communists, AFT leaders looked to the coming years as a time when the union could heal itself, while the war swept up the interests and enthusiasms of teachers everywhere. The postwar decades were marked by an important transformation of the union: from an emphasis on political pronouncements to a more pragmatic and collective-bargaining-oriented trade unionism. The AFT would build its strength to challenge the autocracy of the old superintendency that Margaret Haley had decried. In the NEA the conservative leadership of the Department of Superintendents continued to prevail, although the association would adopt a more activist response to attacks on academic freedom. Neither the AFT nor the NEA could focus on teachers' needs for long, however, as the red scare hit teachers with a force that had not been seen even in the frightening aftermath of World War I.

For most of the postwar era the schools faced a crisis of rapid population growth that overfilled classrooms, opened split sessions, doubled enrollments, and strained every school budget. Efforts to expand the educational budget, however, seemed to provoke an unprecedented negative response from real-estate interests and antitax organizations. This response was soon subsumed in an attack focused on fears of subversion in the classroom. Indeed, the red hunt dampened the teachers' ability to mobilize the community behind educational needs.

Both the NEA and the AFT were keenly aware of the growing crisis in education. During the immediate postwar period both organizations monitored the rising needs of educators while each organization pursued its own organizational agenda. For the AFT the most important issue was to recover a national image of educational responsibility in the wake of its "radical" past. The NEA on the other hand seemed to grow more concerned with teachers' rights while it groped toward a national program of federal funding.

175

The two organizations shared common interests but did not work together and often wound up frustrating each others efforts.

Shortages and Fiscal Nightmares: The Impact of the War

The first years after the expulsion of the three locals in the AFT were marked by terrific growth in membership, generating a new optimism.[1] Wartime AFT conventions reflected George Counts's analysis that without the threat of communism from within, the AFT could now flourish as the maturing liberal leader of democracy in the postwar years. Counts followed his triumph in the AFT by helping to establish the Liberal party in New York State. Lillian Hernstein, John Fewkes, and Paul Douglas, prominent AFT activists, left the union to assume important wartime posts. Eager to claim a leadership role in postwar reconstruction, the union organized a Commission on Reconstruction, which prominently featured Floyd Reeves, Roosevelt's own choice to head his Educational Advisory Committee in 1937. Perhaps overly conscious of the NEA's role in reconstruction planning after World War I, union leaders hoped to proclaim their own reconstruction policy and thereby usurp the traditional NEA role.

For the NEA the same years marked an era of wartime activity and a renewed push for federal funding. This was a period of wartime prosperity, of moves toward national child care, and of widely expressed concerns that the war might tear the family apart. In these circumstances, the prospects for federal aid to schools seemed promising. Executive Secretary William Givens also hoped the NEA's National Commission for the Defense of Democracy would give the association the same prestige that George Strayer had earned as head of the NEA's Emergency Commission on Education during World War I. In 1942 the NEA held a conference with the National Association of Manufacturers to alert businessmen to the teacher shortage. The Roosevelt administration remained cool to federal aid. The NEA noted that with the demise of the NYA and the WPA the federal government was spending less on education. The $310 million spent by the federal government in 1942–43 went to war-training programs at the U.S. Military Academy, to agricultural extension schools, and to the traditional programs of vocational education.[2] Chester Bowles even advised as a wartime measure the temporary closing of schools to save oil.[3]

Eager to prove its ability to influence educational policy, the AFT announced a federal bill that differed little from the NEA's proposals. The

1. Kuenzli to Counts, 6 November 1947, AFT Collection, Series 3, Box 2; Executive Minutes, 11 April 1943, AFT Collection, Series 3.
2. National Commission for the Defense of Democracy through Education, *Defense Bulletin*, December 1941–47.
3. *Defense Bulletin*, 15 May 1944.

union bill required more money—$300 million in the first year, with more to follow—and it earmarked some of the funds for upgrading teachers' salaries. It also hit at the problems of discrimination, carefully picking through the minefield of states' rights, segregation, and separation of church and state. Leaning heavily on the prestige of Floyd Reeves and the Commission on Reconstruction, the union worked for months to unveil its new proposal.

The NEA had its own bill addressing the shortage of teachers, substandard salaries in rural areas, functional illiteracy, and educational inequality. But again the NEA funding proposal would distribute funds through the states and would not fund private education. At first the AFT worked with the NEA and various Catholic organizations to organize a compromise bill. Then in February 1943, just as the AFT was about to present its version of federal aid to the Congress, the American Federation of Labor intervened and wrote a clause into the bill providing that federal money be distributed to all children, including parochial school students. The AFL's insistence on this clause instantly destroyed any possibility for the bill's passage. The old NEA compromise on this issue had been to let each state distribute its federal grant on the basis of its own laws. Heavily Catholic states that provided state funds to religious schools could do so. The AFL insistence on its platform pulled the rug out from under AFT leadership on the education bill. NEA leaders condemned Selma Borchardt for the failure of the bill, to which the AFT lobbyist replied that the NEA was just trying to get funds for school superintendents and segregated states. Even though the union tried the same bill again in 1945, it had no chance of passing Congress.[4]

Married Teachers and the Protection of Teachers' Rights

The war years saw more systematic attempts, especially by the NEA, to codify and defend the rights of teachers. Often the particular issue at stake was an effort by school authorities to prohibit married women, even those with tenure, from continuing in their jobs. Although the question of married women teaching had been a point of contention between young women teachers and school boards since the Progressive era, the dismissal of married women grew rampant during the depression. Frances Donovan found in a 1930 study that nearly one-third of large cities had laws prohibiting marriage for women teachers. "Since the depression," Donovan wrote, "largely for economic reasons, the trend has been against the employment of married women teachers, and many young schoolma'ams have refused to consider marriage for this reason." Many unmarried schoolteachers had to support relatives, especially widowed mothers; this Donovan added, encour-

---

4. Gilbert E. Smith, *The Limits of Reform: Politics and Federal Aid to Education, 1937–1950* (New York, 1982), pp. 125–65; *Defense Bulletin*, 15 May 1943.

aged spinsterhood. "The unmarried school ma'am is also expected to help out in all financial crisis that threatens the solidarity of the family," Donovan reported. Spinster teachers repaid their own education by helping younger brothers, sisters, nieces, nephews, and even cousins. The depression intensified the fiscal burdens of the unmarried schoolteacher. "The unemployed relatives of the unmarried schoolma'am frequently needed aid. Many teachers lost their savings in banks that closed." Even when the deteriorating economic climate failed to keep a teacher from marrying, new school rules appeared to keep school teaching a spinster's profession.[5]

Married women schoolteachers faced a new campaign to eliminate them just as the AFT crisis was heating up in 1938. A survey made that year indicated that of eighty-five cities 60 per cent had a policy—usually an unwritten one—against hiring and keeping married women. By 1939 at least thirteen states had ruled restrictions on marriage unlawful, but most often only tenured teachers came under protection; probationary teachers and prospective teachers had none. The 1938 ballot in Massachusetts carried a measure prohibiting married women in public service altogether, but before a law could pass, state supreme court justices ruled in 1939 that such a statute would deprive women as citizens of their constitutional guarantees.

Although both the NEA and the AFT had convention resolutions decrying the situation, it was the NEA, using the vast resources of its research division, that began to compile systematic coverage of the issue. The NEA Committee on Tenure had long been devoted to strengthening professionalism through the introduction of tenure laws, and state associations had been active, along with AFT local leaders, in sponsoring tenure bills in state legislatures. The first challenge to these bills came in the form of the dismissal of married women schoolteachers. The NEA limited its response, however, to issuing a report in 1940 from the Committee on Tenure. Citing several studies of married women workers, the committee concluded: "Married women who work are not doing anything new. They are making the same contribution to the real income of their families that they have made for centuries." Women were not taking men's jobs, the report noted, especially in view of the way industrialization had taken so much of women's work out of the home and given it to men. Working wives also created jobs for other women by hiring household help. Married women in other countries, with the exception of Hitler's Germany, were being encouraged to enter the work force. Finally the committee concluded, "If higher education necessarily involves celibacy or sterility, the seriousness of the situation for society cannot be exaggerated." The report list eight recommendations from the U.S. Women's Bureau that would strengthen the hand of the married working women, but the report carefully added that these incentives were not endorsed by the committee or by the NEA.[6]

5. *Defense Bulletin,* 30 October 1944, 19 February 1945, 16 April 1946, 11 March 1947.
6. *Defense Bulletin,* 31 January 1950; also Publications of the Committee on Tenure and Academic Freedom, 1911–49, vol. 1.

Another flurry of court cases followed the NEA report. In two Illinois cases courts upheld the dismissal of married teachers, but in Pennsylvania and Ohio the State Supreme Court protected the teachers. In December 1941 the newly created NEA National Commission for the Defense of Democracy began to take a more activist approach in teacher tenure cases. Announcing victories for married women teachers in a number of instances, the editor of the NEA *News Bulletin,* Donald DuShane, urged state associations to strengthen tenure laws by defending teachers in these cases.

The push against married women teachers slackened considerably during the war because of a growing teacher shortage as wartime demands attracted talented prospective teachers into more lucrative fields. DuShane's commitment to strengthening teacher tenure did not abate. Two reports on teacher conditions provided ammunition for his activist approach. In an analysis of school-board rules, published in 1938, the Committee on Tenure identified the main causes of teacher dismissal. Fourth in importance among these were marriage regulations for women teachers. Other infringements on teachers' personal lives included prohibitions on participating in electoral campaigns, engaging in politics at school, becoming a candidate, displaying a flag other than the American flag, giving interviews, incurring debts, attending parents' meetings, contacting parents without permission, tutoring for compensation, and taking more than six units of credit a semester. In the second report, issued in 1945, DuShane studied teacher oaths and found that teachers were asked not only to support the U.S. Constitution but to "discharge faithfully their duties," swear allegiance to the state constitution, the American flag, the state flag, law and order, the government, and all American institutions. In Georgia and Texas teachers took an oath promising to refrain from directly or indirectly teaching theories of government, economics, or social relations inconsistent with Americanism. DuShane became most active in the defense case of Kate Frank, a Muskogee, Oklahoma, high school teacher who was dismissed from her job, along with two other teachers, in 1944 because of her activities in the NEA's Department of Classroom Teachers. In less than three months, DuShane collected $3,786.40 in voluntary contributions for Frank's case. Overwhelmed by the war chest and the NEA's challenge, the Muskogee Board of Education reinstated Frank in the fall of 1945. The war chest was then turned into a permanent fund for the defense of public school teachers and was named for Donald DuShane after his untimely death in 1945.[7]

The Baby Boom and the Financial Pinch

The baby boom was not so much a subject for academic discussion in the educational trade journals as it was an annual surprise, sending school

7. *Defense Bulletin,* 31 January 1950.

principals scurrying for more chairs while they sought to placate increasingly irate teachers. Demographers had casually predicted a small increase in population after the war and were unprepared for the millions who followed. In 1947 the number of children entering kindergarten had jumped 10 percent, and class size in elementary school edged upward from a low of 33.4 in the depression to 36.4. By the 1951–52 academic year schools braced for the baby-boom cohort that would expand elementary school enrollment by two-thirds in the decades from 1950 to 1970; class size rose to levels not been seen since the Progressive Era. The entering cohort of children born in 1946–47 was 38 percent larger than the cohort before it and brought with it into the elementary schools overcrowded classes, split sessions, and a boom in school construction. In the fifties, California opened one new school a week. With every sharp rise in the baby boom, the schools faced a new challenge of expansion and overcrowded classes. Education had become, as President Truman's new commissioner of education announced, "big business."[8]

The scarcity of teachers started in the war but continued throughout the fifties. The age cohort from which new teachers would have come in the late forties was an unusually small one; college enrollment would have shrunk in the early forties even without the war. Most colleges served the military in some capacity during the war just to stay afloat. The consequent scarcity of teachers helped drive up salaries, but a wartime salary increase of 11 percent was not enough to offset a 25 percent increase in the cost of living. Teachers could earn more money working in wartime factories than they could teaching school. In 1941 the average annual wage of a steelworker was $1,580 a year and the average annual salary of a teacher was $1,454. Many teachers switched to other occupations, and only a few returned to education after the war. Although salaries for teachers rose after the war, they did not rise fast enough to attract new teachers.[9]

In 1947 the NEA took the initiative in federal funding away from the AFT and managed to gain the surprise support of former federal-aid-opponent Robert Taft. (The Ohio senator was preparing his bid for the 1948 presidential race.) This time, however, the religious issue heated up, in part because of a Supreme Court ruling that affirmed the power of states to give aid to Catholic schools for the costs of busing children. As a consequence, the NEA moved more in the direction of restricting public aid to public schools only, while Catholic lobbyists held tightly to the commitment of the AFL to give support for all children. Torn by loyalty to the AFL and dedication to the ideal of separate public schools, teachers in the AFT fought bitterly at their 1947 convention: they decided at one point to insist that aid be limited to

8. Landon Y. Jones, *Great Expectations: America and the Babyboom Generation* (New York, 1980), pp. 57–58.

9. Floyd Reeves, "Commission on Reconstruction," *American Teacher,* 32 (December 1948); Irvin R. Kuenzli, "Company Unions and the School Crisis," *American Federationist,* 54 (February 1947), pp. 10–12; Joseph F. Landis, "The AFT Today," *American Teacher,* 32 (October 1948).

public schools, only to reverse themselves and stick with the AFL line. Federal aid became a political football before the 1948 election. Taft tried to seize the initiative from Truman, while Catholic pressure groups, alienated by Truman's leadership and yet unwilling to cross into the Republican fold, seized on the time-honored issue of communism in the public schools. It is not surprising that teachers failed to get a bill through the cost-conscious Congress of 1948, and by 1949 the chances for federal aid were even further reduced by the NAACP's demand that no bill get through Congress without an antisegregation rider. The New Deal was over, Truman's effort to launch his own Fair Deal had failed, and educators were still unable to overcome the original objections to federal aid for education. "The Congress will not enact any bills to provide general federal aid for education," Selma Borchardt announced in 1951. "In fact, we can now say that no Congress for some time to come will enact any bills to provide general federal aid for education."[10]

The fiscal problems of education continued unabated after the New Deal and the war. Cities and towns had grown more reliant on state aid to keep their schools afloat. Between 1932 and 1947, the states' share of total school funding went from 19.5 percent to 41 percent. Even so, in order to keep pace with the new generation of Americans in the baby boom, teachers had to campaign annually for local school bonds. At the federal level, as Washington grew more conservative and tax conscious, aid proposals went nowhere until the Soviet Union startled the world by launching the first space satellite, *Sputnik,* in 1957. Flooded with students and starved for funds, it is little wonder that, beginning in the immediate aftermath of the war, teachers grew more frustrated and militantly demanded higher wages.[11]

Although the NEA's efforts to achieve federal aid were futile, they touched off a reaction that set the association back even further. The National Tax Conference and the U.S. Chamber of Commerce launched an offensive against the NEA's 1943 funding bill and set in motion a half dozen more radical antitax organizations. One of these, the Friends of Public Education, was headed by Major General Amos A. Fries, who charged that the NEA was "completely dominated by communists and fellow travelers." Shaken by the charge, the NEA responded by saying it had a provision in its bylaws prohibiting membership by "any person who favors revolutionary changes in our form of government." But the antitax lobby hailed General Fries's views and used him as a lobbyist against the NEA. He called the NEA a "less extreme group" than the AFT but still an organization of radical propagandists advocating "pure socialism." The famous red hunter Allen Zoll condemned the AFT wholeheartedly but joined in Fries's attack on the NEA, sending letters to American mayors warning them in 1949 about the red

10. *American Teacher,* 36 (October 1951).
11. Smith, *Limits of Reform,* pp. 125–88; Jones, *Great Expectations,* pp. 60–67; *School and Society,* 63:1620 (12 January 1946), p. 22.

teachers' organizations. The NEA *Defense Bulletin* noted with dismay that it had to retain a lawyer to protect the teachers' rights of association while it pursued a 1948 bill to increase federal aid to education. It was no coincidence that the House Un-American Activities Committee (HUAC) began investigating education in 1948 just one month before Congress began considering the NEA's funding bill. One reactionary journal made the connection between the NEA's press for federal educational funding and the growing intensity of the red scare: "We tire of the collectivist plotting of economic planners of the fair deal." The first rumblings of the McCarthy era came with a fiscal crisis that would grow geometrically in the coming years.[12]

The immediate postwar years also made it clear that the AFL would feel the heat of political reaction. The union's Commission on Reconstruction prophetically announced, "The real choice is between American imperialism and militarism, versus a program of international cooperation." On the domestic front, the commission declared, "We shall not have peace within our own country unless we can bridge this gulf of color, and get rid of long standing discrimination and prejudices."[13] It appeared that the union, armed with this sober and remarkably insightful analysis, would cut a distinctively progressive path in the mire of cold war politics. The absence of reflection on the possibilities of a red scare and its impact on the union illustrates perfectly how McCarthyism hit the union on its blind side and steered it off its already compromised progressive course. Despite the ritualistic cleansing of the union and the fanfare of its welcome back into the fold, the teachers could not avoid the smear of the postwar red hunt.

Teachers' Strikes and Militancy

As the fiscal crisis in education deepened, schoolteachers took matters into their own hands. A series of teacher strikes between the fall of 1945 and the late spring of 1948 set the stage for the red scare in education. Given the gloom of the economic picture and the effects of deflation and overcrowding, it is not difficult to imagine why teachers took to picket lines after months of fruitless negotiations. The mass demonstrations of the thirties had helped teachers to become more articulate as a collective of interests. They could also see the greater gains being made by blue-collar unions. Between 1939 and 1946 the average industrial worker's income rose 80 percent in real dollars, while the average teacher's income fell 20 percent.[14]

12. *Defense Bulletin*, 4 September 1946, p. 16.
13. AFT Commission on Reconstruction; Office of Education, *Biennial Survey of Education in the United States, 1946–1948* (Washington, D.C., 1950), p. 41; *American Teacher*, 31 (October 1946).
14. Emery M. Forster, in *Biennial Survey of Education* (1941), pp. 38–124; (1955), pp. 13–21; (1946–48), chap. 1.

An NEA-led strike in Norwalk, Connecticut, was the first and most dramatic because of its success. Teachers in this union town walked out in the fall of 1946 and did not return until they were guaranteed a pay raise and recognition. Although the NEA *Defense Bulletin* denied that this was a strike, the eight-day walkout inspired other small, NEA-affiliated organizations to strike for higher wages. The NEA called these work stoppages "professional group action by professional methods," and tried unsuccessfully to hold the line against strikes in Hawthorne, New Jersey, and McMinnville and Shelbyville, Tennessee. Small, unaffiliated groups of teachers also struck in Wilkes-Barre and Rankin, Pennsylvania. The NEA warned members that they had taken an oath of ethical standards as association members that required them to honor their contracts.[15]

St. Paul teachers in the AFT had a very strong local, years of experience in coping with the Board of Education, and a very specific, public goal in their strike in November 1946. A tax increase, needed to raise teachers' salaries, had lost at the polls in July by a three-to-one margin. They struck for five weeks until reaching an agreement with the board on 1 January 1947 that insured another referendum in February. Furthermore, they were able to negotiate a provision that if a substitute teacher could not be found (a problem in every school district short of teachers), the principal would send the children home from school rather than pack the classrooms of other teachers. This was an important win because it brought the problem of the teacher shortage and classroom overcrowding home to the parents who were turning down tax increases. The teachers lost again in February, but much more narrowly, and a third vote in April won them their pay raise. But the NEA condemned the union teachers, calling their five-week walkout a failure and insisting that the whole affair "confirms the NEA's position that strikes are ineffective."[16]

The St. Paul example certainly helped teachers in Minneapolis, whose strike in May 1948 ended after only a few days when the board tried to literally lock them out and shorten the school year. Minneapolis teachers won raises, as did militant teachers in San Francisco, Jersey City, and Chicago. Teachers in Chicago took their strike vote in the face of the recent AFT convention position upholding the concept of a national no-strike policy. Nevertheless the teachers voted to strike and won concessions before their planned walkout. In Buffalo, twenty-four hundred teachers walked a picket line closing all but nineteen of the district's ninety-eight schools. Most

15. *Defense Bulletin*, 4 September 1946, p. 2.

16. "The St. Paul Story," *American Teacher*, 31 (February 1947), pp. 8–9; "The St. Paul Strike," *American School Board Journal*, 88 (January 1947), p. 62; "Struck Buffalo," *Newsweek*, 3 March 1947, p. 22; "Teachers Strike," *Newsweek*, 8 March 1948, p. 80; "Teacher Strikes," *School and Society*, 65 (19 April 1947), p. 277; "A Teachers' Strike," *American School Board Journal*, 113 (October 1946), p. 54; Maurice L. Hartung, "Strikes by Teachers," *School Review*, 54 (December 1946), pp. 563–66.

of the strikes were one-day affairs although strikes lasted as long as six weeks. The majority of the strikers were teachers, but in some districts students walked out with their teachers, and in McMinnville bus drivers and teachers walked out together. By the winter of 1947, teachers had gone on strike in twelve states.[17]

Most of the strikes had a result that the strikers never intended: state legislatures retaliated with strict antistrike laws for public employees. New York and Delaware were the most vindictive. New York passed the Condon-Waldin Act forbidding strikes after Buffalo teachers struck. At the same time Senator Feinberg led in passing legislation to raise teachers' salaries and thereby hold off any further militant teacher activity. In Delaware, after a half-day strike and march to the state capital for a raise, Delaware teachers were met by a bill calling for a five-hundred-dollar fine and a year's imprisonment for striking public workers.[18]

In the AFT the strike fever was so widespread that the annual convention in 1947 passed a resolution calling for a full discussion on changing the union's no-strike policy. The *American Teacher* carried a debate on the issue. The union was not yet ready to change its policy, but unions like the St. Paul local were given quiet financial help to defray expenses from the strikes. Meanwhile growing militancy among rank-and-file teachers nationwide forced school districts to grant pay raises that pushed teachers' wages up by 13 percent in one year, from 1947 to 1948.[19]

The Red Scare in New York

As teachers kept the heat on for pay increases, tax-conscious organizations and the old patriotic coalitions pressured state legislatures for less rewarding remedies to teacher demands. In discussions of teacher militancy in state legislatures the issues of teacher loyalty were again raised and reexamined. Generally, teacher oaths were revised and directives to school boards outlined methods for ousting subversives from schools. By far the most compelling of these statutes was the Feinberg Law, passed in New York in 1949.[20]

While the rising militancy of teachers and public employees often instigated legislative reaction, the strikes were not solely responsible for the first skirmishes in the red scare that followed. As the cold war deepened, politicians were finding that the search for an internal "fifth column" could be glamorous and popular. It also posed serious dangers for anyone who sided

17. *American Teacher*, 31 (December 1946); *Defense Bulletin*, 3 March 1947, p. 5.
18. *Defense Bulletin*, March 1947, pp. 5–9.
19. *American Teacher*, 31 (December 1946), 31 March, April, and May 1947.
20. Leon Bock, *The Control of Alleged Subversive Activities in the Public School System of New York, 1949–1956* (New York, 1971), p. 46; *NYT*, 4 April 1949.

with "Communists." In New York City the stormy history of Local 5, targeted in the Rapp-Coudert hearings and expelled from the AFT in 1940, was an issue ready to be exploited. Local 5, now renamed the Teachers' Union, was still a major presence in the schools. Moreover, despite its expulsion, its fortunes would remain tied to the AFT: no matter how explicit the AFT was about its past, to the broader public it was the "teachers' union" that had been nailed as a Communist union, and many conveniently chose not to make the distinctions the AFT would have them make.[21]

Old Local 5 was an affiliate of the CIO when it came to the attention of the House Committee on Education and Labor in the summer of 1948. The Teachers' Union, Local 555 of the United Public Workers, CIO, was conducting a strike against the Radio Electronics School, a small, private, technical training school that had grown out of GI benefits. School director Robert Duncan refused to negotiate with the strikers, arguing that they were Communists defrauding the federal government. The strike was settled in November after the school's board of directors removed the flamboyant Duncan from his position. In the meantime, however, the congressional investigation of Local 555 had begun in earnest in September. It headed immediately and unimaginatively into the old Rapp-Coudert material.[22]

Witnesses could provide little in the way of new revelations, yet the hearings introduced three significant characteristics that would stick with the teachers in the next decade of the red scare. The committee called on the New York superintendent of schools, William Jansen, and board member George Timone for their estimation of the Teachers' Union. This was the first time local school authorities appeared before a national investigatory committee of this nature, providing a rehearsal for more dramatic appearances in the early fifties. Second, this was the first time the grievances between factions in the Teachers' Union would be nationally aired. Although Linville had testified at a Martin Dies hearing and the entire story was rehashed thoroughly in New York, it had never been publicly detailed outside the union halls. Finally, it was the first hearing faced by the Teachers' Union without the benefits of Bella Dodd's legal skill. After leaving the Teachers' Union in 1943 as legislative representative, she had risen in the ranks of the Communist party and become a chief proponent of Earl Browder, the party secretary until 1945. Because of Browder's predictions of a peaceful coexistence between Communist and capitalist nations after the war, he became the object of a purge and would be ousted along with many of his supporters,

21. The general studies are Robert W. Iversen, *The Communists and the Schools* (New York, 1959); David Caute, *The Great Fear* (New York, 1978); and Victor Navasky, *Naming Names* (New York, 1980). The best study of McCarthyism in higher education is Ellen Schrecker, *No Ivory Tower: McCarthyism and the Universities* (New York, 1986).

22. U.S. Congress, Hearings before a Special Subcommittee of the Committee on Education and Labor, House of Representatives, 80th Cong. (Washington, D.C., 1948); Teachers' Union Collection, 10/1, Cornell University; Rosalind Russell to Editor, *New York Sun*, 15 December 1948; *Journal American*, 14 September 1948.

including Dodd, in 1949. The alienated Dodd was still nominally in the party in the first of her national appearances; later she would turn on teachers and give names that were used in a city-wide investigation. Disaffected, she had not yet in 1949 defected from the movement. Her appearance later became a fixture of red hunting in the schools.[23]

There was another twist to the hearings that freshened the immediacy of a dramatic retelling of the Teachers' Union story, further nailed the coffin lid for the union, and paved the way for charges that Communist teachers were subverting innocent students in the classroom. Abraham Lefkowitz, Dodd's nemesis and old crony of Linville, had become principal of a high school in which a very political member of the Teachers' Union taught history classes. The head of the history department wrote consistently critical evaluations of the clearly left-thinking teacher, to which the teacher wrote long, elaborate defenses. Lefkowitz became involved when he was attacked, along with his supervisor, in a left publication. Not one to walk away from a dogfight, Lefkowitz published his own defense and his attack on the teacher, providing further fuel for the controversy and ensuring that the issue would come before the superintendent of schools and the Board of Education. The situation added to the tension of the Washington hearings where Lefkowitz, no doubt still feeling that he was under attack by the Communists in his own local, painfully led the committee through the entire history of the AFT, Teachers' Union Local 5, and the Communist party.[24]

The defense of the teachers in the Teachers' Union proved astonishingly inept compared with Bella Dodd's well-orchestrated defense before the Rapp-Coudert Committee.[25] Local president Samuel Wallach responded to Lefkowitz by merely dismissing him: "I want to point out with regard to Dr. Lefkowitz, that he is a pathological opponent."[26] However true that may have become, it hardly explained why the committee should not listen to his testimony. Bella Dodd had done much better on that issue, pointing out the jealousy Lefkowitz expressed when she took over his position as legislative representative for the union and that he had done everything in his power to discredit her in Albany. But this time Dodd's replacement, Rose Russell, had the enthusiasm but not the skill to turn Lefkowitz's damaging testimony around.[27]

The House hearing served the threefold purpose of drawing CIO attention to its affiliate, the United Public Workers (UPW), of testing the propaganda possibilities of looking for Communist party activists in public schools, and, finally, of opening up *both* the Teachers' Union and the anticommunist AFT Teachers' Guild (Local 2) to further action by the Board of Education. The

23. Hearings, pp. 358–61; Teachers' Union Collection, Box 38, Folder 13.
24. Hearings, pp. 107–19; Teachers' Union Collection, 38/13.
25. Hearings, pp. 385–408.
26. Ibid., p. 329.
27. Ibid.

CIO was the first to act. At the November 1948 CIO convention, President Philip Murray began an effort to purge the left-led United Public Workers, the parent union of Local 555 the CIO/UPW Teachers' Union. Finally on 9 January 1950 the UPW was formally tried and condemned by an investigating committee of the CIO, which charged that the union was "consistently directed toward the achievement of the program or purposes of the Communist Party rather than the objectives and policies set forth in the constitution of the CIO."[28] Cut loose from the CIO, the Teachers' Union faced the effects of the Feinberg Law in the first round of red-scare firings three months later.

The Feinberg Law stated that "despite existence of statutes to prevent it," members of "subversive groups, and particularly the Communist Party and of its affiliated organizations, have infiltrated into public employment in the public schools of the state." Aimed at New York City and members of the Communist party there, the law specified that the superintendent of schools should not merely impose a loyalty oath but actively seek out Communists and report the results of his investigation to the Board of Regents.[29]

Superintendent Jansen, like many of his contemporaries in other cities, was under public pressure. In March 1950 a Committee to Rid the Schools of Communists met at the Waldorf-Astoria to proclaim loudly its concern that the superintendent had not yet moved on any teachers. But the committee needn't have bothered: Jansen was well prepared to act against the Teachers' Union. In April he called the members of the union's Executive Board to his office. He told them that he strongly suspected they were members of the Communist party, and he wanted to have them attest to their loyalty. Teachers were given only a few days to reply and were denied counsel at their meetings; although wire recordings of the testimony were made, the teachers had no access to these recordings.

Uniformly, all eight teachers refused to cooperate. They pointed to the fact that the Feinberg Law was being tested in the courts, they argued that they would say nothing without legal counsel, and they demanded open hearings. Because they refused to cooperate with the superintendent they were fired in May. Although their cases were tried individually the following fall, they were permanently dismissed from New York schools in February 1951— while the Feinberg Law was still being tested in the courts and while the red scare was heating up. It was a dramatic beginning.[30]

The eight teachers—Alice Citron, Louis Jaffe, Celia Zitron, Abraham Feingold, Abraham Lederman, Mark Frielander, Isidore Rubin, and David Friedman—provided a stark lesson to the rest of the teaching force. This was especially true of Abraham Lederman, who had been well known in union circles since he joined the local in 1932. An award-winning mathematics

28. Bock, *Subversive Activities,* p. 155; *American Teacher,* 33 (February 1949).
29. Bock, *Subversive Activities,* pp. 136–38.
30. Ibid., p. 138.

teacher who had devised special teaching programs for teachers in the whole system, Lederman was highly regarded in old AFT circles and maintained contact with AFT Local 2 people despite his ouster. His old district superintendent testified as a character witness. His lawyers presented glowing recommendations from supervisors and parents as well.

Others, like Celia Zitron, had been active in the Harlem schools in the thirties and forties and had organized strong parental support for her efforts on behalf of black children. Obviously a Communist activist, Zitron argued that her political views were quite beside the point: she wished to be judged on her conduct as a teacher. Newspaper articles in the *Teachers' News* pointed insistently to the teachers' school record while the superintendent of schools hammered at Communist party affiliation and the formal charge of "conduct unbecoming a teacher." For their refusal to cooperate with the superintendent, the teachers were dismissed. Other less well-known activists in the union could only wait for their summons to the superintendent's office.[31]

The work of Communist teachers in Harlem and Bedford-Stuyvesant was well known in the city. The projects in both areas seemed designed to bridge the growing gap between professionalism and community interests. Reaching out to the parents of disadvantaged children, these Communist organizers hoped to radicalize progressive education and make the classroom a vehicle for social change. In the thirties the strategy had worked well, as a special chemistry of interests fused the Communist teachers with community groups. But after the war the coalition began to fall apart and the teachers grew increasingly isolated. In part some of this was due to the split in the AFT, with Counts's supporter Layle Lane taking an active role in discrediting the Communist teachers in Harlem. Beyond that, progressive education itself had less appeal in the black community. Just as the NAACP had to abandon its coalition politics behind federal funding, black parents looked beyond the promise of progressive education to racial integration as a solution to quality education.[32]

This is not to say that everyone in the black community abandoned the Teachers' Union and its leaders. Indeed, Langston Hughes continued to work with the union to promote black history programs, and when the union teachers were dismissed a storm of protest arose from the community. But the Communist party strategy had been to seek protection in the community from external attacks without recognizing that centralization had long ago destroyed the community's power to protect its interests in teacher selection and retention. Only the union, and the procedures sanctioned by professionalization, could protect teacher interests—and these were sadly weakened by the persistent attack from the right, which connected teachers with

31. *NYT,* 4–20 May 1950; Bock, *Subversive Activities,* p. 157.
32. Mark Naison, *Communists in Harlem during the Depression* (New York, 1983), pp. 309–14.

progressive education and communism without regard to the distinctions within the educational community.[33]

Success in the first move to remove Communist teachers brought more publicity and prompted new national investigations of teachers. A subcommittee of the McCarran Senate Internal Security Committee blew into New York City, taking testimony in the summer and fall of 1951, and again in the spring of 1952. In that same summer, Jansen hired Saul Moskoff to head his investigation, and at that point the hunt took on a new professional look. Each new congressional investigation—the Jenner Committee, a subcommittee of the Senate Internal Security Committee, which arrived in March 1953, the Velde Committee, the House Un-American Activities Committee, which met in April 1954, and so on—invoked a new list of names to be added to Moskoff's file of investigations. Moskoff collected all the lists he could find, from Communist party nominating petitions to license-plate numbers of cars observed at rallies for the Rosenbergs, and he looked for teachers' names.[34]

Charges under the Feinberg Law could not be made until 30 September 1955 because the regents had to draw up a list of subversive organizations. In the meantime, however, teachers could be dismissed for falsification of their oaths, for insubordination, for "conduct unbecoming a teacher" (a relic of World War I once contested by Henry Linville), or for refusing to answer questions.

Teachers seemed to understand before coming into the questioning that Teachers' Guild membership was a good sign and that Teachers' Union membership was the kiss of death. In one case a teacher admitted to being at Communist party meetings, but when asked if he could demonstrate that he was no longer a member, he volunteered that "I am not a member of a certain organization in the teaching field believe me I am not a member."[35] When the teacher mentioned he was a member of the NEA and the Jewish Teachers' Association, his inquisitor admitted, "Well, that is to your credit."[36] One teacher who admitted to past Teachers' Union membership offered that he was now only a member of the NEA and the High School Teachers' Association. Apparently afraid that the superintendent might read his transcript, he quickly added that he was not actually a member of the High School Teachers' Association (HSTA) because he disagreed with them on the issue of salaries. Although the only evidence that Moskoff had on this teacher was his name on a Communist party petition and past Teachers' Union member-

33. Interview with Mildred and David Flacks, summer 1988; see also the correspondence of Rosalind Russell, Teachers' Union Collection, Box 38.

34. Bock, *Subversive Activities*, p. 149.

35. "Hearings and Associated Materials," no. 807, Individual Files, Board of Education Archives, IVE8d, Special Collections, Millbank Library, Columbia University.

36. Ibid.

ship, the teacher still felt it necessary to dissociate himself from anything that would even seem militant to school authorities.[37]

Shortly after fingering the leaders of the Teachers' Union as Communists, the board announced that it would not negotiate with the union, would not allow the union to have meetings in public schools, and would treat the union as an organization "directed towards the achievement of the program of the Communist Party."[38] The Teachers' Union spent the next twelve years devoting itself to defending the legal rights of its members and pursuing legal remedies for teachers caught in the red dragnet.

For the teachers associated with the union, the impact was felt immediately. Teaching merit was never a consideration in their hearings. Only through cooperation with Moskoff, a full "confession," and (after 1955) the naming of other names, could teachers save their jobs.[39] Many teachers resigned before their hearings; others simply never appeared in the school district again. As Teachers' Union lawyer Harold Cammer reported: "Moskoff destroyed the lives of hundreds of teachers. These were people well along in years and careers. Many became menial salesmen, burdens on friends and families, moving about like beggars. Some were totally shattered. And they had all been good teachers, some great."[40] One teacher objected to the publicity given in her case; she reported that "the most horrible rumors became rampant in the neighborhood of my former school; some even saying I was pulled out of school by the FBI and I was now in prison."[41] When she tried to meet with students and parents to explain herself, she was forbidden to do so by her school principal. David Flacks spoke bitterly of the irony that he had planned a class trip to see the Statue of Liberty when he was unceremoniously pulled out of classroom teaching.

Old Teachers' Union members took a certain pride in their role during the red scare. Cecil Yampolsky wrote, "When a nation bent its head in fear, the Union grew in courage."[42] Much later, in 1967, after the investigations had wrought their damage to teachers, a federal court deemed the entire procedure unconstitutional. Restitution for teachers, however, was slow and far from complete.[43]

Several aspects of the Feinberg investigations troubled all teachers and stirred memories of the first red scare. Cammer and Teachers' Union presi-

---

37. "Hearings and Associated Materials," no. 844. The salary issue was a protest against the board's decision in 1949 to go to a single salary schedule and wipe out the pay differential for high school teachers. It was one of the High School Teachers' Association's most popular issues, one that it was now renewing with increasing militancy.

38. Bock, *Subversive Activities*, p. 94.

39. Ibid., p. 86; *NYT,* 24 March 1954.

40. Bock, *Subversive Activities,* p. 149.

41. Correspondence of Rosalind Russell, Teachers' Union Collection, 38/4.

42. Cecil Yampolsky to Rosalind Russell, 6 October 1963, Teachers' Union Collection, 42/1.

43. Lawrence Chamberlain, *Loyalty and Legislative Action: A Survey of Activity by the New York State Legislature, 1919–1949* (Ithaca, N.Y., 1951), p. 192.

dent Rose Russell charged that most of the victims were Jewish whereas charges against Christians were dropped. One board member recalled, however, that "they tried their damnedest to get a Catholic but they couldn't pin it on him."[44] There was a strong connection between board member George Timone, a Catholic board member, and Cardinal Spellman, whose own anticommunist campaign was not devoid of bigotry. The same charges had arisen in 1919 when Henry Linville expressed his suspicion that the victims were all Jewish and union members. Some of the attacks on Jewish teachers were frightening reminders of Nazi hatred. Threatening postcards were mailed to investigated teachers, with the names of family members included in the addresses. Many said that Hitler was right. "Hooked nosed, immoral, money hungry, anti-christian, mongreloid, parasitic leeches and vermin of Delancey Street sewers," said one letter. "Jews don't make good Americans" and "Judas Cow" were other bits of invective. One correspondent said, "First plane for Moskow and Warsaw leaves Monday, hurry hurry, do not miss it as we will not miss you."[45] The ugliness of the campaign and its insistence on connecting communism with Jewish origins became a threat to the entire Jewish community, which remained divided between loyalty to the old Teachers' Union, with its many friends and roots in the Jewish community, and the new Teachers' Guild, which had some important young Jewish leaders.[46]

The conversion of Bella Dodd from Communist agitator to committed Catholic under the tutelage of Bishop Fulton Sheen caused Jewish schoolteachers to wait with great apprehension to see what she would do. Her appearance before the McCarran Committee in New York, in the fall of 1952 and again in the spring of 1953, confirmed their fears. Bella Dodd named over fourteen hundred teachers associated with the union, many of whom were now inside the AFT. Shortly after her revelations George Timone, one of the leading Catholic members of the Board of Education and a staunch anticommunist, insisted that it was not enough that teachers confess their sins of the past and renounce communism. He added that he wanted them to name the names of other teachers. The Teachers' Guild angrily and instantly protested. Charges of anti-Semitism were raised since the hunt would now clearly widen to include most of the teachers who had been in the guild, the membership of which was largely Jewish. Timone and others insisted that the red scare was unrelated: after all, Moskoff was Jewish as were most of the lawyers involved in the Feinberg investigation. The opposition responded by pointing out that these same lawyers worked for predominantly Catholic law firms and that Cardinal Spellman had been in the forefront of the attack on federal aid, even going so far as to attack Eleanor Roosevelt in the process.

44. Bock, *Subversive Activities*, p. 166.
45. Teachers' Union Collection, 21/5.
46. Bock, *Subversive Activities*, p. 161–67.

Others have documented the contribution of a rising Catholic middle class to the intensity of McCarthyism in the fifties. Although the full impact of the religious animosity is difficult to assess, it would be reasonable to suspect that the experience of the red scare helped to bind together the Jewish teachers still in the Teachers' Union. It would seem that the taint of communism could bring with it an American pogrom.[47]

Although the Teachers' Guild opposed the board's policy on investigations and argued that the Feinberg Law was an attack on academic freedom, it refused to work with the Teachers' Union in opposing the investigation.[48] Abraham Lefkowitz called the Feinberg Law an insult to teachers, yet the New York City Teachers' Guild argued forcefully and successfully at the AFT's national convention in 1954 that any teacher who took the Fifth Amendment "as a cloak to hide membership in the Communist Party" should not be defended by the union.[49] Charles Cogen, president of the guild in 1954, argued that locals had a right not to defend a teacher who took the Fifth. Nevertheless, the guild protested some violations of due process and denounced Timone's informer policy as reprehensible. The guild also led the Joint Teachers' Organization to oppose the Feinberg Law and complained when the school principals praised it. The fact that the High School Teachers' Association endorsed the Feinberg Law kept the guild and the association from working together on issues of mutual interest until 1959.[50]

The Red Hunt in the Schools

New York City teachers took the brunt of the red scare accusations and endured an ongoing investigation that carried well into the late fifties. But they were not the only teachers targeted in the red hunt. The exact scope of the red scare for teachers is difficult to assess because the charges were local. In many cases teachers could not face the publicity or the tension of investigation and, when called, resigned without defending themselves. The NEA report of 1949 on Tenure and Academic Freedom reported that 38 states had general sedition laws, 21 forbade seditious teaching, 13 disbarred disloyal persons from public teaching, and 25 had loyalty oaths.[51]

Probationary teachers were, of course, most vulnerable. Describing the dismissal of a probationary teacher in a Utah high school, Superintendent James Glove explained that he could not prove his charges of communism and atheism, but "I have seen Tremayne running around with Jews and

47. Bella Dodd, *School of Darkness* (New York, 1954).
48. Guild Papers, Robert Wagner Archives, New York University.
49. Bock, *Subversive Activities*, p. 168; Guild Files.
50. Bock, *Subversive Activities*, p. 170; *NYT*, 14 September 1955.
51. NEA, *Report of the Committee on Tenure and Academic Freedom* (Washington, D.C., 1949); Teachers' Union Collection, 9/6.

niggers and he voted for Wallace and that's proof enough for me."[52] Without tenure rights, probationary teachers were automatically dismissed, many without a hearing.

In Pennsylvania, forty teachers were called to a HUAC hearing in the fall of 1953, and thirty were immediately suspended by Philadelphia superintendent Louis P. Hoyer. Two other teachers were included in Hoyer's list of suspected teachers and dismissed as incompetent. In contrast to the New York law, Pennsylvania had no category specifying conduct unbecoming a teacher. Hoyer charged, despite the overall superior ratings of these teachers, that their communism impaired their abilities as teachers. One teacher, Herman A. Beilan, challenged his dismissal under the Fourteenth Amendment and won his case in the state supreme court in June 1958. Most teachers had little recourse. Pennsylvania's Pechan Law of 1952 replaced the earlier loyalty oath and again put more force into what legislators declared was an opportunity to "rid the schools of red and pink minded teachers." The American Legion and Blue Star Mothers expressed the desire to "rid the schools of political zionists."[53]

In California the state assembly set up the Tenney Committee to investigate subversion in education. Tenney's commitment to anitcommunism began in 1940, shortly after his ouster as president of the American Federation of Musicians in Los Angeles. Having joined with Sam Yorty to form the "little Dies" committee of California, Tenney ran the committee from 1941 to 1949. Although Tenney focused mainly on people in higher education, he looked into a case of sex education taught in a Chico, California, high school and later held hearings against two officers of AFT Local 430 in Los Angeles, who were accused of spreading Communist propaganda in the classroom.[54]

In some cases, teacher leaders were joined by school superintendents who refused to let investigations go on. Detroit superintendent Arthur H. Dondineau gave such a response in 1953, after Bella Dodd's McCarran Committee testimony. "I have been watching the situation over the last five years and have seen no indication of nests or cells."[55] But not all the pronouncements were as brave as these, and mostly they were inconsistent.

It was impossible for the AFT to distance itself from the many local investigations that multiplied in the late forties. In the Los Angeles case, the national AFT offered defense funds for the accused officers, but then turned its wrath on the Los Angeles local. In February 1949, shortly after a

52. Teachers' Union Collection, 3/12.
53. Ibid., 15/1.
54. Laurence D. Shubow to Harold Cammer, 25 November 1953, Teachers' Union Collection, Box 2; Bock, *Subversive Activities,* p. 170; Edward L. Barrett, Jr., *The Tenney Committee: Legislative Investigation of Subversive Activities in California* (Ithaca, N.Y., 1951), pp. 164–67.
55. *American Teacher,* 37 (February 1953), p. 31; see also the Detroit files at the Walter Reuther Archives. Jeffrey Merril gave me the quotation.

Christmas investigation of Local 430, the AFT Executive Board voted to oust the local on the grounds that it supported other unions in the city that were thought to be associated with the Communist party.[56] The convention thoroughly debated the new ouster, but the decision was upheld. In a similar investigation, Local 61 of San Francisco also came under scrutiny because of its association with the California Labor School, an organization listed by the Tenney Committee as a Communist front. Local 61 was given a warning. In yet a third west coast case, College Local 401 of the University of Washington had its charter revoked. Each local had members called before an investigatory committee.[57]

The AFT's underlying position on government investigations was expressed by the Commission on Reconstruction in 1948: "The Commission recognizes the right and obligation of our government at this time to take dire steps to assure itself of the loyalty of those engaged in public service, including educators."[58] In 1952 the AFT committee on Civil and Professional Rights declared that the AFT did not have to defend Communists, only teachers who were loyal to the AFT charter and were trying to clear their names. In 1953 when a debate arose over the justifiable use of the Fifth Amendment, many teachers wanted to allow its use, while Selma Borchardt and representatives from New York Local 2 opposed it. Urging that teachers testify fully, Borchardt successfully moved for the reconsideration of the issue. All agreed, however, that the procedures of the investigatory committees were "manifestly inadequate to protect the rights of witnesses."[59] As the red scare mounted against all teachers, the union was forced to take a stronger stand against it.

There can be no doubt that the red scare had a demoralizing effect on teachers in both the AFT and the NEA. Both organizations maintained a legal advisor to give general national advice, but the defense of teachers was most often local. Both organizations went out of their way to condemn communism in the schools and Communist teachers. Both organizations also pointed at the same time to the demise of academic freedom and the decline of freedom in the classroom. In a telling 1953 editorial to teachers, Carl Megel wrote about "Another Iron Curtain." He told of how he was watching television in a department-store window; the commentator pointed dramatically at a map and declared, "This is the Iron Curtain." Then Megel glanced down the street at a "screaming headline that read, 'McCarthy To Investigate Teachers.' " The usually conservative AFT president responded, "So it has come to this! If teachers are going to be harassed, if they are going to be stifled and fearful of discussing controversial issues in our schools and colleges, then we, too, will find ourselves behind an Iron Curtain."[60]

56. *American Teacher,* 33 (February 1949).
57. Ibid.
58. Reeves, "Commission on Reconstruction."
59. *American Teacher,* 33 (February 1949); *AFT Proceedings,* 1953, AFT Collection.
60. Megel, *American Teacher,* 37 (February 1953).

The Communist teachers themselves had not appeared to be so very different from ordinary teachers. After all, they had all faced the depression with some compassion for working people, they had all hoped that by drawing closer to the community and the great labor movement they could work out a new accommodation that would embrace the best that progressive education had to offer. Under the strain of the McCarthy era, the divorce of the professional teacher from the community appeared complete. Political advocacy and community involvement spelled isolation against which teachers had only their professional associations for protection, and even these protections were at best flimsy. "The teachers are so afraid," observed AFT secretary-treasurer Irwin Kuenzli. AFT president John Eklund referred to a "wave of intimidation that is sweeping the country."[61]

61. Lawrence D. Shubow to Harold Cammer, 25 November 1953, Teachers' Union Collection, Box 2.

CHAPTER TEN

Civil Rights:
The Contest for Leadership

Collective bargaining and civil rights dominated the minds of both NEA and AFT leaders in the period from 1954 to 1968. As collective bargaining threatened to eclipse the hegemony of the NEA, the issue of civil rights became a weapon in its battle for the sympathies of urban teachers. Although it is difficult, therefore, to separate the histories of the two sets of issues, the issues embodied in both civil rights and collective bargaining deserve separate attention. The union and the association approached these questions with varying degrees of urgency.

In the early years of civil rights activism the AFT took the lead, demonstrating far more resolve with a greater willingness to take risks to achieve integrationist goals than the NEA. But by the close of the sixties it would appear that the NEA had philosophically come to terms with the militancy of the black-power movement and expressed willingness to translate community demands into professional concerns. The AFT, on the other hand, held its strength in urban schools where racial conflict had become explosive and where union ideals met with ugly realities in the streets and in the classroom. The different responses of the union and the association to the civil rights movement reflected the difference in style and structure of the two organizations.

The AFT and Civil Rights

The AFT participation in the cause of civil rights was long and intense. In 1920 the AFT formally asked Congress to support a bill that would give Howard University $1,580,000, thus establishing a long relationship with Howard faculty that led to black leadership on the union's Executive Council in the thirties. The contest between socialists and Communists in the AFT in the thirties led to a series of incidents in which the AFT asserted in no uncertain terms that it would not tolerate various forms of discrimination. Still the union had its own segregated locals, a point that became a hot issue at the 1947 AFT convention. Layle Lane, who continued to head the union's Human Rights Committee, pressed for a program of both integrating the union and working closely with the NAACP on the issue of school integration. By the 1950 convention the issue of segregated union locals was raised again, and in 1951 the AFT Executive Council voted not to charter new locals that were segregated; the following year the successful integration of the Washington, D.C., locals was announced, at the same time that the delegates voted to enter an amicus curiae brief in the case of *Briggs v. Elliott,* a forerunner of the *Brown v. Board of Education* decision. By the time Layle Lane was ready to retire in 1952 the AFT was committed to a fairly extensive program on civil rights.[1]

Prepared to participate in the historic *Brown* decision, the union had no qualms about its role in the push for civil rights. The old socialists like Layle Lane had taken their liberal mandate seriously; they meant to show that the union could be just as reliable (and, they thought, more responsible) in fostering black education as the Communist community organizers had been. The *American Teacher* prominently and regularly reported the progress of the Human Rights Committee, and when the young Dick Parrish replaced Layle Lane it was not hard to imagine that the push for integrated locals would intensify under his leadership. Parrish, a New York City schoolteacher, organized the AFT's summer school in Prince Edward County, where school officials defied the Supreme Court ruling and closed public schools, thus denying black children access to public education. Later, Parrish organized Mississippi Freedom schools which recruited young, well-educated northerners to teach black children in the South. A member of the Socialist party, Parrish became an AFT vice-president.[2]

The AFT's largest southern local, the Atlanta Federation of Teachers, was important to the AFT in a number of ways. The national AFT's first president had been Mary Barker, the Atlanta Local's president who led the union through its darkest hours in the late twenties and early thirties. Second, the Atlanta local was a dual organization of union and association members; it was one of the few locals in the AFT that could claim a majority of teachers in its school district. However, just as the Atlanta schools were strictly segregated, so was the union. The issue in the AFT was whether the local could integrate before the school system without jeopardizing teachers' jobs. Parrish focused on the Atlanta local, and in 1955 proposed an ultimatum that the local either integrate or leave the AFT.[3]

1. Layle Lane Collection, Box 4, the AFT brief on *Brown v. Board of Education;* see also files on civil rights under Series 1, Box 6, AFT Collection.
2. *AFT Proceedings,* 1952, AFT Collection, Series 13.
3. Michael John Schultz, *The NEA and the Black Teacher: The Integration of a Professional*

The problems of local integration, whether for the AFT or for the NEA, should not be minimized in the history of integration. Members of southern locals often faced dismissal from their positions if they belonged to integrated groups or were even thought to sympathize with integration. Pressure for conformity on this issue intensified in the post-*Brown* years as segregationist forces pressed for solidarity behind their states' rights position. In Georgia, for example, a 1955 law required all teachers to swear loyalty to both the state and federal constitutions; the legislature also provided that a teacher could be dismissed for supporting the *Brown* decision or for belonging to the NAACP. In Louisiana teachers were specifically forbidden to belong to integrated organizations, including the NEA, although the state eventually backed down on the association issue. Black teachers suffered job layoffs when the courts forced desegregation, and white teachers were threatened with similarly dire consequences should they defy their state's segregation practices. Southern teachers in both the association and the union strongly resisted attempts to press them into integration in their respective organizations before their schools integrated.[4]

In the AFT, however, Dick Parrish was able to gain support of a resolution for immediate integration in 1955. In part the 1955 AFL-CIO merger was responsible for Parrish's success, for in the year of labor's big merger the UAW's Walter Reuther had made it clear that the CIO would press for union integration as he reentered the official house of labor. President Carl Megel and other AFT leaders supported Reuther's integrationist stance. Unable to comply with the action of the national, the Atlanta Federation of Teachers faced expulsion in 1956. As one teacher argued: "We are just speaking about our Supreme Court decision. I will say this, as I have said previously, that if we do not take a step forward, we are going to have to jump on the bandwagon, because, as it is, they are trying to integrate the schools; and as you know, the NAACP and other organizations are moving in that direction. Frankly speaking, as a teacher I would like to see teachers take a lead in this thing rather than follow."[5]

Megel called upon segregated locals to report their progress on integration, but only five of twenty-five locals answered his call. Parrish as chair of

Organization (Coral Gables, Fla., 1970); Ronald Lloyd Dewing, "Teachers' Organizations and Desegregation, 1954–64" (Ph.D diss., Ball State University, 1967), pp. 63–91. For a general history of desegregation, see Don Shoemaker, *With All Deliberate Speed: Segregation and Desegregation in Southern Schools* (New York, 1957).

4. For more on desegregation, see A. Lee Coleman, "Desegregation of the Public Schools in Kentucky: The Second Year after the Supreme Court Decision," *Journal of Negro Education,* 25 (Summer 1956), pp. 254–61; Albert P. Marshall, "Racial Integration in Education in Missouri," *Journal of Negro Education,* 25 (Summer 1956), pp. 289–98; W. E. Solomon, "The Problem of Desegregation in South Carolina," *Journal of Negro Education,* 25 (Summer 1956), pp. 321–23; Hurley H. Doddy, "Desegregation and the Employment of Negro Teachers," *Journal of Negro Education,* 24 (Fall 1955), pp. 405–8. See also Shoemaker, *With All Deliberate Speed,* p. 29.

5. *AFT Proceedings,* 1955, "Report of the Human Rights Committee," and discussion, p. 852, AFT Collection, Series 13, Box 33/2.

AFT's Committee on Democratic Human Relations submitted a resolution on suspending charters of locals not in compliance with the union's stand on integration by 1 April 1956. In response Megel appointed a committee to visit Atlanta, New Orleans, and Chattanooga, the oldest of the segregated locals. He also sent out a questionnaire to all locals in states where segregation laws applied. In the questionnaire both white and black locals reported the state of the integration issue in their school districts. One white local responded, "Our union hasn't taken a stand on it. If it should there won't be any local to worry about. The NAACP will probably take care of it." A black local in Louisiana said it had not sent invitations to white teachers because "customs of this area are such that racial groups do not meet together." In Atlanta, both the tactics of intimidation and the attitudes of white teachers made integration appear hopeless, whereas in New Orleans the black and white locals worked closely together but were unwilling to step ahead of the school district on integration. Meanwhile in the Atlanta local, AFT stalwarts were unable to pass a resolution to change the segregationist position of the local in the constitution. The AFT Executive Council subsequently voted fourteen to two to recommend expulsion of the Atlanta local. After a long debate the AFT convention voted to insist that locals conform with national policy and integrate. Each local then had to vote on whether to stay in the AFT. On 10 December 1956 the Atlanta local of 1,855 members, finding it "impossible to comply and cooperate with said convention action, mandates, directives and procedures relative to the practice of local's jurisdiction on the basis of race and color," voted to leave the AFT. On 21 December 1956 Carl Megel called a press conference announcing the Atlanta local's failure to comply with the AFT constitution and making public his plans to form an integrated local.[6]

In Louisiana a state law threatened dismissal of public employees who advocated integration or belonged to organizations that were integrated. New Orleans teachers in both black and white unions sent a request to the national for exemption from the convention rule. New York's Rebecca Simonson visited Chattanooga and New Orleans locals, the Executive Council remained firmly behind the integrationist order. The Chattanooga local claimed that it was under the same pressures as the Atlanta local and even requested that the AFT leaders not come to visit the local because a visit would only further polarize a situation that needed to be solved locally.

In 1957 the union further demanded that locals institute civil rights committees to deal with problems of desegregation in their schools, and a national integration committee declared the Chattanooga charter void for noncompliance with the integration order. Black locals that had stayed in good standing through the crisis were allowed to stay in the AFT and reform

6. Dewing, "Teachers' Organizations," pp. 91–92; desegregation files, AFT Collection, Series 5, Secretary-Treasurer's Papers, Box 10–11.

as integrated locals. By the beginning of 1958 the AFT claimed it had lost close to seven thousand members or 14 percent of its membership because of its stand on integration. In actuality the AFT had lost four thousand members because of the desegregation order, but Megel estimated that the entire process, including the integration of some locals as in the Washington area, had led to a significant decline in membership.[7]

NEA organizers have argued that the AFT exaggerated its claims of membership losses and took the dramatic action to attract new members, especially in the South. But the AFT gained nothing by the move. Observers have noted that most rural black administrators belonged to the American Association of Colored Teachers—later known as the American Teachers' Association (ATA)—which held teaching to be a status position in the community. The AFT's militant stand on integration would hardly appeal to this status-oriented group, nor would union affiliation appeal to black teachers anxious to achieve status in the community. The most compelling reason for the AFT action on the issue is the same old reason that Jennie McKeon used in the Chicago Teachers' Federation: it was "the right thing to do." No matter how crassly the AFT would later use its reputation in the field of civil rights, there was no rational organizational advantage that the AFT could have foreseen from this action.[8]

NEA Structure and Style

William Carr's inauguration as executive director of the NEA in 1952 had all the trappings of a college president's inaugural. Reporters pressed the newly installed executive director for his vision of education, his views on the problem of communism in the schools, and his hopes for federal funds for education. Carr brought to office the air of the old NEA, when Nicholas Murray Butler and George D. Strayer had graced the association with their wit and keen intelligence. A student of William Cubberly at Stanford University, Carr had caught the eye of James Crabtree, the NEA's first executive director, after Carr as a young graduate student published his first book on the problems of education. Carr came into the NEA as a protege of Crabtree, but he quickly became William Givens's prime assistant, making his first appearance on the question of school finance before the U.S. Congress in 1935. Allan West, an NEA staff member, remarked that Carr had a great flair for formality and brought with him the airs of the professoriate. He never

7. Megel, Press Conference, December 1957, desegregation files, AFT Collection, Secretary-Treasurer's Papers, Box 10–11.

8. Megel's actions went further than mere pronouncement in favor of desegregation: in 1956 he wrote to John L. Lewis of the United Mine Workers, saying, "I . . . suggest you investigate whether [obstructionists to desegregation] were UMW members." Megel to Lewis, 7 September 1956, AFT Collection, Series 1, Box 6.

failed to address his fellow doctoral colleagues formally as "Dr." and expected as much from others. His leadership of the NEA was shared unequally with the NEA president, whose one-year term of office limited the effectiveness of the elective office. Furthermore, Carr was paid much more than the president, whose equivalent teacher's salary was little over twenty thousand dollars, while Carr's was close to fifty thousand.

Several structural changes came with Carr's inauguration. First he worked with a group he called the cabinet, a small coterie of executive secretaries in various NEA departments with whom Carr consulted. Carr said he regretted the fact that members of the staff began to look upon the cabinet as an upper-level management group, but the fact was that the NEA grew more stratified as Carr fought to preserve the élan of the old professoriate in the NEA.[9]

The second change came with a unification movement and the creation of "dual" affiliates. Although Givens was largely responsible for pressing for members of various state associations to affiliate formally with the NEA national, it was Carr who paid particular attention to organizational growth. Not all local and professional associations were formally affiliated with the NEA, and Carr moved to remedy this situation. Part of this arrangement, however, included the creation of dual affiliates, that is, statewide organizations that were segregated into white and black associations. In 1952 seventeen states were represented by these dual affiliates at the national conventions.[10]

At the same moment that the NEA moved toward further segregation, it grew publicly more vocal in its opposition to racism. But it was only with difficulty that the organization could maintain a consistent position. In 1943 the convention had decided that it would no longer meet in segregated cities, but in 1950 the meeting in St. Louis seemed to break that arrangement. For several years the convention wrangled over the issue until 1953, when the NEA had its first integrated convention in the South in Miami. After that, all NEA conventions were held in cities with no Jim Crow laws. During the course of the war the NEA National Commission on the Defense of Democracy had called on teachers to address issues of racial tolerance in the classroom, but the NEA never moved to support the several legal challenges to school segregation that had begun in the courts.[11]

In 1954, when the Supreme Court decided that the "separate but equal" doctrine no longer applied to America's classrooms, the NEA did not have a defined national position on the decision. Executive Secretary Carr advised

9. Allen M. West, *The NEA: The Power Base for Education* (New York, 1980), pp. 65–93; William Carr, *The Education of William Carr* (Washington, D.C., 1978), p. 274.

10. Carr, *Education*, pp. 353–57.

11. *Defense Bulletin*, October 1945, p. 13; Thelma D. Perry, *History of the American Teachers Association* (Washington, D.C., 1975). The NEA actually met in segregated St. Louis in 1950, but agreed that meetings would be held where "dignity and rights of black members would not be denigrated or diminished." Perry, *History of the American Teachers Association*, p. 275.

the first convention held after the decision that it would be wrong to support or oppose the Supreme Court's ruling until the Court made clear its intentions. The convention passed a resolution that reaffirmed a belief in integration but did not take sides on the Court's decision:

> The principle embodied in the recent decision of the Supreme Court of the United States in regard to racial segregation is reflected in the long established provisions of the Platform of the National Education Association. The Association recognizes that integration of all groups in our public schools is more than an idea. It is a process which affects every state and territory in our nation. The Association urges that all citizens approach this matter of integration in our public schools with the spirit of fair play and good will which has always been the outstanding characteristic of the American people. It is the conviction of the Association that all problems of integration in our schools are capable of solution by citizens of intelligence, saneness, and reasonableness working together in the interests of national unity for the common good of all.[12]

By 1955 the Court had carefully spelled out the provisions of the decision; however, the NEA leadership was still unwilling to move beyond its original statement. Carr again counseled for more time, and the convention accepted his reluctance to act. In 1956 convention delegates were handed a fait accompli when the very large Department of Classroom Teachers, which met before the convention, endorsed the same 1954 resolution. This action closed off the possibility for more discussion on the convention floor. The following year it was difficult for teachers interested in supporting the *Brown* decision to oppose the sense of accomplishment, nostalgia, and unity at the 1957 meeting. Carr had just overseen the completion of the new NEA headquarters, a monumental building dedicated to housing the growing bureaucracy that he so happily served.[13]

Politics in the schools partially shook the NEA out of its complacency. In the three years following the *Brown* decision, teachers had become pawns in the battle over school integration while segregationists rode roughshod over teacher tenure laws. Hundreds of black teachers were fired under a bewildering range of circumstances. In border states where some schools were integrated, black teachers often lost their jobs while white teachers with less experience were kept. Others were fired simply for opposing segregation. In those same years the NEA officially investigated only one case regarding racial discrimination, which charged that some teachers in Clay, Kentucky, had refused to meet with integrated classes. The National Commission on the

12. *NEA Proceedings,* 1954, pp. 124–25.
13. Schultz, *NEA and the Black Teacher,* pp. 71–87; Richard Lugar, *Simple Justice: The History of Brown v. Board of Education and Black Americans; Struggle for Equality* (New York, 1976).

Defense of Democracy found the accusations to be false. Still, times were changing. Congress passed a civil rights bill in 1957, the first since Reconstruction. President Eisenhower sent federal troops to Little Rock, Arkansas, the same year to enforce a desegregation order. It was only with difficulty that the NEA continued to stay the course for gradualism.[14]

In 1958 the NEA was called upon to do more than simply endorse desegregation in the abstract. Integrationists confidently predicted that the association would support the *Brown* decision. Yet, after a pro-*Brown* resolution reached the floor of the NEA Representative Assembly in 1958, hundreds of southern delegates poured out of the room, preventing a quorum. Angry integrationists in the NEA vowed to return the following year and win the issue. Meanwhile, Carr had his hands full with the cases of Little Rock teachers who had participated in the integrationist movement and were being fired for their participation. Quietly, the NEA set up a defense fund to help the teachers defend their tenured positions. Rather than make this part of the normal process of tenure protection, and thereby place the teachers' case under the DuShane fund, Carr preferred to see this as a special case and allocated special collections for the teachers' defense. Later, when the NEA embraced integration, the practice was reversed and the association loudly broadcast the effectiveness of the DuShane fund in bringing teachers legal protection. The point in 1958 was to avoid arousing the segregationist sentiments of white southern members who had bolted the assembly the year before.[15]

To avoid confrontation at the 1959 convention the Resolutions Committee proposed a three-point proposal that provided for the support of the original mild resolution, the support of teachers as citizens (their freedom to discuss political issues and the protection of tenure rights), and the support of public education. For two hours the delegates hotly debated the leadership's proposals. A rival resolution called for recognition of the Supreme Court decision and support for its implementation. In a dramatic speech from Little Rock teachers, members were advised to take this more moderate road, and after further debate the assembly agreed to support the status quo. No support for the *Brown* decision emerged in 1959.[16]

The Sixties

In the early sixties the NEA came under increasing pressure to take a stronger stand on desegregation. Although the Representative Assembly had

---

14. Schultz, *NEA and the Black Teacher,* pp. 72, 77, 81; Myron Lieberman, "Segregation's Challenge to the NEA," *School and Society,* 81 (28 May 1955), pp. 167–68; Doddy, "Desegregation," pp. 406–7.
15. Schultz, *NEA and the Black Teacher,* pp. 87–102; *NEA Proceedings,* 1958, pp. 182–201.
16. Schultz, *Nea and the Black Teacher,* pp. 95–103; *NEA Proceedings,* 1959, p. 225.

failed to vote for a study of integration, the Executive Board ordered such a study in 1960 over the objections of William Carr. Sit-ins in Greensboro, North Carolina, and the promise of civil rights activism at the federal level held out by John F. Kennedy's nomination for president failed to inspire the 1960 NEA convention to come out in support of the *Brown* decision.

The AFT added its criticism in this regard. In 1959 AFT delegates lambasted the NEA for "abdicating its claim to leadership and guidance of teachers in the nation" and reaffirmed the union's own commitment to the struggle for desegregation. Again in 1960 Edwin Irwin, an AFT vice-president, challenged the NEA to compare its civil rights record with the AFT's and pointedly remarked that segregated locals had been ousted from the AFT in 1956. Carr and NEA president William W. Eshelman countered that their dual affiliates allowed teachers to belong to the NEA where segregation was strictly enforced. The continuance of segregated organizations in the NEA, the AFT said, was a "shameful neglect of the principles of democracy." AFT members supported sit-ins and continued to encourage militancy in the cause of desegregation. At the same moment the AFT announced that it would challenge the NEA in a collective bargaining campaign in New York City, where desegregation had been an active and ongoing issue for some time. It was this latter threat that Carr took most seriously of all.[17]

Finally in 1961 the NEA mildly endorsed the Supreme Court decision on desegregation. It was a momentous decision. Southern delegates who for years had threatened to walk out of the convention had little to say, and for the first time major leaders in the Representative Assembly stood against the old gradualism arguments. Arguments for the morality of the decision mixed with arguments about the image of the NEA. Once the principle of support for the Supreme Court decision was adopted, the association had to turn its attention to the internal issue of segregated associations. This was the issue that Carr feared would lead to secession from the organization, but after 1961 confrontation over the issue appeared inevitable.[18]

Because so many state associations were segregated, black delegates had participated in the NEA only as individuals since the twenties, whereas white teachers participated in the Representative Assembly as delegates recognized by their state associations. By recognizing dual affiliates in seventeen states in 1952, the NEA broadened black participation but only along segregationist lines. At the same time the organization was pledged to form a stronger alliance with the American Association of Colored Teachers, or the ATA, with which the NEA had operated in a loosely coordinated fashion since 1926. By the early sixties, the ATA was receiving overtures from the

17. Schultz, *NEA and the Black Teacher,* pp. 107–10; Carr, *Education:* "I never thought that the issue which occupied a substantial part of my time between 1960 and 1967 was whether the initials of the major national teachers' organization would be NEA or AFT," p. 272.
18. Schultz, *NEA and the Black Teacher,* pp. 117–29.

AFT for merger, thus propelling the NEA into its own merger discussions. The ATA, however, was quite adamant that it would join in the NEA only if segregated associations ended. There were eleven such associations remaining in the early sixties when William Carr advocated a program of gradualism and voluntarism in achieving integration. Patience with Carr's proposals was clearly running thin.[19]

The challenge to Carr's protection of the dual affiliates came at the 1964 convention, where a rump caucus, the National Committee of Educators for Human Rights (NCEHR), came into meetings of the Department of Classroom Teachers (DCTA) prepared to set an agenda for the larger NEA meeting that followed. The DCTA set a firm deadline for the elimination of membership restrictions in 1965 and the integration of state and local associations in 1966. It also made Elizabeth Koontz its president elect. She was the first African-American classroom teacher honored with such a high position. Carr faced the challenge of the NCEHR by again warning against an integration-or-else resolution. The actual resolution on integration, which passed within hours of Congress's historic Civil Rights Bill of 1964, did not provide sanctions against associations that failed to comply with the integration order and furthermore left to the Executive Board the enforcement of the deadline provisions.[20]

In 1965 Carr had little to report on the progress of voluntary integration. The merger of the ATA and NEA, he announced, was slated for 1966; however, his report on voluntary action listed endless meetings and the end of membership restrictions in key segregationist associations, but merger of these white associations with black associations was still far off. Meanwhile, ATA leaders faced questions in their own ranks about the merger. Many members worried that the white leaders of integrated statewide associations would ignore the special problems that black educators continually faced in southern schools. ATA president R. J. Martin had to assure his constituents that black executive secretaries and other black organizational leaders would assume leadership positions in the new state associations.[21] The 1966 convention set merger deadlines within one year, after which the Executive Board could determine whether the affiliates had made sufficient progress in the direction of merger. As delegates sang the "Battle Hymn of the Republic," the ATA came into the NEA.

Two other changes took place that promised the end of segregation in the NEA. First, Carr resigned from office in 1966 and was replaced by Sam

19. Perry, *History of the American Teachers Association,* p. 28. At the time of the NEA-ATA merger the NEA had two black professional employees, and none at the managerial or executive level out of over five hundred employees. West, *NEA: The Power Base,* pp. 101–7.

20. Schultz, *NEA and the Black Teacher,* pp. 151–57; Dewing, "Teachers' Organizations," pp. 62–83.

21. West, *NEA: The Power Base,* pp. 120–25; Schultz, *NEA and the Black Teacher,* pp. 125–32; Perry, *History of the American Teachers Association,* p. 374; Dewing, "Teachers' Organizations," p. 32.

Lambert, a staff member far more committed to desegregation. Carr's focus on the AFT rivalry and his concern over membership growth had often led him to neglect civil rights issues in his addresses to the association. He had, however, implemented policy once his advice was overridden. His retirement opened opportunities for the now powerful integrationist group within the NEA. In the same year Mrs. Irvamae Applegate became president of the association. Applegate continued to work for merger of dual affiliates all through the late sixties and early seventies. In 1974 the NEA still had a stubborn segregated Louisiana association, but all other locals and state associations had merged.[22]

The NEA's response to the civil rights movement from 1952 to 1967 can only be described as slow and unenthusiastic. Carr, however, cannot be dismissed as an anomaly, an anti-integrationist crank. It was the survival of the organization that most obsessed Carr, and any threat to the organization's strength he regarded as destructive. He had a tendency to see the history of the organization as a series of crises that had been overcome, from the beginning of Crabtree's reign with the challenge of Margaret Haley to the end of his own with civil rights. These crises were not issues of principles in Carr's thinking, but challenges to organizational survival.

When the NEA nominated Elizabeth Koontz to be its first black president in 1967, it not only moved away from Carr's vision of the organization but it also hoped to assert that the change was genuine and deep. Koontz was a special education teacher from North Carolina who became head of the Department of Classroom Teachers and then of the NEA itself. She became so prominent that President Nixon later appointed her head of the Women's Bureau in the Department of Labor. The president of the NEA, however, still served a one-year term, while the executive directors, of which Carr was the third, seemed to serve for a lifetime. It would take more substantial changes in the NEA before the Koontz election could be seen as more than tokenism.[23]

The AFT in the Sixties

No longer hampered by the issue of internal cleansing, the AFT turned its evangelical mood outward to the civil rights movement. In 1960 the union went on record in support of sit-in demonstrations and, more important, cast its eye on the situation in Prince Edward County in Virginia, where officials had closed public schools in 1959 to avoid desegregation. First the union sent its desegregation message to the governor of Virginia in 1961, but in

22. West, *NEA: The Power Base*, pp. 120–25; *NEA Reporter*, 28 February 1969; AFT Collection, Series 1, Box 21.
23. Schultz, *NEA and the Black Teacher*, pp. 191–202; *NEA Reporter*, 29 January 1969. Koontz became "the symbolic spokesman in government for all working women."

1962 teachers began to protest the fact that seventeen hundred black children were being denied an education. The NEA hesitated to get involved in the Prince Edward County dispute in 1961, but the vocal outrage by most educational groups soon forced it to join the AFT in protest. In the summer of 1963 both the AFT and the NEA moved to take action. The union sent a peace corps of teachers to teach six hundred students in Prince Edward County while the association sent two thousand dollars to the Prince Edward County Free School Association. The different response of the organizations is indicative of their differences in style. The NEA could give money, the AFT could send activists. Teachers in the union pressed the AFT for resolutions supporting the Freedom Riders in the South. In the summer of 1963 the union put its full weight behind the 26 August march on Washington. Providing buses for many groups, the union lent its resources to the organizers of the march, helping to make it a success.[24]

By the early sixties, however, the work of the AFT in civil rights had come under the influence of organizational rivalry. In 1961 the Virginia Education Association suspended the Arlington Education Association when it voted to integrate its membership. In response Carl Megel denounced the all-white Virginia Education Association for its "prejudicial and un-American resolution" and invited the Arlington local to cross over into the union. The national NEA promised an investigation and eventually decided that the Arlington association had a right to its own membership standards, thus mildly chastening the statewide body. In 1963 Virginia's Fairfax County Association one of the largest NEA local affiliates, followed the Arlington route and forced the statewide association closer to desegregation. It would seem that the NEA appeared cornered by the activities of the AFT in Prince Edward County and its intervention in the Arlington affair. In 1965 the NEA was contacted by member Fred Reese in Selma, Alabama, when plans for the famous civil rights march led to Reese's dismissal. The NEA responded quickly to the media-drawing event, and instead of keeping its support of fired teachers in integration cases quiet as it had done in the case of Little Rock teachers in 1958, the association was now willing to have its help publicized. Indeed, by the midsixties the separate voluntary fund for helping teachers in the desegregation wars had been merged with the DuShane fund and became the association's public relations arm in the costly legal battles facing teacher integrationists. In contrast the union had no such fund of resources, but it had the support of major civil rights groups in urban areas, especially the NAACP, the Urban League, and Congress of Racial Equality (CORE). The more activist approach of the AFT was not only cheaper but it was more in keeping with the style and activities of the union. The civil rights movement used all the tactics and organizing skills of the trade union

24. AFT Collection, Series 1, Box 5, Prince Edward County Files; Schultz, *NEA and the Black Teacher*, pp. 135, 157.

movement, and the AFT felt quite at home in its style of activism. All of these activities were decidedly nonviolent, they were part of the integration-ism of the early civil rights movement, and they focused on desegregation in the South. The real difficulties in desegregation, however, were yet to be solved in large cities where the civil rights movement would mature into the black power movement.

CHAPTER ELEVEN /

Collective Bargaining: The Coming of Age of Teacher Unionism

Collective bargaining changed the fundamental relationship between teachers and administrators. It promised teachers more say in the conduct of their work, more pay, and greater job security. It essentially refined and broadened the concept of professionalism for teachers by assuring them more autonomy and less supervisory control. By the late seventies, 72 percent of all public school teachers were members of some form of union that represented them at the bargaining table. Before 1961 unions in less than a dozen school districts could claim they represented only a small fraction of schoolteachers.

For elementary teachers, collective bargaining meant breaks from the constant pressure of being in front of the classroom for six hours; for high school teachers it meant time to prepare for classes; for junior high school teachers it meant relief from extra lunch guard duties. Teachers were no longer told arbitrarily when they had to appear at school and when they could leave; surprise faculty meetings after school disappeared; and administrators could no longer appear suddenly in a teacher's classroom. Teachers still had to report to school at a prescribed time, they still had to attend meetings, they still had to welcome in outsiders to their classes, but what changed was the arbitrariness, the complete absence of control on the job that teachers had incessantly complained of. If the fundamental object of unionism is to give workers dignity on the job, unionization achieved that much for teachers and more.[1]

Of the two teachers' organizations, the AFT was the first to embrace collective bargaining. The NEA thought collective bargaining would destroy professionalism; leaders in the NEA warned that if teachers behaved like

---

1. Robert J. Thornton, "U.S. Teachers' Organizations and the Salary Issue: 1900–1960," *Research in Economic History,* Supplement 2 (1982), pp. 127–43.

210 / Blackboard Unions

trade unionists they would lose all respect and status in the community. In contrast, the AFT pointed out that teachers would gain respect because at last their salaries would be commensurate with their preparation. As collective bargaining laws were introduced, the union and the association began a bitter contest for representation in hundreds of school districts throughout the country. To prove that one organization had more clout than the other, the two organizations became more and more militant, and the number of school strikes rose dramatically. This new teacher militancy often tested old anti-strike legislation for public employees, and as a result of the teachers' contest these laws were liberalized.

Postwar Prospects for Collective Bargaining

Collective bargaining was an issue of discussion within the AFT after World War II, as teachers struck for higher wages. The national acceptance of unionization emboldened the teachers to expect similar acceptance of their desires to fully join the labor movement. As teacher strikes increased, especially within the AFT, a long discussion over strikes ended with the union reaffirming its no-strike policy at the outset of the postwar red scare.[2] Still, strong arguments were raised against the old policy: first, that teachers had a right to a decent standard of living and needed the means to get it; second, that teachers had an obligation to rescue children from intolerable conditions in the schools; and finally, that citizens were so apathetic about school problems that they needed drastic action before they would respond to the teachers' needs.[3] By 1952, even though a divided AFT convention reaffirmed the policy in sweeping language, change was in the air.[4] Carl Megel's election as AFT president that year was seen as a call for more aggressive leadership on economic issues. He began his term by pointing out that "the average salary for teachers in the United States during the past year was approximately $400 less than the income for the average factory worker."[5] Megel did not attack the strike policy right away, but under his leadership a series of articles appeared in the *American Teacher,* between 1954 and 1958, devoted to explaining what collective bargaining was, how it worked in labor, and what teachers could expect.

The union wanted to make it clear that there was a big difference between

2. At the 1947 AFT convention teachers supported a no-strike resolution, believing that it had been in the union constitution since 1919. Abraham Lefkowitz tried to argue them out if it, saying: "The no-strike policy which I helped to draft is merely a policy and not a part of the constitution. It is not even a part of our record unless we reconfirm it at a convention." *AFT Proceedings,* 1947, AFT Collection, Series 13, Box 22, p. 454.

3. *AFT Proceedings,* 1947, AFT Collection, Series 13, Box 22, pp. 426–94.

4. It should also be pointed out that the bigger issue at AFT conventions at that time was how to handle the academic freedom cases of teachers caught up in McCarthyism. *American Teacher,* 36 (January 1952).

5. *American Teacher,* 37 (October 1952), p. 11.

the way that most locals were bargaining (by attending school-board meetings and making formal requests, which were often ignored) and the way most unions bargained, with formal negotiations within a limited time frame. As one Chicago teacher put it, "Collective bargaining is not waiting months for a reply."[6]

In an editorial entitled "Collective Bargaining v. Collective Begging," Megel outlined the benefits that real collective bargaining could bring to teachers once boards of education had to recognize union representatives and bargain in good faith. This program of internal education introduced the prospect of changing the relationships between teachers and their employers. Teachers, often chastened under McCarthyism, cautiously pursued a change in the hierarchical and often destructive line-to-staff methods of supervision in the schools. They were also concerned about their low salaries and their poor working conditions—issues that, since the turn of the century, they had claimed a right to criticize.[7]

In 1958 the AFT urged the repeal of no-strike legislation in various states and edged closer to sanctioning the idea of unlimited collective bargaining, though without mentioning strikes. In contrast, the NEA maintained its no-strike policy: "There is no question of the attitude of NEA members in the past: they have been and remain, preponderantly against the use of the strike by teachers."[8]

The move toward collective bargaining, from roughly the end of postwar teacher militancy in 1952 to the New York City schoolteachers' strike in 1962, can be characterized as a slow, often discouraging, and sometimes extraordinarily frustrating battle of wits between young, dedicated, idealistic organizers and a stubbornly ensconced bureaucracy that was bent on ignoring them. In this important decade teachers were able to gain procedures for dismissal that guaranteed due process, procedures that would have saved the jobs of hundreds if teachers had had such rights before McCarthyism. Teachers were also able to get rid of the discriminatory laws regarding married women teachers while strengthening tenure and pension laws. On the local level, teachers confronted their stringent boards of education and, in an age of the greatest prosperity in the history of the nation, heard fantastic reasons why they could not share in this growth. Sometimes teachers had sufficient luck, organization, and determination to gain small wage increases. Teachers made gains before collective bargaining, but they did so under the slowest conditions imaginable. In this decade, the *American Teacher* faithfully recorded every tedious gain and every disappointing loss.[9]

6. *NEA Journal*, 4 (February 1947), pp. 77–80. Yet this "ingrained" resistance to striking needed to be articulated to teachers by William Givens in 1947 when the strike wave hit.

7. AFT Collection, Series 1, Box 6.

8. "Collective Bargaining v. Collective Begging," *American Teacher*, 41 (October 1956); George M. Harrison, "Procedures in Collective Bargaining," *American Teacher*, 42 (October 1957); see also Megel's files on collective bargaining, AFT Collection, Series 1, Box 6.

9. "Reports from the Locals," *American Teacher*, 1956–60, passim.

The New York Teachers

David Selden was one of the young organizers working to turn the tide for collective bargaining. A schoolteacher in Dearborn, Michigan, Selden was impressed by the success of the United Auto Workers and its president, Walter Reuther. Selden began union organizing in the national AFT office before going to New York City to organize in 1953. At that time Charles Cogen, a scholarly man who had taught in private high schools after several years in the New York City public school system, served as president of Local 2. Selden worked well with Cogen, often pushing his boss to take bold stands for collective bargaining. As Selden describes it, the union was still functioning much as the Teachers' Guild had; that is, it was primarily interested in social issues (opposition to prayer in schools, for example) rather than in bread-and-butter questions of salaries and pensions. Selden argued and won a reorientation of union efforts in the direction of collective bargaining, and then began to press issues that could attract new members. The strength of the union was in the junior high schools, so Selden's goal was to organize elementary and high school teachers. For the elementary school teachers he discovered the issue of having a free lunch period. Elementary school teachers had no break from their early morning arrival until dismissal, often after long faculty meetings late in the afternoon. Selden was able to successfully press the board for free time, while maintaining the goal that teachers would eventually receive a full hour off in the middle of the day.[10]

The high school teachers were a bit more difficult to organize. In New York they had long been organized by the unaffiliated High School Teachers' Association (HSTA). They resisted a move by the Board of Education to introduce a single salary schedule in the schools, a move that many boards of education made in the late forties to equalize teachers' salaries in elementary and high schools. High school teachers, many but not all of whom had more education than elementary school teachers, considered this a further erosion of their status and fiercely resisted it. For the union it was a divisive issue, but because of Margaret Haley the single salary schedule had long been a principle in the organization. The NEA had a similar policy in 1921 and noted that only few schools had this type of schedule. By 1946, 63.9 percent of school districts had adopted preparation-based schedules where teachers were compensated according to educational level rather than grade-level rank, and by 1954 most schools had the system. The change for New York came in 1948, but it was not a welcome one for the male high school teachers who led HSTA.

More men were entering high-school teaching after the war, thus equalizing the numbers of men and women in high school faculties (Appendix, table 1). As the G.I. Bill brought more men onto college campuses they began to

---

10. David Selden, *The Teacher Rebellion* (Washington, D.C., 1985), pp. 21–26.

compete with women for teaching jobs at the highest pay levels. In the same period the ratio of men to women elementary school teachers remained fairly constant, as it did throughout the twentieth century. Nationally men earned more money than women in the schools, but because of the early equal pay suits brought by Grace Strachan in 1910, in most cases this disparity could be explained not by legal differences in allocations but by the different ratios of men in higher-paid high school teaching jobs. Although women teachers tended to be slightly older than men teachers, and to have more seniority, the median income levels were $3,456 a year for men and only $2,394 for women.[11]

Inflation after the war tended to exaggerate effects of the transition from dual salary schedules to single salary schedules. High school teachers noted that elementary teachers had received an increase in income of 62 percent above 1939 pay levels, while high school teachers had received an increase of only 25.6 percent. Chicago high school teachers also gained a substantially greater increase—50.6 percent over their 1939 pay levels—than the usually better paid New York high school teachers. Teachers in both the union and the association raised the question whether they were being adequately compensated for the extracurricular and cocurricular activities they participated in, especially as the nation focused on problems of juvenile delinquency and the need for afternoon activities. The New York High School Teachers' Association boycotted extra duties in 1954, and in 1958 evening high school teachers struck for extra pay. Selden convinced Local 2 to support the strike, and early in 1959 merger talks began which were to culminate in the formation of the United Federation of Teachers (UFT). As part of the merger agreement, the UFT would support salary differentials based on "merit," that is, on level of education achieved.[12]

With these organizing efforts bringing in new teachers and swelling the ranks of Local 2 to five thousand teachers, Selden began to plan a teachers' strike for collective bargaining, to take place on 16 May 1960. Before teachers walked out, the Board of Education agreed to make arrangements for collective bargaining. After a summer of waiting, however, the union leadership announced a strike for election day, 7 November 1960. The strike threat had the Democratic city leadership at the point of despair, but the Board of Education was adamant and the teachers walked out. To be sure, Selden's organizing drive had left many of the city's forty thousand teachers untouched, and many schools were unaffected by the teachers' walkout. But the publicity given the teachers' demands and the effective strikes in junior high schools and high schools forced the city to give in to the UFT. After one day out the teachers returned to work victoriously, knowing that in one year

---

11. U.S. Commissioner of Education, *Biennial Survey of Education, 1953–54*.
12. Teachers' Union Collection, Box 69/6, Cornell University; Selden, *Teacher Rebellion*, p. 40; *NYT,* 27 October and 8 November 1960.

214 / *Blackboard Unions*

an election would be held and that a collective bargaining arrangement would follow. It was a stunning victory that raised teachers' hopes for change nationally.[13]

Collective Bargaining Laws

The daring one-day strike of New York teachers forced a collective bargaining election on the Board of Education in a union town where the city administration under Mayor Robert Wagner was fairly sympathetic to public employee unions. But at roughly the same time other states had begun to recognize the need for collective bargaining for public workers. The first collective bargaining law for public employees had appeared in Wisconsin in 1959. Wisconsin was the state where the first American Federation of State, County, and Municipal Employees organized in 1934. With a long history of progressive public employee unions and a strong lobby in Madison, it was possible to pass a strong collective bargaining law, which was amended in 1961. The new statute gave public employees the right to form their own organizations, and it provided for a form of fact finding in the event of an impasse in negotiations. The law explicitly prohibited strikes.[14]

President Kennedy issued Executive Order 10988, entitled "Employee-Management Co-operation in Federal Service," on 17 January 1962, giving federal employees the right to organize and bargain collectively. The presidential endorsement nudged along the cause of collective bargaining so that by 1966 seven states had collective bargaining statutes on the books. These laws were not uniformly promising for teacher organizations. In California, for example, the Winton Act provided for a council of representatives of all teacher organizations to meet with employers. Administrators were quick to exploit the rivalry between the association and the union and effectively paralyzed negotiations. Other states failed to provide for fact finding or other forms of mediation, thereby leaving the often prohibited strike as the only avenue of resolving disputes. Teachers without collective bargaining laws were able to negotiate grievances and begin informal negotiations, but without an enabling law there was little that teachers could do except force their districts, usually through a strike, to recognize their organizations and bargain with them. The rise in teacher militancy in the midsixties moved other states to revise their statutes and recognize public employee rights. The breakthrough in the sixties came only because of the success of the New York City local.[15]

13. Teachers' Union Collection, Box 79/1, Cornell University.
14. Myron Lieberman and Michael H. Moskow, *Collective Negotiations for Teachers: An Approach to School Administration* (Chicago, 1966), pp. 448–71.
15. Robert E. Doherty and Walter E. Oberer, *Teachers, School Boards, and Collective Bargaining* (Ithaca, N.Y., 1967); Lieberman and Moskow, *Collective Negotiations for Teachers;* Michael

The New York Strike

In the spring of 1961, the New York City Board of Education authorized a collective bargaining election. Despite efforts on the part of the NEA, the old Teachers' Union, and various other teacher factions in the city, the UFT won. The final tally was UFT 20,045, Teachers Bargaining Organization (NEA and affiliates) 9,770 and Teachers' Union (old Local 5) 2,575. Negotiations for a contract began immediately, but the inexperience of both the board and the teachers conspired to slow things to a near halt. By the spring of 1962 it became apparent that New York teachers would go out on strike for their demands. Unlike the election-day strike of 1960 or the various threats of work stoppages in the fifties, this strike would not be symbolic in any way: teachers had to force the Board of Education to make concessions by every means at their disposal. The first contract would set the pattern, the scope, and the degree of latitude for the work force. Just as the auto workers had to illustrate their solidarity and determination in the great sit-down strikes of the thirties, public employees had to demonstrate their mettle to an equally determined Board of Education.[16]

Unlike private sector workers, public school teachers operated under a variety of legal restraints. In New York the particular constraint was the Condon-Waldin law, which passed in 1947 in the wake of the Buffalo strike and set forth a variety of sanctions against public workers who took their grievances to the streets. Under its provisions, teachers could lose their jobs if they struck, and if the board rehired them they would lose all tenure rights for five years and not be able to get a pay raise for six. Condon-Waldin also struck out at union leaders, providing stiff jail terms and fines. Mike Quill of the New York City Transit Workers devoted his energy to narrowing the scope of this legislation. But teachers' strikes had been gestures of defiance of the law, not direct confrontations with it. Work stoppages, boycotts of extracurricular activities, and one-day, no-work demonstrations were means of getting around the law, weakening it to the point where few public officials felt comfortable in applying its stiff sanctions to any public employee group.[17]

The organizational leaders of the union were Cogen, Selden, and Albert Shanker, who joined the staff in 1958. A former junior high school mathematics teacher, Shanker was influenced by Selden, and the two lived in the same apartment building for many years. Assured that they had the majority

Moskow and Robert E. Doherty, "United States," in *Teacher Unions and Associations: A Comparative Study,* ed. Albert A. Blum (Urbana, Ill., 1969), pp. 295–332; Anthony M. Creswell and Charles T. Kerchner, *Teachers, Unions, and Collective Bargaining in Public Education* (Berkeley, 1980).

16. Selden, *Teacher Rebellion,* pp. 61–75; Marschal Donley, *Power to the Teacher: How American Educators Became Militant* (Bloomington, Ind., 1976), p. 49.

17. Selden, *Teacher Rebellion,* p. 75.

of teachers behind them, the two young organizers gambled that they could pull off a more serious strike in 1962. They had reasons to be optimistic in betting that the law would not constrain them. Paramount among these was President Kennedy's executive order in 1962, which broadly defined collective bargaining rights for public workers. Despite this assurance, Kennedy's secretary of labor, Arthur Goldberg, was admantly opposed to public employee strikes and warned the teachers "to resolve your difference by means other than strikes." Union leaders responded militantly to these warnings. "At the present moment," Cogen said, "we are looking for a contract with the Board of Education, not a strike." And yet the UFT president, paraphrasing Kennedy's own language, repeated, "Government must act like government and unions must act like unions."[18]

Twenty thousand teachers struck the New York City public school system on 12 April 1962. It was a surprising turnout of half the teaching force, many picketing the schools while five thousand others rallied at city hall. The issues were very clear: teachers wanted a substantial pay raise, free lunch periods, check-off for union dues, and one hundred and forty-seven other items dealing with work-place conditions. The teachers argued that conditions in the schools had demoralized the staff. Nonteaching chores, inadequate textbook supplies, and detailed lesson plans prepared for visiting administrators were extra burdens that could easily be eliminated. Teachers also focused on supervision as a chief grievance: "Staff conferences often find principals lecturing to teachers dogmatically on organizational details rather than encouraging the kind of academic exchange of views that marks faculty meetings at colleges."[19] With a long list of grievances and a recalcitrant Board of Education, the union decided to focus attention first on the salary issue.

The Board of Education was perfectly willing to settle an amount of money and then go together with teachers to local and state officials to lobby a new budget request. But the UFT pointed out that such an approach had been the practice in times past, when teachers won salary concessions from the local board of education only to find that the coffers were empty. Margaret Haley and the Chicago Teachers' Federation faced the same strategy when they were forced to institute their tax suit. New York schoolteachers argued that with collective bargaining they wanted a contract, a written and legally binding agreement that said teachers would get the money regardless of the lobbying and taxing problems of the local government. Although the newspapers focused on the money issue, they missed this structural change. The change would give organized teachers some guarantees that their organizing efforts would not be wasted. It had been common, since the days of Margaret Haley, for school boards to agree to teachers'

18. *NYT,* 15 April 1962; *Herald Tribune,* 4 March 1962.
19. *NYT,* 12 April and 5 May 1962; especially Fred Hechinger.

demands during election season only to renege on those agreements afterward, when the teachers could no longer mobilize political support for their salaries.[20]

First the union leaders were served with injunctions. Board president Max Rubin announced that all twenty thousand teachers were fired under Condon-Waldin and that the New York State Commissioner of Education was looking into the possibility of lifting the striking teachers' licenses. Union leaders also anticipated jail terms. On the other side of the coin, the schools were in disarray. The teachers were again most effective in the junior high schools and high schools, where disciplinary problems were rampant and baby boomers were overcrowding the classes. Several fistfights and incidents of rambunctious behavior among the undersupervised students had parents worried for the safety of their children at school. Many kept their children at home, thereby strengthening the strike. No injunction was filed under New York's Condon-Waldin Act, thus making it easier for the board and the union to settle their first dispute without long legal battles.

In order to give the raises teachers demanded, the city needed $13 million, money that had been promised to Democratic mayor Robert Wagner for educational improvements but had been cut by the efforts of the Republican governor Nelson Rockefeller. It was rumored that the popular Wagner intended to challenge Rockefeller for the governor's seat. If Wagner could blame the strike on Rockefeller, as he was clearly doing, then Rockefeller's fiscal stringency could backfire at the polls. Rockefeller had begun to pay careful attention to New York City problems.[21]

David Selden suggested that the governor could lend the city $13 million by using a precedent set in the depression when the state had forwarded money based on anticipated income in the following year. It was an emergency measure to be sure, but it put real money on the bargaining table. Mayor Wagner, Governor Rockefeller, and the UFT negotiating team met to make the deal only hours after Charles Cogen had urged the teachers to go back to work. The settlement was a major victory for the UFT. Teachers had won real money on the table, and they had successfully defied Condon-Waldin without tough reprisals. But there was more to this strike victory than appearances. The avoidance of reprisals under Condon-Waldin meant that a new labor law would have to be drawn up, and as it turned out this revision proved no more conducive to labor peace than had previous legislation.[22]

In assessing the strike, it is important to keep in mind that it was not just a local affair. News of the strike "crippling" the schools was a banner headline in the *New York Times*. Hundreds of thousands of other teachers and public employees in other parts of the country looked to the New York strike as an

20. Selden, *Teacher Rebellion*, pp. 69–72.
21. *NYT,* 12 April 1962.
22. Selden, *Teacher Rebellion*, pp. 75–79.

important precedent. "This is the greatest day in the history of education in New York City," Charles Cogen told rallying teacher strikers, but it was also a "turning point," as William Carr referred to it, in the history of education nationally.[23] New York teachers were conscious of playing this role. They spoke of the strike as something revolutionary: "Nothing like this had ever happened before," Simon Beagle recalled.[24]

The event was treated by the newspapers as something catastrophic. Teachers, the *New York Times* lectured sternly, were breaking the law and setting an example of lawlessness to children. The newspapers reported that most of labor in fact did not support the strike. George Meany was silent, while Carl Megel reminded reporters that the national organization had a no-strike commitment and that the parent union would try to urge a settlement. Others spoke out anonymously, such as "highly placed labor executives" who were quoted as calling the strike an "unmitigated disaster." Labor leaders feared that the strike would give unions a bad name, but they did not want to comment lest the union call upon them to mediate as they had in 1960. In fact, it was noted that labor leaders in the 1960 settlement had promised that a strike would not happen again if there was collective bargaining and they were now rather miffed that the teachers had walked out. "Nobody likes the idea," said a unionist in Washington, "but what can you do? The strike is on, and some day it will be over. It's their strike. Let them do the talking."[25]

Strikes and Antistrike Legislation

The strike had legal implications that would affect teachers under similar laws. The New York Condon-Waldin Act was the toughest of the antistrike legislation introduced by several states in the postwar strike boom. When New York City teachers defied it, they opened the doors for teachers in other states to launch similar challenges. Recognizing that the law was so stringent that it would not prevent strikes, school leaders in New York called for a change that would create a legal mechanism by which strikes could be prevented. At first the Board of Education wanted to punish striking teachers despite the settlement, and indeed many principals harassed teachers on picket lines by taking their photographs and later questioning them as they returned to school. But the board quickly stopped the war of reprisals, even as it announced that a commission was being set up to enact new legislation. Finally, the UFT signed an agreement that the union would not strike for the duration of the one-year contract.[26]

23. *NYT,* 12 April 1962; Donley, *Power to the Teacher,* pp. 46–58.
24. Selden, *Teacher Rebellion,* p. 79; interview with Simon Beagle, summer 1974.
25. *NYT,* 12 April 1962.
26. Moskow and Doherty, "United States," p. 303; Donley, *Power to the Teacher,* pp. 68–76.

George Taylor of the Wharton School was appointed to revise the law, with the help of legal counsel Archibald Cox. Their aim was to write legislation that would apply to unions under collective bargaining and use modern methods of labor management to move the bargaining process along while applying the brakes to militant strike action. Although the UFT felt badly constrained by the resulting 1967 Taylor law, it was another innovation that brought public employee unions under constraints similar to those applying to other workers who served the public welfare. The most notable example had been railroad workers, whose rights to strike had been severely limited after the national strike in 1894 but whose rights to bargain collectively and force employers to bargain were liberalized under the American Railway Act in 1926. In other words, the Taylor law treated the UFT as a genuine union, not merely a lobbying group. But, while the UFT was able to prevent reprisals after its first strikes, a feat that emboldened teachers everywhere, it was severely constrained after the Taylor law went into effect. The Taylor law spelled out penalties for strikes that included a $10,000-a-day fine and imprisonment for labor leaders. Shanker, as president of the UFT in 1968, was given a $250,000 fine and a token jail sentence after the teachers' strike. The law did provide for a hearing on whether the unions were severely provoked into strike action by management.[27]

The Taylor law served as a model for subsequent labor legislation. Challenging the issue of strike penalties, Selden suggested that many union leaders might have to go to jail to assert the right to strike. In New Jersey, where state law provided for powerful injunctions and arrests for union leaders, union locals paid stiff fines in legal maneuvers to save teachers' jobs and prevent long jailings. Eventually the law jailed many of the AFT's best organizers, as well as national presidents. In other states there were legal mechanisms to which school districts could appeal to gain injunctions against strikers, and the threat of tougher antistrike laws was often used as a means of preventing collective bargaining legislation.

By 1965 fifteen states had pending legislation concerning some form of collective bargaining; nearly every statute had some form of antistrike provision. In some states school boards were forbidden by statute, court ruling, or the attorney general's opinion from entering into collective bargaining agreements. This was especially true in Alabama, Georgia, North Carolina, and South Carolina. Some states chose to be deliberately silent on collective bargaining, especially New Jersey, Pennsylvania, Ohio, Indiana, and Illinois, and in those state teachers have often gone on strike to gain recognition. But silence on collective bargaining did not mean permission to strike, and thus teachers were placed in the position of testing the law or forcing changes in state law to gain collective bargaining.[28]

27. Diane Ravitch, *The Great School Wars: New York City, 1805–1973* (New York, 1974), p. 397; Moskow and Doherty, "United States," pp. 316–17.
28. Moskow and Doherty, "United States," p. 316.

In November 1960 when the first one-day walkout occurred in New York, there were three teacher work stoppages in the entire nation, and clearly the New York City teachers were the focus of teacher-strike activity. Between 1953 and 1956 there were only fourteen strikes, whereas in 1947, at the height of the postwar strike era, there were twenty strikes involving 4,720 teachers. The New York revolution in 1962 involved 20,000 and opened up a new era of strike activity. In 1964 there were nine teacher strikes involving 14,400 teachers, and in 1965 teachers walked out in nine school districts, including Newark, New Jersey, where union leaders faced stiff jail terms. The big jump came in 1966 when thirty strikes were recorded by the U.S. Department of Labor. "Strikes and threats of strikes by public employees, particularly schoolteachers, are proving a virulent fever," the *Detroit Free Press* observed, "and the fever spreads." In 1967 the number of strikes rose to 105 and the strikes were getting longer. Although there were slightly fewer strikes in 1968, the number of idle teaching days rose to an all-time high of 2,190,000.[29]

Gender and Explanations of Militancy

Although most explanations of teacher militancy were based on economic justice, analysts found that salary issues did not fully explain the rise in militancy, especially since salaries seemed to be on the rise before strike fever hit the schools. The most dramatic structural change in the teaching industry between 1954 and 1964 was the 94-percent growth of the number of male schoolteachers compared with the 38-percent growth of female teachers in the same period. In 1951 men were only 21.3 percent of classroom teachers, whereas in 1964 they were 31.4 percent. We have already seen that most of these new male recruits poured into the higher-paying high school positions, but researchers also found that these men were younger than women in teaching and that 36.2 percent of secondary teachers but only 25.5 percent of elementary school teachers were under thirty years of age. Young people, sociologists have argued, tend to be more militant and radical than older people. An NEA study in 1966 identified an angry young man who had joined a profession with steadily increasing salaries but no longer felt that teaching would provide sufficient financial rewards; since 80 percent were married and 66 percent had children to support, their disillusionment did not come quickly enough for them to switch careers. Finally, researchers found that men were more likely than women to join unions, often concluding that men had greater needs for benefits than female teachers, but also suggesting

29. Donley, *Power to the Teacher*, pp. 106–7; Lieberman and Moskow, *Collective Negotiations for Teachers*, pp. 290–91; Bureau of Labor Statistics, Department of Labor, "Work Stoppages Involving Teachers, 1940–1962" (Washington, D.C., 1963).

that until men became teachers in large numbers, unionization had been insignificant.[30]

None of the researchers in these studies knew the history of Margaret Haley and the early years of the teachers' union; their oversight of the contribution of women to the revival of militancy in the union reinforced cultural stereotypes about women. Some attention was paid to the fact that women tended to teach in the elementary schools, but none of the investigators looked into the issue of union membership and the union's position on single salary issues. In Stephen Coles's study of New York militancy, no mention was made of the issue of single salary schedules, and yet the resentment of elementary teachers can be easily documented. What is surprising is that despite the agreement between the High School Teachers' Association and the Teachers' Guild on salary schedules in 1959, more than 50 percent of elementary school teachers supported the strike in 1962. Another explanation for the sociologists' contention that men had caused teacher militancy was that male teachers came from lower-class backgrounds, whereas women came from higher-class backgrounds. Because teachers who came from lower-class homes were more likely to have fathers who were Democrats and union members, they tended more toward union membership and militancy. But the gender differences in class origins were not as great as the investigators indicated. Coles found that 61 percent of men and 47 percent of women thought of themselves as working or lower-middle class, yet in a footnote he observed that there was only a small difference in actual social origins of men and women teachers: 31 percent of the women were from the working class and 39 percent of the men were from the working class.

Dan Lortie, in a more gender-sensitive analysis of teachers, referred to a 1972 analysis of schoolteachers' origins that found a greater disparity of blue-collar social origins and gender (43.2 percent for men and 29 percent for women), but he did not take into account that the NEA study was national whereas Coles's study focused on teachers in cities where militancy was more pronounced. If the difference in social origins in teachers was negligible, the argument that militancy grew out of male dissatisfaction with teaching as a job is also suspect. Lortie confirms Coles's conclusion that women expressed greater satisfaction with their career choice, but he also puts the conclusion into the context of a labor market in which few jobs were open to women.[31]

30. Stephen Cole, *The Unionization of Teachers: A Case Study of the UFT* (New York, 1969), pp. 87–92, p. 205n; Donley, *Power to the Teacher,* pp. 14–16; Allan Rosenthal, "The Strength of Teacher Organization: Factors Influencing Membership in Two Large Cities," *Sociology of Education,* 39 (Fall 1966), pp. 359–80; T. M. Stinnett, *Turmoil in Teaching* (New York, 1968), p. 4; Moskow and Doherty, "United States," p. 308.

31. Research Division, "Profile of the American School Teacher, 1966," *NEA Journal,* 56 (May 1967), p. 12; William Rabinowitz and Kay E. Crawford, "A Study of Teachers' Careers," *School Review,* 68 (Winter 1960), pp. 380–87; Dan C. Lortie, *School Teacher: A Sociological Study*

If one were to dismiss the gender argument as an explanation of militancy yet agree that economic factors alone did not explain the rising militancy of teachers, there was one other issue, explored in all the studies, that can serve as a less gender-biased explanation of what was happening in the schools. Lortie, Coles, and others found that teachers were fed up with the centralized bureaucracy of the schools. Teachers complained about oversupervision, increasing bureaucratization, inappropriate assignments, and a lack of control over licensing, training, and assignments. These grievances go back to the beginnings of unionization; after tenure laws had been effectively introduced, teachers were willing to strike for those same demands (as well as higher pay) after World War II. Viewed from the historical perspective, teachers seemed to resume in the sixties the militancy of the late forties, which had been interrupted by the red scare.

Organizational Warfare

The first response of the NEA to the 1962 strike was to denounce the tactics of the AFT as unprofessional. NEA executive secretary Carr remarked that "industrial practices cannot be copied in a doctrinaire manner in public enterprises." He specifically directed his comments toward the New York City strike threat in 1962 by saying that such tactics "do not represent values that can be taught to American public school children."[32]

The defeat of the NEA in the collective bargaining election of 1961 seemed especially humiliating to the NEA leadership. T. M. Stinnett, an NEA participant, described how inept the NEA was in the first confrontation with AFT organizers. An AFT plant supplied the union with information on every NEA move, while at national headquarters the ever cooperative Research Division was sending out salary information, which the clever AFT organizers were using in their union publications. Shaken by the experience and pressed from within his own organization for reform on desegregation, Carr delivered what he called his "turning point" speech to the 1962 NEA convention. He said that the NEA had been through three crises before, citing the reorganization after World War I, the depression, and World War II; but the fourth great crisis, he said, was before them. "Some labor leaders may plan to use their considerable economic and political power to affiliate all public school teachers in a white-collar union," Carr warned.[33] The AFL-CIO, he said, had declared war on the teachers and apparently was prepared to attack the NEA at its weakest point: the cities.

(Chicago, 1975); Research Division, NEA, "Report on the Status of American School Teacher" (Washington, D.C., 1971).

32. William Carr, *The Education of William Carr* (Washington, D.C., 1978), pp. 377–80; *NEA Proceedings*, 1962, pp. 18–28.

33. *NEA Proceedings*, 1962, p. 29; Carr, *Education*, p. 380.

In 1964 Carr characterized the union attempt as "an assault on professional independence." He continued, "The AFL-CIO program, as defined by its leadership, would, if successful, destroy the NEA and its state and local affiliates."[34] He urged teachers to keep the educational profession an "independent one" and warned delegates to "know the difference between professional association and a teachers' union and how to tell why the former is better. You should know this as well as your own phone number."[35] He further argued that AFL-CIO labor councils and affiliates had opposed taxes for schools and implied that teachers could expect that once the AFL-CIO had triumphed over the NEA, teachers could expect to live under an "Iron Curtain" of labor control. In keeping with NEA tradition, Carr never mentioned the AFT, which was, after all, the actual source of the challenge to the NEA. The NEA always treated the AFT as though it were a satellite, independent in name only.

The NEA did not stand idly by as the AFT proclaimed its victory in New York. Yet the teachers' strike fever spread so quickly in the cities that the association had difficulty in catching up to the union's impressive takeoff. William Carr was quick to notice that the gains were made in urban areas where the NEA had been weak because of its statewide structures. Most urban leaders considered state executive secretaries to be conservatives, interested only in legislation, and the executive secretaries in turn saw the urban leaders as troublemakers not truly interested in the association. The NEA's Urban Project aimed in part at solving this problem. By 1968 the Urban Project ran on a million-dollar budget explicitly to help organize local city chapters in competition with the AFT.

The NEA also restructured its membership in a unification campaign that would require affiliated associations to pay dues to the national organization. This innovation had begun in 1944 under Executive Secretary Givens's leadership, when Oregon became the first state organization to unify its membership. The movement went along slowly: one state made the change in the decade of the fifties, but in the sixties, thirteen states unified, in 1970–71 a dozen more joined in, and by 1972 it became a requirement that members belong to the national as well as state organizations. The drive increased membership, strengthened the national office, and bolstered local chapter membership in cities. Another step that strengthened the NEA's hand in collective bargaining was the progress Carr made toward widening insurance packages for teachers. Special disability insurance, home insurance, and health insurance were all popular with public school teachers and gave members distinct advantages over union teachers.[36]

A bitter contest between the NEA and the AFT broke out in 1964 when the

---

34. Stinnett, *Turmoil in Teaching,* pp. 73–75.
35. *NEA Proceedings,* 1964, pp. 16–26.
36. *NEA Reporter,* 12 October 1962.

collective bargaining agent for Milwaukee teachers was to be decided. It was the first test of organizational strength since New York, and both organizations coveted victory. T. M. Stinnett, on the NEA staff, recalled, "The AFT brought in big guns—IUD's [Industrial Unionism Department] Nicholas Zonarich and Franz Daniel—to run the campaign."[37] Emphasizing ties to labor in a labor town, the AFT brought in Walter Reuther for a rally of teachers, but the rally was badly organized and the AFT blunder encouraged the NEA to anticipate victory through its "professional negotiations" campaign. The AFT could claim few members in Milwaukee whereas the NEA had long had a strong local that went back to Margaret Haley's day. In the February election the local association trounced the union 2,249 votes to 1,645. In the next three months the NEA picked up six more victories, including teachers in New Rochelle, New York—in the shadow of the New York AFT, as the NEA put it. The NEA's euphoria quickly disappeared on 11 May 1964, when the union defeated the association in the Detroit teachers' election, now representing 11,000 teachers, and in February 1965 crushed the NEA in Philadelphia, a district with 10,676 teachers. The Chicago Teachers' Union had signed a collective bargaining agreement with the Board of Education in 1964 when it could claim 44 percent of the teaching force in its ranks; the NEA affiliate had less than 10 percent of the city's teachers, and most of them were principals and administrators. It looked as if the NEA would continue to pick up teachers in small units while the AFT could count on big wins in the cities where the bulk of the teachers were. For the first time in forty-six years, since 1918, the AFT threatened to surpass the NEA.[38]

To Lobby or to Strike?

Despite its weakness in the push for collective bargaining, the midsixties was hardly a time of gloom for the association. Its major advances came elsewhere, in Washington. Carr had invested heavily in the early sixties in federal legislation. This was his primary program, and indeed it had been the main focus of the organization since it located in Washington in the early twenties. The strength of the NEA was in its ability to lobby, and it had sought a federal education bill since the days of George Strayer and the emergency in education.[39]

37. Carr, *Education*, pp. 372–77.

38. Between 1961 and 1965 there were forty collective bargaining elections involving 96,232 teachers, of which 21,483 voted for the association and 74,749 voted for the union. Lieberman and Moskow, *Collective Negotiations for Teachers*, p. 593. Carr thought that this was the most serious challenge yet to the NEA. "New York was the first engagement in a long war." Carr, *Education*, p. 377.

39. Carr, *Education*, pp. 305–26.

The irony is that federal legislation had been stymied since the early fifties in the last collapse of the coalition of civil rights groups, labor, the NEA, and the AFT. *Sputnik* in 1957 reawakened interest in federal aid and produced the National Defense Education Act in 1958, but this bill fell far short of the goals and expectations of the NEA. Now, with the election of John F. Kennedy, things were looking up for educational funding. In 1962 the Manpower and Development Training Act promised $435 million in funds for vocational schools, a large sum but not what the NEA wanted. Carr and other educational reformers had their eyes on a general school-aid bill that would provide $2.5 billion in aid. Kennedy, who endorsed the bill, visited with NEA leaders shortly before his assassination to discuss lobbying efforts for the bill, but even his tragic death would not save the bill, which was defeated in December 1963.[40]

After years of begging, teachers found a friend in Lyndon B. Johnson. A former schoolteacher himself, Johnson came into office with the promise that he could deliver what Kennedy had failed to accomplish: a federal aid bill for education. Kennedy had been hampered in his efforts to enhance public education by his ties to the Catholic church and Cardinal Spellman. Johnson, on the other hand, brought with him his years in Congress and his knowledge of the power the education lobby could exercise when it was properly mobilized. A beneficiary of Roosevelt's NYA, Johnson was familiar with the old educational squabbles but now as president was prepared to carry the torch of the New Deal on to the classroom.

At first Johnson's aid followed the pattern of the New Deal. Educational programs were attached to his multibillion-dollar war on poverty, especially the Economic Opportunity Act of 1964, which included job corps, work study, and aid to urban and rural community-action programs. Johnson was also able to expand the National Defense Education Act of 1958 to include history, English reading, and geography in addition to mathematics, science, and languages, which had been targeted in the original act. These programs were largely part of Kennedy's unfinished term of office; Johnson's own imprint was really felt only after his 1964 landslide electoral victory. The Elementary and Secondary Education Act of 1965 brought $1.3 billion in grants to schools for textbooks, community centers, and audiovisual materials. "No law I have signed, or ever will sign, means more to the future of America," the veteran congressional legislator, remarked.[41] Annual appropriations of this bill from $5 billion to $7 billion gave education its first general federal subsidy.

Although the Johnson bill was not everything the NEA had hoped for, most educators agreed that it was a major commitment to federal aid to education, the long-sought goal of both the union and the association. In July

40. Ibid., p. 332.
41. Ibid., p. 339.

1965 Johnson was warmly received at the NEA convention to discuss the more than sixty pieces of federal legislation, from Head Start to graduate school programs, that his administration had supported. It would seem to Carr that his patience in lobbying efforts had paid off and all that the association had to do was to maintain its good reputation and the favor of Congress to promote the long-lost dream of the association—a department of education.

Victories in the early Johnson years seemed to reinforce Carr's conservatism. His fears were that the unbridled militancy of the teachers could lead to a cooling off on the part of Congress—and to some degree he was right—but Congress reneged on further educational funding not so much because of the teachers' actions but rather because in the late sixties the prohibitive costs of the Vietnam War had forced Johnson to do what he had been loathe to do: raise taxes to protect his domestic reforms and continue the war. Meanwhile, the NEA lobbyists seemed unresponsive to Johnson's political problem and continued with its general lobbying efforts. The commitment to these lobbying efforts had the effect of hampering the efforts of the teachers, who were counseled to look to legislative victories rather than collective bargaining to achieve their salary goals. Indeed, some of the NEA staff saw the rise in militancy and strikes as dangers jeopardizing years of efforts to gain goodwill. This orientation was not merely Carr's personal style; it was, and remains, one of the chief characteristics of the modern NEA. The whole point of locating in Washington in 1920 was to gain national recognition and federal legislation to improve the profession. The NEA could not shift its orientation from lobbying to collective bargaining without a major internal reorganization.[42]

Professionals into Unionists

The real obstacle for the NEA in its crisis of competition with the AFT was not the union, nor was it NEA weakness in urban centers, nor even the problem of membership. Collective bargaining itself presented the NEA with its deepest concern; it was an ideological construct that fundamentally challenged the association's long-cherished concepts of professionalism. Although the association had affiliates that struck in the late forties, and even though it had representative organizations that regularly petitioned boards of education to adjust salaries, protect teachers' academic rights, and apply grievance procedures, it was anathema to the association to engage in collective bargaining because the term itself was embedded in unionism. Instead it was more in the style of the NEA to declare "professional day" strikes, where teachers would call in sick for one day. Teachers in Kentucky

42. Hugh Davis Graham, *The Uncertain Triumph* (Chapel Hill, N.C., 1984), pp. 179–202.

staged a statewide "professional day" under the auspices of the state association.

Instead of striking, however, the NEA promoted the idea of sanctions, according to which if a state or a district refused to negotiate or respond to demands for higher pay, then the NEA would declare sanctions against that district or state, under which other teachers were urged not to take jobs in the state or district. To facilitate this, in 1967 the NEA set up a computer bank of jobs and teachers, a service that might have better served the growing number of unemployed teachers but was begun to bolster the sagging reputation of professional sanctions. Sanctions did not work because they were difficult to mobilize teachers behind, extremely difficult to maintain, and easily dismissed by cost-conscious districts and states. Sanctions declared against Utah in 1964 lasted for three hundred days when—after teachers helped elect a new governor, a new legislature came to power and after NEA organizers invested a great deal of expense and time—the NEA gained a modest salary increase. Finally, in 1967 the NEA passed a resolution stating that though strikes were to be avoided, the association recognized that under certain circumstances teachers were forced to strike, in which case the association would come to their aid. Even as the association came closer to union activity, the careful language obscured its change in direction. Euphemisms for bargaining activity like "co-operative determination," "collective determination," and "democratic persuasion" preceded the association's favorite euphemism for collective bargaining, "professional negotiations."[43]

However comforting the adoption of indirect language may have been, it accomplished little in the way of confronting the problem that, willy-nilly, the association was being dragged into a process of unionization, and unless it adopted the weapons of labor, it faced oblivion. James Carey, secretary-treasurer of the Industrial Union Department of the AFL-CIO, the same organization that had helped fund the New York City drive, addressed the NEA convention in 1962 and explicitly spoke to this question. "One of the prime troubles—if not the chief curse of the teaching industry, is precisely the word 'profession.' That term, as it is used so frequently here, implies that your craft is somewhat above this world of ours; it implies a detachment, a remoteness from the daily battles of the streets, in the neighborhoods and cities."[44]

Carey's remarks angered some of the association's members, but others were willing to listen and pushed for organizational changes. The biggest push of all came from the successes of the AFT. Between January 1961 and September 1965 the NEA and the AFT completed in forty different elections to determine who would represent teachers at the bargaining table. The NEA

43. Allen M. West, *The NEA: The Power Base for Education* (New York, 1980), pp. 38–58, 104–9.
44. Donley, *Power to the Teacher*, pp. 68–69; West, *NEA: The Power Base*, p. 65.

won twenty-six elections and the AFT won fourteen, but the AFT represented 74,000 teachers, whereas the NEA could bargain for only 21,000 teachers. In suburban and rural districts the association won, but the statistics failed to raise the spirits of association organizers. Association leaders knew that they had to face the AFT challenge more aggressively. Even though they still had a substantial membership lead, 943,000 to 110,000, they could see that the union would gain hegemony if it continued its successes.[45]

In each collective bargaining campaign the AFT made two very effective charges against the NEA which made a substantial difference to urban public school teachers: administrative domination and foot-dragging on civil rights. Well over 85 percent of the NEA's members were classroom teachers, but school superintendents and district supervisors remained prominent in national meetings until the midsixties. Some state associations insisted that local chapters have administrators in their organizations, although some chapters were able to limit membership to classroom teachers only. As for the AFT, it allowed principals into separate locals, but the national constitution specifically forbade membership to supervisors. Teacher unionists were quick to argue that administrators represented management in negotiations and that it was an obvious conflict of interest to allow them into the deliberations of teachers.

The NEA hesitated to adopt such industrial language. Negotiations for teachers were simply discussions between professionals, NEA leaders reasoned, and therefore they could see no value in abandoning their administrators. Yet in 1967, when members of the Association of American School Administrators (AASA) on the NEA Board of Trustees moved to nominate a replacement for William Carr, the Representative Assembly prevented them from acting and thus opened the door for a shift in power within the organization. Internally there was no discussion of the "administrator-dominated organization" charge made by the AFT. The AASA continued to work with the NEA leadership to work out a compromise position and in 1969 went so far as to announce that it would stay in the association even though it deplored teachers' strikes. The drift away from the administrative orientation was just that: there was no final breach. Instead there was a slow shift in emphasis from the more hierarchical educational elite organization to a far more democratic structure that drew more teachers into organizational deliberations.[46]

On the issue of civil rights, the NEA clearly accelerated its integration program in 1965. In the next few years the NEA underwent a complete transformation, a change in structure and outlook that was indeed profound. As time passed, the NEA's ideological barriers to collective bargaining

45. See the Appendix.
46. For the role of administrators, see Edgar G. Wesley, *NEA, The First One Hundred Years: The Building of the Teaching Profession* (New York, 1957), p. 282. For the transition, see West, *NEA: The Power Base,* pp. 135–80.

became psychological barriers, which were more easily overcome. The organization became less reticent about union tactics, and even the term "union" was no longer anathema as it had once been. The last vestige of the old NEA philosophy, the "professional organization," changed in its meaning too, as the competition between organizations heated up in the late sixties. In the race between organizations, the AFT still had an advantage as long as it made no big mistakes.

Sanctions and Strikes: 1968

Nineteen sixty-eight was a turning point in many aspects of political life in America. It was no less for public school teachers. Two events, the NEA's sanctions against Florida and the Ocean Hill–Brownsville strike, stand out as major events in teacher unionism. In Ocean Hill–Brownsville a new local board of education dismissed several teachers, which led to a city-wide teacher strike and lockout that polarized blacks and whites and divided the sympathies of city progressives torn between unionism and black self-determination. For the union the strike had long-term implications. The Florida situation is much less well known, but it did turn the NEA away from its traditional resistance to unionism.

The Florida sanctions began in 1968 after Elizabeth Koontz took office as president and Braulio Alonzo, a school principal, was nominated president-elect. As it turned out, with Koontz appointed by Nixon to head the Women's Bureau and Alonzo taking over her last half year in office, Alonzo had a longer term in office than had been customary. In that same year the NEA changed its bylaws to strengthen the hand of elected officers at the expense of the executive secretary. The status of the Department of Classroom Teachers, renamed the Association of Classroom Teachers, was also elevated. Braulio Alonzo summed up the new changes when he announced that his administration would be marked by militancy. "This is a new day—the day of the new teacher. For too long we teachers have been seen as the meek, mild, passive, acquiescent teachers who will take whatever is given."[47]

The focus of the NEA turned toward Alonzo's state, Florida, where thirty-five thousand teachers packed the Tangerine Bowl in Tampa, Florida and announced that if the legislature did not pass legislation giving school districts funds they would resign en masse. The threat proved powerful, although Governor Claude R. Kirk vetoed a school support bill. A month later the governor agreed to special legislation but stalled by announcing a month later that he would have to wait for a special commission report. By Christmas, the teachers knew they were being stalemated by the stubborn governor.[48]

47. *NEA Reporter,* 15 September and 10 November 1967.
48. Ibid., 15 December 1967, 15 March and 19 April 1968.

In many ways the Florida situation produced the perfect opportunity for the NEA to combine the power of its federal lobbying with the new militancy of teachers. At the moment the NEA passed sanctions against Florida in March, it was pressing for $6 billion in federal aid—in other words, the Florida protest became a kind of theater to dramatize the need for federal funds in education. Instead of a strike, the NEA proposed resignations, and instead of strikers, teachers were actors in the drama of education. While such tactics dramatized teachers' needs, they also placed the teachers on stage, where they were being cornered in a dubious legal situation of escalating threats, which culminated with the dramatic announcement of impending mass resignations and, of course, drastic NEA sanctions.

The deadline for teacher resignations was set for 1 March, when the association estimated that upwards of thirty to forty thousand teachers would resign en masse. The association announced that it would contribute $2 million to the Florida struggle. The Florida Education Association (FEA), however, was unprepared for the vehement reaction to the teachers' drama. At a military base wives who taught school were told that if they resigned their husbands would be sent to Vietnam. Teachers in tears, some fainting, handed in their resignations at an association rally; at home they received personal threats. Estimates of the number of resignations varied from fifteen to twenty thousand out of a total of fifty-eight thousand teachers. The drama convinced the state legislature to pass again the same legislation the governor had vetoed in the fall, which allowed the FEA to quickly announce a victory and call off the protest. But since the teachers had resigned rather than struck, their return to work was difficult, if not impossible to negotiate. With whom would the teachers negotiate? Although the protest was statewide, against the state government, the contracts were local district contracts. One week after the "settlement," teachers in thirty-six out of sixty-seven counties were locked out of their jobs. By 14 March twelve counties settled but seventy-five hundred teachers were still out of their jobs. Three weeks later, five hundred teachers remained out of work. The NEA was in fact embroiled in a legal nightmare.[49]

Having tendered their resignations, NEA teachers avoided breaking the association code of ethics against strikes, but they had broken their contracts under the law, and school districts were not obligated to take them back. Meanwhile, the school aid bill was grounded on the shoals of the Vietnam War and Johnson's more dramatic announcement that he would not run for office after the March primaries. The drama of teachers losing their jobs paled in comparison to the urgency of the war issue. Here, too, the NEA's basic conservatism held the organization firmly in the pro-war camp of the American Legion, which continued as late as 1967 to cosponsor patriotic programs with the NEA leadership. Fortunately for the NEA the Florida

49. Ibid., 19 April 1968.

fiasco was quickly buried in the dramatic events of the spring of 1968, especially the assassination of Martin Luther King. But the NEA was ever keen to the competitive disadvantage Florida brought them in the battle for the hearts and minds of schoolteachers.

In one sense, Florida represented the last attempt to reconcile the old NEA language of professionalism with the language of trade-union action. After Florida, NEA teachers went on strike. On the other hand FEA leaders clearly felt the pangs of defeat and quickly circled the wagons against a union invasion. Florida executive secretary Phil Constans warned against the "empty promises of the AFT as it hovers around the borders of our battleground like a carrion bird."[50] Constans's imagery is revealing because it conveys the sense that Florida was a massacre, with the AFT hanging about ready to reap any gains that the debacle might leave them. Barring any major mistakes, the AFT might have begun to pick up strength in the South by capitalizing on the failure of NEA tactics. Whereas the NEA's problems were staged in a theater far removed from national issues and contained in a narrower educational framework, the AFT's mistakes would be played to a national audience in a drama over the destiny of educational opportunity and the meaning of Martin Luther King's legacy.

Ocean Hill–Brownsville was not just a big mistake for the union; it marked a final breach in the civil rights movement. At the time it happened, in 1968, the union had just negotiated the most important contract in the history of collective bargaining for public workers. This was also a year in which the civil rights coalition was losing its ability to patch over its inner quarrels. The death of Martin Luther King in April seemed to mark an end of the movement itself. A new movement, far more confrontational and disillusioned with passive resistance, influenced educated urban blacks. The teachers' union, with its equally militant stance, headed on a collision course with more radical community groups. But the union was now so professionalized, so tied to the centralized school system, that there was little contact between teacher unionists and community workers. The strike of teachers in 1968 seemed to expose the whole arrangement of a professionalized teaching force under a hierarchical, centralized school system. As difficult as it had been to reformulate procedures so that teachers had a say in the running of schools, the process had fundamentally ignored the community, a point organized schoolteachers had made seventy years earlier.

50. Ibid., p. 2.2.

CHAPTER TWELVE

Black Power v. Union Power:
The Crisis of Race

Civil Rights to Black Power, 1967–1968

Violent eruptions of discontent in Watts in 1965, Newark in 1966, and Detroit in 1967 expressed the frustrations of the urban poor and powerless. Studies of these disturbances pointed to a lack of community control over urban resources and the alienation of neighborhoods from central city administrations. Many cited the city schools as an example of community powerlessness. Jonathan Kozol's *Death at an Early Age* poignantly chronicled the alienation of youth in the educational bureaucracy in an inner-city Boston school. In Kozol's book the young, idealist teacher (the author) is the only hero, and he is beaten down by a system he describes as nearly sinister in intent. The book was influential in several ways. First, it appealed to the younger generation of new teachers who came into a degenerating urban school system where racial strife had become a part of the system itself. Second, it seemed to dramatize the conclusions of the sociological experts who argued that community control, not desegregation, promised the answer to the sense of hopelessness among the urban poor. Finally, Kozol suggested that older teachers were so inured to the educational system that they had become part of the problem. Teachers were perpetuating a racist, class-biased system of education.[1]

1. *Report of the National Advisory Commission on Civil Disorders* (New York, 1968); Jonathan Kozol, *Death at an Early Age: The Destruction of the Hearts and Minds of Negro Children in the Boston Public Schools* (New York, 1967); Herbert Kohl, *36 Children* (New York, 1967); Nat Hentoff, *Our Children Are Dying* (New York, 1966); James Herndon, *The Way It's Spozed to Be* (New York, 1968).

There are many contemporary accounts of the Ocean Hill–Brownsville affair. This is not a definitive list. Most helpful are the newspaper accounts, although they sometimes have errors. Various reports on decentralization are helpful as are a series of documents edited by Maurice R. Berube and Marilyn Gittell, *Confrontation at Ocean Hill–Brownsville: The New York School Strikes*

Kozol's book was published in 1967, right at the time when the sociologists were sifting through urban ruins to explain the explosions in the streets during the "long hot summers" of the sixties. Meanwhile, black organizations were undergoing their own metamorphosis as the emphasis of the civil rights movement changed from integration to black power. It was a time when the Student Nonviolent Coordinating Committee (SNCC) became an all-black organization, as Stokeley Carmichael announced that "integration is irrelevant." CORE rose to new prominence among urban community organizations. Older integration organizations like the NAACP and the Urban League had to reexamine their alliances with white organizations and look carefully at the issue of desegregation versus community control.

Many participants refused to make distinctions—for them, desegregation and community control seemed part of a continuum—while others insisted that what had begun as an integrationist alliance was now an entirely new movement. Black power proved difficult for integrationist whites to come to terms with, but it also opened up the civil rights movement, giving community-based organizations like CORE and the Black Panthers a considerable advantage over older national groups such as the NAACP and the Urban League. Whereas the older organizations maintained an interest in education because of desegregation, the newer organizations were primarily interested in community control and empowerment. When it came to education and the schools, the new advocates of community control could see only the centralized structure ("the establishment") and the oppressed minorities ("the community"). Teachers were normally defined within the establishment.[2]

The New York Case

The educational situation in New York City in the sixties provided a perfect example of how imprecise the labels "establishment" and "community" could be. The establishment was not nearly as perfectly centralized as its

---

of 1968 (New York, 1969). David Rogers, *110 Livingston Street Revisited: Politics and Bureaucracy in the New York City School System* (New York, 1968), recounts thoroughly events leading up to the 1968 strikes; Diane Ravitch, *The Great School Wars: New York City, 1805–1973* (New York, 1974), provides a cogent overview. Mario Fantini, Marilyn Gittell, and Richard Magate's *Community Control and the Urban School* (New York, 1970) offers the perspective of the proponents of decentralization; the union's perspective is handled in Philip Taft's *United They Teach: The Story of the UFT* (Los Angeles, 1974). See also Milton Galamison, "The Ocean Hill–Brownsville Dispute," *Christianity and Crisis*, 12 (October 1968), pp. 239–41. For other useful accounts see Martin Mayer, *The Teachers Strike* (New York, 1968); Barbara Carter, *Pickets, Parents, and Power* (New York 1971). In preparing this chapter I was initially guided by Peggy Walker, who as a beginning teacher marched with Reverend Galamison and left the union over the issues of community control. I am grateful for her time in helping me formulate my ideas at an early stage in this project.

2. Kozol, *Death at an Early Age;* Gary Orfield, *The Reconstruction of Southern Education* (New York, 1969), p. 267.

original architect, Nicholas Murray Butler, had proposed. "They don't really have centralization there," one federal official observed. "They have segmented baronies and fiefdoms that do not communicate with each other."[3] Routine and minor decisions were made centrally, while larger policy questions were often decided on the local level. At the time William Janzen retired from the superintendency in 1958 he was criticized for being too close to the professional staff and not responsive to the lay board. The superintendent worked closely with the Board of District Superintendents.

When the issue of rezoning was proposed to solve the problems of desegregation, Janzen had pointed out that black parents wanted their own schools and not rezoned schools. He failed to mention that the proposal was fiercely resisted by the Board of District Superintendents. In fact it seemed that Janzen's response to desegregation demands was first to deny the existence of segregation and then to explain why the bureaucracy could not handle it. He was most opposed to the idea of busing students out of neighborhood schools. The issue of busing became a central issue of desegregation as superintendents bent over backwards to protect the remaining white minority in the schools by promising to keep the neighborhood school intact. The fear was that busing would accelerate white flight to the suburbs and cause further deterioration of the city's schools. Civil rights leaders focused on this resistance to desegregation, sometimes overlooking the disarray that began to characterize the central administration of the schools.[4]

As the civil rights movement matured, the central bureaucracy of the city's schools seemed to fall into further disarray. Janzen was replaced by John Theobald, who served from 1958 to 1962. In response to desegregation demands, Theobald set up a "black cabinet" of community leaders to advise him on integration, but it soon became clear that Theobald would accomplish little toward achieving the goal of integration. First the city had set up special demonstration schools, loaded with extra free services that would both keep white children and address the needs of minority students. The program soon grew into an underfunded band-aid response to parent protest: school administrators often labeled the schools "demonstration schools" without providing support services. A program of open enrollment also proved a disappointment as many eligible students never heard of the program and fewer than 5 percent of those eligible took advantage of it. In 1961 the board announced that test scores for New York City children had fallen below national averages, while at the same time a state investigatory board found gross irregularities in the construction budget of the schools. The scandal led eventually to Theobald's early retirement. Integrationists could only conclude that the response to their efforts had at best been empty gestures.[5]

3. Rogers, *110 Livingston Street*, p. 325.
4. Ibid., pp. 241–42.
5. Ibid., pp. 242–43; Ravitch, *Great School Wars*, pp. 255–56.

Calvin Gross replaced Theobald in 1963, a year of crisis for the schools as patience with the slow pace of integration from the centralized office wore dangerously thin. Gross not only faced the problem of administering a fragmented, centralized bureaucracy that had been historically unresponsive to desegregation, but also he had on his desk an order from the state commissioner of education calling for desegregation, and outside his office community leaders were threatening to boycott schools in September. Again Gross complained that there was little he could do. He distrusted the lay Board of Education and refused to cooperate with it. He disagreed with the Allen Report, the state commissioner's report on desegregation issued in 1964, and issued his own report, which essentially called for an expansion of open enrollment and demonstration schools. Both of these solutions appeared to be forms of temporizing, though Gross complained that his program of expanded open enrollment was being purposefully undermined at the district level. Some of Gross's unpopularity can be attributed to the presence in his office of Bernard Donovan, who had served as acting superintendent after Theobald retired and had been runner-up to the superintendency against Gross. An insider where Gross came from out of town, Donovan had close ties to the very superintendents whom Gross suspected were undermining his program. Donovan replaced Gross in 1965.[6]

These changes and the slow response to desegregation illustrate that although there was considerable resistance to desegregation at the upper levels of school management, it was the fragmentation and discontinuity of the centralized bureaucracy that prevented real change from occurring in response to integrationist demands. The incompetence of school leadership in these years led to the complete frustration of civil rights leaders, who felt that the establishment had been cunningly astute in avoiding the issue of school desegregation.

In the same period, from 1956 to 1965, the Reverend Milton Galamison led the Parents' Workshop of the NAACP in a campaign for desegregation. Through a series of boycotts and demonstrations, Galamison was able to force various superintendents into negotiations with community groups over school issues. Although Galamison worked to unite community groups in 1963 and actually persuaded Gross to agree in principle with the Allen Report, he was able to hold the citywide coalition together only long enough to carry out a successful school boycott in the spring of 1964. After nearly ten years of engagement, the forces for desegregation had little to show for their persistence. The entry of the militant CORE into school politics after 1963 helped to add to the militancy of Galamison's group, but it also contributed to the fragmentation of various community alliances.[7]

In the midst of the disarray over school desegregation, there seemed to be

6. Ravitch, *Great School Wars,* pp. 267–69; Rogers, *110 Livingston Street,* pp. 243–51.
7. Rogers, *110 Livingston Street,* pp. 101–4; Ravitch, *Great School Wars,* pp. 278–79.

one interest group that was able to be heard by the managers of the system—
this was, of course, the public school teachers. Through a series of dramatic
strikes and demonstrations the United Federation of Teachers, operating in
the same years Galamison had been organizing, had managed to gain collective bargaining recognition and win major concessions from the superintendent and the Board of Education. When the superintendent offered concessions to civil rights groups, it seemed that the teachers refused to cooperate.
For example, as early as 1958 Janzen offered to transfer talented, experienced teachers into schools with disadvantaged children. The UFT quickly
protested the idea, pointing out that arbitrary transfers had long been a
source of punitive action on the part of school supervisors. Such a practice
would enhance the powers of the district superintendents and undermine
procedural agreements made to protect teacher rights. It is unclear just how
Janzen's proposal would have improved desegregation, but civil rights leaders pointed out that it would end the practice of sending the least experienced
teachers into undesirable schools. From the teachers' perspective, the opportunity to transfer into a "better" school was one of the few rewards the
system offered for years of competent service. It was the practice of superintendents generally never to admit that some schools were better than others;
therefore they concluded (and encouraged civil rights leaders to conclude)
that teachers were protecting their own interests at the expense of progress in
desegregation.[8]

The issue of transfers remained the sharpest dividing point between teachers and integrationists; it was also a point that superintendents never failed to
raise, especially when contract negotiations between the union and management were beginning. In April 1965, for example, the board announced a
mandatory transfer plan, which the union interpreted as a move to limit
collective bargaining by turning to civil rights groups and the press for
support. Issues of contention did arise over the teachers' new contracts, and
in 1967 when teachers asked the union to negotiate some form of protection
against assault in the classroom, community members interpreted this again
as the inability of white teachers to deal with their minority students.[9]

The 1967 contract for the union was, indeed, a landmark in gaining
teachers some say in curricular affairs, but again it was interpreted as another
sign of the rise of anti-integrationist forces in the school system. The
negotiators' demand for more protection of schoolteachers from violence in
the schools particularly antagonized community groups. In the summer of

8. Rogers, *110 Livingston Street,* p. 196. It was only in the sixties that superintendents, civil
rights leaders, and teachers were openly discussing teacher transfers and this time offering monetary
incentives but again refusing to recognize that teachers had to have the right to refuse transfers,
especially when they suspected that transfers were politically motivated by supervisory personnel.
Transfers were the issue in the Chicago strike of 1902; the issue arises quite uniformly in AFT
conventions.

9. Taft, *United They Teach,* pp. 162–70; Mayer, *Teachers Strike,* pp. 48–52; Ravitch, *Great
School Wars,* p. 319.

1967 members of CORE occupied UFT offices to protest the union's proposed strike. CORE's demands on the union included: no raises for teachers whose job performance was poor, firing principals whose schools did not maintain national grade levels, an increase in the number of black teachers and administrators, and open hearings on teacher accountability. These demands were brought before Albert Shanker, the tough-talking, politically astute UFT president since 1964. Shanker agreed to meed with CORE representatives and community people on June 26, no doubt to convince them that he did not have the power to agree to all of their demands. At the meeting, however, he was shouted down by members of the audience. Prominent in the heckling were members of the African American Teachers' Association, which had announced its intention to cross picket lines in case of a strike.[10]

Later that summer CORE again demanded that the union create instruction clinics for parents so that in the course of the strike black community leaders could keep their schools open. CORE expressed great contempt for the union's More Effective Schools (MES) program, which called on the board to invest more funds in targeted schools. The expansion of this program was part of the contract negotiations that promised teachers some participation in curriculum projects. Community-control advocates looked upon this proposal as the undermining of their project to assert control over what they considered to be a racist curriculum. Robert Sonny Carson of CORE demanded that all principals in Bedford-Stuyvesant submit plans for bringing up their grade levels to him. "If Donovan thinks we are kidding, he had better wait until September and see what happens when those teachers, those principals try to come back into our community."[11]

The two-week UFT strike in the fall of 1967 proved particularly galling to proponents of community control. In the experimental Ocean Hill–Brownsville district the local school board refused to condone the strike, and after teachers returned to the classroom they were denounced as saboteurs of community control. For the first time, many black teachers in the UFT refused to support the strike and crossed picket lines. They were joined in this strike and later in the 1968 strike by old members of the Teachers' Union whose sense of unionism, community, and professionalism had been offended by the tactics of the UFT. Striking teachers, in their view, were denying black children their right to an education and in that sense were behaving analogously to the officials in Prince Edward County who had earlier defied the Supreme Court.[12]

The main problem between community leaders and teachers in the early sixties, however, was not one particular issue or one particular strike, but

10. Mwlina Imiri Abubadika, *The Education of Sonny Carson* (New York, 1972), pp. 141–43, 145–46.
11. Ibid., p. 147; Rogers, *110 Livingston Street*, pp. 192, 284–85.
12. *NYT,* September 1967; Taft, *United They Teach*, p. 170.

rather the growing sense that while the teachers had benefited much in gaining concessions from the school establishment, community leaders had little to show for their efforts. Although in the early years of integrationist struggles teachers had been firm supporters of the movement, by the midsixties it was not difficult to conclude that the reason for the union's success was that the teachers were primarily white and the community was increasingly black.

The issue of ethnicity in New York education was more complex than simply white against black. In fact, the white Protestants had left the city, and affluent white Catholics either sent their children to parochial schools or joined PAT, the Parents and Taxpayers group that lobbied the superintendent to preserve neighborhood schools. This left only the white Jewish community fully involved in the schools. Tensions between white Jews and Afro-Americans had intensified during the urban riots of the sixties. The stereotype of the white Jewish shopkeeper gouging his black customers had become the typical explanation for rampages against small shopkeepers in the cities. Cultural histories also intensified the enmity. For black Americans, access to educational opportunity was as important as the earlier call for forty acres and a mule. It meant liberation from slavery, it meant citizenship and opportunity. For American Jews, education was no less meaningful. Education had been the primary vehicle for the preservation of Jewish culture, it had provided opportunity for hundreds of thousands of impoverished immigrants, and it promised recognition for merit.[13]

In New York 90 percent of the teachers were white; in the elementary grades over 50 percent of the students were minorities. Critics blamed the Board of Examiners for the slow hiring machinery, the difficult system of testing, and the tedious process of credentialing a teacher in the city system. But the Board of Examiners had been reformed by Jewish teachers in the thirties and had opened up the system. Attacks on the Board of Examiners appeared to be attacks on reform and a promise to return to the old system. For black teachers the examinations were culturally oriented and therefore discriminatory. Few critics took account of the sudden shift from the pre-1960 teacher shortage to the sudden surplus in the late sixties, as baby boomers were now graduating from college and looking for jobs. Finally, black community members could not help pointing out that the UFT was led largely by Jewish teachers. The question of ethnicity, the growing power of the teachers' union, and the persistent inability of the central school administration to address the problems of desegregation led black community leaders to conclude that a deeply racist establishment controlled the city's education. The educational establishment, in their view, included the white, often Jewish, public school teachers.[14]

13. Rogers, *110 Livingston Street,* pp. 79–83.
14. Oral History of Jacob Jablonower, Walter Reuther Archives, Detroit.

Another incident that seemed to paint the UFT into the corner of the educational establishment occurred at Intermediate School 201 in 1966. IS 201 was originally conceived in accordance with the Allen Report of 1964, which recommended intermediate—junior high—schools in a citywide desegregation plan. The construction of the school in East Harlem was immediately controversial as the superintendent and the Board of Education seemed to ignore repeatedly the interests of community groups in the planning of the school. From the selection of the site to the selection of the principal, school management appeared determined to ignore the community. In response, a coalition of various community groups, the Ad Hoc Parents' Council, demanded that the principal of the new school be black. The superintendent appointed instead Stanley Lisser, a Jewish principal from Harlem, who immediately announced that he had a handpicked staff and was ready to open the school. The Ad Hoc Parents' Council managed to delay the opening of the school for a year, but just as the school was about to open Barnard Donovan met with the parents group and promised that he would negotiate the issues before the opening of the school. Meanwhile, parents asked that IS 201 teachers and students be moved to PS 103, a neighborhood school.

While this move was being considered, the record of the negotiating sessions between Donovan and the parents was made public. The record included many anti-Semitic remarks, the idea that a community council could decide on who was hired at the school, and the demand that a black principal replace Mr. Lisser. IS 201 teachers decided they would not teach at PS 103, and, on hearing what they thought was Lisser's forced resignation, they refused to work and set up picket lines. Donovan then abandoned his negotiated settlement with the community council and reinstated Lisser, much to the anger of the community groups. A threatened boycott of the school failed to materialize; however, the issue of IS 201 made union teachers increasingly wary of proposals for further community control, and it convinced community leaders that the UFT was an absolute obstacle to school reform. The stage was then set for the final attempt at community control, an experiment that became known as Ocean Hill–Brownsville.[15]

Ocean Hill–Brownsville, 1968

For the union, the reprise of old battles over priorities in Ocean Hill–Brownsville was like a Greek tragedy, in which its former virtues would be revealed as weaknesses and determine its fate. School centralization, the very issue that launched the union as a protest movement, had become a vested interest for the union leaders. Originally the point of joining the labor

15. Ravitch, *Great School Wars*, pp. 292–319.

movement had been to get closer to children—children of working-class parents—and yet it was the teachers' union in Ocean Hill–Brownsville that seemed to be moving away from children and their parents. The very teachers who had railed against unfair appointments in the school system in the thirties, who had pointed to discrimination against Jewish teachers, now appeared blind to the interests of African-American teachers who were being discriminated against in examinations and licensing. The teachers who first went into the Harlem schools and turned teaching around for young black children, who were educational pioneers in celebrating Black History Week, were being turned away from the Ocean Hill–Brownsville school district because parents and community leaders suspected the teachers' sincerity in developing the minds of minority children. Echoes of the fiasco of the thirties and the fears of the fifties reverberated in the language and action of union leaders. In the community's eyes, the union was just one example of the often reactionary, historically racist, and narrowly economic institutions that had done little to build education.

In the spring of 1968, Mayor John V. Lindsay and the Board of Education fought against Albert Shanker of the UFT in the Albany legislature over the issues of decentralization of the public schools. A proposal by McGeorge Bundy under the auspices of the Ford Foundation promised a hefty grant to school districts that established their own community boards to oversee the running of the schools. The UFT emphatically opposed the Bundy-Lindsay report, which would establish community councils to oversee daily decisions in the local district schools. Although the UFT appeared solely interested in protecting its contract, it consistently pointed to the fact that the decentralization plan had no explicit division of power on the issue of firing and hiring teaching personnel. The Board of Education could gain considerable leverage over the union if it could divide responsibilities for hiring and firing as the report recommended. Finally, the decentralization proposal promised very little funding for quality education programs, a point that the teachers argued spelled failure for school reform. In the original proposal for decentralization, Shanker recalled, fiscal considerations were paramount: the idea was that separate districts could apply for federal funds. The debate, however, was somewhat beside the point. While the battle was being fought in the state legislature, the school districts were already organizing under the generous provisions of a Ford Foundation grant. In the obscure district of Ocean Hill–Brownsville an elected board was ready to assume community control as outlined by the Bundy-Lindsay report.[16]

In April 1968 the elected governing board of Ocean Hill–Brownsville decided to remove thirteen teachers, five assistant principals, and one princi-

16. Ibid., pp. 329–37; Rogers, *110 Livingston Street,* pp. 473–90; Berube and Gittell, *Confrontation,* pp. 217–19; Mayor's Advisory Panel on Decentralization, *Reconnection for Learning* (New York, 1967).

pal. They were accused of sabotaging the project of community control. UFT president Shanker demanded that the teachers receive a hearing, but the teachers in Ocean Hill–Brownsville received no word from their district about their situation.[17]

The strike began on 8 May 1968, when the nineteen educators were dismissed by District Superintendent Rhoady McCoy and sent to the downtown New York office for involuntary transfers. McCoy argued that the teachers were not cooperating with the spirit of the experiment of decentralization in the district. He had not, however, made arrangements for them to be transferred to other school districts, which was the customary practice in school administration. Without assignments in other districts, the teachers effectively had no jobs, although McCoy continued to insist he had not fired anyone. Essentially McCoy was passing the buck to the central office, which in turn took no responsibility for the teachers. In fact, McCoy maintained that he could get no response from Donovan on the transfers. This was precisely the situation the UFT had warned against in the state legislature on the Bundy-Lindsay bill. The point was that decentralization, as designed by Bundy, could undermine the entire structure of collective bargaining. For the frustrated community organizers this prospect seemed a good idea.[18]

The school district, under the centralized Board of Education, had a signed agreement with the UFT, Local 2 of the AFT, which specifically addressed issues of promotion, grievance procedures, and other questions of personnel. Involuntary transfer, an issue discussed in the AFT from the time of the early federations, was a practice the union long regarded as inimical to the best spirit of cooperation between administration and teaching staff. For years such transfers had been used as political punishments for activist teachers—punishments that were, more often than not, meted out to teachers who defended the principles of unionism. The teachers were judged by McCoy to be detrimental to the experiment of decentralization, a judgment that could be made of any union member, as it was well known that the union opposed the Bundy-Lindsay proposal for decentralization.

The dismissal of the teachers seemed to signal an ultimatum to the lobbyists in the state legislature. It was an ominous signal that threatened six years of collective bargaining for the teachers and promised to shatter the remnants of cooperation between teachers and school integrationists. In fact McCoy had been assured that he could remove any personnel from the demonstration districts by merely applying directly to Superintendent Donovan for a small number of transfers. The UFT had approved this agreement. Instead, McCoy had taken the route of transferring a large group at one time. The implication was that the new board and McCoy were looking for a confrontation to test the legitimacy of the decentralized board right at the

---

17. Ravitch, *Great School Wars*, pp. 352–61.
18. Ibid., pp. 358–59; *NYT*, 25 April 1968; Taft, *United They Teach*, pp. 171–73.

time the state legislature was considering legislation that would either legitimize or constrain the actions of the decentralized boards.[19]

The irony of Ocean Hill–Brownsville was that early in the century Progressive administrators had used a similar maneuver as a means of separating teachers from community; a teacher's attachment to community interests and needs had been seen as a sign of unprofessional conduct. Teachers were warned against becoming too close to their students, were discouraged from participating in community politics. In Ocean Hill–Brownsville, the rules were quite suddenly changed for the teachers. Lack of interest in the community, inability to get close to students, and ineptitude in community politics were now issues at the root of involuntary transfers.[20]

The union teachers, after having been ordered to report to the superintendent's office, called their union president. Shanker advised them to report back to their schools; when they did so they were blocked from their classrooms by the school principals. Shanker declared that the teachers faced a lock-out; later the teachers were forcibly escorted by police into their classrooms, whereupon the local board closed the schools. When the schools reopened again, the teachers walked out with 350 sympathizing UFT members in the district. Finally, McCoy brought charges against ten teachers on 27 May 1968. This time McCoy insisted that the teachers had defied his orders and were dismissed for insubordination. Superintendent Donovan questioned McCoy's authority to dismiss the teachers, and Shanker sanctioned a strike of teachers within the Ocean Hill–Brownsville district. Again four hundred teachers walked off their jobs only to find that community members blocked them from returning to school. As far as District Superintendent McCoy was concerned, these teachers were also insubordinate and would have to be transferred from the schools. Shanker insisted that no one could be transferred unless the district superintendent made specific charges and unless there were teaching positions for the teachers in other schools.[21]

Meanwhile, in Albany all hopes for compromise on a decentralization bill had faded. Instead, the demonstration districts had been given a million-dollar grant through the Institute for Community Studies, with nearly one quarter of a million dollars earmarked for the Ocean Hill–Brownsville district. By this time the demand of community control groups was for complete control, while the Board of Education and the state legislature were still behind the original Bundy-Lindsay proposal. The disturbances of May, however, helped to shelve the legislation for decentralization. Change in New York City schools would have to be worked out on the community level. In June 1968 the New York City schools closed for the summer recess with none of the major issues resolved.[22]

19. Ravitch, *Great School Wars*, pp. 360–61.
20. For a variety of teacher views see Berube and Gittell, *Confrontation*, pp. 179–205.
21. Taft, *United They Teach*, pp. 173–81.
22. Ravitch, *Great School Wars*, pp. 360–61.

The issue of community control has too often been confused with mere decentralization. Albert Shanker and the UFT supported decentralization and cooperated in the original plan for the Ocean Hill–Brownsville experimental district. In fact Shanker has pointed out that the proposal for decentralization would have provided additional federal funds for these separate individual school districts. This was the fiscal enticement that drew the union and the board behind decentralization. The union had in fact agreed to some teacher transfers and was encouraging idealistic members to participate in the Ocean Hill–Brownsville district. The point is, however, that decentralization and community control were not the same thing.[23]

"Now how can anybody construe community control as decentralization?" Sonny Carson asks in his autobiography. The Brooklyn CORE leader continued, "Decentralization to my simple mind is a restructuring of a system that's already in operation, and that's not what we're talking about because we're saying there needs to be a new kind of vehicle, with the community determining what it should be."[24] Brooklyn CORE and Sonny Carson helped to organize and elect the community board, which chose Rhoady McCoy as the district administrator of the schools. They organized parent and community leaders, brought the union leadership into the community to explain what was going on, and pressed McCoy to get rid of teachers they felt were against the experiment. For the young activists in CORE, the schools would serve the community, give minority children a positive self-image, teach them the lost history of African-American struggles, and lead them to believe in themselves as the arbiters of their own destiny. The criticism aimed at select white schoolteachers was that they did not believe their minority students were capable of learning and that children responded to these allegedly racist teachers by living up to their low expectations.[25]

There was an element of generational politics operating in this struggle, just as there had been in the early struggle of the thirties. And again the issue of professional qualifications acted to keep young perspectives out of the school system. Jobs again were an issue. Teachers objected to the assignment of McCoy because he was not on the administrative hiring list. Also, by 1968 many young men and women were finding it difficult to get teaching jobs, and if they were placed, they were often given the poorest schools with the most difficult students. Enrollments had begun to decline, except in the city's worst high schools where young black males were staying in high school longer to avoid the Vietnam draft. In the summer of 1968 McCoy hired 350 teachers to replace striking UFT teachers in his district. The majority of these teachers were white and Jewish, although McCoy hired a number of

23. Interview with Albert Shanker, summer 1988.
24. Abubadika, *Education of Sonny Carson,* p. 140.
25. Interview with Peggy Walker, spring 1987.

talented black teachers as well. His criterion was the sincerity of the teachers' commitment to social change. Experience in the Peace Corps, VISTA, or community programs helped applicants. McCoy had qualified teachers but few of them were on the growing eligibility list of the Board of Examiners.

Another generational issue was the Vietnam War. Younger trade unionists were revolting against George Meany's cold war philosophy and his gag on discussion over the issue. Finally, younger teachers, many in the UFT, felt that the union had lost its progressive spirit with collective bargaining. One Ocean Hill–Brownsville teacher who crossed the picket line in 1968 reported, "In six years the UFT has become middle aged. When I started in 1960 it was relevant. But there's no pioneering trade union spirit here anymore. . . . And now they're afraid of black violence."[26] Young community militants shared these sentiments and moreover thought of the union as just as much a symbol of white power as the school administration had been. This inability to distinguish between the union and management infuriated seasoned trade unionists like Shanker, who had spent years at the mercy of powerful administrators who did nothing to advance civil rights. At one point in a series of confrontations, Sonny Carson accused Shanker of being the same as Superintendent Donovan, of signing sweetheart agreements, of being on the same side. In Carson's view the assessment was correct; in Shanker's view it was a deliberate insult.[27]

Other incidents had less to do with the radical perspective of the militants than with plain physical intimidation. Schoolteachers were verbally threatened and physically prevented from entering their classrooms. Carson tells quite gleefully the story of a meeting in Ocean Hill–Brownsville in which militants surrounded Shanker and refused to let him leave the room. Shanker, Carson says, looked quite frightened and demanded to be allowed to leave. It was a triumph for the militants to say that Shanker never again attended a meeting without a bodyguard. Shanker himself recalls the incident and reports that there were many threats on his life and his family's safety, so that armed state troopers were stationed in the Shanker family basement. "Try explaining that to your young children," Shanker adds. The more UFT teachers felt uncomfortable in the community, the more they appealed to the authorities in the central office. It was a standoff between groups, a feud that centered on an angry and disappointed but united black community exercising its power against teachers whom it perceived as holders of absolute control over the system. Ironically, both the teachers in their quest for collective bargaining and the black community in its quest for community control hoped for a new educational system that would give them and public school children a sense of empowerment.[28]

26. Sol Stern, " 'Scab' Teachers," in *Confrontation,* ed. Berube and Gittell, pp. 176–205.
27. Abubadika, *Education of Sonny Carson,* pp. 155–57.
28. Interview with Shanker, 1988; Abubadika, *Education of Sonny Carson,* pp. 145–47.

The issue of physical threats went deeper than the violent flavor of the times—for the union teachers it was a reminder of tougher times, especially the fifties, when the teachers' union was under fire for subversion, and teachers in the city, mostly Jewish teachers, received threats against their lives and were subject to anti-Semitic attacks. It had been an ordeal that the teachers, both in the Teachers' Guild and in the Teachers' Union, shared. But the responses differed. Teachers' Union advocates welcomed CORE's militants while guild teachers shuddered at the prospect of reliving the postwar hysteria. As the black community in New York withdrew to find it roots, so too did the New York Jewish community. When meetings with community leaders led to arguments over who was a racist, union teachers charged that black leaders were anti-Semitic. It was no secret that the UFT (like its predecessors, the Teachers' Guild, the Teachers' Union and Local 5) had a strong Jewish leadership. Attacks on the UFT too often disintegrated into attacks on Jews. Feelings in the union and the community ran high. Hate literature was distributed around the neighborhood of Ocean Hill–Brownsville schools, but the UFT was accused of reprinting the literature and fanning the flames of racial antagonism. The original leaflets were not produced by the major actors in the drama and could be attributed to a few individuals, but they nevertheless furthered polarization. Shanker was often accused of raising the temperature of trade unionists on this issue. He did not have to: the teachers were already conditioned by years of mistreatment. For the black community such accusations of anti-Semitism were disingenuous attempts to sidestep the issue of white bigotry. "Dig that," Carson writes. "We accused the system of bigotry in its miseducation of black children and so instead of addressing themselves to that they turn around and accused us of bigotry."[29]

Shanker's contribution to the anger of the teachers, however, had more to do with a backlash against radicalism itself, directed against militant young teachers who supported community control. It was this tradition of radicalism that Counts had eliminated from the union to protect the movement. Shanker worked in the same way to eliminate this controversial element in the name of ensuring the union's survival. The legacy of George Counts and the Communist purge was definitely an ingredient in the strong UFT reaction against the community militants and their young allies among white unionists in the UFT.[30]

This was the background to the strike in the fall of 1968. Little happened over the summer. Negotiations that started in June broke down over the summer. McCoy and Shanker refused to come together on any issue. When

29. Abudadika, *Education of Sonny Carson*, pp. 143–44; Berube and Gittell, *Confrontation*, pp. 163–67; interview with Shanker; *NYT*, 11 November 1968.

30. Marshall F. Stevenson, "Challenging the Roadblocks to Equality: Labor's Civil Rights Program, 1945–1985" (paper presented at the North American Labor History Conference, 21 October 1988).

school finally opened in September, Shanker announced that the entire teaching force would go on strike in support of the transferred teachers. Risking a jail term, the reputation of his union, and his leadership credibility on this issue, Shanker rose to the challenge of the militants. He would take a strong stand and not allow the school district to renege on its contract in order to satisfy an experiment in education and thereby establish the precedent of allowing a superintendent to use the community against the union. For their part, the community activisits saw this as the critical test of community control over education. If real change were to happen in education, Ocean Hill–Brownsville people had to defend their right to their own kind of education, their own teaching personnel, their own schools. Shanker insisted it was not a test of community control or of decentralization. But television clearly showed the nation an angry community, frightened picketing school-teachers, and the recalcitrant UFT leader denouncing a black administrator, Rhoady McCoy. The architects of the situation, the largely inept, centralized, educational leadership, hid in the downtown offices, away from the camera's eye.[31]

Teachers went on strike, they were locked out, they called off the strike. Arbitrators were called in but the parties failed to come to an agreement. Finally, at the end of November the state commissioner of education stepped in and offered to mediate. He actually sent officers to oversee the Ocean Hill–Brownsville schools to make sure that teachers were not harassed and to make sure that everyone worked hard for the new experiment. Four of these overseers quit before the schools quieted down in late December. The union had won the issue of transfers, while the community experiment continued, and in 1969 a compromise decentralization bill passed the state legislature.[32]

Before the dust had cleared, educational experts were quick to make pronouncements about the terrible power of teacher unions or the divisiveness of community control in education. In retrospect these same experts are now saying that community control has had tremendous successes—especially in those communities where there is political stability, where administrators work well with teachers, where community members are allowed to participate fully in decisions, and where teachers are given freedom to experiment with the curriculum. Teacher unions are no longer the issue.

Chicago v. New York on De Facto Segregation

Though the Ocean Hill–Brownsville affair drew on several typical sources of frustration between community groups and school officials, it did not

31. Carter, *Pickets*, pp. 111–17. See Fred Ferretti, "Who's to Blame in the School Strike?" in *Confrontation*, ed. Berube and Gittell, pp. 293–95.
32. Ravitch, *Great School Wars*, pp. 368–78.

represent an inevitable clash between professionalized public school teachers and radicalized community leaders. In Chicago conflict evolved in a
community where racial tension in the midsixties remained high, where de
facto segregation plagued the school system, and the sociological phe-
nomena of white flight and school deterioration led to extreme tension over
education issues. Yet in two respects the differences between Chicago and
New York were dramatic. First, the proportion of black schoolteachers and
administrators was much higher in Chicago. Entry into the system had never
been reformed as it had been in New York in the thirties. There was no
institution like the New York Board of Examiners open to control by one
ethnic group or another. Standards of professionalism continued to serve as a
barrier to entry, but the union had acted as an advocate of change and had
long demanded the hiring of black faculty and administrators. Second,
Chicago teachers had not been as successful in gaining collective bargaining
as had New York teachers. A powerful Illinois Education Association, which
had built numerical strength through compulsory membership, remained adamantly opposed to collective bargaining. Even though the Chicago Teachers' Union had a majority of teachers in the city, there were several vocal
constituents, including the remnant of Margaret Haley's Chicago Teachers'
Federation, now numbering only one thousand members, that thwarted the
CTU's efforts to become sole bargaining agent. It was clear that if the CTU
were to gain recognition it would be through a dramatic strike, a move that
the membership had been unwilling to take since the 1948 crisis. Aware that
it would need community support, the CTU kept abreast of the civil rights
movement and often found itself on the same side of a closed-door Board of
Education.[33]

This is not to say that the CTU was free from racial conflict. Indeed, the
union and civil rights groups clashed dramatically in 1964, just when the
contours of the civil rights movement were shifting to the left. In March 1964
members of the executive board of the Negro American Labor Council
confronted John Fewkes and CTU leaders in a tense meeting to discuss the
racial attitudes of the leadership. Specifically, Fewkes was being called on
the carpet to explain why, in the wake of a civil rights boycott of schools, he
had appeared on local television and, when pressed by an interviewer,
identified the boycott with the rising problem of violence in the schools.
Fewkes replied that the had only meant that a boycott or a strike would
naturally disrupt the rhythm of school discipline, but black teachers disagreed and declared that the boycotts had not disturbed children. What
disturbed children was racism and segregation. The boycotts, they insisted,
had been a proud moment. "Let me tell you something, Mr. Fewkes,
because you were never a black boy or girl, that was one of the proudest
moments in some of those children's lives that they ever had. They were

---

33. "Proceedings, Chicago Teachers' Union Conference with Negro American Labor Council,"
19 March 1964, CTU Collection, Box 26/4; see also *CT,* 14 February and 7 April 1964.

proud. We were proud to be black." Black teachers and community organizers explicitly threatened to withhold support of collective bargaining for
the CTU if Fewkes could not satisfy them on the issue of racism. Fewkes
responded by pointing to the union's record on civil rights, a record that was
not substantially different from that of New York's UFT. But the black
teachers responded that the urgency of civil rights meant that such resolutions were not enough; they wanted the union leadership to become activist
proponents of civil rights. They pointed to the absence of union leadership at
civil rights rallies, and went carefully over every issue of contention between
whites and blacks in the schools.

Ultimately Fewkes agreed to have a press conference to reiterate his
support for the boycotts and declare unity with the effort for school integration. In 1967, John Desmond, the new CTU president, endorsed the Redmond Plan, a city plan for school desegregation, which included busing.
Finally, in the spring of 1969 teachers prepared a strike call and attracted
eight thousand teachers, including civil rights leaders, to their rally. They
were responding to Board of Education threats to discharge seventy-three
hundred teachers and close summer schools—both issues on which community leaders could back the CTU enthusiastically. In the same year Desmond
was forced to cancel a CTU meeting to which Albert Shanker had been
invited, because black leaders refused to share the platform with the UFT
president and black teachers threatened a boycott. Nevertheless, the teachers' strike in the fall of 1969 proved a success. The issues in Chicago had not
been very different from issues in New York. Chicago schools had violence,
and teachers had included security measures as part of their collective
bargaining demands, but Desmond had been careful to say that the violence
issue was not racial and that black teachers had been victims of school
violence. Desmond's assurances were not very different from statements
made by the New York UFT officers, but in Chicago the issues of racism had
been, since 1964, regularly aired in union circles.

Two other ingredients differentiated the Chicago situation from that in
New York. First, in Chicago the red scare had not prompted a legislative
response as stringent as the Feinberg Law in New York. Second, white union
leaders were not physically threatened at meetings. The tactics of intimidation had not grown to the extent of Shanker's experience in New York. In part
this was because Fewkes and later Desmond consulted frequently with high-
level black leaders who attended the confrontational meetings and who were
members of CORE or had ties in the community. Chicago was hardly an
arena of racial harmony, but on the teacher-union question the schism that
grew out of proportion in New York failed to emerge. When the issue of
decentralization and community control emerged in Chicago, parents and
union teachers found common ground.[34]

34. Memorandum to John E. Desmond, CTU president, from Peter Zansitis, Joint Committee on
Redmond Plan, 27 October 1967, CTU Collection, Box 26; "Why a Strike Against the Board of

Decentralization, Community Control, and Professionalism

The battle over community control was not merely a replay of former efforts to reorganize schools. Decentralization was not merely the reverse of centralization; community control was a call for the empowerment of the community, and it was related to the fact that teachers were being empowered at the same time. It did not suddenly make schools political—they were political all along. In both cities teachers worked to protect their interests in education, but the teachers' organizations in the late sixties were powerful: teachers had tenure laws, legal counselors, and organizational strength to prevent the abuse of power. If anything, the rise of teacher unionism offered a balance of power to the unchecked whims of the intellectual reform elite in the community. Teacher participation in community life today is a significant aspect of professionalism, not a liability. No one has written a book criticizing fully the administrative mishandling of the Ocean Hill–Brownsville affair, although both the community leaders and the UFT leaders felt the need to write their own histories of what happened and why.[35]

It is especially ironic that the contradictions in professionalization and centralization have never been examined. Black teachers now walk the line on the professionalism question. If they are too close to parents, or too close to community political groups, they risk the wrath of a still hierarchical administrative structure. The issues of centralization, professionalization, and community control were central to the entire Ocean Hill–Brownsville episode. Professionalization assured teachers some autonomy, but it also placed them under the mandate of centralized control. The union had decided to embrace professionalism in the late thirties, rejecting the community-organizing style of the Communist party in order to survive in the trade-union movement. Although Albert Shanker said it would be easier to negotiate with small decentralized districts, he was unwilling to relinquish the prerogatives of professionalism to community organizers. He was not just stubborn, insensitive, or racist; he was articulating a fundamental principle that teacher unionists had learned through bitter experience. It seems highly unlikely that under the same circumstances the leaders of the NEA, the professional organization, would have acted differently.

The NEA's Response

The strike at Ocean Hill–Brownsville drew national attention to the spectacle of striking white teachers and militant black community groups.

Education?" 9 May 1969, CTU Collection, Box 63/5; see also CTU clippings, 1969, in CTU Collection.

35. David Rogers and Norman H. Chung, *110 Livingston Street Revisited: Decentralization in Action* (New York, 1983), pp. 1–17, 50, 53, 214–15. See also Ravitch, *Great School Wars*, pp. 381–404. I disagree with Ravitch's historical conclusions although I think her analysis of the problems of decentralization is correct.

The AFT's national reputation as a strong supporter of civil rights plum-meted. Old allies of the union abandoned ship with amazing rapidity. And finally, the NEA, now with its first black president, could respond ag-gressively to the AFT's blunder.

Elizabeth Koontz was not about to abandon the concept of professionalism in responding to the Ocean Hill–Brownsville affair. First, Koontz wanted it known that she did not automatically support decentralization or community control and that she condemned plans that were "a little short of bedlam and complete disorder and a mad scramble for power and influence." She had to admit that the NEA had no position on the issue, but she assured reporters that the NEA would have an Urban Task Force make the study of decentral-ization a priority.[36]

Koontz said, "The school is the public's school, not the parents' school nor the teachers' school; . . . the teaching profession recognizes that the control of education is a legal function of the people." Still, she defended professional prerogatives: "The control of conditions under which teachers enter the profession and practice is a matter of professional self-governance, as in all great professions. Teachers are struggling to obtain the legal author-ity to govern themselves. They need the legal process to protect competent members and to warn, discipline and dismiss those who abrogate their standards or responsibilities." While Koontz stated that "control of educa-tion and governance of the profession are intimately related," she called for a partnership between the public and the teaching profession. She allowed that schools should be able to experiment but the right of teachers and principals to self-determination had to be preserved. Ultimately she condemned "indi-viduals or organized groups" that interfered with such experimental pro-grams. It was not a wholesale condemnation of the UFT and it was certainly not an endorsement of CORE's program. The NEA would not renege on its professionalization project.[37]

In November 1968, as the embattled teachers and community members in Ocean Hill–Brownsville remained locked in conflict, Mario Fantini, the Ford Foundation program officer in charge of the experimental Ocean Hill–Brownsville project, told members of the NEA task force on urban education that "the Black movement is the most creative force in society today." In January the NEA announced that Jonathan Kozol would speak at the national convention. The following February the NEA sponsored a "Critical Issues Conference" in Washington, which prominently featured Whitney Young of the Urban League and James Farmer of CORE. Participants were told that community control was at the forefront of the desegregation movement, and James Farmer predicted that community control would be the wave of the future. The irony was that old Abraham Lefkowitz of the AFT had been one

36. *NEA Reporter*, 4 October 1968.
37. Ibid., 22 November 1968.

of the founders of the Urban League, and many AFT leaders, including Shanker, had been part of CORE-sponsored demonstrations for racial equality at a time when the NEA considered demonstrations unprofessional. Furthermore, the visible appearance of major civil rights leaders in NEA's publications made it appear that the association was endorsing the idea of community control when it had no such position.[38]

38. Two months later, in fact, the NEA intervened in East St. Louis to stop the involuntary transfer of teachers intended to achieve racial balance of teachers in schools. *NEA Reporter,* 25 April 1969.

CHAPTER THIRTEEN /

Professionalism and Unionism in the Seventies and Eighties

The intense competition between the union and the association finally began to drain the resources of the two organizations. Moreover, it was becoming abundantly clear that the costs of the Vietnam War would drain the the nation's treasury, making the dream of further federal aid to education difficult if not impossible. Without Lyndon Johnson's active efforts to unite the two organizations behind federal aid, the NEA and the AFT were weakened by the same disunity that had plagued them since the New Deal. In the face of these problems the AFT made overtures to the NEA about the possibility of merger in early 1968.[1]

Merger and Transformation

The union argued that merger was an economic necessity. "Local sources of revenue were running dry," recalled David Selden, AFT president. "Money for schools would have to come from state and federal sources, which could only be increased through united action by teachers."[2] Besides, within the NEA internal changes had made it clear that the mammoth organization was slowly but inevitably restructuring itself into a union. "Look down the long road and see where you are going," one NEA delegate warned the NEA convention. He urged delegates to "view your changed vocabulary—shop steward, agency shop, collective bargaining, freeloaders, piggyback, war chest, grievance procedures." These, the delegate pointed out, were the words and thoughts of trade unionists.[3] But the NEA had not

1. Movement toward merger talks actually began in 1965. See Michael Moskow, "Transcript of the First Meeting and Reception of the National Committee of Teacher Unity," 30 June 1965, AFT Collection, Series 1, Box 22.
2. David Selden, *The Teacher Rebellion* (Washington, D.C., 1985), p. 132.
3. *NEA Proceedings*, pp. 395–96.

yet embraced the values and viewpoints of trade unionism, and in any case it distrusted the AFT's motives.

In October 1968 the NEA officially rejected a union bid for talks on merger, citing major financial problems within the AFT as a barrier. Selden was not discouraged, partially because his assessment of the school-funding situation was proving accurate. At the same time that the NEA was choosing to go it alone, the Congress voted for a $3.7 billion package, less than half of what the NEA had demanded. In California, in an ominous portent of things to come, voters defeated the first tax initiative (Proposition 13 passed in 1978, a decade later) to cut local property taxes. Few Californians realized that this easy defeat would only serve to educate and prepare a growing property-tax revolt that was brewing in the West and by the eighties would sweep the nation.[4]

Nationally the association played up the rejection of merger, announcing that the Classroom Teachers' Association applauded the dismissal of merger talks. Locally, however, the AFT found it had little to lose by its call for merger. Militant teachers were especially attracted to the AFT call for unity. As early as 1965 teachers in Los Angeles, sharing an outrage at the activities of the Board of Education in the nation's second-largest school district, began to discuss merger between the district's California Teachers' Association chapter and the Los Angeles Federation of Teachers. A joint local conference led to what was seen as a temporary merger agreement. Members of association and union would keep their affiliations, but the new organization, the United Teachers of Los Angeles (UTLA), would unite for bargaining purposes into one organization. UTLA teachers carried out a successful strike in 1970, and their successes stimulated interest in the union for further merger possibilities.[5]

California teachers needed unity because the state's collective bargaining law had been used by school administrators to play off one faction of teachers in bargaining sessions against another. But the next large merger proved a stunning surprise that pointed to a transformation of the entire teacher-union movement.

New York State Teachers' Association president Tom Hobart began negotiations with David Selden and Albert Shanker in 1972. This merger was shaped by the constraints of the Taylor Law, under which a public employee relations board regulated collective bargaining. Teachers needed more political clout on the board to help broaden the scope of bargaining and to bring paraprofessionals into their bargaining jurisdiction. Competition between teachers in New York City and other public workers for the same economic pie had isolated the UFT somewhat, and now Hobart's offer of unity became the promise to break the logjam of isolation and division in Albany between public worker groups.

4. *California Teacher,* 10 (June 1978).
5. See "Report on Merger Talks," AFT Collection, Series 1, Box 22.

The successful unification of the New York teachers produced one of the largest unions in the country, and it instantly catapulted Shanker into national prominence. Hobart, a proponent of unity within the NEA, urged other states to consider merger, but association leaders remained critical of Hobart's move. They pointed out that the union seemed to reap the benefits of the merger while the association's suburban teachers were swallowed up by big city locals.[6] Reaction to the New York merger was so negative in the NEA leadership that after 1972 it declared that all merger talks had to go through the Executive Board and that state federations were not authorized to carry on their own merger discussions.

Although merger talks between the NEA and the AFT continued quietly at AFT president Selden's urging, both organizations held back. Despite this reluctance, the need for merger glared at national leaders amid the problems of the late sixties.

In fact, both organizations staggered beneath the burden of collective bargaining wars and the dramatic rise in strikes between 1967 and 1969. For the AFT, always short of funds and staff, rapid expansion of the union proved expensive. But it was the NEA that had the harder time adjusting financially to the new demands of collective bargaining. New NEA staff members, trained in union organizing and collective bargaining, were crowded into national headquarters. The Research Division remained the most powerful division in the Washington office, where an enormous library—a far better archive than the U.S. commissioner of education possessed—continued to serve all teachers and administrators nationally. The NEA staff numbered between four hundred and five hundred in the late sixties.[7]

In 1970 the NEA held a constitutional convention, which radically restructured its electoral process and opened the way for further internal reorganization. Most important, the convention ("Con-con") allowed for a substantial nationwide dues increase. Under the revised constitution, presidents served two-year terms and could serve consecutive terms, and an elected Executive Committee gained real power. The staff was reorganized so that its myriad of divisions more accurately reflected the permanence of collective bargaining and the strike-related needs of militant teachers. Steps toward becoming a union, however, were not altogether orderly and painless for the association. A staff strike in 1972 forced management to identify its

6. For negotiations, see *NEA Reporter,* 24 January 1969; on the Flint merger, see ibid., 24 October 1970. The UTLA merger involved 19,200 CTA members and 3,000 AFT members. *NEA Reporter,* 23 January 1970; see also Allen M. West, *The NEA: The Power Base for Education* (New York, 1980), pp. 234–36; and Selden, *Teacher Rebellion,* pp. 132–35.

7. For costs, see the discussion of the Newark teachers' strike in Robert J. Braun, *Teachers and Power* (New York, 1972), pp. 267–71. The Newark strike lasted from 1 February to 19 April 1971. The NEA's archives subsequently became part of the Department of Education and are now housed in the AFT's Washington headquarters building, where the Department of Education has leased space.

own interests and separate the interests of the membership from those of the hired staff. The strike also injected the language of unionism into the very sanctum of the NEA. As one NEA staffer remarked, "The staff union should have been paid for giving an in-service workshop, rather than docked for striking."[8]

These internal changes led to a fortuitous alliance that killed the AFT's bid for merger once and for all. The union always had maintained that its affiliation with the AFL brought local support to teachers' strikes and, indeed, local central labor organizations were generous with moral and monetary support in some of the tough struggles teachers had begun to engage in. In the spring of 1971 the NEA struck back. NEA president Helen Bains and leaders of the American Federation of Federal, State, Municipal and County Employees (AFSCME) announced that they had formed a Coalition of American Public Employees (CAPE). The news electrified labor circles, demolished the AFT's claim to trade union solidarity, and made the possibility of merger remote.[9]

Jerry Wurf, head of AFSCME, was responsible for the turnabout. Although once an ally of Shanker and Selden, he had become a rival in the late sixties as competition between the two big public employee unions in New York City forced them to compete for a shrinking pool of public monies. Wurf appeared at the NEA convention in 1972 to explain that the AFT had had the opportunity to join CAPE when the idea was first introduced in 1971, and he expressed his "regrets that that situation got so emotional despite our very best efforts." Wurf went on to say that the differences between the NEA and the AFT were not philosophical. "For the most part, the NEA positions in some areas of the country are as progressive or more progressive than those of the AFT with regard to community responsibility and the well-being of teachers. And I am sure that in some parts of the country the opposite is true, although I am not specifically aware of them. I didn't mean that sarcastically, I really didn't."[10]

From the NEA's perspective CAPE offered an alternative labor support without the need to relinquish Carr's old shibboleth of independence from labor. In other words, the NEA could have labor support without paying dues and could simultaneously build a new coalition for national lobbying. Indeed, Wurf promised that CAPE would support the NEA's long-sought goal of a federal department of education. It appeared that the AFT's support from labor was withering fast. The union was simply not in a position to challenge Wurf's new organization in 1972 because it was by that time embroiled in its own internal wars.

8. Interview with NEA staff, summer 1988; *NEA Reporter,* 18 September 1970, 15 October 1971; *NEA Handbook,* 1971–72.
9. *NEA Proceedings,* 1971, pp. 412–13. The announcement was made on 24 March 1971.
10. *NEA Proceedings,* 1972, p. 76.

Division in the AFT

The defeat of Selden in the AFT election in 1974 marked the end of AFT overtures on merger. The causes of the split between Selden and Shanker are obscure; both men point to the overriding ambition of the other. Together they had created the strongest union in the national. But Selden's defeat came largely because of divisions in the union over Ocean Hill–Brownsville and the Vietnam War.

The immediate impact of Ocean Hill–Brownsville in the union was to set off a protracted battle for control. The recently formed AFT Black Caucus prepared for the 1969 convention, sending out a call for increased black leadership in the union. Members of the caucus, including William Simon, president of the Washington, D.C., local and a national vice-president, were outspoken in their opposition to the UFT strike. Simon pointed out that teachers in Washington supported community control of the schools. In Newark, Carole Graves prominently supported the anger of the Black Caucus. New York's Dick Parrish became a leader in formulating an opposition ticket against the national leadership of Selden, who had been president of the AFT since 1968 and had given Shanker his full support during the strikes.[11]

The Black Caucus gained the support of a small group of left-wing trade unionists in the AFT who were pressing Selden to take a stand against the war in Vietnam. Various state federations and locals in the union had begun to defy George Meany, AFL-CIO president, on the war issue and were visibly present at large antiwar rallies in major U.S. cities. Especially after the United Auto Workers (UAW) left the AFL-CIO in 1968 over the war issue, there was considerable pressure within the internationals to undermine Meany's profoundly anticommunist cold war stance on the issue. In the AFT the antiwar faction failed to get its resolution adopted in 1969 or 1970, but hopes were high for the 1971 convention. Meanwhile Selden was wobbling on the war issue, as were other labor leaders closely tied to Walter Reuther.[12]

11. See the debate on the issue of community control in *AFT Proceedings*, 1968, AFT Collection, Box 38/1, pp. 305–52, 1216–69; also convention leaflets in Series 1, Box 41. Maurice R. Berube and Marilyn Gittell, eds., *Confrontation at Ocean Hill–Brownsville: The New York School Strikes of 1968* (New York, 1969), p. 144. Carole Graves was also outspoken in her support of community control: see Braun, *Teachers and Power*, pp. 266–67. For Dick Parrish's role in leading black opposition to George Meany, see Robert H. Zeigler, *American Workers, American Unions: 1920–1985* (Baltimore, 1986), pp. 174–80. In one incident where A. Philip Randolph was officially censured by the AFL-CIO Executive Council for his criticism of the racial attitudes of union leaders, Parrish heatedly charged that Meany had made "a show of power to demonstrate to Negro union members that they represent nothing when it comes to setting policies . . . even though they pay dues" (p. 176). Parrish was head of the Negro American Labor Council at the time.

12. AFT Resolutions, 1970, AFT Collection, Series 1, Box 42. Walter Reuther broke with the AFL-CIO on the war issue in 1968. See Zeigler, *American Workers*, pp. 170–74. Victor Reuther argues that the break was not a reflection of the antipathy between Meany and Reuther but the response to grass-roots, rank-and-file disgust with the war. See Victor G. Reuther, *The Brothers Reuther and the Story of the UAW: A Memoir* (Boston, 1976), pp. 377–81. See also James R. Green,

The most serious challenge to the union's leadership came not from the Black Caucus nor from the left-wing groups, but rather from AFT organizer Ken Miesen. Miesen himself was no radical, nor did he have an agenda for organizing that could address the problems of unionism and centralization, or community control versus professionalism. But his candidacy against Selden put together an odd coalition of conservative, small locals who were outside the sweep for collective bargaining, along with the Black Caucus and left-wing groups. Resenting the growing power of the New York local, the conservative, small locals saw Miesen as an opportunity to overthrow the hegemony of what they saw as the New York axis between Selden in the national office and Shanker in New York. These locals showed little interest in community control or the Vietnam War; they wanted to hit New York. Miesen came within 106 votes of toppling Selden at the 1971 Pittsburgh convention, pulling 1,462 votes to Selden's 1,567.[13]

More significant than Miesen's showing was the absolute vote for Shanker's most visible opponent, Bill Simon, in the concurrent election of sixteen national vice-presidents. Simon and Shanker shared spots on the Progressive Caucus slate, the slate of the AFT leadership. Simon's supporters in Washington withheld support for Selden and Shanker, thus giving Simon the greatest number of votes for vice-president. Shanker, though reelected as a vice-president, received the fewest votes of those elected. Miffed by Simon's defiance, Shanker demanded that delegates be held accountable to their membership for their votes. This ended the use of the secret ballot at AFT conventions, a twist that Shanker would use effectively in his bid against Selden in 1974.[14]

Miesen's strong challenge exposed Selden's weakness. In the aftermath of the Pittsburgh convention the rivalry between Selden and Shanker intensified. First, Shanker's faithful support of the Vietnam War led to his appointment by Meany to the AFL-CIO Executive Council. Normally only national presidents were rewarded with such important positions, but Meany was suspicious of Selden's now open opposition to the war and his closeness to Reuther. The appointment directly undermined Selden's leadership both in his own union and in the merger talks. Meanwhile, as a national vice-president Shanker had polarized the AFT Executive Council into two fac-

---

The World of the Worker: Labor in the Twentieth Century (New York, 1980), pp. 221–43. Jerry Wurf of AFSCME tried to keep the lid on rank-and-file discontent with Meany's cold war stance until 1969. See Joseph C. Coulden, *Jerry Wurf, Labor's Last Angry Man: A Biography* (New York, 1982), p. 187.

13. AFT Election Folder, AFT Collection, Series 13, Box 42. The *Nea Reporter,* 18 September 1970, suggested that the AFT was staff dominated because Miesen, an AFT staffer, was running against Selden, also an AFT staffer, who replaced Cogen. The observation, still very much part of the collective bargaining, was in response to the AFT's traditional epithet, "administrator dominated," hurled at the NEA.

14. AFT Collection, Box 42, 1970. Miesen received 1,462 votes and Selden 1,567; Shanker received 1,910 votes and Simon 2,134.

tions and gained a majority. Selden complained that he could not conduct the business of the union, to which Shanker's adamant refrain suggested that Selden resign. The contest between the two men came to a head at the 1974 convention, where Shanker won the AFT presidency. After Shanker's election there was a brief flirtation with the merger idea, but the AFT strategy of merger originated with Selden and died with his departure.[15]

The Persisting Issue of Gender

One casualty of the Ocean Hill–Brownsville backlash was the nascent women's movement within the union. Women in both the association and the union benefited greatly in the era of the civil rights movement, although the impact was gradual. Women leaders from both the NEA and AFT had been appointed to Kennedy's Commission on the Status of Women in the early sixties, and representatives from both organizations attended various conferences on the promotion of women to leadership positions. The NEA held an "Education and Women's Leadership Tea" in 1964, but the idea was mostly to discuss how women could advance to administrative posts in education. In both the NEA and the AFT, women were visible and present in leadership positions but were conspicuously absent from the inner sanctum.[16]

Progress accelerated in the late sixties as more women took local leadership roles, especially on collective bargaining teams. These women became concerned with persistent financial inequalities between men and women teachers. Furthermore, the civil rights movement nurtured a cohort of women leaders who moved into issues of women's rights in their respective organizations. In the AFT the Women's Caucus formed at the 1969 convention and in 1970 led a successful floor fight for a set of demands that included the creation of a special committee on women's rights.[17]

At this time, Title VII of the Civil Rights Act of 1964 covered sex discrimination in employment but would not apply to educators until amendments were added in 1972. Some school districts were willing to increase funds for women students, especially in athletics, but they insisted that women educators were not covered. The debate raged until 1975 when, under Title IX, it was determined that school districts could lose federal funds for violating civil rights. Women activists in 1970 could hardly foresee these changes in the law, but they did recognize that the union had to pursue

15. *AFT Proceedings,* Box 46; see also files in the Marjorie Stern Collection, 1974, Walter Reuther Archives, Detroit.

16. *NEA Handbook,* 1973–74; *NEA Reporter,* 18 September 1964; AFT pamphlet, 1973, AFT Archives, Washington, D.C.

17. *Pittsburgh Press,* 21 August 1970. See files in the Marjorie Stern Collection, Series 2, Box 3.

civil rights issues actively in order for women to make gains under the new civil rights legislation.[18]

Feminist demands left the men astonished and uncomfortable. "The AFT adopted its first women's rights resolutions amid snickers, sly looks and boisterous laughter from male delegates who seemed unable to take women seriously," the *Pittsburgh Press* reported in 1970. The women demanded no loss of rights on maternity leave, day care, and equal opportunity clauses in collective bargaining contracts. They urged the national to lobby the AFL-CIO to end its opposition to the Equal Rights Amendment. (Labor had been traditionally opposed to the ERA because it would destroy protective legislation for women.) They wanted vocational counseling that did not limit career choices for young women. But men in the union felt that, given the issues of the war, decentralization, and collective bargaining, the women's demands were frivolous. "I'd be laughed out of Bensalem if I said this is what we did at the convention," one delegate said. "We should get on to something else. This is not the kind of thing we should be addressing." Men were particularly offended when women raised the question of birth-control and abortion counseling. After Alberta Maged of Local 61 in San Francisco informed delegates that in California it was illegal to give contraceptive information in public schools (and some teachers had been arrested for trying to do so), one delegate responded, to the mirth of the men, that teachers had enough clerical duties without having to dispense birth-control pills. "There is enough for us to do in schools today."[19]

One incident brought the house down in laughter. Virginia Mulrooney of Local 1021 in Los Angeles reported to the convention that she and a colleague had been discriminated against in a restaurant-bar in Pittsburgh when they went to wait in the bar and were told, "You can't go in there, we don't serve unescorted ladies." Mulrooney was miffed by the gales of laughter her report received. "I was rather disappointed and surprised and confused that the reaction on the floor was laughter. I didn't know if it was because of a relief of tension or what. Now, I think it was laughter on the frivolousness and foolishness of women." One delegate recalled that during the discussion of maternity leave "I noticed those around me nudging each other so that any talk about pregnancy, maternity and so forth was treated as if someone was telling a dirty story. It was a puritanical reaction."[20]

Most of all, women wanted to establish an AFT policy to negotiate these issues in collective bargaining contracts. The men, who had to face men from school boards across the bargaining tables, feared they would look ridiculous negotiating for birth control and what they perceived as frivolous female issues. Bargaining could be rough and extremely sexist, as Carole

18. Diane Ravitch, *The Troubled Crusade* (New York, 1983), pp. 297–304; Marjorie Stern Collection, Series 2, Box 3.
19. Ibid; ibid.
20. Ibid; ibid.

Graves, president of the Newark local, could attest. In a 1970 bargaining session a district negotiator had pointed to the local's demand to include teachers' honeymoons among absence-with-pay provisions. He leered at Graves, who was the only female negotiator, and said, "Hey, honey, you want we should buy you the hot water bottle, too?" Instead of solidarity, however, one of the union negotiators joined in the administrators' laughter. Aware of the resistance they were receiving to their demands but nonetheless clutching the proposals the convention had passed, the women leaders marched into the postconvention Executive Committee meeting to insist that their resolutions be implemented. In January 1971, President Selden appointed Marjorie Stern to chair a Women's Rights Committee, giving official notice that the women were being taken seriously.[21]

In 1971, resolutions on women's issues were assigned to the Civil Rights Committee, prompting the Women's Caucus to ask for its own convention committee. Resolutions providing child care for women delegates, for a regional conference on women's rights, for creating women's rights committees at the state and local levels, for seeking income-tax relief for the costs of child care, for the promotion of women to administrative and staff positions, and for sending women to AFL-CIO educational courses all passed. But endorsement of the ERA again caused trouble. In 1971 the UAW endorsed the ERA, thus further widening the gap between Reuther and Meany. Like the war issue, the ERA was becoming another litmus test to determine whether one sat on the left or the right in the house of labor. Stern, with Selden's support, tried to get the AFT to endorse the ERA but was stymied by opposition from the New York locals until 1972, when the convention finally voted its endorsement; the AFL-CIO changed its policy in the same year.[22]

Women teachers were particularly angered by the AFT's failure to act. Objecting to a watered-down ERA that would cover protective legislation, one teacher complained to Stern: "I fail to understand why there have to be any strings to equality. Either a person is equal or the person is not. I am not. I can strike with men, I can picket with men, I can be sentenced to go to jail with men. But when it comes to being equal before the law, I cannot be so. I learned this on the day I was sentenced to jail. The men who were sentenced got to stay together in comfort. I had to wait alone with no company. Thank you AFT." But Stern was pushing the national to hire more women, to institute local women's rights chapters. In 1973 Stern managed to conduct a survey of women's activities in the locals, and she allied herself with Selden's bid to retain the presidency. When Shanker was elected in 1974 Stern left the national office and was informed that the union would not pay her way to the national meeting of the Coalition of Labor Union Women.

21. Ibid; ibid.
22. Ibid; ibid.

CLUW represented a national coalition of union women which Stern and other women teachers helped found. Although the Women's Committee continued to meet, no one replaced Stern in the national office.[23]

In the NEA, which endorsed the Equal Rights Amendment wholeheartedly, women were enhancing their internal role. For example, Margaret Stevenson, the executive secretary of the Department of Classroom Teachers, was offered a position on the NEA Executive Committee when the department was being dissolved as a separate unit and incorporated into the NEA. Her promotion marked the introduction of women into the upper echelons of the NEA staff. Both organizations prepared curriculum packages on issues of sexism in education, and both organizations lent their support to various national organization for women. Along with the merger discussions Marjorie Stern attended NEA meetings to make alliances with women's rights advocates.

The big change for women in education came with the addition of Title IX to the Education Act in 1972. Title IX simply stated that women could not be discriminated against in education programs. It soon became a rallying point for women in both the association and the union. Title IX gave women educators a direct legal foundation for further negotiating women's issues in their contracts as well as for using federal power to force schools to give women equal opportunity. The enthusiasm with which women embraced Title IX can only be matched by the disappointment they expressed in the eighties when the Supreme Court narrowed the application of Title IX in the Grove City case (an important civil rights decision that narrowed the application of Title IX). In 1988, over the objection of the Reagan administration, the Civil Rights Act was amended to overcome the implications of the Grove City case.[24]

Race, Class, Gender, and the Redefinition of Professionalism

Although teachers could point to some progress toward equality in their organizations and their classrooms, there remained fundamental contradictions between the push for equality and the pursuit of professionalism. Inherent in the professionalism ideal was the triumph of merit. In the early civil rights era this concept was not in opposition to the push for equal opportunity. Equality and merit came into conflict later as reformers tried to address the historic barriers to equality and correct for them; in the process they often ignored the implications of these corrections for principles of merit as well as for safeguards to ensure fairness.[25]

23. *AFT Proceedings,* 1971; Marjorie Stern Collection, Series 2, Box 3; interview with Marjorie Stern, summer 1988.
24. Cynthia Stoddard, *Sex Discrimination in Education Employment: Legal Strategies and Alternatives* (Holmes Beach, Fla., 1981), pp. 18–19.
25. J. Harvie Wilkerson III, *From Brown to Bakke: The Supreme Court and School Integration,*

Conflicts between reformers and educators after 1968 appeared to have class connotations just as they had in the reform era of the 1890s. The triumph of professionalism over community interests in the Ocean Hill–Brownsville case was not the final victory predicted by the proponents of centralization at the turn of the century. Indeed, it appears that in class terms professionalism failed to transform the population of teachers as reformers had hoped. Though no longer mainly the sons and daughters of farmers, schoolteachers were still recruited from manual laboring and clerical families. The element of class antagonism remained close to the surface in the Ocean Hill–Brownsville conflict, much as it had been in the student strikes in Chicago. White schoolteachers resented the "limousine liberals" for imposing values of progressive educational change on their lives.[26]

Referring to the "upper-middle-class person and intellectual" whose jobs was not threatened by Ocean Hill–Brownsville, a union schoolteacher named Patrick Harnett defended the teachers' strike, arguing against "a tolerance for, at times even an encouragement of, unquestionable violations of the professional and human rights of one people in the professed interest of promoting the human rights of another." He pointed to the ministers, poets, and intellectuals who would abstract the situation into a conflict in which white, working-class bigots denied black people their rights. "Everyone knows that the slave-owning Southern gentleman was less bigoted than the non-slave-owning white." To Harnett the real bigots were New York's upper-crust liberals who belittled the teachers by accusing them of behaving "like plumbers" in that they were not "dedicated." But Harnett reminded his readers that teachers were drawn from the working class: "They are people who did not have things and now they want things, the same things that

---

1954–1978 (New York, 1979), p. 293. Oddly enough, the issue of meritocracy, equality, and civil rights has not been addressed by historians of professionalism. See Gerald L. Gerson, *Professionalism and Professional Ideologies in America* (Chapel Hill, N.C., 1982), in which it is argued that the collection of essays holds a "skepticism" toward existing models and a "reluctance to indulge in 'conspiratorial' histories of the professions" that interpret the pursuit of professionalism as "mere verbal smokescreens designed to disguise the self-interest of those who construct them." Professional ideologies, however, are *constructed* within a historical context of social hierarchy. The issues of civil rights, community control, and social justice challenge the rationale of professionalism, exposing the need for self-interest incorporated in the professionalization rationale. Professional ideology incorporated racist and sexist ideas in a scheme of merit that was challenged by notions of equality and social justice in the early seventies in affirmative action programs. That the key court cases on affirmative action (with the exception of *Webber v. Kaiser*) involved the professions— education, medicine, law—should come as no surprise. Because the issues are debated in courts of law (one of the most elite segments of the professional community), lawyers, often with conflicting values on questions of social justice, attack the issues with ambiguous and conflicting results. For a classic statement of this ambiguity, see the cover of *Time:* "Quotas: No/Race: Yes," as noted in Ravitch, *Troubled Crusade*, p. 288.

26. Dan Lortie, *School Teacher* (Chicago, 1975), p. 35; NEA, *The American Public School Teacher* (Washington, D.C., 1963); NEA, *Status of the American Public School Teacher, 1970–71* (Washington, D.C., 1972), p. 15.

everybody in our consumer culture wants—and if they have to act like members of an electricians' union to get them, they will."[27]

Responsibility was a key issue in the controversy. Regardless of the anger of black parents, teachers simply did not feel that they had to take responsibility for a system they did not control. They felt victimized because the administrative blunders that led to Ocean Hill–Brownsville had occurred outside their control. The teacher, Harnett insisted, "does not feel that he should be made the scapegoat to assuage the guilt felt by much more affluent whites over their much larger role in committing those crimes." Racial polarization, Harnett charged, was more the creation of Mayor Lindsay and the liberal press than Shanker and the union. "I am convinced that both strikes were brought about by a mayor who has catastrophically botched every labor dispute he has stepped into. . . . Lindsay is not a friend of black people by being the enemy of white, unionized teachers." Harnett pointed to the bitter irony that blacks long had been denied racial integration because school administrators wanted to keep whites in the schools: the same whites who fled to suburbs. "The white liberal intellectual living in his Connecticut Shangri-La" wanted to impose his vision of racial harmony on the lower-middle-class white, "whose life is most immediately affected by the struggle of blacks for social justice."[28]

Harnett's argument articulated some of the same resentments teachers had felt against Nicholas Murray Butler's social elite and its concern over reshaping the class values of schoolteachers. Dan Lortie confirmed much of Harnett's conclusions: "Teaching appears to be one of the more important routes to the middle class." Studies made by the NEA in 1967 pointed to the fact that nearly one-third of the male teachers came from blue-collar backgrounds. This is not to argue that social mobility was the sole reason for entering the field; in fact these surveys demonstrate that the desire to serve was still a powerful motive; the point was that teachers now had a vehicle, the union, to express their material interests as well.[29]

The 350 replacement teachers hired by Superintendent McCoy in 1968, black and white, were a diverse group. Some were former organizers for the Mississippi Freedom Democratic party, others had experience in the Peace Corps, Head Start, and various community-action programs sponsored by President Johnson's Office of Economic Opportunity. Nearly one-quarter of them had no previous job experience, which in the stiff competition for teaching jobs in the late sixties represented a tremendous opportunity for

27. Patrick Harnett, "Why Teachers Strike," in *Confrontation*, ed., Berube and Gittell, pp. 205–14.

28. Ibid., pp. 193–205.

29. Lortie, *School Teacher*, p. 35. Thirty percent of teachers came from blue-collar backgrounds in 1973, or approximately six-hundred thousand teachers who, in Lortie's terms, "crossed the boundary between blue-collar and white-collar work."

young, gifted, inexperienced teachers. "Nearly all were committed to social change," writes one teacher-participant in the experimental district. McCoy, as a district superintendent, was rewarding the very leftism that the school system had rooted out a generation earlier. He recruited the very well educated young idealists whose families had either fled the system for suburban schools or had blocked integrationist schemes fifteen years earlier. These new teachers came precisely from the population that Nicholas Murray Butler would have approved of; it was a triumph of administrative professionalism over union professionalism.[30]

The class issue was important in under the growing conflict between equality and merit. Women and minorities regarded their pursuit of equal opportunity through affirmative action as an adjustment to assure them a place in competition, whereas white males (who often experienced more subtle class discrimination) felt that the system was an elitist solution to destroy the concept of merit. The Horatio Alger concept of class mobility was a powerful aspect of this perspective on merit, and in the union it was particularly powerful because only by erecting procedural safeguards against administrative prerogatives had the union been able to protect its members.

The confrontation over equality and merit came with the case of *Bakke v. Regents of the University of California* in 1977–78. Allan Bakke. a white student, charged that he was discriminated against when he was twice denied admission to the University of California–Davis medical school. A special dual-admissions program of the medical school reserved sixteen places for minorities and eighty-four places for white students and accepted different levels of test scores in the two groups. A sharply divided U.S. Supreme Court, in a "Solomonic compromise," upheld Bakke's claim in 1978. Although most civil rights organizations and women's groups opposed Bakke's suit, AFT president Shanker entered an amicus curiae brief on behalf of Bakke, based on the union's opposition to quotas. Shanker's position on *Bakke* further alienated the union from minority groups and tended to confirm harsh judgments made about the union in the Ocean Hill–Brownsville affair. This happened despite the fact that some minority spokesmen claimed that nothing had been lost with Bakke's victory in the courts: Vernon Jordan saw it as "a green light" for affirmative action. Again the NEA was quite willing to exploit this difference in the two organizations.[31]

---

30. Charles Isaacs, "A JHS 271 Teacher Tells It Like He Sees It," in *Confrontation,* ed. Berube and Gittell, pp. 198–200.

31. "Among the many defenders of the University of California's special admissions procedure were many private universities, the Justice Department, the American Civil Liberties Union, the NEA, the Association of American Law Schools, the Association of Medical Colleges, and civil rights groups. Bakke's position was defended mostly by Jewish organizations, white ethnic groups (of Italian, Polish, and Ukrainian descent), and conservatives." Ravitch, *Troubled Crusade,* p. 287. See also Terry Eastland and William Bennett, *Counting by Race: Equality from the Founding Fathers to Bakke* (New York, 1979), pp. 173–76. More friend-of-the-court briefs (fifty-eight) were submitted in the Bakke case than in any previous case. Ravitch, *Troubled Crusade,* p. 281.

What changed in the transition to collective bargaining was that women and blacks found a new voice in educational politics. Whereas the professionalism of the Progressive Era was decidedly white and male, the new professionalism accommodated formerly disenfranchised minorities who were more representative of the community teachers regularly serve. Just what this will mean in determining the new definition of professionalism under unionism remains to be seen. It is no longer a case of a handful of alienated union women marginalized by Gompers's condemnation of "brain workers" versus manual laborers, or the complete dismissal of a teachers' union because educational concerns seemed distant, feminine, and radically alien from bread-and-butter unionism. Collective bargaining is no longer seen as a masculine pursuit. The real problem women teacher unionists face is how to integrate women's concerns into the broader framework of the union movement.[32]

Unionism, professionalism, centralization, and community control have continued to confound the efforts of black and other minority teachers. Black teachers walk the line on the professionalism question. If they grow too close to parents, or too close to community political groups, they risk the wrath of a still hierarchical administrative structure. But that administrative structure is no longer exclusively white. They also run the risk of losing their professional identity, but again, that professional identity is no longer exclusively white. As long as the instruments of educational change are not closed to minorities, that is, as long as the unions, the administration, and a teacher's entree into education remain open, the task of balancing professional identity with community identity is a manageable problem for women and minorities. Teaching is far better integrated, in race as well as gender, than other professions. The persistence of the demographic profile of teachers over the last ninety years and the varying interpretations of the meaning of that profile should assure us that teachers make their own history; they have defied the predictions of their examiners.

Professionalism, then, can move in one of two directions: either it broadens to obscure the division between teachers and the community or it narrows to focus on an exclusive core of highly trained, expert teachers operating in the midst of teacher aides and paraprofessionals whose presence separates the teacher from the client community. The direction of professional change will be determined by its practitioners in relation to the options open in society. Since African-Americans and women continue to dominate in the field, they have the most to contribute to this debate.

The paradox of Shanker's role in the *Bakke* decision has been that in running the AFT he has promoted more women to leadership positions in the

32. See CLUW files in the Marjorie Stern Collection; also Ruth Milkman, "Women Workers, Feminism, and the Labor Movement since the 1960s," in *Women, Work, and Protest*, ed. Ruth Milkman (Boston, 1985), pp. 300–323.

union than previous presidents. Several women leaders head large local unions and are in a position to assume leadership of the union should Shanker step down. Nevertheless, Shanker avoids calling this affirmative action; he insists that he has simply chosen the best qualified candidates for the job. He articulates the class interests of his constituency in ways reminiscent of Margaret Haley, while he remains firmly in the Gompers-Stillman tradition of male trade unionism.

Fiscal Crisis in New York and the Nation

Shanker's new leadership of the AFT marked a definite shift in AFT politics. The dominance of the New York City local in the AFT brought a climate of conservative action to the union, while collective bargaining fights for smaller suburban locals drained the energies of any opposing leadership.

Shanker's triumph in office proved short lived, for no sooner had he become president in 1974 and weathered the storm of fall teachers' strikes, which had become a seasonal pattern, than the fiscal crisis in New York hit the UFT in the summer of 1975. Stunned by the bankruptcy of the city, New York labor leaders did their best to salvage what was left of their agreements. Civil servants' wages were frozen at the third step of their increments, but for teachers with fifteen steps and sabbatical leaves the policy of cutbacks yielded close to a 19 percent cut, while other city services were cut between 3 and 8 percent; fifteen thousand teachers and paraprofessionals lost their jobs in 1975. As the layoffs began, the city's teachers' seniority law protected teachers for only the duration of their current teaching license, not for the number of years they were on the payroll. Thus teachers with thirty-two years of seniority but only two years of service on a particular license were laid off. But minorities were still the hardest hit; African-American teachers in 1975 were only 11 percent of the teaching force, while African-American students composed 37 percent of the student body.[33]

In San Francisco, after the passage of Proposition 13 by California voters in 1978, half the public school teachers received layoff notices. The California Federation of Teachers responded immediately by calling statewide meetings to address the crisis. In New York the oil crisis and problems with commercial banking sparked the municipal bond crisis. Unable to honor $792 million in mature securities, New York city placed its finances under quasi receivership and, like Chicago in the thirties, took orders from the city's banking establishment. The UFT launched a short strike, but Shanker urged teachers back to the classroom with a contract that affirmed the bitter

33. Mark H. Maier, *City Unions: Managing Discontent in New York City* (New Brunswick, N.J., 1987), pp. 174–77.

conditions the fiscal crisis had imposed. Teachers voted 10,651 to 6,695 to accept the unpopular contract after which union officials sang "Solidarity" and rank-and-filers shouted "sellout." Other communities began to feel the same fiscal pinch as declining birth rates began to affect school enrollments.[34]

Proposition 13 in California spawned similar tax-limitation programs in Michigan, Wisconsin, and Massachusetts, and other states instituted some form of tax limitation through their state legislatures. A full-scale tax revolt coupled with the ascendancy of Ronald Reagan to the presidency cast a note of gloom among schoolteachers everywhere. The magic of collective bargaining had evaporated. Teachers now had to look to leadership to protect their hard-won gains and to maintain their concept of professionalism as it had survived the introduction of unionism.[35]

In this period of contraction, teachers' unions and associations began a defensive war to protect the gains of collective bargaining while they set up procedures for layoffs and retrenchment. School boards, in Shanker's words, "were no longer soft on unions." It became progressively more difficult to gain concessions; strikes lasted longer and increasingly were defensive responses to recalcitrant boards of education.[36]

The NEA response to the contraction of the midseventies was to seek greater political power. Observers in most state capitols regarded state education associations as among the most powerful lobbyists. In 1976 the association entered the national political realm by publicly endorsing Jimmy Carter for president and pressing for a cabinet-level department of education. Carter promised a generous educational package but proved incapable of delivering congressional approval. One thing he did gain for NEA in return for its support was the creation in 1979 of a department of education. For the NEA this was a singular triumph. Although much of the Carter term was distracted with defensive actions against tuition tax-credit plans, the NEA leadership claimed that the new cabinet post was just the opening goal of a national program that was still the centerpiece of NEA activity. The NEA's visible presence in the 1980 campaign became part of the Republican party's charge that the Democratic party was devoted to "special interest groups," yet the NEA was doing no less than what the labor movement had begun to do under Samuel Gompers's leadership during Woodrow Wilson's administration. In 1976, 265 association delegates attended the Democratic convention, and in 1980 464 association delegates attended the convention, tempting Daniel Moynihan to quip, "The Carter delegation is a wholly-owned subsidiary of the NEA." In 1980 the AFT had 94 delegates, more

34. Eric Lichten, *Class, Power, and Authority: The New York City Fiscal Crisis* (South Hadley, Mass., 1986), pp. 95–126; William K. Tabb, *The Long Default: New York City and the Urban Fiscal Crisis* (New York, 1982).

35. Interview with Raoul Teilhet, summer 1988; see also *California Teacher*, 10 (June 1988).

36. Interview with Albert Shanker, summer 1988.

than the American Federation of State, County, and Municipal Employees AFSCME (64) or the International Association of Machinists (IAM) (91), and just shy of the UAW (100). Ronald Reagan's genius was to turn the NEA's new-found power against itself by throwing the reactionary, back-to-basics William Bennett into the post of secretary of education. Shanker had warned against cabinet status for just this reason—that a political appointee could harm educational programs.[37]

By the midseventies it became common practice for the NEA to be referred to as a union, and the executive secretary, Terry Herndon, expressed no great anxiety about the usage. Miffed by the NEA's loose use of the term union while it ignored the AFL-CIO, AFT leaders pressed for the NEA to file under the Landrum-Griffin Act, which the NEA was forced to do in 1979. Despite this acceptance of unionism and its practices, the leadership of the NEA still insisted that merger discussions with the AFT could only proceed with the promise that the NEA would not have to join the AFL-CIO. Herndon remarked when he came into office in 1973 that he considered merger of the two organizations inevitable and foreseeable. By 1980, however, Herndon was less than sanguine. It appears today that only an organizational crisis could revive the notion of association/union unity.[38]

The New Environment

Finally, the unions had to think creatively in the face of the tide of reaction that severely restricted the potential of collective bargaining to give teachers more than simply monetary gains. Given the fiscal restraints of the late seventies and the eighties, teachers' organizations have had to form coalitions in communities, participate in local elections, and press for alliances not just with labor organizations but with businessmen and other professionals just to make their needs known. In other words, collective bargaining has made teachers assume a much more aggressive political stance and forced a new definition of professionalism. As community organizers press for the divorce of politics from education, unionized teachers must take leadership in political battles lest power over education fall into the hands of real-estate speculators and tax-conscious corporate interests. Teachers have always been in a bind over the issue of public school finance, but only in the age of collective bargaining have their demands been legitimized, not as luxuries, but as necessities in the overall bill of quality education.

Having gained greater control over their profession, teachers have begun to debate issues of responsibility. Community-control critics in Ocean Hill–

---

37. Theodore H. White, *America in Search of Itself: The Making of the President, 1956–1980* (New York, 1982), pp. 334–35.
38. West, *NEA: The Power Base,* pp. 242–55.

Brownsville persistently argued that the union was not taking responsibility for incompetent or apathetic teachers. The charge was that someone should be held accountable for the decline of public education. Community leaders wanted the unions to assume that role but the unions were still unsure of their power under collective bargaining. The fear of the union leadership was that community control would undermine collective bargaining and destroy the teachers' efforts to gain control over their profession. Conservatives, alarmed at the decline of American productivity relative to Japan's, demanded accountability in the schools in exchange for tax dollars. For teachers this meant performance evaluations, testing, and merit pay. The NEA has strongly opposed this move, whereas the AFT has embraced the idea of accountability.

The terms of this debate were set during the late sixties but in the nineties, in the aftermath of severe urban fiscal crisis and tax revolt, when collective bargaining between teachers and schools is no longer a novelty at best and a criminal activity at worst, the attitude of the teachers' unions has matured. Shanker has consistently argued that teachers need to set standards for themselves, accept testing, and welcome the opportunity to weed out their weaker members.[39] Mary Futrell of the NEA disagrees and argues that this process only caters to the budget cutters, the administrative zealots who would use testing as a means to eliminate teachers. At first glance it seems quite a reversal in roles for the NEA and the AFT. Perhaps one should view this disagreement as an issue in the redefinition of professionalism after collective bargaining. This redefinition will not come simply from the unions, whether AFT or NEA, but also from community groups and parents interested in public education.

The fundamental difference between this focus on professionalism and the original calls for professionalism in the days of Margaret Haley is that teachers now have a greater sense of responsibility for their own destiny. Shanker's proposals for reform address a world in which the majority of teachers have the protections of collective bargaining. The NEA leadership's caution reflects a basic lack of confidence in the powers of unionism to protect teachers' interests. Shanker's proposal, on the other hand, may reflect an unwarranted confidence in the power of the unions. Though the New York City local remains strong, other bargaining agents have not fared as well.

The union's position on accountability is a measure of the degree to which teachers have been able to take control of their profession. Self-governance has its potential pitfalls, but it cannot be said that it has been tried. In the heat of the Ocean Hill–Brownsville controversy it was significant that NEA president Elizabeth Koontz insisted that self-governance was at the crux of the matter. "The control of conditions under which teachers enter the profes-

39. Interview with Shanker.

sion and practice is a matter of professional self-governance, as in all great professions. Teachers are struggling to obtain the legal authority to govern themselves. They need the legal process to protect competent members and to warn, discipline and dismiss those who abrogate their standards or responsibilities."[40]

Conclusion

In May of 1974 the California Federation of Teachers held its annual meeting in Fresno, California. The meeting came on the eve of the final showdown in Shanker's campaign to wrest the AFT presidency from Selden. Both Selden and Shanker attended the CFT convention, and word leaked out that state president Raoul Teilhet would become Selden's campaign manager. As the convention progressed over a long spring weekend, the California delegates coalesced into an anti-Shanker faction opposed to the big city locals of San Francisco and Los Angeles, both of which had AFT vice-presidents, Jim Ballard and Larry Sibelman, respectively. Late on Saturday evening a resolution was introduced on the floor that condemned the action of the national Executive Board in defying Selden's leadership. Through a clever floor maneuver the enthusiastic anti-Shanker forces managed to pass the resolution over the objections of the two large city locals. In triumph the session adjourned to an informal rally in support of Selden's candidacy, although most delegates understood that Shanker already had the votes lined up.[41]

At almost the very time the California federation was meeting, the state legislature passed a law guaranteeing collective bargaining rights for teachers throughout the state. The law touched off the greatest AFT-NEA jurisdictional battles in the history of blackboard unionism. The California contest between the association and the union was fought district by district between the passage of the collective bargaining law in 1974 and the passage of the statewide tax initiative in 1978. In those five years, costly collective bargaining campaigns and strikes drained both union and association treasuries, as similar battles had on the national level in the late sixties. Finally, in 1978, as the CFT asked for a dues increase at its annual convention, it also asked delegates to welcome Shanker as the guest speaker to the convention. Humbled by the need for finances to keep its collective bargaining campaign afloat, the delegates welcomed the same man they had defied four years earlier. For Shanker the issues were clear, and he came into the convention supporting Allan Bakke's case and opposing quotas in affirmative action programs. For the opponents of the Vietnam War, dissenters from the union's

40. Ibid.; *NEA Reporter*, 11 November 1968.
41. Interview with Teilhet.

activities in Ocean Hill–Brownsville, and proponents of affirmative action, Shanker's visit was a bitter pill to swallow.

In a sense the experience of the CFT encapsulated the changes that collective bargaining had brought to teachers. First, the defiance of Shanker was the last gasp of gadfly union politics. The old radical politics of the union could not be accommodated, as collective bargaining had changed the needs of the unions themselves, binding them more powerfully to their national organizations and forcing them to approach more pragmatically the issue of survival against competition from the association.

After the defeat of this idealism, however, the union and the association in each district had to appeal to the solidarity of teachers to negotiate with the now-experienced and management-trained new school administrators. In consequence teachers in California have persistently sought unity between union and association members. The CFT continues to seek some form of merger with the California Teachers' Association.

It would be far too simplistic to conclude that the introduction of collective bargaining made teachers more conservative, or that it remade teacher unions into vehicles for preserving the status quo. The California experience—and indeed the national experience—in collective bargaining must be viewed as a historic process firmly rooted in the struggles of the past and engaged in the changes of the future.

Unfortunately, neither the union nor the association is prepared to come back to the problem of centralization, which is linked to professionalization and will continue to haunt teachers in their dealings with the community. As long as schools remain isolated from community interest groups, the heritage of Nicholas Murray Butler will overshadow the heritage of Margaret Haley. Parents must feel comfortable in the schools; they must be part of the educational endeavor. But responsibility must be shared. As Elizabeth Koontz said in 1968, "The school is the public's school, not the parents' school nor the teachers' school."[42] Decentralization has begun to address the problem of shared responsibility. The mechanism most likely to confront union teachers and community groups with the need for coalition is taxation. All the hopes for successful community control rest on the ability of those communities to gain needed tax dollars to pay for quality education. The fiscal crisis in education, allowed to fester since the disappointments of the New Deal, worsens as affluent parents seek private education as an alternative.

In the final analysis the tax issue is not at all a teachers' problem, or particularly a union problem, or particularly an educational problem. It is an issue about wealth distribution, about opportunity structures, and finally about the class structure of American society. The teachers' union was not being perverse when it attracted municipal socialists to its ranks before World War I or when it championed the same causes as the Communist party

42. *NEA Reporter,* 11 November 1968.

in the thirties. Nor was it being paranoid in the age of McCarthyism, nor can it be argued that it was the naive politics of the UFT that threw it against the radical black community organizers of CORE in the late sixties. Strife associated with the intersection of teacher unionism with the great ideological debates of the twentieth century cannot be explained alone by a facile dismissal that intellectuals and unions should never mix (at least on this side of the Atlantic). The point is that since education is the foundation of the state, as Socrates said, teachers operate within the state apparatus, and thereby they are tied to it. As the state grew more powerful, not just the national government, but state and local governments as well, education grew in importance—and it grew in terms of cost. As early as Margaret Haley's tax campaign, American businesses and the wealthy wished to cap the costs of education and shift its burden onto individual property owners. This move was largely successful and culminated in the assurances of the New Deal that education would remain fundamentally a local tax affair. The injustice of this system was most glaring with respect to black illiteracy in the South, but the solution to this problem challenged the entire racial status quo in the nation. *Brown v. Board of Education* broke the logjam on federal aid to education and fueled the challenge to white male supremacy in American political life. As the injustices of race and gender became part of the national discourse in the age of Martin Luther King, Jr., it is little wonder that schools came under close scrutiny, and with this examination the issues of inequality, opportunity, and redistribution of wealth surfaced. Teachers were not innocent bystanders in this debate. They were actors, and in the case of union teachers, they were activisits for social change just as they had been in the social turmoil of the Progressive Era. Their persistence in confronting the chronic fiscal crisis of education lends further credence to their avowal of a belief in the fundamental value of the services they provide.[43]

This is not to argue that teachers will always represent a progressive force. By looking at the genesis of both the AFT and the NEA in the twentieth century we can identify a shift in political perspectives regarding collective bargaining. The association and the union have nearly switched roles, with the NEA taking bolder, more progressive positions on a range of social issues, while the union looks for creative yet conservative solutions to educational problems. For example, the NEA has been vocal against U.S. military involvement in Nicaragua and Central America, while the AFT leadership has supported the Republican administrations policies. The divide between the two organizations may be inevitable. Because teachers reflect the composition of the community, they also reflect the fundamental division between conservative and progressive political forces. Teachers' unions in France and Great Britain show a similar division, although the historic paths of unionism in these countries were quite different from the U.S. example.

43. Ibid.

On the other hand, competition between the union and the association, now no longer contained within the dichotomy of trade unionism versus professionalism, may deter the development of progressive trade unionism. When the AFT was most progressive, the NEA had an alliance with conservative forces within the AFL to block radical educational reform in the thirties; now, though the NEA is most progressive, it still refuses to align itself with the AFT and is therefore effectively blocked from uniting with the labor movement. In this regard it is worth noting that Shanker still volunteers to step down from office in the AFL if the NEA wishes to merge and the NEA continues to insist on its independence and takes the union offer as disingenuous.

Merger seemed most feasible when the two organizations were undergoing their deepest internal turmoil as a result of ten years of intense competition. Furthermore, the NEA's deepest crises seem to occur when the AFT threatens its hegemony, as it did with Margaret Haley's challenge in 1919 and again in 1926 with the AFT's New York City victory. The initial impetus for this competition, however, was based on differences regarding professionalism, centralization, and unionism. The NEA *was* led by new administrators; the AFT *was* trying to unite class interests and teachers' interests. Today union and administrative differences are gone; the raw ideological questions come to the fore. In this sense Shanker is taking the Charles Stillman line that teachers are basically conservative, while Mary Futrell has her feet firmly planted in the tradition of the women classroom teachers.

It is possible to overemphasize the significance of the teachers' union in relation to the rest of the labor movement, but the conventional wisdom tends to err in the opposite direction and underestimate the significance of public employee unions in general in determining the direction of the labor movement as a whole. Yet the major struggles in trade unionism in the eighties have been over the rights of public employees to strike, and the greatest growth in union membership remains in the sector of public workers. The teachers' union is the oldest of these public employee unions, and its history extends the history of American unionism beyond the era of industrial union organizing into the present era of public employee unionism.

Appendix Tables

Table 1. Number of public school teachers employed, 1929–1958

Year	Elementary		Secondary	
	Men	Women	Men	Women
1929–30	68,705	633,819	82,689	152,405
1939–40	70,187	569,860	138,384	192,023
1949–50	58,407	607,258	158,536	207,741
1955–56	95,540	719,970	223,330	237,603
1957–58	105,066	784,421	253,682	257,916

Table 2. Distribution of classroom teachers by sex, 1870–1964

Year	Men teachers (%)	Women teachers (%)
1870	38.7	61.3
1900	29.9	70.1
1930	16.6	83.4
1950	21.3	78.7
1964	31.4	68.6

Table 3. Salaries of instructional staff, 1929–1980

Year	Average annual salary ($)
1929–30	1,420
1933–34	1,227
1937–38	1,374
1939–40	1,441
1943–44	1,728
1949–50	3,010
1959–60	5,174
1969–70	8,840
1972–73	10,633
1974–75	12,167
1975–76	13,124
1976–77	13,840
1979–80	16,175

Source: U.S. Department of Education, National Center for Educational Statistics, 1988.

Table 4. Salaries of teachers and wages/salaries in all industries, 1930–1960

	Average annual wages/salaries ($)	
Year	Teachers	All industries
1930	1,420	1,368
1936	1,283	1,184
1940	1,441	1,300
1946	1,995	2,356
1950	4,010	3,008
1956	4,156	4,042
1960	5,174	4,702

Source: Robert J. Thornton, "U.S. Teachers' Organizations and the Salary Issue, 1900–1960," *Research in Economic History,* 4 (suppl. 2, 1982).

Table 5. Salaries of teachers and salaries in other occupational categories, 1929–1953

	Average annual salaries ($)				
Year	Teachers	All	Manufacturing	Federal service	Lawyers
1929	1,400	1,405	1,543	1,933	5,534
1930	1,425	1,368	1,488	1,768	5,090
1933	1,385	1,120	1,150	1,824	4,156
1935	1,255	1,137	1,216	1,759	4,272
1940	1,450	1,300	1,432	1,894	4,507
1944	1,765	2,108	2,517	2,677	6,504
1946	2,080	2,356	2,517	2,736	6,951
1950	3,050	3,008	3,300	3,504	8,540
1953	3,617	3,590	4,051	4,103	9,227

Source: Bernard Yabroff and Lilly Mary David, "Collective Bargaining and Work Stoppages Involving Teachers," *Monthly Labor Review,* 76 (May 1953), p. 479.

Table 6. AFT and NEA membership, 1916–1980

	Number of members	
Year	AFT[a]	NEA[b]
1916	4,500[c]	—
1917	2,403	8,466
1918	1,500	10,000
1920	10,000	53,000
1930	7,000	172,000
1940	30,000	203,000
1950	41,000	454,000
1960	59,000	714,000
1961	61,000	766,000
1962	71,000	812,000
1963	82,000	860,000
1965	110,000	943,000
1968	163,000	—
1970	205,000	1,100,155
1980	551,359	—

Source: CTF Collection; AFT Collection; *NEA Handbook.*

[a]Includes classroom teachers, some principals in a few locals, and college teachers.

[b]Includes classroom teachers, school administrators, college professors, and specialists in schools, colleges, and educational agencies.

[c]Includes members of the Chicago Teachers' Federation before the Loeb Rule.

Index

Academic freedom, 101, 103–4, 175; Chapters 5, 6, 8, 9, passim
Addams, Jane, 9, 30, 67
Affirmative action, 264, 266, 270, 278
African American Teachers' Association, 237
Allen Report (New York), 1964, 235, 239
Alonzo, Braulio, 229
Altgeld, John Peter, 26
American Association of Colored Teachers (AACT, later ATA), 147, 200, 204, 205
American Federation of Labor, 102–6, 108–11, 113, 115–17, 120–21, 123; and communism issue, 150, 152, 159, 161–63, 166–70, 173, 177, 180; in early AFT history, 80, 85–86; in early federation history, 62, 65, 67, 72–79; merged with CIO, 198, 222, 223, 256; women and, 259, 260, 268
American Federation of State, County, and Municipal Employees (AFSCME), 109, 214, 255, 269
American Federation of Teachers, 2–6, 80–87, 89, 90, 93, 97, 99, 101–3, 132–49, 150–74, 255, 257, 260, 268
    and academic freedom, 95, 97–98, 104–5, 184–92
    and American Legion, 122, 138
    and civil rights, 196–208, 236, 239, 250–51, 260, 264–68
    and class relations, 111, 261–66
    collective bargaining, 3, 209, 227–29, 236, 239, 266–67, 270, 272
    Commission on Reconstruction, 176, 182, 194
    and Communist party, 155, 158–59, 160–61, 164–71
    and Congress of Industrial Organizations (CIO), 146, 186–87
    in depression, 133, 150

and federal aid, 114, 145–46, 149, 180–81, 252
fiscal crisis, 175, 180
gender issues, 107–10, 172–74, 220–22, 258–61, 265–66
junior high schools, 112–13
legislative lobbying, 113–15
locals:
    (1) to 1917, Chicago Teachers' Federation (CTF), 107, 109, 112, 216, 247; after 1937, Chicago Teachers' Union (CTU), 163, 247–49
    (2) Chicago Mens' High School Teachers' Federation (merges in 1937 with CTU), 118; after 1941, New York City Teachers' Guild, 161, 163, 169, 170, 186, 189, 191, 212–13, 245. See also United Federation of Teachers
    (3) Federation of Women High School Teachers (after 1937, CTU), 118–19; after 1941, Philadelphia Federation of Teachers (see Local 192, below)
    (5) New York Teachers' Union 65, 97, 102, 116, 151–61, 163–71, 174, 185. See also Teachers' Union
    (8) Washington, D.C. Teachers Federation, 102, 116
    (24) New York City Vocational Teachers, 164
    (61) San Francisco Federation of Teachers, 194
    (77) Los Angeles Federation of Teachers, 194. See also Local 430, below
    (189) Atlanta Federation of Teachers, 197–99
    (192) Philadelphia Federation of

279

Library of Congress Cataloging-in-Publication Data

Murphy, Marjorie, 1947–
   Blackboard unions : the AFT and the NEA, 1900–1980 / by Marjorie Murphy.
     p. cm.
   Includes bibliographical references and index.
   ISBN 0-8014-2365-1
   1. Teachers' unions—United States—History.   2. Collective bargaining—Teachers—United
States—History.   3. American Federation of Teachers—History.   4. National Education
Association of United States—History.   I. Title.
LB2844.53.U6M87   1990
331.88′113711′00973–dc20

                                                             89-46175